The Traditional Trade of Asia

The Traditional

Foreign trader with Chinese attendant and ox cart
(T'ang, fifth century A.D.). *Seattle Art Museum*

Trade of Asia

C. G. F. SIMKIN

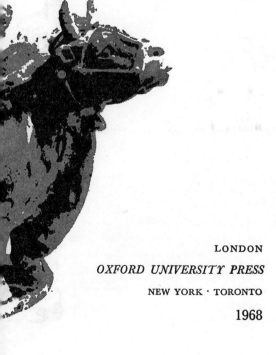

LONDON

OXFORD UNIVERSITY PRESS

NEW YORK · TORONTO

1968

Oxford University Press, Ely House, London W.1

GLASGOW NEW YORK TORONTO MELBOURNE WELLINGTON
CAPE TOWN SALISBURY IBADAN NAIROBI LUSAKA ADDIS ABABA
BOMBAY CALCUTTA MADRAS KARACHI LAHORE DACCA
KUALA LUMPUR HONG KONG TOKYO

PRINTED IN GREAT BRITAIN
BY EBENEZER BAYLIS AND SON, LTD.,
THE TRINITY PRESS, WORCESTER, AND LONDON

Contents

Illustrations   *page* vii

Preface   xi

ONE The shaping of traditional trade   I
  1 Townsmen and nomads, 1
  2 Iranian imperialism, 5
  3 Hellenic enterprise, 8
  4 Indian enlightenment, 15
  5 Chinese superiority, 28
  6 Rome's Asian trade, 38

TWO Medieval changes   49
  1 Nomad havoc, 49
  2 Byzantine and Sassanian monopoly, 54
  3 The eastward sweep of Buddhism, 61
  4 The Islamic conquests, 73
  5 The glory of T'ang and Sung, 85
  6 Korea and Japan, 99
  7 Srivijaya and Ankor, 111

THREE Mongolian conquests and their aftermath   127
  1 The Khanates and the landways, 127
  2 China's maritime expansion, 137
  3 Japanese piracy, 145
  4 Burmese and Thai, 153
  5 Majapahit and Malacca, 161
  6 Moslem and Mughal India, 167

FOUR Intrusion, withdrawal, and disintegration   181
  1 Portuguese and Spanish enterprise, 181
  2 The Dutch and English East India companies, 191

3   Japanese withdrawal and Chinese restriction, 202
4   Indochina's relative immunity, 215
5   Indonesian disintegration, 224
6   The collapse of Mughal India, 235

FIVE   The passing of traditional trade   251
1   The historical constant, 251
2   Agents of change, 260
3   China eroded, 270
4   India transformed, 285
5   Plantations and mines, 301
6   The rice trade of Indochina, 328
7   The modernization of Japan, 351

List of Sources   371
Chronological Table   *between pages* 384-5
Index   385

Illustrations

Foreign trader with Chinese attendant and ox cart (T'ang, fifth century A.D.) *frontispiece*

1 Darius giving audience (from the Treasury at Persepolis) *facing page* 66

2 Gandhara Buddha 67

3 Chinese cavalryman. (T'ang, fifth century A.D.) 82

4 Indian ship of the eighth century (from the Stupa, Borobudur, Java) 82

5 Arab ship of the thirteenth century (from a manuscript of al-Hariri's *Maqâmat*) 83

6 The Polos on their way to China (from *Carla Catalana*, 1375) 162

7 Near-Eastern merchant in China (T'ang, fifth century A.D.) 163

8 Jayavarman VII (from Ankor Thom) 163

9 Akbar receiving the Persian ambassador (from the *Akbarnama*) 178

10 Portuguese ship in Japan (early seventeenth-century Japanese Namban or South Barbarian screen) 179

11 Batavia (from Valenjin, *Oud en Niew Oost Indien*, 1721–6) 258

12 East Indiamen at Calcutta (water-colour by J. Baillie-Fraser from 'Views of Calcutta and its Environments', 1820) 259

13 Chinese–English naval clash in Anson's Bay, 7 January 1841 274

14 Coffee plantation in Ceylon (engraving after C. O'Brian, 1864) 275

Maps

Trade routes in A.D. 100   *facing page*   I
Asia in the reign of Kublai Khan and later sea voyages   127
European penetration in Asia, 1900   *pages* 382–383

To my friends in Asia

Preface

In 1961 I went to Bangkok as a consultant to the Economic Commission for Asia and the Far East. There I had the good fortune to be closely associated with Raj Desai who taught me much about Asian economic problems, and whose wife, Toshi, aroused my interest in her own studies of cultural links between India and Thailand. Through these good friends I began to see Asia in a double perspective—present affinities between widely dispersed countries and traditional connections which have helped to shape those affinities. In each of the following three years I returned to ECAFE, partly for work on Asian trade, and gained further insights through this work as well as from brief visits to other parts of Thailand, Cambodia, Laos, Hong Kong, Malaya, and Singapore. Asian colleagues generously encouraged a growing interest in the traditional, besides the contemporary, trade of Asia, and I remember with particular gratitude a visit arranged by Whatana Bulsuk to Sukhothai, the cradle of Thai civilization in Indochina.

A large field of historical reading was opened as it became an absorbing hobby to sort out the development of trade which did much to foster not only economic but also cultural and political relations between Asian countries. I found nothing ready-made for this purpose as few scholars have attempted very extensive studies of Asian history and no such study bears directly on economic aspects. An opportunity came to arrange my own notes, and to expand them by reading in British libraries, during 1966-7 when I was Commonwealth Visiting Professor at the University of Essex and free from teaching duties. Most of the book was written there and at Oxford where, for some weeks, I enjoyed the academic hospitality of Nuffield College; I am most grateful to Essex and Nuffield for making this possible.

I have tried to write in a straightforward way on the great theme of trading relations between all the countries of Asia from remote beginnings to the momentous changes which came in the nineteenth century. For that reason I hope the book will appeal to those who have a general interest in Asia. I hope also that it may be of interest to fellow economists in giving some glimpses into old connections between trade, security, technology, and affluence as well as into periods of economic progress which occurred long before the industrial revolution, even if progress never became self-sustaining and was all too often followed by periods of miserable poverty. In particular, the book may give a useful historical perspective to those who, like myself, are working on current problems of a semi-traditional Asia; a major reason, indeed, for writing it has been to gain such a perspective for a projected sequel on the contemporary trade of Asia.

But I do not claim to have made any contribution to historical scholarship. This is the work of an economist whose interest in Asia has led him well beyond his own field and who, lacking contact with specialists or knowledge of Asia languages, has made an amateur exploration of sources which are, in the main, secondary and sometimes even tertiary. Although I have done what I could with limited opportunities and time, I fear that the book has more errors even than might be expected in a work of such diversity and scope. More important, there can well be criticism about balance or selection of material; the book is directly concerned with Asian trade yet gives much space to religious or political conditions as well as to internal economic changes in the various countries. I admit occasional indulgence of a personal, if inexpert, enthusiasm for some aspects of Buddhist pilgrimages, Chinese culture, Ankorian theocracy, and Thai life, while hoping that such indulgence does not exceed tolerable bounds. But I do not see how to give a meaningful account of traditional trade without a good deal of reference to the great religions which had such diffuse repercussions upon Asia, or to the despotisms upon which trade so heavily depended. In writing about such matters I have had in mind ordinary readers rather than those who have no need nor liking for potted histories but, in order to give historical flavour, I have liberally quoted from primary sources, and, to help comprehension of a complex theme, have provided maps and a chronological chart.

Difficulties inevitably arise about spelling Asian names in our alphabet. I have followed the *Oxford History of India* for South Asian names, Ghirshman for Iranian names, Hitti or Hourani for Arabic names, Prawdin for Mongolian names, Reischauer and Fairbank for East Asian names, and Hall for South-east Asian names, although I have preferred recent official publications for Thai names. (The above works are included in the list of sources.)

In many ways I am sorry to have had to finish this book; writing it has been a pleasurable and rewarding experience. It has been made the more pleasurable by the sympathetic encouragement of my wife, whose careful scrutiny of successive drafts has eliminated many slips or clumsy expressions. I have also been fortunate in having the help of two splendid typists, Mrs E. Bennett and Miss J. Irwin, and that of the Press staff at Ely House in preparing the book for publication.

C.G.F.S.

University of Auckland
January 1968

Acknowledgements

Acknowledgements are due to the following publishers for permission to quote material: George Allen and Unwin Ltd. and Random House Inc., New York (from J. Mirsky, *The Great Chinese Travellers*), Routlege & Kegan Paul Ltd. (from H. Giles (trans.), *The Travels of Fa-Hsien*, and R. Grousset, *In the Footsteps of the Buddha*), and Cambridge University Press (from T. Pires, *Suma Oriental*).

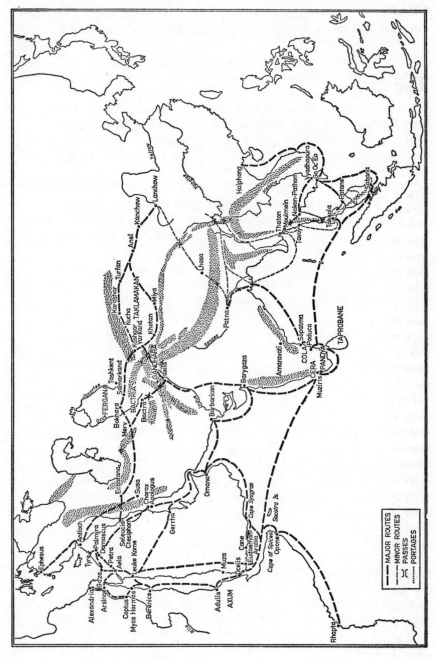

TRADE ROUTES A.D. 100

CHAPTER ONE

The shaping of traditional trade

1. *Townsmen and nomads*

Trade is probably almost as old as society itself, but it could become regular and extensive only after that neolithic economic revolution which made a basic division between settled cultivators and nomadic pastoralists. Cultivation with early tools of wood, stone, or soft copper was most rewarding in the alluvial soils of great river valleys and there, after men had developed laborious arts of controlling water, agricultural surpluses grew large enough to support urban civilizations. Villages developed into fortified towns, and these into city states which, in time, became grouped into kingdoms or modest empires. It was in this way that urban life spread along the Nile and the Tigris-Euphrates and, about a millennium later, along the Indus and the Huang Ho.

Egypt and Mesopotamia were connected by the Fertile Crescent, along which emerged a ribbon of derivative civilizations and through which came the first international highway, supplemented by easy coastal shipping. Trade, indeed, had about as much as agriculture to do with the rise of Phoenicia and Syria. North-west India, however, was separated from Egypt by the steppe-enclosed deserts of Arabia and by the sterile ranges or deserts of Makran. It was also separated from Mesopotamia by the formidable Hindu Kush, intervening arid steppes, and the mountains encircling the dry Iranian Plateau. North China, at a much greater distance, was separated both from India and Iran by the great meridional range of the Pamirs, 'the Roof of the World', and the vast desert depression of the Tarim basin, itself shut off by the Kunlun chain in the south and by the T'ien Shan in the north.

The steppes and deserts between these first civilizations were dominated by nomads or semi-nomads who were often predators upon them but also partners and even connecting links. Nomads, so far from being mere barbarians, had an economic organization of some complexity, well adapted to steppe conditions and able to provide for most needs except in times of drought. Stock-breeding appears to have developed about the same time as settled cultivation and from a common root of primitive agriculture that became associated with domestication of animals. A choice thus arose between two directions of specialization—growing cereals in confined areas of irrigated land, or herding animals over wide areas in a complex grazing cycle, adjusted both to the long cropping of cattle, horses, or camels and to the short cropping of sheep or goats. At suitable places within their grazing lands, moreover, there was some cultivation to provide additional fodder for animals or a more varied diet for men. Nor were nomads backward in the fundamental crafts of spinning, weaving, felting, pottery, and working wood, leather, or metals. But their small migratory groups could not produce so fine or abundant a range of manufactures as those catering to the luxurious courts of urban civilizations, and they needed at least occasional supplements of grain or other crops. Failing pillage, they could give in exchange surpluses of wool, hides, or livestock, as well as such specialized products of their territories as Arabian incense, Iranian copper or tin, Altai gold, Khotan jade, or Siberian furs.

Nomad tribes bartered with one another, especially in gold, copper, and tin during the Bronze Age, and in iron later. Transit trade developed over considerable distances, linking urban civilizations not only with adjoining pastoral tribes but, indirectly, with more distant tribes and through them with other, far distant, urban civilizations. A vital part was played here by nomads' animals. Even sheep and goats, coming down from summer uplands to winter lowlands, can carry some wares. But cattle, camels, horses, asses, and mules can be used both as pack animals and to draw wagons loaded with a tribe's tents, weapons, stores, household equipment, or treasures. Where opportunity coincided with inclination, such animals were also used for transporting trade goods.

Bedouin, who still call themselves 'people of the camel', early used it for developing caravan trade along the wadis of Arabia to link the Levant with the Yemen, and the Red Sea with the

Persian Gulf. When nomads on the Iranian Plateau had tamed an indigenous small horse, they used it for bringing to Mesopotamia, not only Iranian gold, tin, and turquoise, but Armenian lead, Afghan lapis lazuli or rubies, and even cotton textiles from the cities of the Indus valley. The horses, however, for which both Arabia and Iran later became noted, were first obtained from Indo-European tribes who had mastered the fine species in the region east of the Caspian Sea. Some of these tribes—the Iranians—penetrated the Plateau about 1800 B.C. and were soon supplying horses to the Kassites and Hittites, who in turn supplied the Arabs. From Central Asia, too, came the Bactrian camel, important for early transport between this region and India or China. Iranian turquoise, Afghan lapis lazuli, Khotan jade, and Altai gold had long percolated to China through nomads of the Mongolian steppes. But the Aryans' horses and camels so quickened communications that, by the fifth century B.C., China's previous technological lag behind West Asia was overcome.

The horse was also associated with an important change in military power during the period between 1500 and 500 B.C. Used first for driving carts and chariots, it began to be ridden in the Near East and used for cavalry. Newly mounted warriors from Transcaucasia and North Iran attacked both urban civilizations in the Near East and steppe tribes, who had then to become mounted warriors themselves. Requirements for pastures enormously increased and there was warfare on the steppes as one Royal Horde after another imposed a feudal type of rule over other tribes, and levied tribute from settled cultivators. The Cimmerians came to dominate the Pontic steppe, between 1250 and 750 B.C., the Iranians the Caucasian steppe, the Scythians the Volga steppe, and the Sarmatians the steppes of Central Asia. But the Sarmatians pressed upon the Scythians, and they upon the Cimmerians who thus penetrated Asia Minor and the Iranian Plateau. The Sarmatians also showed the advantages of horsemanship to the Mongols, who then became an increasing danger to China's emerging empire.

Archaeologists have discovered a good deal of evidence for early contacts between nomads and urban civilizations, and for their role as a link between distant civilizations. Very early indirect contacts between India and China are suggested by the use of cowrie shells from the Maldive Islands at the first stage of the Huang Ho civilization. Similar connections between the Indus and Mesopotamian civilizations are suggested by excavations at both places, revealing distinctive objects from the other region. Stein's expedition to the Makran yielded pottery that showed a connection between India and Iran in chalcolithic times. Saka remains in Central Asia show that they imported timber from India and arrows and beads from Mongolia. Royal tombs of the Scythians contained a mixed collection of northern and Near Eastern objects, in which Greek artifacts of gold, silver, and ivory were prominent. Soviet workers found Chinese knives in Bronze Age graves of the East Urals, and Chinese silk, lacquerware, bronze mirrors, and jade carvings at early Iron Age graves west of Lake Baikal. Moreover, the art of the first Scytho-Siberian nomads of the Altai region shows clear signs of borrowing from both China and Iran and, through the latter, from the East Mediterranean.

This is not to say that all early transit trade depended on nomad initiative. City merchants participated by going into nomads' territory to trade with them, by crossing it to reach mining areas, or, in West Asia, by taking caravans through it to other cities. These merchants were supported by royal masters who often waged campaigns against nomads in order to subdue them or to annex desired territories. The Pharaohs conquered Sinai nomads who had supplied Egypt, from prehistoric times, with copper and turquoise. The kings of Assyria, early in the Iron Age, began a long series of attacks upon Iran, partly for control over transit supplies of this revolutionary metal, together with terminal supplies of copper, lapis lazuli, and horses; Tiglath-pileser I (1116–1093 B.C.) was, for a time, master of the main trading routes across West Asia. But Syria was soon lost to Semitic nomads, known as the Arameans, who made Damascus a great trading city and, until the fourth century B.C., were the principal merchants of the Fertile Crescent. So, too, the Nabataeans, another tribe of nomadic Arabs, after taking Petra from the Edomites, made it a splendid junction to either Egypt or the Levant for the caravans which they brought up the Red Sea coast from Aden. Trade, if not agriculture alone, could thus settle or civilize nomads, as was later shown by the Parthians in Iran, the Kushans in Central Asia, and, much later, the Mongol Khanates.

Trade with nomads, or across their lands, was far from negligible, even in prehistoric times. But it was limited by their meagre numbers or poverty, and always liable to interruption from tribal wars. Contact, moreover, was dangerous because of the nomads' constant temptation to attack cities, caravans, or ships. Pliny spoke of the Arabs as addicted to trade and theft, and Hitti remarks that the Bedouin was 'a land pirate or broker, or both at once'.[1] In the Red Sea and Persian Gulf the Arab was also a pirate–trader, as were the Phoenicians or Greeks in the Mediterranean. If drought wiped out the nomads' thin margin above subsistence, or if bad government weakened the urban civilizations, attack was almost inevitable, as the history of both India and China abundantly shows. The whole Indus Valley civilization, indeed, was wiped out by a wave of invading Aryans about 1500 B.C.

There could, then, be no large, dependable, international trade until strong empires arose to protect caravan routes or to clear sea lanes of pirates. Both the Assyrian Empire (1900–605 B.C.) and the Babylonian Empire (1625–538 B.C.) had achieved a limited and brief control over the trade of the Levant. But the first empire to extend sovereignty far beyond the confines of the old river valley civilizations was, ironically enough, created by another branch of those Aryan nomads who had destroyed the Indus civilization. They provide the first great example, too, of the ease with which conquering nomads could adapt to urban civilization, and greatly extend its scope.

2. *Iranian imperialism*

The Persian Empire of the Achaemenian dynasty (559–330 B.C.) had its origin in a small kingdom carved out by Achaemenes during the seventh century B.C. at Parsumash, to which his son added the province of Parsa (Fars) and other territory. These first two kings had been vassals of Media, a similar but larger Aryan kingdom in Iran. The third, Cyrus the Great (559–530 B.C.), reversed this position and, by subsequent annexations or conquests, bequeathed to his son, Cambyses, an empire including not only Iran but all Asia Minor, Mesopotamia, and Central Asia as far as the Jaxartes River. Cambyses

[1] Hitti, *History of the Arabs*, p. 23.

added Egypt, together with Greek colonies in Africa, but lost his throne while returning from an unsuccessful campaign against Ethiopia and died before he could reach Iran. His army wisely chose a young noble, Darius (521–486 B.C.), to succeed him. Darius soon put down the usurper and pacified an empire now torn by revolts. After that he went on to conquer much of North-west India but failed, at Marathon (490 B.C.), to conquer Greece.

It was the great achievement of Darius to devise and apply a successful method of controlling a vast empire on the basis of powerful centralization. Satraps of its twenty provinces, each supervised by an imperial secretary, were directly responsible to him as were two corresponding provincial officers, the military commander and the treasurer. Travelling inspectors made surprise checks upon provincial administrations. Unity was imposed on areas as diverse as highly sophisticated Babylon or Egypt, commercialized Phoenicia or Syria, agricultural Media or Bactria, and the nomadic steppes of the Caspian region or the Iranian uplands. Central power was carefully limited nevertheless; it seldom interfered with social life in the various provinces, but rather sought to pacify or protect them by strong garrisons connected by good roads.

The most important roads were the Royal Road of 1,677 miles between Ephesus and Susa, and the even longer road from Babylon to Hamadan, subsequently extended as far as Kabul in order to reach the Indian satrapy. Nor was sea transport neglected. Ports or quays were built along the Empire's coasts and navigable rivers, new vessels were developed, some as large as 500 tons, and a ship canal, begun by Pharaoh Necho, was completed to link the Nile with the Red Sea. Scylax, a Greek of Caryanda, was ordered to lead a fleet from the Indus for a thorough exploration of coastal routes as far as the head of the Red Sea; it must have been thoroughly done as the fleet took two and a half years to reach Arsinoe. Thereafter Arab, Greek, and Phoenician sailors were able to maintain more or less regular connections between India, the Persian Gulf, the Red Sea, and Mediterranean ports.

The considerable taxes that the Empire levied on land, farms, herds, mines, industries, trade, and ports were thus used not only for maintaining its government and army but also for works of great utility. These included, besides transportation, irrigation schemes drawing upon the subterranean waters of the Iranian Plateau and the Syrian desert. Irrigation, of course, was not new to Iran, where it has been practised from prehistoric days, and the Achaemenians had learnt from the big works made by Van kings during their temporary occupation of North-west Iran. Cyrus and his successors carried much further the difficult construction of subterranean canals in both Iran and Syria, and may have extended or improved irrigation works based on the Oxus and Jaxartes in Chorasmia.

Darius was responsible for introducing useful plants, trees, and animals throughout his empire. Greece acquired lucerne, the food of Fergana's horses, together with the domestic fowl and the peacock. Mesopotamia acquired rice, Aleppo the pistachio, and Egypt sesame. Fruit trees from Babylonia were transplanted to eastern provinces. Timber resources were also better managed as Darius drew upon Lebanon cedar, Indian teak or ebony, and trees of Crete and Asia Minor for his great palace at Susa and other royal buildings.

A further notable reform was adoption of the Lydian bimetallic currency and promotion of a monetary economy. Many taxes were levied in silver talents, one-third of which came from the Indian province. Spread of monetization is also indicated by a change in wage payments on public works;—these had been entirely made in kind but, by the end of Xerxes' reign (486–465 B.C.), two-thirds were being paid in coin. One important consequence of this monetization was the extension of private banking, first developed in seventh-century Babylon; Achaemenian banks became active in lending, accepting deposits, and even in providing a cheque system.

Besides standardizing money, Darius appreciated the importance of uniform and sound weights or measures. The 'king's measure', of approximately 1 bushel, replaced varying private measures and a 'royal cubit' of 18 inches became standard. A new weight, the *karsha* of 22 lb., was the most important innovation among avoirdupois measures.

Strong, efficient government, good transport, agricultural and industrial promotion, monetization, banking, and standard measures all helped trade to surpass any previous level in the Ancient World. Internal trade grew in every province of a prosperous empire. International trade reached out to countries which had never been in commercial contact, such as Greece and Babylon, and extended, far beyond the Empire's limits, to the peoples of the Rhine, Danube, South India, and Ceylon. Luxury goods were still important: Egyptian drugs, linens, and glassware, Arabian frankincense and myrrh, South Indian pepper and scented barks, Greek wines and oil, or amber and furs from northern lands. But much trade now took place in grain, cheap clothing, household pottery, and other everyday requirements. Pressure of trade led to a sharp rise of commodity prices and interest rates, although land values fell and improvements in smelting or transport reduced copper and iron prices.

3. *Hellenic enterprise*

Darius had shown what a great empire could do for the trade and prosperity of the Near East. But after his death political, and so economic, conditions slowly if irregularly declined. The Achaemenian Empire became externally threatened by the rising power of aggressive Greek city-states, and internally weakened by a corrupt, divided court unable to cope with increasingly autonomous satraps. In the end it fell easily to Alexander the Great (336–323 B.C.) when he crossed the Dardanelles to begin his conquest of West and South Asia.

He was master of the whole Empire within four years of this crossing, but spent two more years putting down revolts of the Sogdians in Central Asia. Descending then into India, he reached, after another two years of hard fighting, the five rivers of the Punjab. There, however, his homesick troops demanded return to Iran, and all that he could persuade them to undertake further was an advance down the Indus. They built a fleet of about 2,000 ships to fight their way to the delta, where Alexander partly built a large port. After dividing the Punjab and Sind into five provinces and appointing governors, he sent heavy troops across Baluchistan, other troops by the ships to Diridotis, on the Gulf, and led the remainder along the arid Makran coast. They rejoined at Susa, having proved three routes to India besides that through the Khyber Pass.

Impressive as Alexander's conquests were, and also his skilful political measures, they hardly surpassed those of the great

Achaemenians. Except for Greece, his empire was little bigger than that of Cyrus, and his political measures did little more than restore the sound administration of Darius. Alexander might well have gone further, in both directions, but for premature death within a year of returning from India. As it was, his successors became selfishly involved in a forty-year struggle for power, during which economic conditions again suffered and the Empire was divided up. The Ptolemies (305–30 B.C.) took Egypt, and the Seleucids (305–127 B.C.) what had been the Achaemenian Empire. Seleucid territory, however, was soon reduced as Chandragupta expelled the Greeks from India in 321 B.C., and the ambitious governor of Bactria successfully revolted, in 250 B.C., to found his own dynasty there.

Alexander's most durable achievement was not the politico-economic reunion of the Near East but rather its Hellenization. This process was begun by the progression of a large army with numerous camp-followers over the Near East, by the military colonies Alexander transplanted from Egypt and Asia Minor to Afghanistan and India, and by the immediate influx of Greek merchants anxious to grasp dazzling new opportunities for trade. It was carried much further by the Ptolemies and Seleucids, both concerned not only to exploit their kingdoms but to stabilize and develop them along Greek lines with the help of fellow Greeks. They had, of course, to rely upon their own soldiers for securing these kingdoms, and to reward them with grants of land or other privileges. But they also used Greek administrators for transforming the effective routines of Achaemenian government into something more creative and less burdensome to the throne; in particular, such men were used for royal economic monopolies and extensive economic regulation of agriculture, industry, and trade. In order to avoid lapsing into orientalism, these kings promoted and fostered Greek education, professionalism, and culture. Philosophers, scholars, teachers, poets, artists, actors, engineers, lawyers, and physicians were successfully induced to work in Egypt or Iran. There they served both Greek residents and the many local people who sought Hellenization, either because of the intrinsic appeal of Greek culture or because of its manifest social and economic advantages to the subject of a Ptolemy or Seleucid.

Nowhere was Hellenization more marked than in economic

life, where it had two aspects. One was penetration of Greek merchants to transform the business centres of Egypt and Iran. These men brought not only the original outlook fostered by their culture but also the commercial acumen and experience of a country whose meagre resources had long made colonization and trade necessary even for survival. Greek accounting and business methods came as improvements, but more important still were better knowledge of western markets and contacts making for easy trade with the Aegean, then the biggest area for international trade. All this, as Rostovtzeff points out, effected an economic union of the Ancient World as compensation for its shattered political unity.

The other aspect of Hellenization in the economic sphere related to the development of royal monopolies and revenues. Both Ptolemies and Seleucids regarded themselves as ultimate owners and active chief stewards of their kingdoms. They sought and used Greeks with business ability or experience to organize and to develop economic resources for the benefit of the royal treasuries. The Ptolemies, besides owning great estates and collecting many taxes, controlled land registration, irrigation, salt pans, mines, timber resources, oil mills, breweries, leather works, linen factories, and paper mills. They monopolized the entire Egyptian trade in wares from East Africa, Arabia, and India, competing here vigorously with the Seleucids and with Arab merchants. The Seleucids, similarly, although making land reforms which helped Iranian peasants, controlled estates, salt pans, mines, forests, fisheries, other sources of raw materials, and some important manufactures. Both kingdoms provide interesting examples of early planned economies, even if the evidence is rather fragmentary.

Consider, first, Egypt, a productive land exporting much of the corn Greece exchanged for wine, oil, and manufactures, paper from the papyrus which it alone could grow successfully, many fine linens, and various types of glassware. But it lacked minerals or timber, and had strong demands for imports of aromata, elephants, camels, and horses. The most important mineral deficiencies were gold, used for coinage or plate, and iron which came into widespread use under the Ptolemies. These two metals reached it from Nubia, the southern land between the two Niles, and from Meroe, the Abyssinian kingdom further south. Nubia in addition supplied copper and some gems. Meroe controlled the great caravan route through Central and East Africa, bringing slaves, elephants, ivory, ebony, ostrich feathers, hides, and oil. Arabia furnished the few of its own products for which it had long been noted—frankincense and myrrh, gold and pearls—and now also exported horses for the Egyptian army and camels for the caravans introduced by Philadelphus, the second Ptolemy (285–246 B.C.). More important was Arabia's function as an entrepôt for Indian and Iranian wares. Indian wares included rice, cassia, cinnamon, pepper, indigo, ivory, pearls, tortoiseshell, muslins, and silks, all of which were brought, in easy stages often involving transshipment, by Arabian, Ethiopian, Indian, or Iranian merchants to Aden, the only good harbour of Arabia, or to Socotra, the island below this port. From Socotra shipments were made not only to Aden but to Meroe through East African ports. From Aden goods could reach Egypt by ships going up the Red Sea, but this was not usual owing to foul winds, reefs, shoals, and pirates. Most exports from Aden, accordingly, went by caravan up the west coast of Arabia to Petra, and thence across Sinai to Alexandria or west to Gaza and the Levant.

These caravan routes, and the great trading city of Petra, were in the hands of the Nabataeans, a strong Arab tribe whose piracy discouraged Red Sea shipping. Philadelphus tried to break their monopoly. He built desert roads for the camel caravans which he introduced to develop trade with Meroe both in African wares and in Indian wares. His main attempt, however, was opening up the Red Sea to merchants. After sending a fleet to put down Nabataean piracy he went on to build a series of ports; Berenice (Ras Benas) served a new caravan route to Coptos on the Nile, Mussel Harbour was free from shoals, Berenice Trogodytica served gold mines at Jebel Allaki, Berenice Epideiris was west of Bab al-Mandab, Ptolemais Theron (Epitheras of the Hunts) was a collecting point for elephants or ivory, and Berenice the All Golden (Massawa?) later became the Abyssinians' port of Adulis when they grew strong enough to capture it from Egypt. Philadelphus also restored an old canal between the Nile and the Heroonpolite Gulf in the hope of further encouraging trade with Socotra or Aden. His successor, Euergetes II (145–116 B.C.), advanced the same policy by sending an expedition to India. Soon after it returned with rich cargoes there were direct sailings from Egypt to North-west India, and the Ptolemies appointed 'generals in charge of the Red and Indian Seas'.

The Seleucids, too, had a sea-route with a parallel land-route up the Persian Gulf and, just as the Nabataeans had dominated the Red Sea, so another Arab tribe, the Gerrhaeans, dominated the Gulf. Their port, Gerrha, was the starting point of a caravan route which crossed Central Arabia to connect with the Nabataean route from Aden to Petra. The Seleucids maintained a fleet to check the Gerrhaeans' piracy but had little success in wresting a share of their trade.

From Iran, in any case, the land-routes were far more important. All roads to Bactria and India crossed the Plateau except for a northern route to the Kingdom of Bosporus. The major route ran from Seleucia, the capital and the great clearing centre for trade, through Ecbatana and Merv to Bactra. Seleucid control never extended beyond the Hindu Kush as, two years after Alexander's death, Chandragupta I (321–297 B.C.), founder of the Mauryan dynasty, expelled the Greeks from India and then repulsed an attempt by Seleucus Nicator to regain it. The two rulers, however, quickly established sensible relations for commercial and cultural intercourse between their countries.

Before long Seleucid territory shrank further. The Ptolemies took Phoenicia in 272 B.C., and Pergamum broke free in 262 B.C. Struggles followed with the Ptolemies for Syrian ports, and Antioch had to be developed as an alternative outlet for the empire; it later became the Seleucid capital. Then came the loss of Bactria as Dodotus, its ambitious satrap, took advantage of Seleucid weakness to found his own Greek dynasty (250–139 B.C.) in a new kingdom extending from Merv to the Pamirs and from Samarkand to the Hindu Kush. This area had long been important as a source of Ferganan horses and Bactrian camels, and as a complex junction of caravan routes from Siberia and China to India and Iran. An early system of irrigation, improved by the Achaemenians, had made it rich in crops and fruits. The Greek kings of Bactria took further measures to develop its agriculture, industry, and trade, and protected these by a close network of military colonies. Bactria thus became known as the 'land of a thousand cities' and its capital, Bactra (Balkh), as a 'paradise on earth', famed for great bazaars. Soon cut off from the Seleucid Empire by the Parthians, Bactria came to lose much of its Hellenism, but its rulers succeeded, as the Seleucids never did, in achieving a remarkable fusion of interest with their subjects, a fusion which led to a distinctive blending of Greek with Iranian culture.

The Parthians were a Caspian tribe which, under the leadership of Arsaces, took two other provinces from the Seleucids, in 249–247 B.C., and made these into another independent kingdom. His successors took advantage of every opportunity to enlarge it, becoming ultimately masters of all Iran. The Seleucids were, accordingly, pressed by the Ptolemies in the north, by the Parthians in the east, and later by the invincible power of Rome. Nevertheless, until a few decades before its end, their empire was a strong one and, in spite of wars and territorial losses, remained prosperous.

Like their Achaemenian predecessors and their Ptolemaic rivals, the Seleucids promoted economic development. Agriculture was improved by a number of innovations in ploughing, cropping, and viniculture, and by further work on irrigation. Industry was fostered in order to lessen dependence on Egypt or other foreign suppliers, so that pottery, glassware, parchment, woollens, and chasing of gold or silver became important manufactures. Old roads were improved and made thoroughly secure within the Empire. New roads were built to Antioch after the Ptolemies took Syria, and to the Black Sea after the Parthians became a menace. Great attention was paid to coinage; excellent and abundant issues were widely circulated, not only within the Empire, but also throughout the Hellenic world.

The main issues were silver, strictly minted to the Attic standard from ores of mines in Asia Minor. Gold coins were minted but their issue sharply fell when Siberian gold was cut off soon after Bactria became independent, although lesser supplies continued to come from Armenia, India, or the Caucasus area. The Ptolemies, however, were vigorously exploiting Nubia's gold mines and the flow from them, together with that of silver from Seleucid mines, made the precious metals so abundant that their value halved.

Such monetary expansion, and rapidly growing demands from Rome for foreign goods, help to explain the commercial prosperity of the Hellenic world. Rome's entry also helps to explain a shift of trade from the former predominance of every-day wares to what Gibbon called 'the splendid and trifling objects of Oriental trade'. Iran's exports included both types of goods; seed corn and drugs, woollen textiles and fine carpets, horses and pedigree dogs, lead and turquoise, coin and gold- or silver-ware. Trade in Asian wares was no less important to the Seleucids than to the Ptolemies. Seleucia handled great quantities of aromata, spices, drugs, dyes, gems, cottons, mus-lins, and silks from Arabia, Bactria, India, and China, many of these products being re-exported to the Mediterranean.

This transit trade was profitable and important, but the Seleucids had difficulties in maintaining it because of pressures from the Ptolemies and the Parthians. Tiridates (247–212 B.C.), the second king of Parthia, after annexing Hyrcania, the Cas-pian province, transferred his capital to Hecatompylos on the caravan route from Seleucia to Bactra, an indication of Parthian interest in profits from Asian trade. The Seleucids recovered this territory, but lost it again when the Parthians took advant-age of the struggle between Antiochus III (223–187 B.C.) and Rome. After the Roman victory at Magnesia (190 B.C.) Seleu-cid control weakened over the eastern provinces, so that Mithridates I (171–138 B.C.) was able to annex Media, Elam, Persis, Characene, Babylonia, Assyria, and Gedrosia. Seleucid power was then pushed back to the Tigris, where the Parthians made a large camp that later became their capital, Ctesiphon. Here, too, they sought to preserve trade, and so reached a *modus vivendi* with the merchants of Seleucia across the river. This was disturbed by two attempts to recover the Empire but, after a final defeat at Ecbatana (129 B.C.), the Seleucids gave up. Indeed, they retained Syria only because the Parthians were attacked by invading Sakas—who had already extin-guished Greek rule in Bactria (139 B.C.). But the respite was brief; Rome, after making Pergamum and Pontus its own Pro-vince of Asia, took Syria from the Seleucids in 64 B.C. The Ptolemies fell thirty-three years later after Octavian's victory at Actium.

The Greeks thus lost all the great power gained for them by

Alexander, and were not to recover any of it until the days of Byzantium. Their political disasters, however, did not halt the process of Hellenization. Under the *Pax Romana*, Greek bankers, merchants, and sailors were all able to advance much further the trade between Asia and the Mediterranean. Beyond the *Pax Romana* Hellenism did wane, largely because Greeks were too thinly spread over the new Parthian Empire. But even the Parthians styled themselves 'Philhellenes', and Greek kings were to rule briefly over North-west India, where their sculptors made a great and permanent contribution to Buddhist art.

4. *Indian enlightenment*

Gautama, the Buddha, attained Nirvana in 483 B.C. after teaching for many years, over North India, a simple, ethical doctrine of individual liberation from evil and suffering through enlightenment. This doctrine, like the almost contemporary Zoroastrianism of Iran, was a reaction against the cruel features of the old Aryan religion and, at the same time, a rejection of the Brahmans' elaboration of this religion into the caste-bound, pantheistic rituals of Hinduism. Immediately after their great teacher's death, five hundred disciples wrote down his precepts, dividing the books into three *Pitakas* or baskets which contained his rules for monks, his sayings, and his philosophy. They made numerous converts but, at a second council held in 376 B.C., unity was threatened by demands for relaxing discipline and extending doctrine in the direction of Hinduism. Such demands were again made, and rejected, at a third council convened by Asoka (269–232 B.C.), grandson and successor of Chandragupta I.

His own conversion is said to have followed personal revulsion at the carnage of the battle which, by adding Orissa to the Mauryan Empire, extended his rule over all India save the three small Tamil kingdoms at its southern tip. After that battle he devoted a long and brilliant reign to a very different conquest of men's hearts by the Law of Duty or Piety—obedience to parents, reverence for teachers, courtesy to relations, and adherence to truth. Buddhism spread over his vast domain, and missions were sent to border tribes, the Tamil kingdoms, Ceylon, Lower Burma, and even to the Greek courts of Egypt,

Epirus, Syria, Crete, and Macedonia. These missions, besides showing Asoka's zeal for the new faith, indicate the development of communications since his grandfather's day and the friendly relations that had been maintained with the Seleucids. Communication by land with East Asia was still infrequent because of the terrible rigours of any crossing over the high, bleak Pamirs or through the long desert wastes of the Tarim basin. Tibetan sources, it is true, say that Asoka did visit Khotan, and there is another legend that this oasis city was founded by his son Kustana; but there is no firm evidence of Indian culture in the Tarim oases before the first century A.D.

Asoka's zeal for Buddhism did not prevent him from being an efficient ruler who strengthened, as well as humanized, the remarkable administrative system Chandragupta had partly copied from the Seleucids. Highly centralized, it depended on a standing army of about 700,000 men, a widespread secret service, and a large, well-paid bureaucracy. Law and order were strictly kept, and economic affairs were regulated in considerable detail. The king was served by thirty ministers whose departments both administered Magadha and supervised the provinces, each of which came under a royal viceroy with a parallel set of ministries. Asoka added an inspectorate which made quinquennial checks upon provincial governments. Magadha and the provinces were divided into municipalities and rural districts, and the latter into groups of villages. Headmen of villages were responsible to the group treasurer and tax-collector, who took a quarter of the crops as land tax. Municipalities had six boards, each comprising five of the thirty ministries, all of which had important economic functions.

These have been described by Megasthenes, the Seleucid ambassador to Chandragupta I. The first board dealt with crafts, most of which came under guilds, and regulated wages together with standards of work. The second registered foreign visitors and arranged for their care. The third registered births and deaths, perhaps in connection with a poll tax. The fourth licensed merchants, who were also organized in guilds, and controlled weights and measures. The fifth supervised the quality of products sold, and prevented old goods from being passed off as new. The sixth collected a sales tax of 16⅔ per cent. In addition, the general commission of all ministers was collectively responsible for roads, irrigation systems, drains, fire brigades, and other public works.

Many new roads were built, especially in the south, and old roads were improved by placing milestones or providing resting places. They were much used by merchants whose 'long lines of two-wheeled carts, each drawn by two bullocks, were a distinctive feature of the times'.[1] In all districts they had to pay duties and the cost of volunteer police to protect their convoy. But the roads did not extend everywhere and for journeys across waste places, jungles, or hills, dominated by tribesmen, merchants organized themselves into caravans under a captain and with a guide who could find the way by the stars. Coastal or river traffic must have been active as there were elaborate regulations for shipping. Following Asoka's highly successful mission to Ceylon, and the co-operation of its king for the spread of Buddhism, there was close contact with this rich island. Indian ships also plied to Lower Burma from Tamralipti, the Ganges port. Within India, long distance trade was mainly in luxury wares. From the south came pepper, other spices, pearls, and gems, and from the north, muslins, other cottons, and Chinese silk woven or fashioned by Indian craftsmen. Most regions had to import iron, chiefly from Orissa, and copper from the Himalayan area or Rajisthan. Inland regions needed salt from the coast, and some rice was sent to the north-west to relieve the monotony of a diet based on wheat.

Foreign trade increased considerably under the Mauryas. Indian ships regularly went to the Persian Gulf, South Arabian ports, Aden, or Socotra, just as foreign ships frequented western or southern ports. Caravans from Taxila connected at Bactra with others leaving for, or coming from, Seluecia. Many splendid coins were thus brought to India from the fine mints of Iran and Bactria; for, although the Mauryans made big issues of copper, their silver coins were crude or soon debased, and they struck no gold. The court, together with its wealthy bureaucrats and the rich merchants, had demands for foreign luxuries. One Greek visitor described Chandragupta's palace as excelling even the splendour of Susa, and Megasthenes wrote of Magadha's handsome bazaars thronged by Indian and foreign traders who had assembled all the precious wares of India and the Near

[1] Rhys Davids, *Buddhist India*, p. 98.

East; silks, muslins, cutlery, armour, brocades, embroideries, rugs, perfumes, drugs, ivoryware, jewellery, and gold.

Yet this empire, where 'the great mass of the people were well-to-do peasantry, or handicraftsmen mostly with land of their own',[1] survived Asoka by only half a century. The reason may have been that Buddhism had both affected political loyalty and provoked a strong Hindu reaction, or that personal, highly centralized rule made the Empire very susceptible to weakness in succeeding rulers. Little is definitely known beyond the fact that the last Mauryan emperor was slain by his com- mander-in-chief who then established a Sunga dynasty (185–73 B.C.), during whose brief rule there was strong support for the Brahmans.

The Sungas, however, were soon confined more or less to the Ganges area because Bactrian kings took over the north-west. Demetrios, the fourth king, after annexing South Afghanistan, overran much of the Punjab and most of Makran. While his general, Menander, was attacking Magadha, Demetrios, who had returned, was dethroned. Refusing to acknowledge the usurper, Menander made himself king of a realm from Kabul to Mathura and from Kashmir to Cutch.

He has an enduring fame in Indian history because of a spectacular conversion to Buddhism, recorded in the Socratic *Questions of King Milanda*, although he may well have been influenced here by a desire for closer identification with his new Indian subjects. The book gives information about his kingdom and describes its capital, Sagala (Sialkot), as a great trading centre.

Well laid out are its streets, squares, cross-roads and market places. Well displayed are the innumerable sorts of costly merchandise with which its shops are filled . . . . Shops are there for the sale of Benares muslin, of Kotumbara stuffs . . . and sweet odours are exhaled from the bazaars where all sorts of flowers and perfumes are tastefully set out. Jewels there are in plenty, and guilds in all sorts of finery dis- play their goods in bazaars which face all quarters of the sky.[2]

If the Greeks in India had adopted a new religion, they had obviously kept up their old interest in trade. But Greek rule,

[1] ibid., p. 102.
[2] Quoted in Rawlinson, *India: A Short Cultural History*, pp. 90–91.

both in Bactria and India, was swept away between 140 and 120 B.C. by Scythian nomads from the Caspian region. These Sakas, as the Indians knew them, had themselves been displaced by another nomadic people whom the Chinese called the Yueh-chih and who had been driven out of Mongolia by the united Hsiung-nu. The Sakas quickly settled down in North India to establish an administration copied from their old neighbours, the Seleucids. The Yueh-chih, now known as the Kushans, followed to take over Afghanistan and Kashmir; before long there was a Kushan Empire over most of India above the Deccan and west of Benares.

The most notable ruler was Kanishka (c. A.D. 120–c. 140) whose campaigns brought Kushan power to its greatest extent. Although his coins suggest favour for a number of religions, Indian, Iranian, and even Greek, he gave a strong impetus to the northward spread of Buddhism. His capital, Peshawar, had remarkable Buddhist temples, and his encouragement of the Indo-Greek sculptors of Gandhara who were making the first images of the Buddha, led to wide diffusion of a great and enduring art form over all East Asia. The spread of Buddhism, and its new art, owed much to the fourth Buddhist council which Kanishka organized at Kashmir. It authorized commentaries on the Scriptures and arranged missions to Central Asia. Soon afterwards Kanishka took a large army over the difficult Pamirs to subdue the rulers of Kashgar, Yarkand, and Khotan in the West Tarim basin, until recently tributaries of Han China.

But as Buddhism rapidly spread north it suffered a basic change from the pure Hinayana or Theravada form that has continued in South-east Asia and Ceylon. The new Mahayana form which evolved in the north infused Buddhism with Hinduism and, to some extent, with western elements, so that the dead Teacher of truth became a living God of salvation with a hierarchy of lesser gods, one of whom, Amida, the Buddha of Boundless Light, could help believers to rebirth in a western paradise. Images proliferated and, with books and paintings, were to add a marked Buddhist component to the trade of Asia as the Mahayana faith swept north and east.

The high tide did not come until the seventh century but the first seepage of Buddhism to the oasis principalities of the Tarim

3

basin began in Kanishka's day. Indians could reach these principalities by a number of routes but all of them presented great difficulties. The shortest route began at Srinagar in Kashmir, proceeded up the Gilgit valley to Yasin, crossed the icy Darkot Pass (15,400 feet) and so came to Sarhad in the Wakhan valley. Alternatively, Sarhad could be reached from Taxila (Peshawar) by traversing the Khyber Pass (3,400 feet) to Kapisa (Begram), going up the Panjshir valley and over the Anjuman Pass to Chitral, then up the Swat valley and over the easy Dorah Pass to Ishkashm at the western end of the Wakhan valley; Sarhad (10,500 feet) was then reached by ascending the Wakhan for about 140 miles. From Sarhad the route continued east over the terrible Wakhjir Pass (16,200 feet) and then swung north to Tashkurghan (12,000 feet) beyond which it branched, at Yangi Hisar, to either Yarkand or Kashgar, two of the largest Tarim principalities. There were two other alternatives after reaching Ishkashm from Kapisa. One was to proceed up the Wakhan valley only to Kila Panja, and then to ascend the Great Pamir valley, passing Lake Victoria (13,400 feet), 60 miles beyond which the route could split south to Tashkurghan through the Naiza Tash Pass (14,900 feet) or else proceed more directly to Kashgar past Little Karakul Lake and down gorges of the Gez river. This Great Pamir route was longer than the Wakhan route, and more exposed to constant, freezing winds, but had the advantage of better grazing for pack animals. The other, much less used, alternative from Ishkashm was the Alichar-Pamir route, reached by going north to Khorog, then proceeding east along the Ghund river and crossing over the glacier-clad Sarikol to Little Karakul. The easiest and commercially most important route, but much the longest, was through Kapisa and over the Khawak Pass (13,000 feet) of the Hindu Kush to Bactra (Balkh); then one could join the great Silk Road which went along the Alai valley to Daraut Kurghan (*c.* 8,000 feet), which Sir Aurel Stein took to be the site of the Stone Tower mentioned by Pliny as the meeting place of Iranian and Chinese merchants.[1] From Daraut Kurghan the route climbed to the Taun-murun saddle (11,200 feet) to Irkishtam and thence over the Trans-Alai range to Kashgar.

[1] Warmington apparently erred in identifying it with Tashkurgan, *The Commerce between the Roman Empire and India*, p. 23.

This Alai route was open eight to nine months of the year, had good grazing and the distance over which it offered no shelter was only 70 miles or three days' journey.

By these various routes Buddhism and other aspects of Indian culture reached the Tarim oases. It is impossible to date this arrival, but it may have preceded Kanishka's subjugation of Kashgar, Yarkand, and Khotan. Stein found at Niya, an oasis 170 miles east of Khotan, a room filled with tablets in Kharoshti script, an early Indian form associated with the Kushan kings and seeming to give credence to legends that Khotan was colonized by Indian migrants during Asoka's reign. He found, too, the same script used in documents excavated at Loulan, at the far eastern entrance to the Tarim, as well as wooden carvings at a Buddhist shrine there showing distinctly Graeco-Buddhist motives. Many other expeditions—German, French, Russian, Japanese, and English—have also found in the Tarim oases ample evidence that Indian culture and religion flourished there up to the tenth century, when Buddhism was replaced by Islam. The results of these finds have been well summarized by N. P. Chakravarti, a member of the Pelliot mission:

Numberless manuscripts have been discovered in Sanskrit, Prabrit, Sogdian, Manichean, 'Runic' Turkish, Uigur, Tibetan and Chinese and the long forgotten languages of Khotanese and Kuchean or Tocharian as well as in scripts which have not yet been deciphered. Hundreds of specimens of arts, pictorial and plastic, mostly Buddhistic, have been recovered and thousands of other articles of archaeological and ethnographical significance have been unearthed which, by their characteristics, mark Chinese Turkestan as the meeting ground of Hellenistic, Indian, Persian and Chinese currents of civilization.[1]

Buddhism, and Hinduism, also spread from India to the east by other routes through South-east Asia. There are Chinese records of a trade route from Bengal through Upper Burma to Yunnan as early as the second century B.C., and Majumdar believes that this route was used by Indian colonists to Burma; he also refers to a legend of Nanchao, the old Thai kingdom of Yunnan, that it, like Khotan, was founded by agents of Asoka.[2] The legend seems far-fetched, but there was a little contact between India and China by this route as early as 128 B.C., and

[1] *India and Central Asia*, p. 15.
[2] Majumdar, *Ancient Indian Colonies in the Far East*, p. 12.

Roman envoys used it to reach Yung-ch'ang in A.D. 97. I-ching, the Buddhist pilgrim, says that it was used by twenty Chinese monks at the end of the third century A.D. It may, too, be significant that late Han cave reliefs, found at Ma Hao in Szechwan, include a figure of the Buddha. This route, however, was not known to the Chinese court until the return of Chang Ch'ien, the Emperor Wu-ti's ambassador to the Yueh-chih, who had concluded from a sighting of bamboo and silk in Bactria that these must have come through India from Szechwan via Yunnan. The envoys whom Wu-ti sent to find this route were killed or captured by tribesmen of Yunnan, but in A.D. 69 the Chinese set up a prefecture at Yung-ch'ang in order to protect a route from the Upper Mekong, through Lower Burma, to one or more of the four passes into Assam. It could not have been an important route as, although Chinese records of the third century A.D. apparently refer to a Buddhist kingdom in Central Burma, no evidence of Indian culture has been found in Burma dating from before the sixth century.

The great expansion of Indian culture to South-east Asia came by sea, as a consequence of growing demands in the early Roman Empire for Asian luxuries and the thrust of its shipping from Egypt to South India and Ceylon. This thrust was associated with the major innovation of monsoon sailing across the Indian Ocean. Until Graeco-Egyptian mariners took this up, trade between Egypt and India had been largely in the hands of Arab seamen who, as they still do, clung to the coasts of Arabia, Iran, and Pakistan, or else, falling away from the Hadramawt, came over on the north-east monsoon. Hippalus, a Greek pilot, has been credited with the first real use of the far more boisterous south-west monsoon in order to reach the Malabar coast directly from the Red Sea. This route both avoided pirates and gave a relatively fast trip of forty days from Ocelis to Muziris (Cranganore), but only solidly built Roman ships could withstand the associated rough seas and weather; Arab ships, held together by coir, were fair-weather craft. Monsoon sailing began on a large scale during the reign of Augustus (27 B.C.–A.D. 14), and so vigorously that Strabo reported 120 ships a year leaving Myos Hormos for India as compared with only a few in the days of the Ptolemies.[1]

[1] Warmington, *The Commerce between the Roman Empire and India*, pp. 8–9.

South India had long had trading relations with the West through transhipments at northern ports; its cinnamon, ginger, pepper, rice, coral, pearls, beryls, and tortoiseshell had been important to the Ptolemies and Seleucids, and before that the Bible speaks of ships sent by Hiram of Tyre for ivory, apes, peacocks, almug trees, and precious stones. But the new direct access to Egypt, coupled with greatly increased demands of Rome for Indian wares, had an enormous impact on South India. Tamil kingdoms became prosperous and encouraged sea trade by developing harbours and by providing quarters, complete with warehouses and workshops, for Roman sailors and merchants. For a time the new trade exacerbated their chronic strife, but Chola gained a supremacy over Pandya, Chera, and Ceylon, and used it for a joint development of ports on both coasts as well as for an overland route across the Coimbatore Gap, where most of the Roman coin hoards have been found. This overland route was obviously popular, once Chola could keep it open, because it avoided the dangers of sailing around Cape Comorin. As we shall notice further, mariners of ancient days had a strong aversion to sailing round capes.

One reason for fostering trade with Rome was to compensate for the Siberian supplies of gold that had been interrupted by conflicts between the Sakas and the Yueh-chih. Rome, indeed, had to export so much gold in payment for Asian wares that Tiberius (A.D. 14–37) tried to restrain his subjects from wearing silk, and Vespasian (A.D. 69–79) tried to halt outflow of bullion. His efforts must have been rather successful, judging from the scarcity of issues later than those of Nero (A.D. 54–68) among the many hoards of gold coin unearthed in South India. But, as trade with Rome increased, India found it harder to supply the very products that it exported for gold.

In these circumstances, Indian merchants naturally looked towards South-east Asia. Their ancient books called it Suvarnabhumi, Land of Gold, and their names for its various ports—Takkola, markets of cardamoms, Karpuradvipa, camphor isle, or Narikeladvipa, coconut isle—indicated that it was also a land of spices. Because the various recensions of these books may have been added to later, it is hard to date their references to South-east Asia, and there is no archaeological evidence for Indian contacts with this area before the Christian era. Nevertheless, authorities seem agreed that such contacts were made well before then, and that the contacts were far from being one-sided; Malays, after all, are known to have sailed as far as Madagascar.[1]

These voyages, however, must have been infrequent and of little consequence beyond giving Indians and South-east Asians some vague knowledge about each other. It was not until Roman days that South-east Asian trade became important. By the end of the second century, according to Pliny's information, voyages between India and South-east Asia had become frequent, and, again, there is evidence that they were not one-sided; Malays or Indonesians also participated in the growing traffic.

The South Indian ports which are known to have traded actively with South-east Asia were Muziris (Cranganore), Poduca (Pondicherry), and Sopatma (Markanam), but other ports further north also participated—Tamralipti (Tamluk) at the mouth of the Ganges, and Barygaza (Broach). It was mainly from them, and through the settlements of Indians at new trading ports in the Malayan Peninsula or the Indonesian Archipelago, that Indian culture peacefully, but extensively, deeply, and permanently, penetrated South-east Asia. Trade, that is, was here associated with the rise of Hinduized kingdoms, familiar with India's sacred law, using Sanskrit language and writing, steeped in the mythology of the Mahabharata and Ramayana epics, fervently accepting both Buddhism and the Hindu trinity of Brahma, Vishnu, and Siva, and building fine temples in the Indian style to express this devotion.

It is natural to suppose that Indian culture would have first reached Burma, Thailand, and Malaya before spreading further east to Vietnam or Borneo. Proof is lacking because there are no Indian records, and the first Hinduized kingdom with which the Chinese came into contact was Funan, in the lower reaches of the Mekong River, i.e. across lower Cambodia and Cochinchina. From their account it appears that Funan was founded in the first century A.D., and a neighbouring Hindu-ized kingdom of Champa, on the coast of the China Sea, a century later. No archaeological evidence has yet been found

[1] Coedès, *The Making of South East Asia*, p. 50; Hall, *A History of South-East Asia*, pp. 12–15; Wheatley, *The Golden Khersonese*, pp. 177–85.

to support these dates, for none of Funan's buildings have survived except traces of port buildings at Go Oc Eo, where
cameos were found with inscriptions in Brahmi of the second
to fifth centuries, and the first inscription found at Champa cannot be dated earlier than the fourth century. The fact, therefore,
that the first Chinese references to Burma and Malaya relate to
the third and the fifth centuries, and lack of epigraphical evidence before the fourth century in Malaya, or before c. A.D. 500
in Burma, by no means counts against the supposition.

It appears, from later Chinese references, epigraphical find-
ings, local chronicles, or mere traditions, that there were two
Hinduized kingdoms in Burma, one of the Pyu people in the
middle reaches of the Irrawaddy and the other of Mon people
around the port of Thaton. The Mon kingdom was connected
in some way with other Mon settlements in the basin of Thailand's Menam River, where archaeological evidence from
Si T'ep, P'ong Tuk, and P'ra Pathom can be dated to the early
sixth century. These places, in the seventh century, were certainly part of a Mon kingdom of Dvaravati. Trade was probably a strong connecting link between them as they lay on the
overland route from Thaton, Martaban, and Moulmein across
the Three Pagodas Pass to the Menam basin, and in those days
P'ra Pathom was a port. It may well have been these states
which the Liang History describes as 'the mart where East and
West meet together'[1] and as one of the conquests of Fan Shih-
man (c. A.D. 205–c. 225), the fourth of Funan's kings. The
evident later prosperity of the Mon kingdoms was also connected with overland trade from Tenasserim ports to Cambodia.

The Mon ports would have been in touch with Indian
settlements in Malaya. According to the Liang History, Fan
Shih-man's nephew and successor sent to India an embassy
which left from a port, Chu-li, in the Malay Peninsula, perhaps
in one of ten kingdoms which it says this great king conquered.
Two fourth-century inscriptions in Sanskrit have been found
near Kedah, and a Chinese report of the fifth century says about
a place somewhere in the Peninsula: 'There are over a thousand
Brahmans from India; the people practise their doctrine and
give their daughters to them in marriage, so that many

---

[1] Quoted in Hall, *A History of South-East Asia*, p. 26.

Brahmans stay there.'[1] During the fifth century China itself established diplomatic, and so commercial, relations with two Peninsular kingdoms, one called Langkasuka situated around Patani and the other called P'an-p'an just north of it. The Liang History says that Langkasuka had been founded three centuries earlier.

These Indian settlements or Hinduized Malayan kingdoms were associated with important routes over the Peninsula, some going across the narrow Kra Isthmus, but the more used routes were between Kra and the pirate-infested Straits of Malacca. Langkasuka controlled at least the terminal portions of routes coming up the Kedah and Perak rivers to the east-coast ports of Patani and Ligor. Ships from Orissa or Madras favoured these portages because they avoided the difficulties of the Straits, where ships could be becalmed or attacked by pirates, and because they shortened the trip to Funan or China by 1,000 miles. Indian merchants established settlements between anchorages on each coast of Malaya, put up warehouses, organized cross transport by river boats or elephants, planted rice fields, erected temples, and invited Brahmans to serve them. The settlers obviously intermarried with local people, and acquainted them with most aspects of Indian life,—agriculture, handicrafts, trade, writing, literature, religion, and culture. One reason for not favouring the Kra route was its restricted hinterland for settlement.

For similar reasons, including the need for food and shelter between the stages of a round trip that, because of the different monsoons needed for sailing from India to China, could take more than a year, Indian settlements were made in other parts of South-east Asia. It was probably in this way that both Funan and Champa became Hinduized, and the process is indicated by a charming legend, reported by Chinese ambassadors, about the origin of Funan. A Brahman, led by a vivid dream, sailed to it from India and soon after his arrival married the daughter of the local snake-king who, as a wedding gift, swallowed up Funan's marshy water so that their descendants might have proper cultivation. The legend clearly points to one of the greatest boons of Hinduization—skill in the kind of irrigation that had done so much for South India and Ceylon: in the

[1] Quoted in Coedès, *The Making of South East Asia*, p. 52.

Mekong delta the Khmers made a great network of canals that washed out salt from the ground, drained it, provided fish, and connected their settlements by boat transport. These canals, indeed, linked to the rivers of Cochinchina, formed a maritime highway which enabled trading ships to 'sail across Funan', thereby avoiding the storms of Cape Ca-mau and some of the pirates from Champa.

By the time Chinese envoys came to Funan, in the middle of the third century, Hinduization was far advanced there, and they heard that it had been founded during the first century. They were much impressed, and described it as a land where gold, silver, pearls, spices, and perfumes were plentiful. The people practised agriculture, were addicted to cock-fighting or pig-fighting, and used boats as large as 90 feet by 7 feet. They worshipped Siva and other Indian gods, and made bronze images to represent them. The king had many slaves, lived in a multi-storied palace, used an Indian script, rode an elephant, and kept a mystic splendour. Fan Shih-man had built a large fleet to dominate the seas and used it to subjugate ten kingdoms; he thus extended Funan's power over the Malayan portages and the Menam basin. His successors dispatched embassies to India in A.D. 225, and to China in A.D. 243, received a return mission from China between A.D. 245 and 250, and sent there three further embassies between A.D. 285 and 287.

Relations with China were complicated by friendship with Champa, which had resisted Chinese expansion into Annam. The Chinese give A.D. 192 as the foundation date for this kingdom in the region around present-day Hué, and there is no evidence for earlier Hinduization. But Indian traders would have been attracted to this narrow coastal strip, not only as a staging post on their quest for Chinese silk, but also because of the aloeswood, spices, and ivory from its confining mountains. Sanskrit inscriptions dating from the fourth century show the predominance in Champa of the cult of Siva and Uma, his wife; and Chinese reports of about A.D. 230 indicate a Hindu-ized kingdom of 'cruel and warlike' people. Their limited agricultural resources drove them to trade and piracy. Nevertheless they kept on good terms with Funan, if only because of frequent clashes with Chinese garrisons in Annam.

Sanskrit epigraphs of the late fourth century have been found on the west coast of Borneo, one of which mentions a king, Mulavarman, of a Hinduized state on the Mahakam river. Besides these inscriptions there were found sandstone figures of Siva, a golden image of Vishnu, and ruins of a Hindu temple.

China had no direct commercial contact with any part of Indonesia before the fifth century, when Straits traffic became important; before then most trade between China and India crossed the Malayan portages. But there are indirect reports of *c.* A.D. 250 about an important trading area somewhere on the south-east coast of Sumatra, which the Chinese knew as Ko-ying. The earliest works of Hindu art date from the third century; Amarvati Buddhas found at Palembang and at Sempaga in Celebes. In Java the earliest evidence comes from Sanskrit epigraphs of *c.* A.D. 450 found near Bogor and near Djakarta; they relate to a King Purnavarman of Taruma, who promoted irrigation and practised Brahmanical rites. The possibility of earlier Hinduization is not, of course, ruled out, nor is that of active contacts made by Indonesian sailors with South India. Van Leur and his followers have made much of this possibility, arguing that Indonesians had long been bold sea-farers, and that low-caste merchants or sailors could have been in no position to transmit the higher elements of Hindu culture or religion.[1] That, he thought, must have come from successful invitations to Brahmans by Indonesian rulers, who charac-teristically led their people in trade as well as in war. It could have happened in this way, among others, but it seems just as likely that settlements of Indian traders would have sent for Brahmans to keep them, and even more their children, in touch with Hindu religion. However this Hinduization took place, there can be no doubt of its association with a great extension of Indian trade, not only to South-east Asia for gold and spices, but also to South China for the silks so eagerly sought by Roman customers.

5. *Chinese superiority*

China was for very many centuries a strong magnet for trade, and this attraction, notwithstanding remoteness and serious ob-stacles to communications, brought about a commercial unity

[1] Van Leur, *Indonesian Trade and Society*, ch. 3.

of the Old World that endured long after the discovery of the New. Every part of Asia sought Chinese products, especially silks, jades, lacquers, and ceramics, and so, at least from Roman times, did Mediterranean countries. The Chinese were themselves comparatively inactive over foreign trade, leaving most of the initiative to those who prized its wares. Their civilization, based on the largest and perhaps the most industrious population of any state, and directed by the most cultivated and carefully selected of all governing classes, added to the technological superiority of Chinese products an exquisite artistry of restrained naturalness that commanded wide appreciation. The vast Celestial Empire was remarkably self-sufficient in both the necessities and refinements of life, having little need for other countries' wares beyond the jade it prized so highly and the horses which enabled it to fight off predatory nomads.

This superiority, however, had not been reached without help from foreign contacts. At the beginning of the second millennium B.C. China was without writing and used metals only for colouring purposes, whereas the Near East had, for many preceding centuries, used a variety of scripts and had moved from a Bronze to an Iron Age. It was only under the semi-legendary Shang (c. 1523–1028 B.C.) that the newly unified city–principalities around the Huang Ho and its tributaries developed a remarkable system of writing and took up bronze casting. Chinese writing owes nothing to any external influence and, although bronze casting may somehow have permeated from the west through the nomads from whom the Chinese had diverged, Shang bronzes have a quality and design surpassing those of any other time or place. Jade objects, in the form of nephrite, had reached China as the finest products of neolithic craftsmanship, but Shang artists brought jade carving to a high standard, long associated with the veneration of ritual forms.[1] The main source of nephrite was in the mountain slopes and river beds at the west end of the Tarim basin, and Shang China received it by bartering with the Yueh-chih then settled around the Kansu corridor. Much progress, too, was made in sericulture and in spinning or weaving silk, also a prehistoric product

[1] The spinach jade of Lake Baikal did not reach China until the fifth century A.D., nor jadeite until the eighth century (Willetts, *Chinese Art*, p. 156).

of the Shantung area. The silk moth is a native of other areas, including Assam and Bengal, but only the Chinese discovered, and long kept to themselves, the arts of obtaining undamaged cocoons and of unreeling them so as to get unbroken threads that gave silk its strength, elasticity, fineness, and high suscepti- bility to dyes.

At the beginning of the first millennium B.C. Shang China was conquered by the Chou, a half-nomadic people from the Wei valley, whose chariots won them most of the North China plain. There they established a sort of feudal system but, from the eighth century B.C., this disintegrated into a number of con- tending States during a period of social and political upheaval. It was, nevertheless, a period of rapid economic progress. Iron replaced bronze for even ordinary tools, the traction plough and the water buffalo came into use, large-scale irrigation developed, and also the construction of transport canals, silk became so abundant as to replace, together with metal ingots, cowrie shells as a medium of exchange, trade grew rapidly, and towns be- came commercial centres. These developments were partly the result of contacts with India or Iran, and occurred, significantly enough, after Darius had unified West Asia and part of North India. Wheat reached China from the Near East, and both the water-buffalo and the domestic fowl reached it from India. From South-east Asia came the cultivation of wet rice and the lacquer tree, whose juice was used to make fine wares that gave scope to the pictorial genius of the Feudal Age. About this time, too, the Chinese began establishing their superiority in ceramic wares.

When the nomads became horsemen communications be- tween west and east were so quickened that China overtook the technology of India and the Near East. But the nomads also became far more dangerous. Chariots could not withstand mounted archers, nor ordinary towns the swift attacks of nomad cavalry. Border states began constructing large walls to hold back nomads, and the Chinese were forced to become horsemen themselves. These changes, and the development of the cross- bow, helped to protect exposed areas, but there was always a real difficulty in obtaining a sufficient supply of horses to match the nomads' inexhaustible herds.

In these circumstances border states became semi-military,

and conquered richer kingdoms of the plain. The process was completed when the Lord of Ch'in subdued all other states, proclaimed himself Shih Huang-ti, First Emperor (221–210 B.C.), and, by further conquests, expanded his empire south to Canton. In the west he consolidated and extended earlier defence works into the Great Wall of China, and manned it to contain the nomads. It is not impossible that he followed the example of Darius in substituting imperial provinces for feudal kingdoms, in connecting these provinces by arterial roads and posts, and in standardizing weights, measures, and coins of copper cash. He is said to have standardized writing, and attempted at least a pruning of the luxuriantly brilliant philosophies of the Feudal Age. Although execrated by scholars for a burning of books, Shih Huang-ti succeeded in imposing upon the Chinese mind the important notion of unity between all peoples 'within the wall', in making men's basic loyalty to Chinese civilization itself. But his iron rule of heavy sacrifice inspired little loyalty to his house, and the imperial throne was soon lost by an incompetent son.

Several years of anarchy followed until a peasant adventurer succeeded in imposing his own rule over the whole empire, and founded the glorious dynasty of Han (206 B.C.—A.D. 221). Kao Tsu (206–195 B.C.), the High Progenitor, largely restored Ch'in administration, although having to make a concession, that fortunately proved temporary, to his followers by allowing some feudal fiefs. He was less successful against the Hsiung-nu, most formidable of all Mongolian nomads. Maudun (or Modun), between 183 and 174 B.C., welded them into a disciplined fighting force which expelled the more Aryan Yueh-chih from the region of Kansu and sent them wandering towards Bactria. It also gained him control over much of Manchuria, western Siberia and the Tarim basin, as well as over Mongolia. After Maudun's death there was more or less constant fighting between the Hsiung-nu and the Han, whose first four emperors had to mix active defence with appeasement by gifts or subsidies, in which silk was the biggest item.

The fifth emperor, Wu-ti (140–87 B.C.), set out to break the Hsiung-nu by bold campaigns of a new cavalry into the nomads' own territory. Soon after the first defeat inflicted upon the Hsiung-nu in the border area, Chang Ch'ien was sent on an embassy to the Yueh-chih for an alliance against the common enemy. He was immediately captured, and held by the Hsiung-nu for ten years before he could escape to reach the Yueh-chih in Bactria. Well content with their new home, and fearful of the Hsiung-nu, they declined the proffered alliance. Chang Ch'ien was again captured on his return journey, but when he did finally reach the Han court he had important news to give.

First, that Fergana had wonderful horses, powerful chargers which could carry heavily armoured men against nomads mounted on Mongolian ponies. Second, that in Bactria he had seen bamboo and silk, Chinese products which must have travelled from South China through India, as no traffic could pass through Hsiung-nu territory. Wu-ti, as has already been mentioned, sent envoys to find this southern route, but they disappeared among the dangerous tribesmen of Yunnan. Horses, in any case, were far more important, so that Wu-ti redoubled his efforts against the Hsiung-nu in order to establish contact with Fergana.

This meant sending, not an embassy, but an army across the Tarim basin and, even without attacks from the nomads, that was a matter of great difficulty. The first victory, which had cleared the Hsiung-nu from the northern slopes of the Nan Shan mountains, was immediately followed by the dispatch of 700,000 soldier-settlers to colonize the Kansu corridor and safeguard this new limit of the Empire. Protection was completed by an extension of the Great Wall as a line of small forts to Yumen-kuan, Barrier of the Jade Gate, through which the lovely mineral had been brought by the Yueh-chih. Beyond the gate there was a 150-mile journey across a salt-encrusted sea-bed to Loulan, then an oasis town on the edge of the Taklamakan Desert, a 700-mile long and 300-mile wide area of shifting sand dunes. Around its long perimeter there were more than fifty little oasis principalities, practising an agriculture based on irrigation and supplemented by game, furs, timber, and minerals from enclosing mountains. The biggest oases were on the northern or western rims, Karashar, Kucha, Turfan, Kashgar, Yarkand, and Khotan, but those on the north were exposed to raids by nomads from Dzungaria, coming through the gaps of the T'ien Shan mountains.

Embassies were sent to these oasis principalities in order to secure their allegiance or friendship to China, so that their nobles received handsome gifts of silk, bronze mirrors, lacquer-ware, ceramics, and other Chinese products. Even if Wu-ti had been primarily interested in trade with the Tarim, the oases had too small populations and too insignificant courts to make such trade important. His main interest in the Tarim was as a transit route to West Asia—and especially to Bactria which had such wonderful horses. As Ssu-ma Ch'ien, the great Han historian, put it:

After his victories over the Huns the Chinese Government founded the province of Chiu-ch'uan so as to keep in touch with the lands to the north-west. For this reason embassies were again sent to An-hsi, T'iao-chih and other countries. But the Son of Heaven greatly loved the horses of Kokand, and embassies set out one after the other on the road to that country. The largest of them comprised several hundred men; the smallest fewer than 100. Some years the Chinese court would send off ten embassies or more; in other years the number would be five or six. The ambassadors returned from their missions to the most distant lands in eight or nine years; it took them but two or three years from nearer countries.[1]

Ssu-ma Ch'ien went on to relate how the people of Kokand were reported to have 'a great number of magnificent horses' that they kept hidden from the Chinese ambassador. Another embassy was sent to demand them in exchange for rich gifts. But the elders argued thus:

China is far off and the road is long; travellers lack both fodder and water; in the north they run the risk of being attacked by the Huns; in the south there is neither water nor grass. Moreover, as the country along the roads is but thinly populated, the travellers themselves are often short of food. The Chinese ambassadors bring with them a suite of several hundred men, and they are always so short of food that about half of them die of starvation. How could an army ever reach us?[2]

So they refused the demand. Wu-ti thereupon sent an army under Li Kuang-li but its experience only confirmed the pre-diction. It was throughly exhausted by the arduous crossing, and the remnant that reached Fergana was easily routed. Imperial pride, no less than his great love for horses, then made

[1] Quoted in Boulnois, *The Silk Road*, pp. 33–34. [2] ibid., p. 35–36.

Wu-ti organize all his resources in order to send a second army of 60,000 men, 30,000 horses, 10,000 mules, asses, and camels, and 100,000 cattle for food across the Tarim to Fergana. Only half the men arrived but, after a long siege, finally took Kokand. They exacted a tribute of 3,000 fine stallions, deposed the king, and established a puppet. On their return journey all the little Tarim principalities offered submission to China which, for more than a century, had effective control over this lengthy and desolate way to the west.

The Hsiung-nu remained a menace and, during the reign of the interloping Confucian, Wang Mang (A.D. 8–23), the Tarim was abandoned to them. But Wu-ti had a worthy successor in Ming-ti (A.D. 57–75) who sent the brilliant general, Pan Ch'ao, to reconquer Central Asia. Before long he accomplished this and was made Protector-General of the Western Region, with headquarters at Kucha in the middle of the northern rim; Turfan had already been occupied in A.D. 60, in order to give flank protection against the Hsiung-nu. By bold diplomacy, as much as by often meagre force, this tireless warrior-statesman kept the Tarim under Chinese control during his three decades of service there. His hold over the large western oases of Kashgar, Yarkand, and Khotan was more precarious than over the eastern and northern Tarim, but was strengthened by defeat of a strong Kushan invasion in A.D. 90; after that the Kushan Empire paid tribute to Han. Pan Ch'ao also led an army across the Pamirs to the Caspian Sea, thereby establishing direct and friendly contact with the Parthian Empire. He even sent, in A.D. 97, Kan Ying to make contact with Rome but, at some northern place on the Persian Gulf, the wily Iranians dissuaded the ambassador from going further by exaggerated accounts of the journey's difficulties.

Although diplomatic relations were never properly established between China and Rome, the great civilizations at the two extremities of the Ancient World had become linked by active transcontinental trade since the first through caravan from Lanchow crossed the Tarim in 106 B.C. Caravans had also to cross Bactria and Iran, but both the Kushans and the Parthians were concerned to foster, and to exploit, transit traffic through their territories. The Han and the Kushans had had friendly relations since Chang Ch'ien visited the Yueh-chih in their new dominions, and defeat of the Kushan invasion of the Tarim meant only a temporary disturbance because the Kushans had to concentrate their forces in order to hold off the Parthians. Following Pan Ch'ao's expedition to the Caspian, China and Iran maintained good relations with each other by exchanging embassies. Rome also sought good relations with the Kushans to lessen dependence on the Parthians for Chinese silk. Through Bactria goods could come down to North Indian ports, or else avoid Parthian control by a route via the Caspian and Black Seas. But Parthia was itself an important customer for Indian and Chinese wares, and the best routes to the Mediterranean still went across the Iranian Plateau to Roman Syria. In spite of political difficulties, therefore, the Kushans and Parthians had to co-operate over trade, and stablized their frontier. The Parthians, in particular, paid much attention to communications because taxes on transit trade were an important source of revenue. Roads in Iran were never better maintained nor protected, and various specialist centres developed to serve transit trade by providing warehouses, mercantile or financial services, caravan leaders, boatmen and other personnel, as well as animals and equipment. The least satisfactory relations were between Rome and Parthia. These were good from the time of Augustus, who was content to have buffer states between Roman Syria and the Parthian Empire, until the reign of Trajan (A.D. 98–117), who launched a three years' war during which the Romans took Ctesiphon, the Parthian capital. This was only a temporary victory and Hadrian (A.D. 117–38) again accepted the old *status quo*, but the Parthians were disturbed by an attack on Syria, in A.D. 155, after which frequent and serious warfare weakened both empires. The troops of Verus (A.D. 162–5), after sacking Ctesiphon, brought back a terrible plague which seriously depopulated Italy and, in A.D. 226, the Parthians were overthrown by an Iranian dynasty of the Sassanians (A.D. 226–651), who restored the Empire to Achaemenian proportions.

Trade across the Iranian Plateau must have been strictly confined to Parthian subjects. That seems clear from the fact that Ptolemy, the Alexandrian geographer, visiting in A.D. 140, could draw on only one account of a Roman merchant's expedition along the Silk Road. He obtained it from another geographer, Marinus of Tyre, to whom Maes Titianus, a

4

Macedonian merchant, gave the report of agents whom he had sent to explore the route. They went via Ecbatana and Merv to Bactra, after which they went along a route 'exposed to the storms of winter', probably the Alai valley, to reach a stone tower which was the eastern limit for Parthian merchants. It is not clear whether they went further but, as Marinus complained, 'from their seven-month journey they brought back not a single piece of worthwhile information'; like most merchants they had little concern for geography. Pliny obtained additional information from a Ceylonese embassy to the court of Claudius (A.D. 41–54). Goods carried to the Pamirs 'are deposited on the further side of a certain river beside what the Seres have for sale, and the latter, if content with the bargain, carry them off'.[1] This silent barter trade, similar to that described later by Cosmas, in his *Christian Cosmography*, as taking place between Axumite merchants and nomads of Sasu, could not have been with Chinese merchants but most likely with the Hsiung-nu.

Kushan merchants sent some caravans to Lanchow, or intermediate Tarim cities, and Chinese caravans may have proceeded, like Chinese embassies, beyond Kashgar or Khotan to Bactra. But the nomads were still playing their historic role as traders across the steppes and deserts. Nothing makes this plainer, and also the overriding importance of silk, than a speech by the Lord Grand Secretary to the Han Council in 81 B.C.

A piece of Chinese plain silk can be exchanged with the Hsiung-nu for articles worth several pieces of gold and thereby reduce the resources of our enemy. Mules, donkeys and camels enter the frontier in unbroken lines; horses, dapples and bays and prancing mounts, come into our possession. The furs of sables, marmots, foxes and badgers, coloured rugs and decorated carpets fill the imperial treasury, while jade and auspicious stones, corals and crystals become national treasures.[2]

Foreign products were also beginning to flow in through southern ports. Wu-ti had recaptured Nan Yueh, the old kingdom from Canton to Haiphong, the port of North Vietnam. Wang Mang, about A.D. 3, dispatched envoys to Huang-chih,

---

[1] Quoted in Hudson, *Europe and China*, pp. 80–81.
[2] Goodrich, *A Short History of the Chinese People*, p. 41.

which scholars have variously identified as being in Malaya, India, or even Africa; the envoys certainly returned with pearls, glass, gems, and rare birds or animals in exchange for gold and silk. But they probably went in barbarian ships as Chinese mariners do not appear to have ventured on the high seas before the fourth century A.D. Indian ships, however, began sailing to South China in the first century A.D., and a few may have reached it earlier. Most shipping in Han times was, as we have seen, conducted by South-east Asians who brought goods from Haiphong to the entrepôts of the Malayan portages. A Chinese account of the fifth century A.D. describes one of these as still being a rendezvous for Indian merchants: 'Its market was a meeting ground between the east and west, frequented every day by more than 10,000 men, including merchants from India, Parthia and more distant kingdoms who came in large numbers to carry on trade.'[1]

Further evidence of the entrepôt activity of South-east Asians came to light, in 1944, through excavations at Go Oc Eo, the port of Funan. Besides many Khmer objects there were artifacts from India, Rome, and China: gold rings, jewellery, carvings in semi-precious stones, tin amulets with symbols of Vishnu or Siva, a Buddha head of Gandhara, and merchants' seals in Sanskrit; a Roman medal dated A.D. 152, a coin issued by Marcus Aurelius, and intaglios of glass or semi-precious stones; a fragment of a Han mirror and Buddhist statues of the Wei period. Some Indian wares would have reached Go Oc Eo directly, but it is unlikely that any wares were brought by Roman ships. There were Roman factories in South India, but Roman geographers and merchants had only a vague, hearsay knowledge of sea routes or places further east.

Besides making the Tarim basin safe for land trade between China and India or Iran, and opening up sea trade with South China, the Han dynasty was associated with further developments of Chinese products. Bronzeware had declined from the superlative standards reached in Shang days, but there were wide demands, at home and abroad, for beautifully worked bronze mirrors with elaborate designs of some cosmological significance. Ceramics advanced through better kilns, which made higher firing possible, and the use of glazes taking a wider range of

[1] Quoted in Majumdar, p. 8.

colours, so that Han craftsmen produced lovely proto-porce-lains, much ahead of anything in the West. Han textiles were also centuries ahead and, in the later period, a water-powered mill was used in the imperial factories which turned out great quantities of fine brocades, crêpes, damasks, gauzes, reps, and taffetas, all woven into striking but subtle patterns, and dyed over a fairly complete range of colours. Greater supplies from Khotan stimulated jade-carvers to higher levels of artistry, as well as to increased output, and much the same is true of jewel-lers, who were receiving bigger supplies of Altai gold and Indian or Iranian gems. Lacquerware was produced in greater quan-tity and better quality. In this period, too, the Chinese invented a pure rag paper that was welcomed as an improvement on slits of bamboo or wood; more than a thousand years passed before Europe learnt how to make such paper. Another Chinese improvement, well in advance of the west, was the breast-strap for draught animals. China made some permanent gains from foreign trade; the soyabean was probably introduced during this period, together with lucerne, the food of Fergana horses, grape-vines from Iran, and the p'i-pa, a Bactrian lute. Best of all were the horses, which went to imperial stud farms in which Wu-ti took the greatest interest.

6. *Rome's Asian trade*

Under the Julian-Claudian emperors (A.D. 14–68) Rome's for-eign trade began a remarkable expansion and, by the second century, had become worldwide. It was, according to Wheeler, based on five commodities, essential to the Empire's luxury: German amber, African ivory, Arabian incense, Indian pepper, and Chinese silk.[1] But these were supplemented by many less important wares. Egypt, which had long been a big supplier of wheat, linen, and building stones, and the sole provider of papyrus and mosaic glass, now became the great entrepôt for Rome's African and Asian trade. This hinged upon Alexandria, a city of about 500,000 inhabitants, and a great processing as well as a great trading centre. Its linen industry made special cloths for Asian trade, and its weavers also worked on Indian cottons and Chinese silks. Gold- and silversmiths made quanti-

[1] Wheeler, *Rome Beyond the Imperial Frontiers*, pp. 176–81.

ties of plate for African or Asian potentates. Perhaps in association with its fine medical school, Alexandria developed a pharmaceutical industry processing Arabian, Egyptian, and Indian drugs. There was also a perfumery industry, based on Asian imports and supplied with fancy jars and bottles by a vigorous glass industry. This glass industry was more important as supplying beads and imitation gems for African and Asian trade.

Rome not only added a large and growing demand for goods reaching Egypt but strengthened and protected ports or roads built by the Ptolemies. Axum, the Abyssinian kingdom which controlled trade with East and Central Africa, was made an ally. Escorts of troops protected the caravan route from Berenice to Coptos, and a river police the Nile and its canals. Petra was manned as a fort and, after Trajan had conquered the Nabataeans (A.D. 98), he built another road from Petra to Aila with the consequence that this port superseded Leuke Kome. Trajan had another canal dug to link Alexandria with a new port of Clysma. By this time a Roman fleet was patrolling the Red Sea in order to give protection from pirates, and its control extended to the Arab anchorage at Ocelis, where Rome had trading rights secured through costly gifts to the local ruler.

Monsoon sailing had not seriously affected the Arabs. They had founded Axum; frankincense and myrrh were still important monopolies; they still controlled Gerrha and the caravan routes through the Peninsula and were active at the twin ports of Charax and Apologus, at the head of the Persian Gulf. They continued semi-coastal voyaging to East Africa, Iran, and India, and preserved monopolies of trade with the Mediterranean in ginger and cinnamon by concealing their sources from Roman subjects, and even making them believe these sources were in East Africa and Arabia. Persian sailors were not much in evidence before Sassanian times, but Indians regularly voyaged from Barygaza (Broach) to Omana (Muscat?) on the Persian Gulf or to Socotra and Aden; there was, too, a colony of Indian merchants at Alexandria. It is possible that Indian ships were trading on the East African coast as far south as Madagascar, because there is a tradition that settlers came to it from Mangalore on the Malabar coast.

But Graeco-Roman merchants and sailors had, since the

discovery of monsoon sailing and the advances in Roman ship-building, become the most active of all Red Sea traders. We owe to one of these sailors an informative handbook, *The Periplus of the Erythrean Sea*, for voyages from Red Sea ports to both coasts of India. Its information was later supplemented by Ptolemy's *Geography*, written when Rome's Asian trade had already passed its peak; Ptolemy gave little more information than the *Periplus* about trade, but showed better knowledge of the interiors of India and Ceylon, as well as of places further east.

The *Periplus* begins with two 'designated' ports in Roman Egypt, Mussel Harbour (Myos Hormos) and Berenice, the boundary of the province and so a limit of the Empire. Sailing 450 miles south one came to Ptolemais of the Hunts, where the Ptolemies had formerly sent hunters for elephants or ivory but which now supplied only a little ivory or tortoiseshell. It had lost trade to Adulis, 'a port established by law' in Axumite territory 330 miles further south; the reason was that Adulis was only three days' march from Coloe, 'the first market for ivory', and only eight from Axum, the great centre for ivory and rhinoceros horn (used by the Romans for making oil flasks). These products could be obtained in exchange for undressed cloth, robes of Arsinoe, poorer quality cloaks, articles of flint glass or murrhine (its substitute), brass, copper, iron, axes, adzes, swords, Greek and Italian wines, olive oil, and gold and silver plate (presents for rulers). At Red Sea ports Roman traders needed only 'a little coin', so that this trade must have been nearly self-balancing. For similar wares Roman traders could obtain from Arab ports on the opposite shore, Leuke Kome and Muza (Mocha), such Indian goods as iron, steel, cotton, broad cloth, muslins, girdles, and lac.

Around the Horn of Africa there were various Berber towns having only roadsteads: Avalites (Zeila), Malao (Berbera), Mundus (Bender Hais), Mosyllum (Ras Hantara), the Market and Cape of Spices (Guardafui), Opone (Ras Hafun), the Pyralcae Islands, Menuthias (Pemba or Zanzibar), and Rhapta (Dar-es-Salaam), 'the very last market town on the continent of Azania'. These East African places supplied some ivory, tortoiseshell, and rhinoceros horn, a good deal of frankincense or myrrh and re-exports of the Indian products cinnamon,

copal (a gum used both as an incense and as a drug), and macir
(a medicinal bark). The *Periplus*, misled by Arabs, took East
Africa to be the source of cinnamon, much prized in Rome as a
perfume, incense, condiment, and medicine. In return for such
products, Roman merchants exchanged cloaks, cloth, tunics,
glassware, copper, iron, and tin. The East African places also
imported, from India, rice, wheat, sugar, ghee (clarified
butter), sesame oil, cotton cloth, and girdles.

Eudaemon Arabia (Aden), with its good anchorage and
watering facilities, had been a great entrepôt for Asian trade
but, at the time of the *Periplus* (*c.* A.D. 60), it had recently been
sacked by Arab tribesmen from the north. Much of its trade
had, accordingly, gone to Dioscorida (Socotra), the largely
desert and thinly peopled island 600 miles to the south. Here now
came traders from Egypt, East Africa, Arabia, and India in
order to exchange their own wares, and to procure the island's
supplies of tortoiseshell and dragon's blood (a red gum used for
dyes, paints, and medicines).

Most of the frankincense or myrrh of the Hadramawt came
to Cana (Hsin-al-Ghurab) which traded, not only with the Red
Sea and the Persian Gulf, but also with Barygaza and other
ports of North India. Arab seamen had long traded further
south, too, if only to get from Malabar the timber lacking in
Arabia for their ships. Other Hadramawt ports for collecting
frankincense and transhipping goods, to or from the east, were
Syagras (Ras Fartak) and Moscha (Khor Reiri). Cana received
frankincense or myrrh that had been collected at these minor
ports, together with tortoiseshell from the island of Sarapis
(Masirah). Egypt supplied Cana with cheap clothing, copper,
tin, coral, storax (the medicinal sap of the liquidambar), a little
wine or wheat, and gold- or silverware for the king, together
with other luxuries. Some aloes (an aromatic wood also known
as agal-, aghil-, eagle- or aloeswood, and lignaloes) were
obtained at Cana but, like cinnamon and ginger, came there
from India.

The *Periplus* mentions two ports on the Persian Gulf. Omana
was six days' sailing from the entrance and on the Arabian
shore; Apologus, at the head, was 'a market town designated by
law'. Large vessels, sailing regularly from Barygaza, brought to
these Gulf ports copper, blackwood (an East Indies rosewood

often sold as ebony in Rome), ebony itself, teak, and sandalwood (a native tree of South India). They exported many
pearls, 'but inferior to those of India', great quantities of dates,
wine, some gold and clothing, and a purple dye. Omana exported 'sewn boats' to Arabia, carvel-built hulls of teak or
coconut wood (imported from India), the planks of which were
held together by fibre stitches; they had the advantage of a
certain flexibility for coping with shoals or reefs, but were too
frail for monsoon sailing.

The only port mentioned on the Makran coast was Oraea, 'a
little market town' in a country yielding much wheat, rice,
dates, and wine. More important was Barbaricum(Bahardipur)
on the marshy delta of the Indus. It exported cotton cloth,
indigo, bdellium (an aromatic gum), lycium (a plant dye), and
nard (a highly prized oil used as a condiment and for ointments
or medicines); also lapis lazuli from Afghanistan, turquoise
from Iran, silk yarn from China, and 'Seric skins' (skins or furs
from Central Asia). It imported much thin clothing, figured
linens, the fine, red coral of the Mediterranean (in demand
among wealthy Indians), topaz, storax, frankincense, glass
vessels, a little wine, and gold or silver plate. But Barbaricum
did not compare with the great port of Barygaza, which drew
produce from secondary ports around the Gulf of Cambay as
well as from the interior: bdellium, lycium, nard, costus (a root
from Kashmir with similar uses to nard and also used for preserving fruits); agates, carnelians, and ivory; all kinds of cotton
and silk cloth; and long pepper (*piper longum*) used in medicine.
To Barbaricum Graeco-Egyptian merchants brought antimony,
copper, tin, realgar (red sulphide of arsenic, used in medicine);
flint glass, coral, and topaz; storax and sweet clover (made into
chaplets and thus re-exported); inferior clothing, wines, and
various other luxuries including, for the king, beautiful maidens
or singing boys.

Muziris (Cranganore) 'abounds in ships sent there with cargoes from Arabia and by the Greeks'. To it, and other Malabar
ports, they brought 'a great quantity of corn', thin clothing
('not much'), and figured linens; as well as some wine and
wheat for sailors of their ships or merchant colonies of Roman
subjects established in South India during these early days of
monsoon sailing. The chief Malabar exports were pepper (used

by every respectable Roman household), great quantities of fine pearls, diamonds, sapphires, ivory, and tortoiseshell; malabathrum (cinnamon leaf much used for ointments), nard (from the Ganges area), and silk cloth (from China but re-exported from the Ganges). Many of these products came from Ceylon, but the *Periplus* makes no mention of any port on this island because it was only later that Roman ships began visiting it.

On the Coromandel coast were Camara (Karikal), Poduca (near Pondicherry), and Sopatma (Madras), all of which had similar exports or imports to Muziris, but in bigger quantity; for 'the greatest part of what is brought at any time from Egypt comes here'. Quite large ships left these ports for the Ganges from which they brought malabathrum, nard, pearls, and 'muslins of the finest sort'. They also left them for voyages to 'Chryse' (Malaya) which had 'the best tortoiseshell of all places on the Erythrean Sea'. North of the Ganges was 'a great inland city called Thinae, from which raw silk and silk yarn and silk cloth are brought on foot through Bactria to Barygaza, and are also exported to Damirica (South India) by way of the river Ganges. But the land of Thin is not easy of access; few men come from there, and seldom.'

Ptolemy Claudius compiled his account of eastern lands (*c.* A.D. 150) from reports made by later voyagers, and he says something about Ceylon. Pliny records that the Emperor Claudius (A.D. 41–54) received a mission from the King of Ceylon, and it would be after this that Roman ships went to the resplendent island. The most eagerly sought of its exports were pearls and gems (both royal monopolies): chrysoberyls, rubies, sapphires, and such semi-precious stones as garnets, moonstones, spinel, topaz, tourmaline, and zircon. The Romans may have obtained cinnamon leaf from Ceylon or South India, but the Arabs apparently still managed to conceal the source of cinnamon shoots (*cinnamomum*) and cinnamon bark (cassia). After the death of its great king, Dutthagamini (101–77 B.C.), Ceylon became virtually a dependency of Chola.

Tamil kings encouraged western trade. Mention has already been made of their improvements to harbours, the linking of Malabar and Coromandel ports by the overland route through the Coimbatore Gap and the facilities provided for Roman merchants. In 1945 archaeologists systematically investigated the old site of Poduca at a place called Arikamedu, and were able to identify warehouses or industrial quarters of about the first century A.D.[1] A great quantity of red-glazed Arretine ware proves that this old port had been frequented by Roman traders, as did many wine-amphorae, some lamps, glass, crystal intaglios, and Graeco-Roman carved gems. Yavanas, as the Indians called the Greeks or other westerners, also came to the Tamil kingdom as soldiers, engineers, or even bodyguards.

One reason for Roman warehouses or workshops on the Coromandel coast was an extension of shipping towards the source of silk. The Parthians were putting high charges on goods coming through Iran, and Rome desired silk above all other Asian wares. Ptolemy makes it clear that Roman subjects were active at the mouth of the Ganges, and he mentions another land route from China. 'They say there is not only a road from these lands to Bactriana by the Stone Tower but also one to India through Palimbothra' (Patna). Hudson held that this was the present route from Kansu via Lhasa and Sikkim to Patna,[2] a view which Needham receives with caution.[3] Needham, however, is more definite, because of Chinese sources, about a third land route from Yunnan via Bhamo in Upper Burma to two ports, Sabana and Takkola, both mentioned by Ptolemy. Following Hudson and Wheeler, he takes Sabana as having been near Moulmein and Takola as having been near Rangoon. Wheatley, on the other hand, argues that Ptolemy's Golden Khersonese, in which the geographer placed both ports, must have been in South Malaya, not Lower Burma, and so thinks Takkola must have been on Malaya's west coast and Sabana at its tip.[4]

Ptolemy also mentions Kattigara, 'the harbour of the Sinae', which was visited by a certain Alexander after touching at another port, Zabae. His visit, according to Han records, was followed by an embassy from Marcus Aurelius bringing the, by

---

[1] Wheeler, *Rome Beyond the Imperial Frontiers*, Ch. XII; see also Adhya, *Early Indian Economics*, pp. 150–51, for a few similar finds of Roman products at Bombay and at Akota in Baroda.

[2] Hudson, *Europe and China*, p. 88.

[3] Needham, *Science and Civilization in China*, vol. i, p. 182; Adhya, op.cit., p. 163, accepts this view.

[4] Wheatley, *The Golden Khersonese*, pp. 144–7 and 151–2.

then, unexciting tribute of ivory, rhinoceros horn, and tortoise-shell. Hudson put Zabae at Saigon and Kattigara at Hanoi,[1] but Needham thinks Kattigara may have been in Kwantung.[2] Toussaint puts it at Go Oc Eo, the port of Funan,[3] but excavations there did not bring to light many Roman articles and these, in any case, could have been brought by Indian or Cambodian merchants. Wherever Kattigara was, the Han record makes it clear that Tongking had a port for southern trade, not supplanted by Canton until centuries later. To it, presumably, Wu-ti's envoys returned with exotic tribute: pearls, gems, glass, rare birds, and a live rhinoceros.

We have only fragmentary indications about the magnitude of Asian trade in this early period. Pliny, a well-informed adviser of Vespasian (A.D. 69–79), reckoned that each year Indian trade drained Rome of 12,500,000 denarii and the Arabian and Chinese trade together of at least another 12,500,000 denarii. The denarius was a silver coin—perhaps it was helpful that Rome preferred silver to gold while India had the opposite preference—and in Pliny's day had a content of 3.1–3.3 grams. The aureus had a gold content of 7.3 grams so that, as an aureus was worth 25 denarii, the two metals had an exchange ratio of 1:11, as against 1:27 in 1967. Our price of gold has been fixed at $35 per troy ounce since 1934 and, at this price, the denarius would be worth about 28 d., so that Pliny's estimate of the total gold drain to Asia becomes about £3,000,000. If allowance were made for the rise of commodity prices since 1934 the figure would be nearer £10,000,000.

By modern standards this is not a large drain for a great empire, but it was substantial for the Ancient World as a few comparisons may indicate. It has been estimated that, between 200 and 150 B.C., the Roman Republic obtained 261,000,000 denarii as booty or indemnities from the Mediterranean conquests, Gaul, Asia, and Spain's gold-mines, the chief western source. This works out at 50,000,000 denarii a year, twice Pliny's estimate of the annual loss to Asia. The Emperor Tiberius, moreover, a frugal man, left his successor only 750,000 denarii. In China, the usurping Emperor Wang Mang, by A.D. 23, had accumulated a gold treasure of 156,200 kilograms

[1] Hudson, op. cit., p. 89.   [2] Needham, op. cit., p. 178.
[3] Toussaint, *Histoire de l'Océan Indien*, p. 40.

and so equivalent to 540,000,000 denarii, or about twenty-two times Pliny's estimate.

The crucial question, of course, is the relation of Rome's gold drain to its Asian imports. Rostovtzeff held that 'the goods of the east were paid for, without doubt, partly with silver and gold coins, as Pliny says, but mostly by goods produced in the Empire, especially in Alexandria'.[1] No evidence is adduced for this view but it is, perhaps, supported by the apparent success Vespasian had in halting the outflow of coin to India. Although, too, the *Periplus* refers to 'a great quantity of coin' being sent to South India, and a profitable exchange for gold and silver at Barygaza, it does not mention significant exports of coin to other ports of the Erythrean Sea and lists many exports from Rome or Egypt. Goitein, moreover, reporting about Jewish trade between Egypt and India during the eleventh and twelfth centuries, says that 'payment was largely made in kind';[2] what was possible then could also have been possible in the first century. Chwostow has calculated that Europe's adverse balance with India during the period 1788–1810 was about the same as Pliny's estimate of 12,500,000 denarii for Rome, and so supports a conclusion reached by Beloch that Indian imports per head of population in the Roman Empire were at least 70 per cent of what they were for Europe in 1835. Warmington endorses this conclusion, although he thinks Pliny's estimate may have omitted South India by including this adverse balance in the other estimate for Arabia and China.[3] We might, in the light of these considerations, guess that Rome's Asian imports were around four times its adverse balance, and so about £40,000,000 in 1967 values, with corresponding exports of about £30,000,000.

Even if that were the case, Asia's export receipts would have been considerably less. What Rome paid for Asian wares had to cover not merely their market price in the lands of origin but also levies of tariffs or tolls, and transport costs including allowance for risks from shipwrecks, storms, pirates, or brigands. The *Annals of the Later Han*, referring to the Silk Road, allege that goods sold in Syria for ten times their cost in China, and the *Chin-sha Annals* allege for a hundred times this cost. The

---

[1] Rostovtzeff, *The Social and Economic History of the Roman Empire*, vol. 1, p. 67.
[2] Goitein, 'Mediterrenean to India'.   [3] Warmington, op. cit., p. 276.

Arthasastra, reputedly written by a minister of Chandragupta I, recommended a just rate of interest at 15 per cent a year for ordinary secured loans but at 5 per cent a month for trade loans, 10 per cent a month for caravan trade, and 20 per cent a month for sea trade. Such were the comparative risks of the two modes of transport, and the profits expected from trade.

Pliny gives information about the prices charged for Asian spices and aromata in the Roman market. They are in denarii per pound and may be compared with an average daily wage of 1–2 denarii.

Arabia and Abyssinia		India	
Cardamom	3	Amomium	
Cassia	5–50	(cardamom)	49–60
Cinnamon Oil	35–300	Bdellium	3
Frankincense	3–6	Costus	5½
Ginger	6	Indigo	20
Laudanum	2½	Malabathrum	c.300
Myrrh	3–50	Pepper, white	7
Serichatum (?)	6	black	4
		Spikenard (nard)	100

The only other extant price list is from Diocletian's famous Edict (A.D. 301), issued in an unsuccessful attempt to halt inflation. As it puts the wage of unskilled labour at 25 denarii per day, and that of skilled labour at 50, prices must have risen twenty-five times since Pliny's day. The text has survived only in fragmentary form so that, although we have prices for about nine hundred items, many prices are missing. This, however, does not explain the surprising omission of Indian cottons among related references to linens and woollens. Chinese silk, moreover, is mentioned only twice; white silk at 12,000 denarii a pound, against 1,200 for the best linen yarn, and purple-dyed raw silk at 150,000 a pound, three times the price for purple-dyed wool. The famous purple from the shellfish of Tyre was an even more expensive commodity than silk.

The most extensive list of prices for other Asian goods relates to spices and aromata, but strangely omits pepper.

Bdellium	100
Cinnamon (root, bark, and wood)	125
Frankincense (finest)	100
Ginger (prepared)	50
Malabathrum (leaf)	60
Myrrh (oil of)	600
Roses (oil of, first quality)	70
Saffron (from Arabia)	2,000
Storax (from Antioch)	200

Comparing these prices with those given by Pliny, it appears that ginger had become relatively much cheaper, and cinnamon or malabathrum relatively cheaper still.

The Edict throws interesting light upon transport costs within the Empire. It fixed freight rates at 20 denarii a 1,200-pound wagon load, at 8 for a 600-pound camel load, and at 4 for an ass load. This gives, on converting Roman pounds into avoirdupois, a rate of 40 denarii a ton-mile, or just above the daily wage of unskilled labour, allowing for maintenance. It is not far from the relative cost of goods transport on the first British railways which, in 1856, charged about 45d. per ton-mile as against a daily wage of 35d. for unskilled labour.[1] It would seem, from this comparison, that it was not the cost of transport so much as the high risks merchants had to run which made the movement of goods over long distances so expensive in the Ancient World.

---

[1] Mitchell and Deane, *Abstract of British Historical Statistics*, p. 312.

CHAPTER TWO

Medieval changes

1. *Nomad havoc*

Asian trade had reached an apex during the second century B.C. because the prosperous empires of Rome and China both created and supplied large demands for foreign wares, and because their own protection of trade routes was reinforced by that of the Parthian and Kushan empires over the 2,500 miles between Syria and the Tarim basin. All these empires sustained a heavy burden of defence against various nomads threatening their northern borders. China's Great Wall had to be manned from South Manchuria to the Kansu corridor, and garrisons in the isolated Tarim oases held off the Hsiung-nu and other tribes in Dzungaria. The neighbouring Kushans inherited and improved a ring of large brick fortresses to the north of Chorasmia, where soldiers kept watch on Sakas menacing both their own and the Parthian empire. Parthia had no standing army, relying instead upon powerful feudal families to oppose Roman and Kushan forces. It did Rome a great, if involuntary, service by restraining the Alans and other invaders from the Caucasian or Caspian steppes, so that Rome's Asian provinces were little troubled by nomads. From the Danube to the Rhine, however, Rome had to build palisades or stone walls against dangerous northern tribes, and to man them with legions which, like those of Han China, were increasingly recruited from barbarians themselves.

Han military strength and diplomacy succeeded in dividing the Hsiung-nu during the first century A.D. into a southern group around the Empire's Mongolian border and a northern group which had gone to Dzungaria. The southern group became colonists within the Empire, garrison soldiers or semi-agriculturists under Han control. In Dzungaria the northern group was troublesome until, during the second century, they were expelled by another nomadic horde, the Hsien-pi. They

then moved into Central Asia, where one branch mingled with
Iranian nomads of the Sarmatian steppes, and with Mongols of
the Siberian forests, to form a people known later as the Black
Huns, while another branch, the White Huns or Ephthalites,
kept to the region south-east of the Aral Sea.

Meanwhile adverse changes were taking place in both China
and Iran. The Han had become weakened by poor rulers, corrupt officials, ambitious generals, and the heavy burden of
defence. Demands for taxes and corvée labour so impoverished
peasants that two great rebellions broke out, in A.D. 184, and
took over thirty years to put down. Generals became so powerful
that in A.D. 220 they deposed the last Han, and three of them
then divided the Empire into kingdoms of their own. They
maintained for a time, and even extended, Chinese control over
the border provinces or commanderies in the south, the west,
and Korea, in spite of almost constant warfare among themselves. The Kingdom of Wei gradually gained ascendancy and
one of its generals, after seizing the throne, managed for a few
years to restore the Empire under a brief Chin dynasty (A.D.
280–316). But the Hsien-pi, the Hsiung-nu, and two Tibetan
tribes, who had all been swarming over the Tarim, took advantage of renewed civil war to invade North China in A.D. 304.
There they fought with one another as well as with the Chinese,
many of whom fled to the southern empire of Eastern Chin
(A.D. 317–420). Nevertheless the invaders became, in varying
degrees, sinicized and some attempted to carve out a northern
empire of the Han type. None had much success until the
T'o-pa, as the Hsien-pi were now called, united the whole north
under a Wei Empire (A.D. 439–535). It, in turn, had to cope
with fresh nomads, the Juan-juan, and so controlled the Tarim
only briefly and intermittently.

Iran, too, had serious trouble from nomads as well as frequent
warfare with Rome and its eastern successor, Byzantium, but
managed to hold them off under a new Sassanian dynasty (A.D.
226–642). This dynasty arose through the refusal of Artabanus,
the last Arsacid emperor, to recognize usurpation by an Iranian
family of an important fief in the province of Fars. A son of this
family, Ardashir (A.D. 226–40), took over the province, added
to it, and defeated Artabanus. Almost immediately the king of
Armenia, supported by Rome, led a coalition of Scythians and

Kushans against Ardashir; he beat it and went on to make a highly centralized empire from the Euphrates, through Merv and Herat, to Lake Hamun. The second emperor, Shapur I (A.D. 240–71), after conquering Samarkand, Tashkent, and Bactria, deposed the line of Kanishka. He then fought two wars against Rome capturing, in the second, the Emperor Valerian and 70,000 troops, most of whom were sent to build military or civil engineering works in Iran. A further Roman war, during the next reign, coincided with a serious revolt in the eastern provinces, backed by the Kushans. It was not put down until Shapur II (A.D. 309–79) had conquered the Kushans and reduced their territory to a province of the Empire. They, however, soon made an alliance with the Ephthalites, and were subdued only when the Sassanians allowed the Ephthalites to settle in Kushan territory as 'confederates' of the Empire. The newcomers soon evicted the Kushans, and began to make an empire of their own while the Sassanians were desperately engaged in new struggles with Rome. Shapur III (A.D. 383–8) eventually came to terms with Byzantium, which agreed, to pay a contribution for Iranian protection of the Caucasian passes against the Black Huns, now threatening both empires. Vahram V (A.D. 420–40) was able to check Ephthalite expansion, and Peroz (A.D. 459–83) later felt able to attack in force. But he lost his life in a defeat which almost reduced Iran to a vassal of the Ephthalites. The yoke was not thrown off until Chosroes (A.D. 531–79), in alliance with the Western Turks, succeeded in crushing them.

This defeat was a relief to India as well as to Iran. There the Gupta family, after gaining control of the Kingdom of Magadha in A.D. 300, had largely succeeded in restoring an empire over North India. Samudra Gupta (c. A.D. 335–80), the second king of this line, began a process of expansion, and Chandra Gupta II (A.D. 380–415) completed it with conquests that brought the Empire's limits from Cambay to Bengal and from Kashmir to Madras, although much of this territory included States which merely paid tribute, and most of Central or South-west India remained outside it. The Gupta period (A.D. 300–700) has been called the Classical Age of India, remarkable for its culture and, in particular, for the development of Hinduism, as well as for prosperity and peace. Skanda Gupta repulsed, in A.D. 455, a

5

great raid of the Ephthalites but, after his death, they wrecked the Empire. The collapse of Iranian power as a result of the defeat inflicted upon Peroz's army, left India fully exposed to their pressure, so that they poured over the Hindu Kush, took North-west India and made Sialkot their new capital. With them came a number of other nomadic peoples, who moved south and east to form Gujarati settlements in Cambay or to found Rajput families. The kings of Malwa and Magadha combined forces to push the Ephthalites back to Kashmir, in about A.D. 528, and soon afterwards their power was completely broken by the Iranians and Western Turks.

The Black Huns, whom the Iranians also withstood, moved into Europe. Balambar, their king, led them in a destruction of the Ostrogoths' kingdom between the Don and the Dnieper, and then drove the Visigoths from the region of the Dniester. Rome, foolishly as things turned out, allowed the fleeing Visigoths to settle in its Balkan provinces. The Huns, after bringing Alans and other Sarmatian tribes under their command, advanced into Hungary and began raiding further Balkan provinces. Attila (A.D. 432(?)–453) welded the Huns, the Sarmatians, and some Germanic tribes into a crude empire, roughly modelled on Sassanian lines. He led them against Constantinople, which was spared only on payment of a huge tribute, and, after probing Rome's weakness in the Balkans, attacked Gaul and North Italy. He was turned back from Gaul at a battle near Orléans and soon withdrew from Italy, probably owing to another heavy bribe. Two years later Attila died, and the Hun Empire quickly fell apart.

Rome had serious trouble with barbarians from the reign of Marcus Aurelius (A.D. 161–80), when Germanic tribes began raiding both the Balkans and North Italy. Under their increasing pressure the Empire's boundaries were contracted to the Danube and the Rhine, and defended by barbarian troops or colonists. Italian vigour was being undermined by disastrous plagues and a too luxurious or parasitic way of life. Authority waned as the throne passed, often infamously, to men entirely dependent on semi-barbarian armies and having to appease them with lavish concessions. Prosperity decayed as taxes were increased and coins debased to meet these concessions and growing costs of defence. In the third century, it seemed that the

Empire was breaking up under the double strain of barbarian attacks and civil disorders. For a time, it was saved by the drastic reforms of Diocletian (A.D. 284–305) who, after repulsing barbarians and restoring imperial authority, took direct control of the Empire's eastern half and placed the west under a co-emperor. When, however, he had to repel a Gothic invasion of Italy, he found it necessary to take over the whole Empire again. Further barbarian raids during the next few reigns, and further political troubles, led, in A.D. 395, to the Empire's final division.

Byzantium, the Eastern Roman Empire, survived a thousand years of successive pressures from nomads, Sassanians, and Moslems; and was eventually destroyed, not so much by Turks, as by Christian Crusaders. The Western Empire, on the other hand, hardly lasted another century. In A.D. 410 the Visigoths descended upon North Italy to sack Rome and, after taking over Gaul, founded a Kingdom of Toulouse. The Vandals, who had simultaneously left Spain for Africa, took over Carthage; but re-crossed the Mediterranean, in A.D. 455, to pillage Rome. Some twenty-one years later Odovacar, the Visigoth, deposed the last, feeble Western Emperor and Europe, overrun by Germanic tribes, slumped into a brutal feudalism, relieved by Byzantium's long hold on parts of eastern or southern Italy.

By the opening of the fifth century A.D., therefore, North China and Western Europe had passed from the ordered rule of great empires, with all that such rule meant for prosperity and trade, to the ravages of contending barbarians, some of whom, after destroying the Kushan Empire, were also to destroy the Gupta Empire of India. The only stability on the landways between Europe and Asia was provided by the Byzantine and Sassanian empires, and they were in frequent conflict. In these circumstances, it was natural for Asian trade to become increasingly sea-borne; Egypt was under Byzantine control, neither South India nor South China were touched by nomads, and a great trading empire, Srivijaya, was developing in South-east Asia.

2. *Byzantine and Sassanian monopoly*

A first consequence of crumbling Roman power was a serious decline in the great part played by Egypt in Roman trade, a decline associated with the meteoric rise and fall of Palmyra. This Arab city, with a mixed population that included Greeks and Iranians, had become, by the second century A.D., a more important entrepôt than Petra for such Asian trade as came up the desert routes from South Arabia or crossed between Egypt and Syria. Because of its location on the edges of the hostile Roman and Parthian empires, Palmyra held a semi-independent position as a feudatory city, and emerged as a military power in A.D. 260 when its chief, Odaynath, drove from Syria Shapur, the Parthian conqueror of Valerian. In the following year Odaynath crushed a revolt by Roman troops in Syria against the new emperor, Gallienus, who then made Odaynath *dux Orientis*, master of Rome's eastern legions. The Egyptian prefect revolted, and was crushed after fighting which destroyed a good part of Alexandria. But Odaynath and his son were treacherously assassinated, possibly at Rome's instigation, and his able queen, Zenobia, on taking the succession, abandoned all faith in the Empire. A fresh revolt in Egypt gave Palmyreans the chance of occupying the whole country save Alexandria, which was held by a Roman garrison. The energetic Aurelian, however, quickly reconquered Egypt, captured Palmyra, and led Zenobia in golden chains to adorn a magnificent triumph. These events had had such a disastrous effect on Alexandria's industries that its merchants and manufacturers conspired with Palmyra to shake off Roman rule. Aurelian grimly put down both revolts, and utterly destroyed Palmyra.

Palmyra's trade passed to the Ghassanids, another Arab tribe which soon controlled a large strip from Sinai to the Euphrates. They became rapidly Syrianized and adopted Monophysite Christianity. During the fifth century A.D. they were under Byzantine influence and served as a buffer against the Bedouin. Their prosperous kingdom was destroyed by Byzantium in the following century, because of strong support for the Monophysite heresy, and the Syrian desert then lapsed into an anarchy which was not remedied until the Islamic conquest.

Alexandria survived but did not regain its former commercial supremacy, partly because it was also weakened by Axum. This kingdom, which Arabs had long ago established in the northern highlands of Abyssinia, was an ally and trading partner of the Roman Empire. In the third century A.D. it began a vigorous expansion which brought its limits to the Nile and to the Straits of Babal-Mandab, forcing chiefs to pay tribute and to protect land or sea routes that were important for entrepôt trade with East or Central Africa. Adoption of Christianity in the following century did not prevent the Abyssinians from invading the Himyarite kingdom in the Yemen. They held it for thirty-eight years during which they dominated Red Sea trade. Himyarite kings recovered the Yemen in A.D. 378, but the Abyssinians again occupied it in A.D. 525. Fifty years later an Iranian expedition expelled them, and the Yemen soon became part of the Sassanian Empire.

Decay of Roman power in the Red Sea meant a decline of voyaging by Graeco-Egyptian sailors to India. In the sixth century A.D., accordingly, Cosmas Indicopleustes, who wrote *The Christian Topography* in order to prove the flatness of the earth but who had some experience of sailing, at least along the Hadramawt coast, reported only rare visits by Roman merchants to Ceylon, then the great entrepôt for western and eastern merchants. Rome's former Asian trade was now shared by Abyssinians and Iranians, who had reached an understanding that the sea-trade in spices or aromatics was left to Abyssinia and that in silks to Iran, thereby strengthening its more important monopoly of overland trade in Asian wares. Alexandria continued to receive, and to process, African or Arabian wares as well as some Indian wares. But it now received very little silk, and the bulk of Indian or Chinese wares came to the West through Iran. Diocletian and Narsah actually made an agreement, in A.D. 297, that Nisibis, in Iranian Mesopotamia, should be the only centre for Byzantine purchases of silk; in A.D. 408 another agreement nominated two other such centres, Callinicum, also in Mesopotamia, and Artashat on the Araxes River.

Byzantine emperors sought to reduce dependence upon both Egypt and Syria, provinces whose heresy often made them insubordinate, and which were always liable to attack by Iran because of frequent Sassanian attempts to recapture Syria. Naval power was used to divert trade from Alexandria, Tyre,

Beirut, and Antioch to Constantinople and, even before the Arab conquests, Syria's control over Mediterranean shipping was further challenged by Byzantine ports in southern Italy, such as Amalfi and Naples. Syria's dominant position in silk manufacturing was also broken. Soon after Constantinople was founded, it had five separate guilds concerned with trading or processing silk and, from the fifth century A.D., there were imperial gynaeceums—large workshops in which many women were kept, under strict conditions of security, to weave increasingly elaborate silken fabrics for the Court, the Church, and higher officials. Before long Tyrean dyers were hit by a reservation of purple fabrics to the gynaeceums, and other Syrian weavers by a similar reservation of gold brocades. All private manufacturers, moreover, were exposed to sharp fluctuations of supply because imports of raw silk could be bought only by official *commerciarii*, who saw to it that the gynaeceums' requirements were met first. An acute shortage developed in A.D. 540, when Justinian ordered *commerciarii* to pay no more than 15 gold nomismata (or solidi) for a pound of raw silk, and the Sassanians refused to sell at this price because of an outbreak of war with Byzantium. Syrian manufacturers demanded a corresponding rise in the controlled price of their finished silks, but Justinian forbade a sale at more than 8 nomismata a pound. Manufacturers naturally ceased producing and tried to sell off their stock at black market prices. The court then made the entire silk trade a royal monopoly, which was run so avariciously that private manufacture had to be abandoned. 'All those who had devoted themselves to the silk trade were reduced to beggary', said Procipius, the Byzantine historian. 'Many of them emigrated and went to take up refuge among the Persians.'[1]

But the gynaeceums throve as oriental standards of luxury gripped Byzantium. Mosaics of the period show the long silken robes favoured by rulers and priests, and then by upper-class men and women; even the dead were clothed in silk under the new Christian ritual of burial. Cloths were becoming more luxurious, too, as the gynaeceums acquired higher skills in weaving to produce beautiful gold brocades or the fabulously expensive *opus plumarium* of interwoven feathers from tiny birds. Nor had demands for silk abated in Western Europe. There the

[1] Quoted in Boulnois, *The Silk Road*, p. 144.

conquering barbarians quickly adopted the sumptuous tastes of the Roman upper classes for Asian luxuries. Alaric, for example, exacted from Rome a ransom which included 4,000 silken tunics and 3,000 lb. of pepper, and Byzantine envoys had to soothe Attila's court with gifts of silk and Indian gems. To the demands of new barbarian rulers in the West were added those of the rapidly expanding Christian Church for incense, costly vestments, and altar hangings. Both these western demands were, of course, influenced and strengthened by the deliberately impressive luxury of Byzantium. The gynaeceums thus furnished large exports which the emperors controlled, not only as a source of valuable profits, but also as an instrument of diplomacy over peoples who depended upon Byzantium for highly prized silks.

For all its concern with religious matters, Byzantium was fundamentally a commercial state like its rival, Sassanian Iran. The capital, Constantinople, was magnificently sited for trading with the Aegean, the Levant, Iran, and Russia; the Black Sea area supplied amber, leather, furs, dried fish, and slaves, and its commercial importance grew as time went on. Emperors levied a 10 per cent duty on both exports and imports, and received large profits from the gynaeceums or other state enterprises. Constant wars, however, both in the West and the East, and the high cost of Court, Church, and Government imposed great financial strains, which were aggravated by a continuing, heavy adverse balance on eastern trade. Byzantine's handsome gold nomismata of 24 carats were eagerly sought in Asia; Cosmas Indicopleustes reported that all merchants around the Indian Ocean conducted their trade with these coins, and that the King of Ceylon valued them above all others. Byzantium had to manage its trade so as to finance huge imperial expenditures and to redress the adverse balance with the East by favourable balances with the West and North. 'If', Runciman says, 'Byzantium owed her strength and security to the efficiency of her Services, it was her trade that enabled her to pay for them. Her history is fundamentally the history of her financial policy and of the commerce of the Middle Ages.' Ostrogorsky adds that it was not trade with the impoverished West which enriched Byzantium but rather its trade with the East.[1]

[1] Runciman, *Byzantine Civilization*, p. 130; Ostrogorsky, *History of the Byzantine Empire*, p. 68.

Byzantine monopoly in supplying Asian wares to Europe was itself subject to Sassanian monopoly of their supply to Byzantium. The Sassanians further improved ancient land routes to Asia across Iran by providing more caravanserais, watering places, and customs or toll stations to cope with increasing traffic. They sought to breach the Byzantine monopoly of supplying Europe by constant yet unsuccessful attempts to regain Syria. Land traffic must have suffered when nomads overran the Tarim and North China, but revived when the Sassanians conquered the Kushans and established good relations with the new Gupta Empire of India. There was a further commercial setback when the Guptas were wrecked by the Ephthalites, but overland trade from China was then recovering under the Wei dynasty. The Ephthalites soon became a menace to the Sassanians who, for reasons of security, stopped all trade with them. This stoppage badly hit Sogdia's merchants so that their ruler, Khan Dizibul, authorized a commercial mission to Byzantium. Justin II (A.D. 565–78) gave it an attentive reception, and made a military as well as a commercial alliance with the Ephthalites against Iran. The route by which the Sogdians brought Chinese silk, and their own renowned ironware, ran from the Aral Sea to the north shore of the Caspian Sea and thence across the Caucasus to Trebizond, on the south-west corner of the Black Sea. Although the new trade began well, it was soon terminated as the Ephthalites became incensed with Byzantine trickery and even attacked Bosporus.

The reason for the Sassanians being able to cut off trade with the Ephthalite kingdom was that they had a flourishing sea trade with India and Ceylon. Iranians had not been active seafarers before this dynasty, but its emperors, from the outset, developed ports and encouraged shipping so as to reinforce their monopolist control over Asian wares coming by the land routes, or to have an alternative to these routes. They were, no doubt, impressed by the way Roman shipping had weakened their Parthian predecessors' control over Asian trade to the West, and anxious to profit from the decline of Red Sea trade with India. Sea-trade, too, had become more important because of the impetus it had given to development in South India and Southeast Asia and to an extension of shipping to South China. When, under barbarian pressure, Chinese civilization retreated below the Yangtze, South China made rapid progress and sought sea-trade as compensation for blocked access to land routes. By the fifth century A.D., accordingly, the whole western trade of the Indian Ocean came into Persian hands, except for the spices and aromatics which Abyssinians brought to the declining marts of Egypt.

Ceylon was then the great centre of exchange between West and East, as Cosmas reported:

> From all India and Persia and Ethiopia many ships come to this island, and it also sends out many of its own, being in a central position. From the further regions, that is Tzinista (China) and other exporting countries, Taprobane (Ceylon) imports silk, aloeswood, cloves, sandal-wood and so on, according to the production of the place.[1]

Justinian attempted to break this reinforced monopoly by appealing to the King of Axum, a fellow Christian, to purchase silk in Ceylon for delivery to Byzantium. The King agreed but did not succeed because, so he said, his merchants were out-manoeuvred by those of Iran. Yet, as Hudson points out, the Abyssinians could surely have bought silk in Ceylon and, it may be added, delivered this to Egypt, if they had really wished. Ceylon was not under Iran's sway, nor could the Sassanians have effectively policed the vast Indian Ocean. It is more plausible to suppose an agreement allowing the Abyssinians to bring spices to the West if they would leave silks to the Iranians; collaboration to exploit Byzantium was better than damaging competition to supply its insistent demands for Asian goods.

Cosmas makes it clear that, at least up to his day, land trade in silk was much greater than the corresponding sea trade. 'It is obvious', he said, 'that anyone who comes by the overland route from Tzinista to Persia makes a very short cut; which accounts for the fact that such quantities of silk are always to be found in Persia.'[2] The sea route which the Iranians successfully dominated thus served mainly to tighten their control over the supply of silk to Byzantium and, through it, to the whole of Europe.

Like the Byzantines, the Sassanians needed trading profits in order to finance great military expenditure and a costly

---

[1] Quoted in Hudson, *Europe and China*, p. 111.
[2] ibid, p. 111.

administration. No less than nine wars were fought with Byzantium over Syria; Caucasian passes had to be defended against the Black Huns, and the Oxus frontier against the Kushans, and then against the Ephthalites. In order to carry out these demanding tasks, the Sassanians had to have a permanent army, in place of Parthian feudal levies, and a far more centralized administration. The army was made expert in siege warfare and supplemented by military colonies of border peoples to guard the frontiers. Emperors could not fully restore the government of the great Achaemenians, but they weakened and diminished the power of feudal nobles by making royal princes or army officers governors of important provinces, and by establishing a stable, efficient civil service. This was headed by a vizier and secretaries or ministers responsible for posts, appointments, justice, war, and finance. The secretary of finance was especially important as his large force of accountants, agents, and tax-collectors had to raise huge revenues for the court, government, army, fortifications, shipping, and such public works as irrigation or improvements to transport.

The most important taxes were those on land and trade. Land tax, plus the exactions of the men who collected it, bore heavily upon peasants, and could take up to one-half of their produce. Although nominally free, most peasants had become serfs, and the state added to exactions of feudal masters by levying various kinds of extraordinary service for public works or royal enterprises, and by requisitioning grain and animals at low prices. The peasant's dark situation was relieved only a little by better irrigation, which considerably increased agricultural production, by help from state granaries in times of famine or scarcity, and by occasional cancellations of rural debt. Some improvement, however, was effected by Chosroes (A.D. 531–79) when he converted the land tax-in-kind to fixed money payments on area and produce.

Merchants and manufacturers were also heavily burdened by customs, octrois, tolls, or forced requisitions, and subject to state monopolies in silk and some other products. Nevertheless, there was a great expansion of trade and industry under the Sassanians. New towns sprang up, urban populations increased, and much was done to improve urban amenities, including water supplies and schools, as well as to improve communications. Industrial growth, and state supervision over prices and wages, led to a marked development of guilds. As both foreign and urban transactions were now on a monetary basis, there were large issues of silver and copper coins, and a further development of banks and credit instruments in response to growing needs of trade and industry. The bill of exchange became a legally valid claim and banks, run by Iranians or Jews, developed other monetary instruments so effectively that our world is indebted to the Pahlavi language for such terms as 'cheque' and 'avaliser'. A far more immediate consequence of this financial activity was the introduction, by Syrian traders, of the Iranian bill into Merovingian Europe.

3. *The Eastward sweep of Buddhism*

If the Sassanians did not fully succeed in re-establishing the centralized empire of the Achaemenians, still less did the Guptas succeed in re-establishing that of the Mauryas. Chandra Gupta II (A.D. 375–415), Sun of Prowess, was direct master of all North India and, to a lesser extent, of the West Deccan, but he restored Mauryan administration only in the Ganges Valley where his power was firmest. Even there the Guptas left much to provincial or district officials, whose independence was strengthened by grants of land in lieu of money salaries. Such a policy, no doubt, was the result of insufficient political or military strength, but it reflects the Guptas' tolerant desire to avoid needless interference, shown by their encouragement of representative local government. Villages were largely controlled by councils of elders under a headman of their own choice, and towns by municipal councils which included representatives of guilds. Within their own spheres of trading and manufacturing, moreover, guilds had become virtually autonomous.

By Gupta times guilds embraced most merchants or artisans and, besides making or enforcing rules for conditions of work, standards of products, trading practices, and price regulation, had developed wider functions. These included technical education, welfare measures and, as guilds became wealthier, banking and trustee activities. Many guilds made big contributions to charitable or religious works, as did kings and nobles. The main beneficiary was the Buddhist Sangha (monastic organization) which, by Gupta times, was itself something of a landlord, banker, and investor in commercial projects.

There was much scope for commercial enterprise in Gupta India. Mauryan communications had survived largely intact, and were so restored or further developed that goods moved fairly easily and safely over the whole country. The ports of West and South India were busier than ever, as were their associated industries. They had received an impetus from Rome's Red Sea trade, and continued to benefit as this passed to Iranians and Abyssinians. Indian ships were also crossing to Arabia and the Persian Gulf, but the big expansion of their activity was from west coast ports to South-east Asia as Indianized kingdoms developed there and traded increasingly with South China. Good relations with the Sassanians encouraged more overland trade with Iran which, after its conquest of the Kushans, had become the neighbour across the Indus. Overland trade with North China revived after the Wei dynasty reunited it and restored some order in the Tarim, especially as the oasis towns were now strongly Indianized. So much silk, indeed, appears to have come from China that at least one important guild of silk weavers in West India broke up, its members being fortunate enough to enter other callings, all of higher status. Gupta India, nevertheless, produced great quantities of silks, muslins, cottons, calicoes, linens, and woollens, and the metallurgical industries made further progress, especially with regard to bronze casting. One indication of increased trade and prosperity was a sharp fall of interest rates from Mauryan levels; against the previous rate of 240 per cent a year for loans on foreign trade the legal rate fell to 20 per cent. Other interest rates were never so high as to exceed, on cumulation, the principal owing.

Besides importing greater quantities of Chinese silks and South-east Asian aromatics, spices, and gold, Gupta India increased imports of horses and camels from Arabia, Iran, and Bactria, and imports of ivory from Abyssinia or South-east Asia. There was not much change in India's exports to the west, but a marked change in those both to the north and to South-east Asia, owing to the spread of Buddhism or Hinduism there. Bronze images of the Buddha and Hindu deities must have been shipped in large quantities from West Indian ports, especially casts from Amaravati, to South-east Asia, and such images, together with carvings in wood or ivory, paintings, books, and religious jewellery went over caravan routes to the Tarim oases and North China. Close links of most Indian merchants with Buddhism, of course, helped this dissemination, but it also owed much to the princes of areas which had become Indianized, and to the activities of Buddhist missionaries or pilgrims. The extent to which Buddhism had spread eastwards by the fourth century is shown in a remarkable book written by the pilgrim, Fa-hsien, about his journey to India.[1]

Buddhism seems to have reached China during the first century A.D. through traders or missionaries who brought it by both the land and the sea route. A Parthian prince is known to have come as a missionary to Loyang in the latter part of the following century, and many Buddhist scriptures were translated by Kumarajiva whose father had married a princess of Kucha in the Tarim, and whom the Chinese brought back, about A.D. 382, after their occupation of Kucha. The faith made such progress under royal patronage, both in North and South China, that by A.D. 381 nine-tenths of the north-west were said to be Buddhists. Its greatest patrons were the Wei dynasty (A.D. 386–534) who built the magnificent cave temples at Yun-kang and Lung-men. Fa-hsien was one of their subjects and a monk at Ch'ang-an when, 'distressed by the imperfect state of the Buddhist "Disciplines" ', he set out in A.D. 399 upon a fifteen-year journey to seek proper rules from India, and to absorb other wisdom from foreign Buddhists.

Before reaching the Great Wall he was joined by disciples and, supplied by the friendly governor, set off across the Gobi Desert, guided only by 'the rotting bones of dead men'. After seventeen days they came to the region of Lop Nor where the king had become a Buddhist and there were over 4,000 monks of the Lesser Vehicle (Hinayana). They rested, and then took fifteen days to reach Karashar, which also had 4,000 priests of the Lesser Vehicle. Its people, however, 'did not cultivate politeness nor duty to one's neighbour', so that some of Fa-hsien's party had to go back to Turfan in order to raise funds, while he and the others proceeded south-west on a thirty-five days' journey. After hardships 'beyond all comparison', they

[1] Giles [trans.], *The Travels of Fa-hsien.*

reached Khotan (presumably via the beds of the Yarkand and Khotan rivers), and had a rewarding experience.

This country is prosperous and happy, its people are well-to-do; they have all received the Faith, and find their amusement in religious music. The priests number several tens of thousands, most of them belonging to the Greater Vehicle (Mahayana). . . . They prepare rooms for travelling priests, and place them at the disposal of priests who are their guests, together with anything else they may want. . . . Fa-hsien and the others, wishing to see the processions of images, stayed on for three months.[1]

From Khotan another journey of twenty-five days brought them to Karghalik, a smaller Buddhist kingdom with only 1,000 Mahayana priests, and, after a further rest, they made a four days' journey across the Pamirs to Tashkurgen where they went into retreat. After that they went north to Kashgar, making another twenty-five days' journey and rejoining their companions from Turfan. They were in time to witness the great quinquennial assembly to which the king invited monks from all quarters; 'and these collect together like clouds'. Fa-hsien was impressed by this festival but found Kashgar 'mountainous and cold', unable to ripen any grain but wheat. It took a full month to cross the Bolor Tagh range, covered with perpetual snow and inhabited by 'venomous dragons, which, if provoked, spit forth poisonous winds, rain, snow, sand and stones. Of those who encounter these dangers not one in ten thousand escapes.'

Once over this dreadful range the pilgrims were in India, but still had to go south-west for another fifteen days 'over a difficult, precipitous and dangerous road, the side of the mountains being like a stone wall ten thousand feet high'; the crossing was made possible only by numerous steps or ladders. A rope suspension bridge finally brought them to the other side of the Indus to spend a summer retreat at Udyana and make a brief visit to Gandhara, both places being given to the Lesser Vehicle. The party then came down the Khyber Pass to Peshawar, but soon re-entered Afghanistan in order to see various famous shrines. It was only at the end of another summer's retreat that Fa-hsien came back to the Punjab and, after a warm welcome there, made a slow trip down the Ganges valley.

[1] Giles, op. cit., pp. 4–5.

His valuable description of the Tarim routes and oases was now supplemented by almost the only contemporary account of Gupta India. It delighted him.

The people are prosperous and happy, without registration or official restrictions. Only those who till the king's land have to pay so much on the profit they make. Those who want to go away, may go; those who want to stop, may stop. The king in his administration uses no corporal punishments; criminals are merely fined according to the gravity of their offences. . . . Throughout the country no one kills any living thing, nor drinks wine, nor eats onions or garlic. . . . As a medium of exchange they use cowries.[1]

This description applies more particularly to what Fa-hsien called 'the Middle Kingdom', south of the Jumna River, but his highest praises were reserved for Magadha: 'Of all the countries of Central India, this has the largest cities and towns. Its people are rich and thriving and emulate one another in practising charity of heart and duty to one's neighbour.' Throughout North India he observed admirable charity: 'The elders and gentry of these countries have instituted in their capitals free hospitals, and hither come all poor or helpless patients, orphans, widowers and cripples. They are well taken care of, a doctor attends them, food and medicine being supplied according to their needs.'[2]

Fa-hsien could not visit the Deccan which is 'mountainous and its roads difficult', because he lacked money for paying escorts; so he returned to the Middle Kingdom in order to copy a text of the Book of Discipline as approved by the First Buddhist Council. Journeying then to the mouth of the Hooghly, he took a passage to Ceylon, arriving there after fourteen days, thanks to the favouring winter monsoon. Ruled from the mainland, Ceylon had a flourishing agriculture and produced many pearls and gems, now that it had been freed from the demons or dragons with whom, long ago, Indian merchants had conducted a silent barter trade. Fa-hsien found Buddhism well developed in this agreeable climate, but he had been so many years away from his home that, 'when he saw a merchant make offering of a white silk fan from China, his feelings overcame him and his eyes filled with tears'.

So he embarked on 'a large merchant-vessel, on which there

[1] Giles, op. cit., pp. 20–21   [2] ibid., pp. 47–48.

were over two hundred souls, and astern of which there was a smaller vessel in tow, in case of accident'. Within three days the ship sprang a leak during a storm, and the terrified merchants threw their goods overboard. This awful gale blew for thirteen days before they could beach the ship for repair on an island; but the gale may have saved them from the pirates who infested this sea and 'to meet whom is death'. They went on through bad weather until the sky cleared sufficiently for the captain to tell east from west and, after more than ninety days, to bring the ship to Java, a heretical place where 'the Faith of Buddha was in a very unsatisfactory condition'. Five months later Fa-hsien took another ship which set a north-east course for Canton, but after a month's sailing its captain lost his way in another bad storm. When seventy more days had passed, and provisions were nearly done, the course was changed to north-west and a further twelve days' sailing brought the pilgrim to the south coast of the Shantung promontory, 15° north of the original destination. If the land route to India was appallingly difficult, the sea route was then just as perilous. The odyssey, however, ended well; the prefect gave Fa-hsien a most honourable reception, after which he went to Nanking, the southern capital, in order to hand over there the *Sutras* and Disciplines he had so heroically and devotedly collected.

Perhaps Fa-hsien's picture of Indian social life is superficial and idealistic, but there is little else against which it can be checked. Gupta records are meagre, and the best support for this pilgrim's accuracy comes from excavations and contemporary literature. The excavations show that urban luxury was of a high standard and not narrowly restricted. A good account of the daily life of a well-off man is the *Kamasutra* (Art of Love), which describes a gentle refinement in comfortable surroundings. For the upper classes, at least, there was sufficiently widespread wealth to make the Gupta age the greatest period of Indian cultural achievement. Large universities were thronged with students from many lands, important progress was made in mathematics and astronomy, the six Brahmanical philosophies were developed, and the great epics or *Puranas* were put into enduring literary form. Kalidasa wrote plays for a lively theatre, the Ajanta caves were decorated with magnificent paintings, and all the plastic arts came to full Hindu flower.

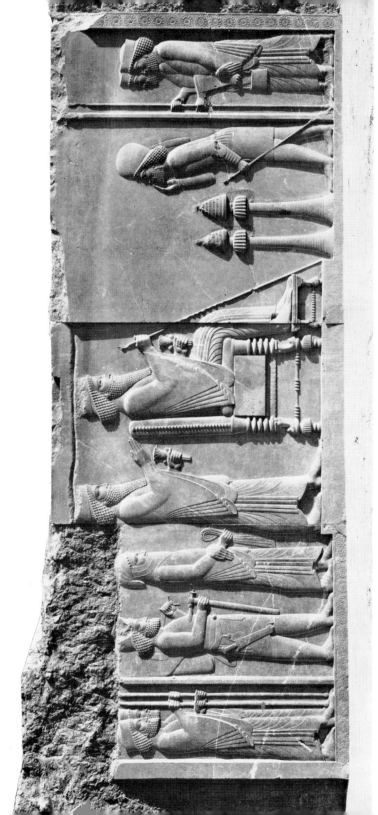

1 Darius giving audience (from the Treasury of Persepolis)

Oriental Institute, University of Chicago

2 Gandhara Buddha *British Museum*

Political confusion descended upon North India during the fifth century when the Huns came down the passes, and continued when they were driven back, a century later, after the Turks and Sassanians had dealt them a fatal blow. Petty kingdoms then took over the Gupta inheritance until they were once again welded, by Harsha (A.D. 606–47), into a rather loosely feudal empire. But other aspects of Gupta civilization survived, and recovered, during his long and fruitful reign. They have been well described by the most famous of all Chinese pilgrims, Hsuan-tsang (b. A.D. 602), the T'ang Master of the Buddhist Law.

Already highly esteemed as a scholar and monk at the age of 29, he petitioned his new emperor. T'ai Tsung, who was restoring the Chinese Empire and clearing Turks from the Tarim, for leave to visit India where he wished to consult pure texts that would resolve confusion over rival Buddhist philosophies. Permission was refused because of dangers on the overland route but, strengthened by a vision of success, he set out alone from Chengtu in Szechwan on travels that would keep him from China for sixteen years.

Avoiding various officials who had been warned to stop him, he set off across the Gobi to reach Hami where three monks gave him hospitality and where an invitation came from the Buddhist king of Turfan, a flourishing oasis deeply imbued with Sanskrit culture. So taken was this king with the pious learning of his guest that he wished to keep him as a permanent spiritual director, and Hsuan-tsang could leave only after a serious threat of fasting to death. The king then equipped him for crossing the T'ien Shan and the Pamirs, and sent an escort to ensure him good treatment from the Western Turks. The whole court, *sangha*, and people saw him off and, after some dangers, he crossed the 'mountain from which silver was dug' and came to the even more prosperous oasis of Karashar. He saw there ten monasteries and 2,000 monks, but stayed for only a single day, after which he left for Kucha, perhaps the most important of all Tarim principalities.

The capital is from 6 to 7 miles in circumference. The soil is suitable for red millet and wheat. It also produces rice of the kind known as keng-t'ao, grapes, pomegranates, and a large quantity of pears, plums, peaches and apricots. There are gold-mines, as well as copper, iron, lead and tin. Its climate is mild. The morality of the people is high. Its alphabet has been borrowed from India.[1]

Although royally welcomed, he did not find the Hinayana Buddhism of the court to his liking, but had to spend more than two months at Kucha because of heavy snow on the T'ien Shan.

So cold and bitter was the 40-mile crossing that Hsuan-tsang's party lost fourteen men and many horses and oxen. At the Issyk-kul (Warm Lake) they came to the hunting camp of the Khan of the Western Turks, and were impressed by his fine horses, clothing, tents, and food. The Khan entertained Hsuan-tsang generously but warned him against going to India; the country was too hot and the people were too much like savages to be worth visiting. This advice was, of course, politely refused, and the Khan helped the party to reach Samarkand. Hsuan-tsang praised this town highly.

It is completely enclosed by rugged land and very populous. The precious merchandise of many foreign countries is stored up here. The soil is rich and productive, and yields abundant harvests. The *shen* horses are bred here. The inhabitants are skilful in the arts and trades beyond those of other countries.[2]

After making some converts, Hsuan-tsang set off for Bactria via the Iron Gates, a famous defile on the caravan track from the Oxus. Bactria's old canals were still intact so that the Master found 'the plains and adjacent valleys unusually fertile', but made little comment on its trade beyond noting that 'in commercial transactions they use gold and silver alike'. At Bactra (Balkh) there were 100 monasteries and 3,000 monks, all devoted to the Lesser Vehicle, but he had a pleasant stay with them before crossing the Hindu Kush to Bamyan.

The Snowy Mountains are high and the valleys deep; the precipices and crevasses are very dangerous. A blizzard keeps on without intermission; the ice remains through the full summer and the snowdrifts fall into the valleys and block the road. The demon spirits send, in their rage, every kind of calamity; robbers waylay and kill travellers. Going with difficulty the six hundred *li* or so, we gradually arrived at Bamiyan [*sic*], a kingdom located deep in a valley of the Hindu Kush. The capital leans on a steep hill bordering on a valley. On the north

---

[1] Quoted in Grousset, *In the Footsteps of the Buddha*, p. 53.
[2] Mirsky, *The Great Chinese Travellers*, p. 53.

it is backed by high precipices. The country produces spring wheat and few flowers or fruits. It is suitable for cattle, and affords pasture for many sheep and horses.[1]

Although its people were uncultivated, they were good Buddhists and had carved two colossal, impressive statues of the Buddha into a cliff.

Hsuan-tsang then crossed the Shibar range to Kapisa (40 miles north of Kabul), commanding the major passes to India and so a great trading centre. It produced cereals and many fruits as well as breeding horses. Here the Master spent an agreeable summer among 6,000 monks of the Greater Vehicle, before crossing the Kabul River to enter the Buddha's own country. It had been greatly damaged by Hunnish raids. At Peshawar the monastery built by Kanishka was almost deserted, and at Udyana the university which used to have 20,000 monks had become silent and empty. When they reached the Indus the party turned north, using footbridges of rope or iron and climbing up many ladders set in the cliffs, before coming to Kashmir.

The soil is fit for producing cereals, and abounds with fruits and flowers. Here also are dragon-horses, the fragrant turmeric and medicinal plants. The climate is cold and stern. . . . The people wear leather doublets and clothes of white linen. They are light and frivolous, and of a weak, pusillanimous disposition.[2]

Yet they were handsome, loved learning, and supported 100 monasteries and 5,000 monks at Srinagar, the capital. They gave the Master a splendid reception, and the king placed twenty scribes at his service for copying the many sacred books of its great libraries besides introducing him to a leading Mahayana philosopher. So rewarding was all this that Hsuan-tsang spent two years in Kashmir.

It was not until A.D. 633 that he entered Harsha's restored empire. Another two years were spent in further study at various monasteries in the Punjab. From there he went to visit the holy places in Nepal associated with the Buddha's life and enlightenment, experiencing deep religious emotion to strengthen intellectual insight. Further enrichment came from five years spent at Nalanda, the great Buddhist university where the leading master instructed him further in idealism and where he perfected his knowledge of Sanskrit.

[1] ibid., p. 57.   [2] ibid., p. 63.

From Nalanda he went down the Ganges Valley, crossed Bengal, and visited Assam, which he heard was only two months' journey from Szechwan. At Tamralipti, on the mouth of the Ganges, he learnt of Burma and other kingdoms across the sea, but was dissuaded from embarking for Ceylon as this would be better reached from a southern port. And so he travelled through Orissa, where he noticed that cowrie shells and pearls were still in use as currency, and through Andhra, visiting Amaravati, the great centre of religious art. Eventually he reached Kancipura in the Pallava country, but was further disappointed about visiting Ceylon. Refugee monks told him that it was torn by civil war and gripped by famine. Some of them accompanied him across the Deccan to the Gulf of Cambay where he saw the famous port of Barygaza (Broach). 'One sees in this kingdom piles of merchandise from foreign lands. There are more than a hundred families whose fortune amounts to over a million ounces of silver.'[1] There, too, he heard about Iran, a country from which there came woollens and silken brocades, pearls, and other precious wares, besides fine horses and camels.

Going again down the Ganges Valley he visited a number of holy places and scholars before returning to Nalanda for further studies in grammar and logic. By this time Harsha, an enthusiastic Buddhist, was anxious to meet the renowned pilgrim and instructed the King of Assam to bring Hsuan-tsang to Kajangala. There Harsha prostrated himself at his guest's feet, held a great welcoming banquet and summoned 1,000 monks together with 500 Brahmans or Jains and many laymen to two philosophical tournaments. At these Hsuan-tsang overcame all opponents and won victory for the Mahayana faith. Harsha, in zealous elation, distributed all his treasure to the priests and consented to the Master's departure most reluctantly.

Hsuan-tsang clearly admired Harsha's administration and the 'happy prosperity' of his Empire.

As the administration of the country is founded on benign principles, the executive is simple. The families are not entered on registers, and the people are not subjected to forced labour. The crown lands are divided into four parts. The first is for carrying out the affairs of state; the second, for paying the ministers and officers of the crown;

[1] Grousset, op. cit., p. 188.

the third, for rewarding men of genius; the fourth, for giving alms to religious communities. In this way, the taxes on the people are light, and the services required of them moderate. Everyone keeps his worldly goods in peace, and all till the soil for their subsistence. Those who cultivate the royal estates pay a sixth part of their produce as tribute. The merchants who engage in commerce travel to and fro in pursuit of their calling. Rivers and toll-bars are opened for travellers on payment of a small sum.[1]

Early in A.D. 644 Hsuan-tsang crossed the Indus, accompanied by Kings of Kashmir and Kapisa, an indication of their respect for Buddhist learning—and of the growing power of T'ang China over the Tarim basin. A difficult journey by tortuous paths through ice and snow brought the Master to Badakashan where he spent another month with the Khan of the Western Turks. He then went up the Wakhan Valley to Tashkurgen past the Great Dragon Lake (Lake Victoria): 'these sombre valleys and dangerous peaks are covered with eternal snows and ice, and a cold wind rages around them'. There were other dangers, too; robbers attacked the party and its elephants were lost when, in panic, they plunged over a cliff. More hardships followed before the party reached Kashgar, where Hsuan-tsang noted the people's skill in making felt, woollens, and other textiles but was saddened by their devotion to the Lesser Vehicle.

He turned south for a return journey along the Tibetan rim of the Tarim basin. Khotan, long famous as a source of both black and white jade, gave him a royal welcome and hospitality for eight months. Its people pleased him; for they observed justice and the rites, esteemed scholarship and music, and showed a probity that marked them off from other barbarians. He admired their textiles, including silks which they owed to a Chinese royal bride who, in about A.D. 440, had smuggled both silk-worm eggs and mulberry seeds in her head-dress; the Khotanese long remembered her gratefully.

On his way from Khotan to Niya, Hsuan-tsang found evidence of the slowly increasing desiccation that was to overwhelm many oases; a river which had ceased flowing and towns which were already under the sands. The desert was, indeed, fearsome: 'Travellers have only the bones of men and animals left by

---

[1] Quoted in Rawlinson, *India: A Short Cultural History*, p. 115.

preceding caravans to guide them. Nowhere is there a spring or
pasturage. Frequently a burning desert wind blows, and then
both men and animals fall stunned to the ground.'[1] At last the
party reached Tun-huang, some miles west of Yumen, and
Hsuan-tsang waited there for a reply to his petition for re-entry
to the Empire which he had left, sixteen years ago, in defiance
of T'ai Tsung's orders. The reply was gracious, the mandarins
of Ch'ang-an prepared a fine reception and he deposited his
treasures—150 relics of the Buddha, six statues, and 657 volumes
carried by twenty pack-horses. He then hastened to Loyang
where the Emperor personally welcomed the monk who had
become his most famous and revered subject.

It is plain from Hsuan-tsang's account that Buddhism flourished throughout the Tarim. During his lifetime it also came to
full flower in China, and stimulated contacts with India as other
pilgrims went there for instruction or inspiration. Buddhist
images, paintings, and books became a significant feature of the
traffic which the T'ang had restored on regaining control over
the Tarim. China itself now became a transmitter of Buddhist
culture to Korea and Japan. Buddhism had reached the two
Korean kingdoms, Koguryo and Paekche, in the fourth century,
and although it was much later in reaching Silla, the third kingdom, it was made the official religion when Silla unified Korea
in A.D. 668. Numerous monks and lay students then went to
China, and Korean fervour for Buddhism led to a glorious period
of religious art, fostered by many important monasteries
throughout the country as well as by the Court.

Buddhism, too, was, for Japan, the most appealing of all the
seductive aspects of Chinese culture. It had first spread there
from Korea, and made such rapid progress that it became
Japan's official religion in A.D. 587. Embassies, accompanied by
many Buddhist students, went to T'ang China with the result
that Japan also brought Buddhist philosophy and art to high
levels. This noble faith, moreover, did something to reduce the
harsh militancy which marked Japanese social life.

But while Buddhism, fifteen centuries after the founder's
death, was benevolently conquering the Far East, it began to
weaken in India. Both the Guptas and Harsha were obliged to
be politically impartial between Buddhism, Hinduism, and

[1] Grousset, *In the Footsteps of the Buddha*, p. 239.

other sects, and by Harsha's reign the Hindu Renaissance was already in full swell. Under the Rajput kingdoms, which divided up North India after Harsha's death, the new trinity of Hindu gods and Hinduism's new practical answers to the problems of life and salvation quickly gripped the country. Within the next few centuries Buddhism had hardly any adherents in India, and was soon to yield in Central Asia to the blazing crusade of Islam.

4. *The Islamic conquests*

Muhammad (A.D. 570–632), a young merchant of Mecca, had revelations which made him preach to the pagan or pantheistic Arabs a single omnipotent god. When his first followers were persecuted, he went to Medina and soon became the leader of a new commonwealth of Islam, based on his own revelations and on the customary law of the tribes. Both a religion and a social organization, Islam proclaimed Six Beliefs—one God, his angels, his prophet, the Day of Resurrection, predestination, and the Koran. It has also Six Duties—the profession of faith, attesting the unity of God and the mission of Muhammad, five daily prayers, fasting in the month of Ramadan, pilgrimage to Mecca, and the Holy War against infidels. Although based both on Judaism and Christianity, Islam broke sharply from them and sought converts by the sword as well as by the word.

Its first victory was over Mecca, which the prophet-prince capured in A.D. 630, and he quickly gained the allegiance of about one-third of Arabia. However, he died of a sudden illness within two years of this triumph and, during disputes about his successor, many tribes broke away from Islam. The succession went to his aged father-in-law, abu Bakr (A.D. 632–4), during whose brief reign Khalid subdued not merely defectors but the whole of Arabia.

The warlike tribes had now to find other outlets for their military talents than in fighting one another. They found them, during the Caliphate of Umar (A.D. 634–44), first Prince of the Faithful, in conquering Syria, Mesopotamia, Egypt, and Iran. Byzantines and Sassanians had weakened their great empires by internecine wars and the Arabs, poor as well as zealously militant, were avid for their riches. Conquest of Syria was made easier by its detestation of Byzantine overlords, who had imposed heavy taxes, persecuted Monophysites as heretics, and neglected frontier defences. Khalid promised lighter taxes and religious freedom, so that Syria quickly fell to him in A.D. 636. Both Egypt and Mesopotamia were also soon detached from the Byzantine Empire. It was more difficult to conquer Iran, as the last Sassanian army was not defeated until A.D. 641, and the stubbornly resisting Iranians were not subdued until a decade after that. But, when Iran was at last theirs, the Arabs commanded an Asian Empire almost as large as that created by Alexander.

Equally important, and also surprising, was that the Arabs became the greatest naval power of the Middle Ages. On capturing Alexandria they took over the main dockyard of the Byzantine Empire, and used it to create the first Arab fleet. This fleet took Cyprus in A.D. 649, three years later repulsed a Byzantine fleet off Egypt, then pillaged Rhodes and, in A.D. 655, destroyed the Byzantine navy of 500 ships. That ended Byzantium's domination of Mediterranean shipping, and meant the loss of its African territories.

Arab unity, however, was being injured by characteristic dissensions. Umar was assassinated and then Uthman (A.D. 644–56), his elected successor, a Caliph notorious for favours to greedy relatives. Ali's succession was next disputed and no sooner had he put down a civil war that Mu'awiyah, governor of Syria, joined another revolt, at the indecisive end of which Ali was also assassinated. Mu'awiyah then took over the Caliphate as founder of the Umayyad dynasty (A.D. 661–750). During his reign North Africa was conquered up to Algeria, and Central Asia as far as Kabul, but a long attack on Constantinople finished in a pact for a thirty years' peace. Civil war raged again after his death, and under successors who had very brief reigns. It was not until Caliph Abdal-Malik (A.D. 685–705) that the Empire was mastered and given an efficient administration. He reduced Carthage and, by further eastern conquests, extended the Empire to Kashgar, part of the Punjab, and all of Sind. After his death the Arabs invaded Spain and then swept into France until they were repulsed by Charles Martel at Poitiers.

By this time Islam was again torn by dissension. There were revolts in North Africa, Syria, Mesopotamia, and Iran. They ended in the slaughter of the Caliph and Umayyad princes by the followers of abu-al-Abbas, founder of a new Abbasid Caliphate (A.D. 750–c. 1100). It did not become secure until his successor, al-Mansur (A.D. 754–75), had crushed other revolts and murderously repulsed a Byzantine invasion. But thereafter the new capital, Baghdad, became the centre of a golden Arab age under such brilliant Caliphs as Harun al-Rashid (A.D. 786–809) and al-Mamun the Great (A.D. 813–33).

Abandoning that simple austerity which had been upheld by the Orthodox Caliphate, and enjoying greater security than the Umayyads, the Abbasids transformed Islam's vast conquests into a cosmopolitan empire along Persian lines. Baghdad soon became a fabulous centre of power, luxury, and intellectual activity, avidly absorbing the legacies of Greece and Iran, freely borrowing from India and reinvigorating everything absorbed with the energy of Arab nationalism. Even Byzantine envoys were awed by the Caliph's huge palace with its sumptuous furnishings, and by his grand parade of 700 chamberlains, 7,000 eunuchs, and 160,000 troops. Scholars were equally dazzled by the House of Wisdom which, combining the functions of a library, translation centre, and academy, became the towering centre of medieval philosophy and science, destined to play a crucial role in the later Renaissance of Europe. Poetry has always been important to the Arabs, and both theology and jurisprudence became important with the advent of Islam. These all reached high levels under the Abbasids, as did belles-lettres, architecture, ceramics, and painting through contacts with and contributions by Iranians and other subject peoples of the Caliphate.

Such achievements depended upon good administration and economic prosperity. Administration was mainly a blending of Islam with the proven methods of Iranian or Byzantine government. The Caliph was both the head of Islam and the ruler of its empire over many subject peoples. Moslems were privileged; only they could bear arms or be appointed to high offices, they were exempt from poll tax and some other taxes imposed on non-Moslems, and all revenues collected from them had to be spent for the benefit of Islam, as well as some part of the revenues from infidels. Benefits included care of the poor, orphans, and volunteers for a holy war, and ransom of captured Moslems.

But Islam was open to all converts, whatever their race or nationality, and considerations of self-interest helped a rapid Islamization of the Empire's towns and large pastoral areas. The Arabs rapidly took to industry and trade but, true to their nomadic traditions, looked upon agriculture as below their dignity. Agriculturists, who formed the bulk of the Empire's population and provided most of its revenue through land tax, were thus not extensively converted, and were left free to follow their own religions or cultures. Even in the cities Jews, Christians, and Zoroastrians held important offices, and were active in commerce and finance; although later they were mostly superseded by Moslems as a result of conversions and extension of Arab activities.

The Caliphate was partitioned into twenty-four provinces under governors and independent judges. In spite of repeated attempts at tight central control, and legal dependence of provincial officers upon the vizier's own appointment, governorships, at least in the remoter provinces, tended to become hereditary and quasi-independent. The vizier, as the Caliph's deputy, presided over a cabinet of ministers for finance, audit, police, posts, espionage, and grievances—an Umayyad inovation for appeals against political or administrative bodies. Justice came under a *qadi* appointed from the theologians, and serving also as trustee for pious foundations, Moslem orphans, minors, and lunatics. Military organization, in spite of the Abbasids' dependence on arms, was looser. Caliphal guards were the only standing army and served as a well trained and equipped nucleus for armies raised, in times of danger, by general levies of Moslem troops.

The imperial revenues seem to have been highest during the first century of Abbasid rule when they reached about 390 million dirhams, including revenues-in-kind. As the dirham (Greek, drachma), the Arab silver unit, had a value of around 10*d*. in 1938, this revenue would be about £40 million in current values. Mesopotamia contributed 78 million, Khurasan (Afghanistan) 45 million, Egypt 38 million, and Syria 30 million. There are no comparable figures for expenditure but there must have been large surpluses of revenue because, when Harun al-Rashid died, the treasury contained over 900 million dirhams. Moslems paid only *zakah* (alms), a tax of around 2½ per cent levied on all forms of property capable of growth by natural increase or investment. In practice, it was levied on arable lands, herds, and merchandise, and the proceeds had all to be spent for the good of Islam—for the care of the poor, for rewards to volunteers in holy wars, and for ransoming captives. Non-Moslems paid a poll tax, land tax, and a tithe upon their merchandise. Other revenues came as tribute or truce money, often paid by Byzantium.

Although Islam's military conquests caused some desolation, Caliphs quickly saw that agriculture was the basis of the Empire's wealth and set about restoring it. Damaged or deserted farm lands were everywhere brought back to cultivation, and irrigation works were both repaired and extended. Much of this restoration was in Mesopotamia, which had been damaged most, but, as the large revenue from Khurasan indicates, areas as remote as Central Asia were by no means overlooked. Arab geographers described Sogdiana as a marvellous garden that yielded almonds, apples, apricots, basil, cucumbers, dates, egg-plants, figs, grapes, lemons, melons, oranges, pomegranates, and roses. It was through the Arabs, moreover, that citrus fruit reached Spain, and sugar-cane reached Syria.

Mineral resources were also well exploited. Central Asia sup-plied gold, silver, mercury, and marble; Iran, antimony, azur-ite, kaolin, lapis lazuli, lead, mercury, rubies, silver, and turquoise, as well as pearls; Georgia, bitumen and naptha; Syria, iron, marble, and sulphur; and the Yemen, carnelians. These, and imported gems from South India or Ceylon, were used for an extravagant climax of the jeweller's art. Al-Mamun and his bride knelt on a gold mat studded with pearls and sap-phires as their wedding ceremony culminated in a shower of 1,000 choice pearls; al-Mutawakkil's gorgeous banquet was served with golden tables and trays all richly studded with gems; al-Muktafi left 200 million dirhams' worth of jewellery and perfumes; and a Baghdad jeweller refused 7 million dir-hams for a single box made of precious stones.

Manufactures flourished and gained from imperial luxury. West Asian looms were busy making carpets, prayer rugs, tape-stries, woollens, cottons, brocades, and silks. Their most expen-sive product was probably the rug, decorated with gold, rubies, and other gems, ordered by a royal lady at a cost of 130 million dirhams. Glass works made great progress, too, as Syrian glass was in demand for enamelled sconces or mosaics in mosques and palaces, and inspired the stained glass used later in European cathedrals. Iranian glazed tiles, beautifully figured and coloured, were in similar demand. The busy scientific and literary activity of the Abbasid age led to great demands for paper; that of Samarkand was especially prized, but there were also papermills at Baghdad and in Egypt, Morocco, and Spain.

But no economic development of the Abbasid Empire was more striking than that of its trade. The Arabs had always been keen merchants along the caravan routes of their own Peninsula or the Levant, and South Arabians had early developed a coastal shipping trade to East Africa and North-west India. Now they were masters of the whole network of caravan routes from the Pamirs to the Mediterranean and knew how to use them. The site of Baghdad itself was carefully chosen with keen awareness of its commercial advantages on the rich plains of Mesopotamia between the Tigris and the Euphrates. Several canals were built between these rivers, and one connected with Baghdad. Roads were built to link the capital to Syria, Arabia, and Egypt. The great trunk roads of Iran were further improved as was the postal system. Extending over the whole Empire, having an office in every provincial capital, and using pigeons as well as relays of horses or camels, this postal system helped merchants as well as the state which it primarily served. It carried some of their correspondence and supplied itineraries showing distances between stations. These itineraries, and also the more generous provision of cisterns, hospices, and caravanserais along the main roads, were designed to help pilgrims as much as merchants; for the Islamic duty of a visit to Mecca was quite as powerful a stimulus to improvement of communications as was Arab enthusiasm for trade. Land trade gained enormously from the security given by unified command over all the routes from the Mediterranean to the Pamirs and the Punjab. Only Alexander had previously been able to control so extensive an area, and his control was very brief. Land trade also gained much, between A.D. 648 and 751, from the T'ang restoration of Chinese control over the whole Tarim basin. The Arabs destroyed that control by inflicting a defeat on the Chinese at the momentous battle of the Talas River, when they came to the aid of the Prince of Tashkent. But overland trade must have been very considerable after the Chinese lost the Tarim, because the revenues from Khurasan, 45 million dirhams, referred to the first half of the tenth century and exceeded a similar estimate for the reign of al-Mamun (A.D. 813–23) by one-half. Khurasan included Merv, Herat, Balkh, and Kabul, all of which were important trading centres, although most of their trade would have been with India.

But if trade had never been more active between West and Central Asia than under the Abbasids, a far more important development was the sudden rise of Arab seafaring. Besides acquiring Byzantine's dockyards and ports along the Mediterranean littoral, the Arabs took over the whole Persian Gulf and the mercantile marine that had been built up by the Sassanians. Little was done about this in the austere and disturbed times of the Orthodox and Umayyad Caliphs, one of whom, Umar I, showed uneasiness at maritime activity when he told his Governor of Egypt, 'Let no water intervene between me and thee.'[1] This ineffective prohibition, however, applied to the Mediterranean, in contrast with which the Indian Ocean was a sea of peace. Ancient rivalry between the Red Sea and the Persian Gulf was ended by their co-ordination under the Arab Empire, and by the elimination of the old political barrier between Iran and Syria which had made the Red Sea dominant in Roman days. Now natural facilities alone counted, and its barren shores, bad winds, and dangerous reefs told heavily against the Red Sea, not to mention its distance from the Empire's centre of economic gravity.

Ships continued, of course, to bring grain from Egypt to food-deficient towns on the Arabian shore, but even pilgrims to Mecca preferred to reach it by caravan routes across the desert, so that there was not much activity in the upper part of the Red Sea. There might have been more if Harun al-Rashid had proceeded with an idea for a Suez Canal, but he was deterred by the consideration that the Byzantines might then be able to raid Mecca. Abyssinians still dominated the East African shore, and their ports were thronged by Moslem traders, mostly from Gulf ports. Aden was probably avoided because of the activity of

[1] Hitti, *History of the Arabs*, p. 168.

Indian pirates based on Socotra. Juddah, on the middle of the
Arabian shore, became a considerable port largely because it
served as an entrepôt for wares coming from Persia. Neverthe-
less some ships leaving Juddah went to Aden for voyages to
India or China, and contemporaries went so far as to describe
Aden, exaggeratedly, as 'the gateway to China'.

A good proportion of the trade through this gateway was conducted by Jewish merchants. There had been Jews in Egypt from
the fifth century B.C. and they were protected by the Ptolemies
who employed some as tax-gatherers. Most, however, were
agriculturists, more noted for poverty than for wealth. As
Josephus said, in the first century A.D., 'Neither commerce nor
the intercourse which it promotes with the outside world has
any attraction for us'; the Talmud, moreover, prohibited usury,
even from Gentiles, unless a Jew lacked another source of
income. The position, of course, changed after Judea's unsuccessful revolt against Rome and the subsequent Diaspora or
scattering of the Jews over the Near East and Europe. Egypt
acquired a million, mostly settled in Alexandria, but it was not
until the fourth century that they obtained a real share of the
trade in Asian goods to Europe. Their trade depended upon
connections in Europe, Arabia, Iran, India, and China; there
were Jewish merchants and physicians in Muhammad's Medina, Jews in Indian ports soon after the Diaspora, and Jews at
Canton before its sack in A.D. 879. Ibn-Khordadhbeh gave an
account of the ninth-century activities of these multilingual
organizers of a trade which, based on Egypt, went from France
to China.

These merchants speak Persian, Roman, Arabic, French, Spanish,
and Slav languages. They go from West to East and East to West,
now by land, now by sea. From the West they bring eunuchs, female
slaves, boys, silks, furs and spices. They embark in the country of the
Franks, in the Western Sea, and go towards Farama; there they load
their wares on to the backs of pack animals and come by land to
Kolzoum (Suez), five days' march to the south, at a distance of 20
parasanges. They embark on the Eastern Sea (Red Sea) and go from
Kolzoum to al-Djar and Juddah; then they go to Sind, India and
China. For the return journey they load musk, aloes, camphor, cinnamon and other products of eastern lands, and come back to Kolzoum and thence to Farama, where they once again embar kon the

Western Sea. Some sail for Constantinople so as to sell their goods there; others go to the land of the Franks.[1]

Jewish trade also went from France to Antioch, across Syria to the Euphrates, down the river to al-Ubullah and from there to India or China.

Much the greater part of Asian trade was conducted by Arabs from the Persian Gulf as a development of Sassanian hegemony over the Indian Ocean. Siraf, despite its position on the barren middle reach of the Iranian shore and the consequent necessity of provisioning it by sea, became the Gulf's new deep-water port from which big vessels left for long voyages. There cargoes were transhipped by smaller vessels to Suhar or Masqat on the Arabian shore and, much more important, to al-Ubullah (the old Apologus) at the head of the Gulf. Al-Ubullah was connected by canal to al-Basrah, a great commercial centre, and thence by the Tigris and connecting canals to Baghdad. Its miles of wharves received hundreds of vessels unloading wares from East Africa, South Arabia, India, Ceylon, Indonesia, Cambodia, and China. As al-Mansur is supposed to have said: 'This is the Tigris; there is no obstacle between us and China; everything on the sea can come to us.'

It was the remarkable achievement of Arab seamen to inaugurate and maintain direct voyages from the Persian Gulf to South China. The first Moslem ships must have reached Canton before A.D. 671, the year in which the pilgrim I-ching embarked there on a Po-sse (Persian) ship for Sumatra, and a Chinese account of A.D. 727 describes big Arab ships sailing to Ceylon, Malaya, and thence 'straight to Canton for silk piece-goods and the like ware'. The History of the T'ang records that, in A.D. 748, 'the Ta-shih (a Persian tribe) and the Po-sse together sacked and burned the city of Kwangchou (Canton) and went back by sea'. After that Canton was closed to foreigners for forty-four years, during which Haiphong was used as a terminus. Regular convoys did not leave the Gulf for China until the ninth century, but soon became so large and frequent that a contemporary geographer could describe the Gulf as the 'Sea of China'.

These convoys, leaving Siraf in November, crossed on the

---

[1] Toussaint, *Histoire de l'Océan Indien*, pp. 50–51.

north-east monsoon to Quilon in Malabar, but were less concerned with Ceylon than the Persians had been because direct sailings reduced its importance as an entrepôt for Chinese or South-east Asian wares. Towards the end of November, when the cyclone season was over in the Bay of Bengal, they would cross from Malabar to Kalah Bar, which many writers have taken to be Kedah but which Wheatley argues is more likely to have been near Mergui on the Tenasserim Coast.[1] This stage would take a further month, and some time was spent at Kalah Bar replenishing water and other supplies or in rendezvousing with ships coming back from China. Ships proceeding to the next stage would leave soon enough to use the last of the northeast monsoon to carry them through the Malacca Strait, and then wait to catch the south monsoon of the China Sea. A month's sailing would bring them to Sanf-Fulaw, an island off Champa, from which another month's coasting would bring them, via Haiphong, to Canton. There they had to register with a Superintendent of Maritime Trade, who collected duties and so controlled their cargoes that these were sold when the last foreign ship had arrived for the season. Only then could they legally dispose of the cottons, linens, woollens, carpets, ironware, horses, coral, or silver they had brought from the Gulf, and the drugs, spices, gems, or other wares they had bought in Malabar, Ceylon, or Malaya. Nor could they load silk, camphor, or other Chinese products until export dues had been paid, and checks made for illegal exports.

Some Arab ships went to Yangtze ports, or even Korea, but most of them spent the summer in Canton. Sailing back on the north-east monsoon they would reach Kalah Bar again about November, having also acquired South-east Asian wares around the Malacca Strait. They reached Quilon in January, took on Malabar wares and arrived at Masqat or Siraf during April. The round trip thus took about eighteen months. Some Siraf merchants were said to have 'spent their lives on the water', but they were well rewarded. The home of an average merchant was worth more than 100,000 dirhams and many merchants had fortunes exceeding 40 million dirhams—fabulous, even by modern standards.

These figures, if trustworthy, point to a very considerable

[1] *The Golden Khersonese*, p. 224.

3 Chinese cavalryman ('T'ang, fifth century A.D. *British Museum*

4 Indian ship of the eighth century (from the Stupa, Borobudur, Java) *Ministry of Information and Broadcasting, New Delhi*

5 Arab ship of the thirteenth century (from a manuscript of al-Hariri's *Magâmat*)
Bibliothèque nationale, Paris

Gulf trade. That part which was conducted with East Africa gained both from the weakening of Abyssinia and the development of trade in slaves. Relations between Islam and Christian Abyssinia, at first friendly, deteriorated in the eighth century, when the Abyssinians took to piracy and had their ports occupied by the Arabs. Although the Abyssinians regained them in the tenth century, they then came under pagan pressure which drove them southwards and the conquering pagans became converts to Islam. Moslem control spread from East African ports to the caravan routes from Central Africa. Down them came large numbers of captives for a slave trade, immemorially old, but well organized by the Arabs on a large scale. They transported slaves over the whole Indian Ocean, even to China, but most went to the Persian Gulf to join Turkish or Christian captives in the Caliphate's slave markets. One caliph is reported to have had 11,000 Greek and Sudanese eunuchs, and the prevalence of slavery is also shown by a terrible revolt of slaves at Basra in the eleventh century.

But the greater part of Gulf trade was with Indian ports. These had long been the main providers of eastern luxuries to the West—cottons, muslins, drugs, spices, and gems. Their trade now increased, not only through the luxury demands of Abbasid society, but also through far greater Arab requirements for teak and other timbers needed for building ships or houses. The Gulf area lacked durable timber so that the merchants of Siraf had to import teak from India and South-east Asia for their shipyards at al-Ubullah and for their own residences or warehouses. Coconut wood was also much used, so that the Maldive and Laccadive Islands became shipbuilding centres, loading the finished vessels with timber, coir, or fruits for carriage to the Gulf. Coir was important because Arab ships were still 'sewn', i.e. their planks were held together with fibre and the seams blocked by a mixture of resin or pitch with whale oil. Whatever the advantages of such construction in shallow waters or reefs, it was frail for violent winds or waves, and shipwrecks were frequent. Nor could large vessels be built in this way, although Hourani mentions a length of 76 feet and ships carrying 400 men.

How important was Gulf trade with China? One contemporary says Chinese goods were scarce in Iran or Mesopotamia

7

because of fires at Canton, shipwrecks, pirates, tolls, and diver-
sions to such ports as Aden because of unfavourable winds.[1] But
another criticizes this statement by pointing to the great movement of Gulf shipping to the Far East and the estimate of
120,000 Moslems, Iranians, Jews, and Christians killed at
Canton, in A.D. 878, by rebel forces under Huang Ch'ao.[2]
When this 'disaster reached (even) the captains and pilots of
Siraf and Uman' they gave up direct voyages to China, becoming content to meet Chinese merchants at Kalah Bar, just as the
Iranians had formerly met them at Ceylon. Jewish merchants,
however, continued to send ships from Aden or Uman to Canton and, as Egypt gradually displaced Mesopotamia as Islam's
economic centre, Red Sea trade revived while Gulf trade
declined.

The Arabs, however, found immediate compensation in
greater trade with South-east Asia by making direct, regular
voyages to Sumatra or Java. These voyages were also made by
Arab merchants who had settled in western and southern ports
of India as well as in Sind. For Arabs displaced Indians in the
sea trade to the East as well as in that to the West, partly
because they were strong and enterprising, and partly because
of a new, Brahmanical ruling that Hindus sinned by travelling
on the sea.

So marked was Arab domination of the Indian Ocean that
the dinar (Latin: *denarius*, equivalent to 10 or later to 12 dirhams) became the international currency of the whole area.
This would point to the same adverse balance of trade for the
west as had plagued Rome and, to some extent, Byzantium later.
But the drain might not have been serious for the Caliphs as
they do not seem to have attempted to check it. Jewish trade
certainly had no such problem. Goitein has investigated the
archives (Geniza) of an old synagogue at Cairo, and these throw
much light upon Jewish trade between the Mediterranean and
India during the eleventh and twelfth centuries.[3] He is emphatic
that it was one-way only in certain periods; normally, 'payment
was largely made in kind'. One reason for such a change from
Roman conditions would have been lessening dependence on

---

[1] Quoted in Hourani, *Arab Seafaring*, pp. 76–78.
[2] Quoted in Goodrich, *A Short History of China*, p. 125.
[3] Goitein, 'Mediterrenean to India', pp. 75–91.

China for silks, owing to the spread of sericulture to Iran and Byzantium, but another would be the considerable advance of manufactures in the Near East since Roman days.

5. *The Glory of T'ang and Sung*

No civilization has ever attained the comprehensive brilliance of the Second Chinese Empire, the most populous and wealthy part of the medieval world. The First Empire, like that of Rome, had succumbed to barbarian attacks following upon internal divisions but China, after five centuries of dividing strife, restored its empire along traditional lines and, within them, brought a superior culture to wider reaches or further refinements. Under the T'ang and Sung emperors, indeed, Chinese society developed so perfect a balance between high cultural ideals and traditional limits of technology as to achieve a commanding stability which survived all but the external catastrophes of the nineteenth century.

Restoration was first effected by the Sui Dynasty (A.D. 581–618) which had the energetic ability to reunite China, annex Taiwan, subdue Annam, pillage Champa, and repulse the Eastern Turks. Its major economic achievement was to rebuild Ch'ang-an and Loyang and then to link them, at enormous cost, by the first Grand Canal between the Huang-ho and the Yangtze. But these campaigns and public works caused much suffering, and discontent was increased by successive failures against Koguryo, then extending its power over Manchuria. Li Shi-min persuaded his timid father, the Count of T'ang, to attempt the Mandate of Heaven and, after seven years of intricate fighting, overcame all rivals. Soon after his father became emperor, Li Shi-min had to disperse the Turks, who had been tempted to attack by China's anarchy, and before long his father abdicated in favour of so able a son. T'ai Tsung (A.D.629–49), to use his posthumous name, then began a glorious reign during which the Empire was firmly reorganized, restored to Han limits by conquest of the Tarim basin, and extended beyond them by the absorption of Mongolia. His successor, Kao Tsung (A.D. 649–83), after inflicting another defeat on the Turks, carried Chinese sovereignty over the Pamirs. Tashkent, Bokhara, and Samarkand itself became his vassals so that two new protectorates were created, one north of the T'ien Shan range and the other south of it. Kao Tsung also conquered Manchuria, helped Silla to overcome Koguryo and Paekche (defeating a Japanese fleet that came to Paekche's aid), and thereafter had Silla as a loyal subordinate of T'ang. Towards the end of his reign, however, the Tibetans partly overran the Tarim, and the Turks, recovering Mongolia, continued their ravages until the reign of Hsuan Tsung (A.D. 712–56). It was he who brought the T'ang Empire to its widest limits, not only restoring suzerainty over the Tarim and Fergana, but extending it over Gilgit, Balkh, and Kabul; even princes in the Indus Valley became his vassals.

T'ang control of routes across the Tarim and over the Pamirs coincided with Arab control of those from Syria across Iran. Both new empires were keenly interested in trade, and exchanged embassies to promote good relations. Never had the Silk Road been so busy; soldiers, ambassadors, governors, monks, scholars, merchants, and entertainers crossed it on innumerable journeys between China, India, and Iran. All served as models for the expressive art of the T'ang potter, and the Court also sent painters to depict the exotic foreigners who thronged the great caravanserais of Ch'ang-an. This western capital, as Obata says, became 'a great cosmopolitan centre where Syrians, Arabs, Persians, Tartars, Tibetans, Koreans, Japanese, and Tonkinese and other peoples of widely divergent races and faiths lived side by side, presenting a remarkable contrast to the ferocious religious and racial strife then prevailing in Europe'.[1] The Court itself had cosmopolitan interests, being receptive to embassies and encouraging its officials to return information about the distant lands towards which their duties took them. The knowledge thus acquired was used for constructing a huge map, 30 by 33 feet, showing both Chinese and Barbarian Peoples within the Four Seas and the seven great trade routes which connected them.

Buddhist interest in contacts with India and Central Asia was shown by Hsuan-tsang's journey. It inspired many other pilgrims who brought back, not only relics and scriptures to strengthen the Faith in China, but images and paintings to inspire visual arts, psalmody to enrich music, and many schol-

---

[1] Quoted in Goodrich, op. cit., p. 120.

arly contributions to medicine, astronomy, and mathematics. Iran also made important additions to Chinese culture; Zoroastrianism was brought by refugees fleeing the Arabs, Nestorian Christianity by a monk to whom T'ai Tsung allowed freedom of preaching, and Manichaeanism (a blend of Zoroastrianism with Christianity) became the faith of the Uighurs upon whose alliance the T'ang depended in Central Asia. Iranian decorative motives began to appear in Chinese art—peacocks, winged horses, framed medallions, and the motifs of Sassanian gold- and silversmiths. Chess and polo also reached China from Iran, as did backgammon. Many entertainers or servants came to Ch'ang-an seeking employment by wealthy Chinese; for example, Syrian actors and singers, Indian acrobats and jugglers, and Central Asian grooms and camel-drivers. The Silk Road, too, brought China many useful plants; before T'ang days, the broad bean, chive, cucumber, flax, onion, pea, pomegranate, safflower, sesame, and shallot; and, during them, the almond, date, fig, jasmine, lemon, lettuce, olive, pepper, saffron, spinach, and sugar-beet.

Chinese reciprocal influence was very widespread, as its civilization was highly admired and its products widely appreciated. Sericulture, it is true, had, in the fifth century, spread to Khotan through that resourceful princess-bride who smuggled silk-moth eggs and mulberry seeds in her headdress. Two monks from 'Serinda', according to Procopius, came in A.D. 551 to Justinian offering to give relief from Sassanian extortion by bringing silk-moth eggs to Constantinople. Promised a good reward, they returned two years later with the eggs hidden in their staffs. Sericulture also spread to Iran via Merv, and found an especially favourable environment in the Caspian Plain. Nevertheless it was a long time before these countries could produce much silk, which remained the Celestial Empire's major export.

Two new exports, however, porcelain and tea, were now developed and later became very valuable. Glazed ware, perhaps copied from the West, had been made in Han times and, towards the end of that period, successful experiments with kaolin clay in high-fired furnaces had resulted in proto-porcelain, a hard, impermeable pottery usually having an olive-brown glaze. Further developments under the T'ang led to true porcelain—hard, white, translucent, and ringing when struck.

Such vitrifaction required high-temperature glazes which could fuse with the body as a glassy band, and they were associated with a far wider range of colours. This technical advance was matched by a new functional form of virile beauty which also extended to lower-fired pottery. Much of the pottery that has survived comes from graves, as part of the furniture for the dead, and provides delightful illustrations of what T'ang China found most interesting—women, foreigners, and horses. True porcelain was seldom used for such statues but rather for bowls, cosmetic boxes, vessels, spitoons or for reproducing, in various ways, the forms used in contemporary silverware. It soon commanded the world's admiration and was especially sought in the Near East, which itself had a great ceramic tradition. 'To have a cabinet of Chinese porcelain has long been a mark of good taste in the Near East and Moslem India, and was a necessary adjunct to any palace.'[1] As export demands swelled those of an opulent society, the potters of Chekiang, according to Lu Kuei-meng, 'despoiled the thousand peaks of their colours'.[2]

China had long used pottery to enhance delight in wine or food, and the output of porcelain was stimulated by a new demand for tea and the ritual developed around its consumption. This beverage was first used in Szechwan during the third century and came into general use from the eighth century. The T'ang made it a state monopoly like salt and liquor, a good indication that it had become familiar to ordinary people; they drank it in the new tea-shops where they were entertained by professional story-tellers. The upper classes, of course, provided most of the demand for porcelain teaware. Lu Yu's *Tea Classic* of A.D. 780 judged porcelain solely by its use for tea bowls; they should be 'of ice and jade . . . which impart a tint of green to the tea'. Although tea exports began under the T'ang, and China had another monopoly in this product, they did not become considerable until Sung times. Zen monks probably introduced tea in Japan early in the ninth century, when it also reached Tibet, but tea did not become popular in Japan until the thirteenth century, and the Mongols, later heavy consumers, ignored it even during their occupation of China in the fourteenth century. Europe did not take to tea until the seventeenth

[1] Speiser, *China: Spirit and Society*, p. 144.
[2] Quoted in Goodrich, op. cit., p. 137.

century, although Arab traders at least knew of its use eight centuries earlier. One important benefit of tea to Asia was protection against epidemics through the necessity of boiling the water which it flavours so fragrantly.

Another important development, following upon the old invention of paper, was the introduction of block printing during the seventh century. Thousands of textbooks were thus produced for the new T'ang civil service examinations, and countless papers or charms printed for Buddhists and Taoists. Block printing was well suited to the numerous characters used in Chinese writing, as well as for illustrations, but movable type was also introduced during the eleventh century. Chinese books and reproductions went in ever-growing quantity to Japan, Korea, and Central Asia. Stein discovered the world's oldest surviving book (of A.D. 868) at the Monastery of a Thousand Buddhas near Tun-huang (beyond Yumen), among many other books which had been hidden by monks when threatened by a nomad attack. Although paper is not very suitable for transport over long distances, Arab merchants brought it from China to Baghdad, but after their capture of Samarkand they brought from there some Chinese paper-makers to start the industry at the Abbasid capital. One prisoner who escaped after eleven years reported that other Chinese artisans were also working for the Arabs: silk-weavers, goldsmiths, and painters among them. Islam, nevertheless, missed the significance of gunpowder, another T'ang invention, because until the twelfth century its use was confined to fireworks, originally for religious ceremonies.

Silk, of course, was not the only old Chinese export sought by foreigners. Bronzeware, gold- and silverware, lacquerware, jade carvings, and scroll paintings were the most important manufactures. China, it may be noted, exported few primary products—some minerals, such as gold, silver, lead, and tin, and a few spices or medicaments, such as cinnamon and rhubarb. Primary products, on the other hand, made up most of China's imports: camels, horses, and jade from Central Asia; furs, hides, and gold from Siberia; gems, pearls, ivory, rhinoceros horn, tortoiseshell, aromatics, drugs, spices, and precious woods from South-east Asia, India, and Arabia. Carpets, tapestries, and jewellery were imported from Iran and India, but by far the largest manufactured import was the fine cotton textiles of India.

Some trade went down to India through Tibet. There Srong-tsan Gampo (A.D. 629–50) had not only welded his wild tribes-men into a kingdom but had made this kingdom strong enough to annex Nepal and to harass the T'ang in the Tarim. He obtained a Nepalese and a Chinese princess as wives and, both being devout Buddhists, they persuaded him to protect and spread their faith so successfully that it obtained a powerful grip over the whole kingdom. Princess Wen Chan also introduced some Chinese arts and crafts, and the King is said to have sent sons of nobles to China for education. He is credited with having imported the Tibetan alphabet from India, and with founding Lhasa. In A.D. 822 he and T'ai Tsung made a treaty of friendly alliance, 'being in the relationship of nephew and uncle', and thus agreed to respect faithfully each other's frontiers so that 'between the two countries no smoke nor dust shall be seen'. But the 10,000 years of peace invoked by the treaty did not reach much beyond their deaths. In A.D. 670, after half a cen-tury of fighting, the Tibetans took Kashgar, Khotan, Kucha, and Karashar. The T'ang regained them twenty-two years later, and subsequently improved relations with Tibet for a further half century by sending another princess-bride to Lhasa. Her son, however, joined the Arabs (A.D. 747) in an attempt to wrest control of the Pamir passes. General Kao Hsien-chih broke them up, and went on to overbear Tashkent, whose prince soon appealed to Islam for help. The Tibetans joined the Arabs at the Talas River, where the Chinese suffered a momentous defeat that undermined their whole position in the Tarim. The Tibetans made frequent raids both upon it and Kansu until, during the next century, they became exhausted by internal dissensions, which destroyed their kingdom.

Chinese power, after seeming to be gloriously invincible, sud-denly weakened towards the close of Hsuan Tsung's long reign. In the same year, A.D. 751, at the battle of the Talas River, the Khitan defeated a Chinese army in Manchuria, and the new Thai Kingdom of Nanchao expelled Chinese garrisons from Yunnan. The Khitan divided up Manchuria with the P'o-hai; and the Thai, maintaining their hold on Yunnan, later went on to raid Annam. The Tarim, despite Tibetan attacks, was not completely lost, but its control now depended upon an alliance with the Uighur Turks who had become masters of Mongolia.

They served as guardians of the North-west until they were supplanted, in A.D. 840, by the Kirghiz. So far, indeed, were the Turks, or even the Arabs, from exploiting Chinese weakness in the Tarim that both helped Hsuan Tsung's son to obtain his throne by sending forces to put down a serious revolt of Chinese troops. Some of these Arab helpers stayed in China to form the peaceful nucleus of a not unimportant Moslem community.

The great administrative system of the T'ang, after little more than a century, had fallen into a most critical condition. It had been based on two main principles—an identity of interest between peasant and state, and centralized government under scholar-administrators, carefully chosen by competitive examination. Identity of interest between peasant and state was to have been ensured by combining an 'equal field' system with a militia system. Land held by nobles or officials was classed as 'rank' or 'office' land and, together with areas under mulberry or other trees, was regarded as 'permanent'. The remainder, however, including much land that had been abandoned during the civil wars, was subject to periodical redistribution so as to ensure each free peasant family about 19 acres for the working lifetime of its head. In return, peasants had to pay a *per capita* tax, in addition to a much lighter land tax which estates had also to pay, and to render militia service as well as labour for public works when required. As the T'ang developed a bureaucracy of talent, far beyond the limits reached under the Han, there was a great expansion of government schools, a well-developed examination system, and recruitment of most top officials, as well as nearly all minor officials, through this system. The legal code was both elaborate and humane, officials were carefully controlled by an Imperial Secretariat, which originated policy, an Imperial Chancellery, which could refer back edicts for reconsideration, and a Secretariat of State Affairs, which controlled six ministries: Personnel, Revenue, Rites, War, Justice, and Public Works. In addition, there was a powerful Board of Censors to discover treason or maladministration.

All this led to a well-governed and prosperous nation, until the resulting growth of population, and the increasing military burden upon peasants in North China, led to breakdown of the equal field and militia systems. By the close of the seventh century, population growth made it impossible to give peasants anything like 19 acres each, and the difficulty was considerably aggravated by the passing of much land, legally or illegally, into wealthy estates. The Treasury also suffered thereby, especially as peasants, faced with a higher burden of *per capita* tax and onerous service in the militia or corvée labour, transferred their holdings to an estate, or even abandoned them. Degeneration was so rapid in the eighth century that the Government was forced more and more to substitute mercenaries for militia and paid workers for corvée labour, all of which strained the imperial finances further. At the same time, mercenaries developed loyalties to their leaders, instead of exclusively to the throne, and regional commanders, especially in remote border areas, became increasingly intransigent or independent. All this coincided with strain at the centre because of factionalism between T'ang nobles and scholar-bureaucrats.

Disaster came at the end of what had been a glorious reign. Hsuan Tsung, in his old age, became infatuated with a beautiful young wife, Yang Kuei-fei, a good theme for poets and painters. She promoted her greedy family's interests as well as those of various favourites, the most important of whom was the barbarian soldier, An Lu-shan. The Emperor put him in command of all forces on the north-east frontier but in A.D. 755 he revolted, took Ch'ang-an and Loyang, and drove the Emperor to Szechwan. There the imperial troops insisted upon the execution of Kuei-fei and her unscrupulous brother, whereupon the heart-broken old man abdicated. An Lu-shan was soon killed by his own son but the revolt went on until A.D. 763 and, as has been seen, was ended then only with Turkish and Arab help.

Although the T'ang Government never fully recovered from this disaster it gave China another century of relative peace and stability, largely because of the reforms made by two statesmen. Liu Yen restored the basically important transport of grain to the capital along the Grand Canal by completely replacing corvée labour and making various improvements to such transport. Yang Yen consolidated all peasant taxes into a uniform tax on the land itself, a reform which had the immediate effect of redistributing the burden of rural taxation from peasants to estate owners, but the long-run effect of promoting landlordism instead of peasant proprietorship. His fiscal reforms included new taxes on wealth and commercial transactions, as well as the revival and extension of imperial monopolies. But further population growth led to new strains, and administrative efficiency again declined. Peasants became seriously indebted or rack-rented, and merchants so heavily taxed that Ch'ang-an was said to have been as empty of goods as if the barbarians had pillaged it. Bad weather led to famine conditions in North China in A.D. 874, and there were great peasant risings. These came under the leadership of Huang Ch'ao, an embittered intellectual whose ambition for an administrative career had been frustrated. His bands sacked Foochow and Canton, and took Loyang and Ch'ang-an. He was eventually put down, in A.D. 884, with help from Turks who had already moved into Shansi and had to be rewarded with its formal possession. Chinese generals and governors then parcelled out the Empire. The last T'ang emperor was assassinated in A.D. 907, and China was given up to the half-century of political anarchy of the Five Dynasties and Ten Kingdoms.

So durable, however, had Chinese civilization become that the south continued to prosper and even the north was not badly disturbed. Before long the Empire itself was restored by Ch'ao K'uang-yin (A.D. 960–76), during whose reign a new Sung dynasty was firmly established. By the time of his death all China had been pacified and reunited, save Chekiang and Shansi, the Khitan state of Liao in Manchuria and around Peking, the Thai Kingdom of Nanchao in Yunnan, and Annam which had broken free from more than a millennium of Chinese rule. His able successor regained Chekiang and Shansi, but failed against the Khitan and had to be content with the mere vassalage of Dai Co Viet, as Annam was now called. The third Sung emperor, Chen Tsung (A.D. 998–1022), also fought the Khitan but had, in the end, to accept stalemate based upon a Chinese subsidy. During the struggle, moreover, he lost Kansu and the Ordos region to the Tangut, a Tibetan people, to whom he had also to pay a subsidy. They barred China from even the approaches to the Silk Road, and its traffic accordingly suffered.

One reason for lack of military success was Ch'ao K'uang-yin's clear appreciation of the dangers to the Empire's stability from strong regional commanders, such as those who had so badly weakened the T'ang. He limited their commands, transferred the best troops to the capital, and put the provinces increasingly under the control of civilian officials. At the same time, important measures were taken to strengthen the civil service and its recruitment from scholars. High standards of efficiency and conduct were developed for, and within, this civil service, and the main organs of government were recast to strengthen a professional centralization under the Emperor's own supervision. He was now advised by two or three Chief Councillors and a Board of Academicians, and served by a Privy Council concerned with military affairs, a Board of Finance, and a Chancellery which supervised the various ministries and courts. The Board of Censors developed an elaborate system of checks upon the whole administration, and there were other bodies for the same purpose. An important consequence of this use of trained scholars was the spread of education; public schools were established in every sub-prefecture, and were supplemented by many private academies which became institutions of research as well as of teaching. China had never been better governed, better educated, nor more intellectually active.

A further reason for military weakness was loss of grazing areas to the Liao and Tangut, so that the Sung lacked horses upon which both Han and T'ang had relied for overcoming the nomads. Defence was somewhat improved by the development of gunpowder as a weapon, but became increasingly expensive in terms of soldiers, recruited from paupers, despised by scholars, and far from having high morale or efficiency. This army grew from 378,000 in 976 to 1,259,000 in 1041, when it absorbed about four-fifths of state expenditure. State revenues had also risen under the early Sung, reaching the equivalent of 150,850,000 strings of cash in 1021, a much greater figure than any for the T'ang. (A string of cash was worth approximately 1 oz. of silver or nearly 10s.) By 1065, however, revenue had fallen to 116,138,405 strings and there was a deficit of 15,000,000.

Revenue fell because the very prosperity of the Sung's first century led to such a growth of population as to diminish the average size of farm and so peasants' ability to pay taxes. Expenditures rose because of the bigger army and civil service, and because of the increasing demands for tribute by the Tangut (now the Hsi Hsia) and the Liao. In this crisis Wang An-shih, a new Chief Councillor, attempted bold reforms: abolition of remaining corvée labour, state loans to peasants at 20 per cent interest and similar loans to craftsmen, graduated land taxes, state purchases to stabilize crop prices or to equalize supplies between provinces, and assessments of private wealth. These and other reforms, such as a more modern curriculum for the state examinations, were opposed both by the rich and by conservative officials; they were able to thwart complete application, to force Wang An-Shih's resignation and then to reverse his reforms. Economic and administrative difficulties thus reappeared, and there were a number of peasant risings.

Before these risings could become dangerous, a new attack by nomads stripped the Sung of their Empire's northern half. When the Khitan were attacked by a subject people, the Jurched or Chin, the Emperor Hui Tsung (1100–25) made an alliance with them in the hope of recovering Chinese territory. The Khitan were defeated and forced to move to the Ili Valley, where they became converted to Nestorian Christianity and known to the West as Cathayana (from which is derived an old name for China). But Hui Tsung quarrelled with his dangerous new allies over an inadequate transfer of territory, and so lost his throne as the Chin began taking over all North China. His son continued the struggle, but unsuccessfully, as the Chin captured even Hangchow and Ningpo. A treaty was eventually made in 1141, fixing the northern boundary of the diminished Sung Empire at the Huai River and obliging it to pay the Chin tribute. There were further troubles, but these diminished as the Chin became rapidly sinicized.

Despite great losses of territory and population, the Southern Sung (1127–1279) ruled so benevolently and wisely over a territory four times the size of France that population trebled to over 60 million people. Prosperity was soon regained, and advanced to levels which made this period the greatest in China's rich cultural history. Several new cities were founded, and at least five of them had over a million people. The capital, Hangchow, as Marco Polo later testified, was 'without doubt the finest and most splendid city in the world'. There went the Imperial Academy, founded earlier at Kaifeng by Hsuan Tsung, and it brought painting, allied to calligraphy and poetry in an 'epitome of all the arts', to a full maturity, especially notable for hauntingly philosophical treatment of landscapes. Poetry also flourished, but the Sung era is more remarkable for prose works of wide range and high quality—encyclopedias, standard histories, and works on philosophy, natural science, and political economy. The neo-Confucianist philosophy then developed by Chu Hsi was to become the orthodoxy of China until the present century; and, in the fields of science and technology, according to Needham, it is always in the Sung dynasty that one finds the focal point of Chinese thought.[1]

There were no striking new inventions, perhaps, but rather a widespread improvement of existing technologies and crafts. Rice production was greatly increased, to match rapid population growth, by a quickly maturing variety introduced from Champa, and by some 496 major hydraulic works which added both to the size and efficiency of paddy fields, especially in Kiangsi, Chekiang, and Fukien. Food resources were also augmented by green lentils, introduced from India by imperial edict in the eleventh century, and by the gardens or orchards of the well-to-do that dotted the luxuriant areas below the Yangtze. On the hillsides tea production greatly expanded, and cotton became a usual crop. There were further improvements in processing cotton and silk, especially in regard to the brocades now sought for European churches. The production of both ceramics and lacquerware reached still higher levels; no celadons or porcelains surpass the delicate outputs of Sung potters. The state encouraged high or honest standards of craftsmanship by regulating guilds, each of which selected a head responsible to the government for collecting taxes or maintaining standards of work, prices, and wages.

The most impressive economic development, however, was a sort of 'commercial revolution', in which merchants, breaking free from previous state restrictions upon market-places, lined city streets with shops, spread their activities over the whole Empire, proliferated their guilds and developed a considerable specialization from wandering pedlars to large-scale wholesalers. Some of the biggest merchants belonged to a guild which formed one of the state monopolies for salt, liquor, incense, and tea, or which supplied state enterprises and the armed forces. Local tax-gatherers often became wholesalers through disposal of surplus goods in their districts to travelling merchants. Other

[1] Needham, *Science and Civilization in China*, vol. i, p. 134.

travelling merchants brought supplies of both manufactures and required agricultural products to local shopkeepers or pedlars.

A number of circumstances favoured or assisted the commercial explosion. Basic, of course, was the good order and prosperity of the Southern Sung and good transport facilities of the long Yangtze River, the many canals in its lower plains, roads to the interior or to the coastal provinces and, along 2,000 miles of coastline, many harbours for small ships. Trade was helped by an extensive monetization of the economy. The traditional coinage was copper cash, the issue of which rose from 130,000 strings in T'ang days to 310,000 strings. Nevertheless it was still in relatively short supply, despite increased outputs from government mines, a ban on exports of copper, and a 50 per cent duty on exports of cash. Silver ingots had to be cast for large transactions, and their issue rose from 800,000 in 1021 to 10,000,000 in 1180. Even when supplemented by gold dust these issues proved insufficient and the state turned to paper instruments. The T'ang had used 'flying cash' for payments to distant areas, and the Sung greatly increased these drafts to an annual level equivalent to 2,500,000 strings of cash, redeemable in salt or tea; it was not until 1265–74 that the state issued notes which were convertible in gold or silver. Private merchants found these state issues of paper convenient for transferring credits, and various bankers arose to supply the same need by certificates of deposit. Those of Chengtu bankers became so popular that the state took them over in 1024, limiting the issue of this first paper money to 1,256,000 strings of cash and holding a reserve of nearly 30 per cent as backing.

Loss of control over the Silk Road was amply compensated for by development of sea-borne foreign trade. Such trade had hitherto been dominated by aliens. Koreans, using Shantung, had largely monopolized the trade of the Yellow Sea, and Iranians, then Arabs, that of South China. Under the Sung, however, China captured the coastal lanes and took over the route to India from the Arabs. An important factor here was the building of the first Chinese navy which grew, between 1130 and 1237, from eleven squadrons of 3,000 men to twenty squadrons of 52,000 men. It not only suppressed pirates in home waters but led to the construction of large junks for distant voyages. These almost square vessels had a raised prow and poop, saiis of cloth and mat, but also eight to ten pairs of oars, a balanced sternpost rudder, and watertight compartments for safety. The largest had several dozen cabins, could carry up to 600 people with corresponding supplies of goods, and towed a boat containing wood and water. Such advanced vessels were quickly used for commerce, and have been vividly described by Chou Ch'u-fei: 'The ships which sail the Southern Sea and south of it are like houses. When their sails are spread they are like great clouds in the sky. Their rudders are several tens of feet long. A single ship carries several hundred men. It has stored on board a year's supply of grain.' Another twelfth-century writer, Chu Yu, said of their navigation: 'The captain ascertains the ship's position, at night by looking at the stars, in the day time looking at the sun; in dark weather he looks at the south-pointing needle.' There were, of course, astronomical and marine charts to help further.[1]

Canton had quickly recovered most of its foreign trade after being re-opened in 998, but was overtaken by both Ch'uan-chou and Foochow on the coast of Fukien, close to the main centres producing porcelain and tea. These, and Hangchow itself, were designated official ports under local Superintendents of Merchant Shipping who gave passes, registered the dimension of a vessel together with its cargo and crew, and collected both anchorage fees and taxes of 10 to 20 per cent *ad valorem*. The government became so interested in foreign trade that, from 719 on, it tried to monopolize the considerable profit from it. Although the attempt was far from being completely successful, trade receipts rose from about 500,000 to 65,000,000 strings in 1189—nearly twice the entire state revenues for 1065. Taxes on commerce, indeed, together with profits of state monopolies, became far more important than land taxes, the traditional prop of Chinese treasuries.

The Sung Annals for 999 record exports of gold, silver, copper, cash, lead, piecegoods, and porcelains against imports of incense, drugs, rhinoceros horn, ivory, tortoiseshell, amber, carnelians, coral, crystal, pearls, ebony, sappanwood, cottons, and steel. The export of gold and silver was associated with an adverse balance of trade so heavy that, in the twelfth century, a ban was placed on imports of luxury goods. Chinese copper

[1] Goodrich, *A Short History of the Chinese People*, p. 151.

coins were in strong demand by Korea and also Japan where, until the sixteenth century, they formed the main currency; they even went to such distant places as Zanzibar and Somaliland. Silk piece-goods were still a very important export, but became surpassed by the porcelains which were increasingly sought by all of China's trading partners. The list omits books and paintings, which were imported in considerable quantity by Japan and Korea. Fine cottons were still the largest import, in spite of a growing Chinese industry, but it is significant that the list also omits the horses which had been so important to Han and T'ang. Some horses, however, and hides and skins, must have reached the southern Sung through the Kin or the Tibetans.

The extent of China's trade is shown by the work compiled by Chao Ju-kua; a thirteenth-century Superintendent of Chu'anchou, from information given by Chinese and other merchants or sailors. He presents detailed accounts of the geography, peoples, and products of Indonesia, Ceylon, South India, Arabia, Somaliland, and even Sicily. It is clear that Chinese merchants were regularly sailing as far west as South India; for ibn-Battutah, who travelled to China in the fourteenth century, observed that only Chinese junks carried goods from Malabar ports to those of South China. But there is no reliable evidence that Chinese junks reached the Persian Gulf before the third cruise (1412–15) of the great Ming admiral, Cheng Ho.

6. *Korea and Japan*

Both Korea and Japan, at the far eastern fringe of the medieval world, derived the more important features of their social organization and culture from China. The scale, splendour, and richness of its civilization inevitably had a dominating influence upon these small countries, both naturally adapted for agriculture, the fundamental occupation of China, and remote from the influences of other civilizations. Neither had developed a proper alphabet and, although their spoken languages are very different from Chinese, they readily adopted China's writing in order to become familiar with its law, philosophy, and literature. Korea was not often exposed to nomad incursions and Japan, separated by a safe distance of sea, was quite immune from them. Both had, accordingly, an isolation which enabled

8

them to develop, for their own purposes, many features of Chinese culture. For centuries the only influence to reach them from other civilizations was the Buddhism which they so fervently embraced; but that, too, came indirectly from China. Islam did not touch them, beyond a few commercial contacts with Arab seamen. Even the Mongol raids, which badly damaged Korea and also threatened Japan, disturbed, but did not fundamentally alter, their derivative civilizations. Kublai Khan himself soon became a convert to the Chinese way of life.

The first central governments in Korea and Japan coincided with the early years of the Second Chinese Empire, and both drew consciously and heavily upon T'ang models. There had, of course, been contacts long before. Korea had begun to acquire agriculture and metal-working as early as the third century B.C. from the north-eastern Chinese state of Yen, and the Han commanderies, established after Wu-ti's conquest of Korea, had spread other Chinese crafts together with writing and Confucianism, especially to fertile Koguryo. When, in the fourth century A.D., Koguryo gained independence, it adopted a Chinese type of administration and public finance, established an academy for teaching Confucianism and Chinese history, and began a rapid conversion to Buddhism. The south-western state of Paekche, with iron deposits as well as good land, early developed a maritime trade with China, made similar cultural borrowings, and also adopted Buddhism in the fourth century. Silla, in the rather barren south-east, had maritime contacts mainly with Japan, and did not follow its neighbours in adopting Chinese institutions or Buddhism until the sixth century. Its people, however, developed military prowess through frequent struggles against the other two kingdoms and Japan, so that Silla became a valuable help to the T'ang when they attempted reconquest of Korea. But after Koguryo and Paekche had been overcome the two allies fell out and Silla, with help from other Koreans, eventually managed to expel T'ang forces and unite the whole country south of the Taedong River into an independent kingdom. It became, nevertheless, a tributary of T'ang, sending annual embassies to Ch'ang-an and, for cultural as much as political reasons, made Korea a very faithful replica of T'ang China; large numbers of Buddhists went to China for periods of study. Ministries, provinces, prefectures, and subprefectures were constituted on Chinese lines, but neither Confucianism nor a bureaucracy recruited from scholars made much headway in a society dominated by clannish nobles.

Japan's history is obscure before the sixth century A.D. but appears to have had some parallels with that of Korea. Agriculture reached Japan about the third century B.C., probably from South China or Indonesia, and the bronze culture of North China soon after, partly brought, no doubt, by refugees from the feudal wars that preceded the First Chinese Empire. Iron-working came through the Han colonies in Korea, with which tribes in Kyushu had begun trading across intervening islands. Han records mention an official Japanese embassy coming to Ch'ang-an in A.D. 57, and also thirty 'communities' having some relations with Chinese authorities in Korea. Because of its proximity to Korea and China, Kyushu developed Japan's first concentration of politico-economic power. From it went many embassies, between A.D. 238 and 247, to the Chinese governor of Korea appointed by the Wei kingdom, whose records describe the route to Kyushu and tribes under the suzerainty of a single queen. Her people practised agriculture, fishing, spinning, and weaving, and were strictly governed within a rigid hierarchy. After the Chinese lost control over Korea in A.D. 313, the Kyushu tribes established, by conquest, a small coastal colony, Mimana or Kaya, between Paekche and Silla, thus intensifying direct contacts with Korea and indirect ones with China. There were further refugees into Korea and Japan during the savage conflicts of China's First Partition, and they were probably responsible for introducing sericulture. Silk was especially important for Japan owing to its lack of grazing areas for wool-bearing animals, but it was long before Japanese silks could compare with those of China.

Kyushu leaders and their followers seem to have crossed to Honshu, which was much better suited to rice cultivation. At any rate, kings at Yamato were soon vigorously extending their control over the island's central area. They furthered contacts with China by sending embassies to Nanking, where the Sung History records them as having subjugated many communities to the east and west, and also in Korea (Mimana). But the strongest of all Chinese influences upon Japan reached it from Paekche. In return for help given against Koguryo, in A.D. 391,

the King of Paekche sent scholars who took the Chinese alphabet to Japan and began recording its history. In A.D. 552 a later
King of Paekche, desperately seeking help against Silla, sent a
Buddhist image, some Buddhist scriptures and a personal letter
commending the faith as excellent above all others.

These gifts came at a time when Japanese leaders were impressed by the rising power of the three Korean kingdoms, and
critical of the lagging political organization of Japan, bedevilled
as this was by acute clan rivalries. The Soga family, prominent
among those seeking reform, favoured adoption of Buddhism
and, when conservative clans opposed this, obtained the
Emperor's permission to take the image and became Buddhists
themselves. There was soon a dispute over the succession, during which the Soga overthrew rivals, put their own candidate
on the throne, and made a member of their family Chief Minister with effective powers of government. Thereafter Buddhism
spread rapidly, especially when the Sui adopted it on re-unify-
ing China into the Second Empire. It had a double appeal to
the upper classes of Japan as a noble religion and as a valuable
aid to strong civilization. While beautiful temples and images
made Buddhism appealingly familiar to ordinary people, they,
too, welcomed it as giving blessed comfort in lives of hardship.

Further assimilation of Chinese influences was checked by
serious disputes between the now overweening Soga and other
leaders. It was not until the Soga were overthrown, in another
succession dispute, that a bold attempt was made to apply T'ang
methods of government, land tenure, and taxation. These were
announced in the famous Taikwa Edict of A.D. 646, drafted by
the Crown Prince, later the Emperor Tenchi (A.D. 661–71), and
by Katamari, founder of the great house of Fujiwara, both of
whom had led the overthrow of Soga. The Edict announced
abolition of private titles to land or estate workers and replacement of old taxes, together with corvée labour, by *per capita*
taxes on free peasants. It also ordered registers of population for
a more equitable allocation of rice lands, established a metro-
politan area, and divided the country into provinces and districts under imperial officials. Within the limits to which a not
very strong government could push them, the reforms were
accepted, largely because members of landed families were
appointed to the new imperial posts in provinces or districts.

Further reforms came, in A.D. 702, under the Code of Taiho which completely re-organized central government on the T'ang model, according to Confucianist moral and political principles; this proved its most enduring feature.

The Japanese were also impressed by another aspect of the T'ang Empire—its ability to defeat the fleet which they had sent to help Paekche. The Court decided on a defensive policy and sought good relations with China. Official embassies were exchanged in A.D. 664 and 665, and others followed at irregular intervals. But private visits to China were far more important, and increasingly frequent after the capital was moved from inland Asuka to Heian-kyo on the Yodo River. Numerous monks and novices, teachers and students, artists and craftsmen, lawyers and other professional men went to China, and some stayed for considerable periods. They brought back knowledge that was useful to the Court as well as to monasteries, schools, and workshops. Buddhism was, naturally, a main factor in these importations and, as Sansom remarks, 'It was the development of the great Buddhist foundations as much as the work of political reformers that fostered the growth of a national state with a relatively stable government.'[1]

Communication with China, however, became more difficult as relations with Korea changed for the worse. At first content to accept inferiority, Silla's kings soon demanded equal status with Japan's emperors, and consequent bad relations made Korean waters unsafe for Japanese ships. So, early in the eighth century, embassies began direct sailings to China across 500 miles of open sea, without prevailing winds and subject to hurricanes or other storms, in inferior Japanese vessels. They required, for this purpose, four newly built ships which together could not carry more than 600 men.

Following a brilliant first century of Silla rule, Korea began a rapid deterioration. Adoption of Chinese institutions had altered but not removed the selfish struggles of clan nobles. No longer united by a national cause, they contended for official positions or other privileges in an increasingly bitter and dividing factionalism. After a series of revolts the king was assassinated in A.D. 780. During the next 155 years further rebellions or *coups d'état* placed on the throne no fewer than twenty different

[1] *A History of Japan*, vol. i, p. 81.

Silla princes, as nobles fought for power. Social order collapsed, and the resulting economic deterioration weighed heavily on the lower classes. Some took up banditry, and others piracy or trade. By the ninth century the seafarers had become so successful as to dominate the three-way trade of Korea, China, and Japan. Sailing from Korea with cargoes of iron, horses, furs, silks, and even paper, which was highly regarded in China, they brought back a variety of Chinese wares in which copper coins, porcelains, incense, books, and paintings bulked large. To Japan they carried similar exports or re-exports, and brought away timber, gold, mercury, swords and weapons, fans and screens. Groups of these low-born Korean merchants had their own settlements along the southern coast of the Shantung Peninsula or the lower reaches of the Huai River. One of their leaders, Chang Po-go, lived like a prince at headquarters on an island off South-west Korea, even succeeding in putting a contender on the throne; but when he overreached himself by seeking to marry his daughter to the new king in A.D. 841 the outraged nobles killed him.

Some of these Korean merchants also settled in Japan, which appreciated their better ships and help in building up its own mercantile marine. Although Japanese were mainly interested in voyaging to China for knowledge or culture, there were strong associated demands for imports of goods. The Court, for example, in A.D. 874 organized a special mission for purchasing incense, perfumes, and medicines. Similar demands came from monasteries or wealthy families. Other main imports from China were Buddhist images or paintings, scrolls relating Buddhist sutras or Chinese classics, and books of verse and prose. They were, apparently, in short supply because the government ordered returning ships, under pain of severe penalties, to reserve cargoes for first choice by officials. In fact, however, wealthy people sent agents to the ports whenever they heard of a ship's arrival in order to bid immediately for its cargoes.

During the ninth and tenth centuries foreign trade fell off, both for Korea and Japan. Restoration of royal power by Wang Kon, founder of the Koryo dynasty (A.D. 918–1392), was associated with a collapse in the activities of Korea's seafaring merchants. Kaesong, the capital, became a magnificent city, imitating Ch'ang-an, and the new administration was more closely modelled on T'ang lines than ever before, including even the Chinese examination system as a method of selecting officials. But all power, society, and wealth were heavily concentrated in this capital, whose palaces and great houses contrasted sharply with poor hovels throughout the rest of the country. Only the capital had shops; trade in the countryside depended on periodic rural markets and itinerant pedlars, catering for far from prosperous peasants. A tightening of class distinctions was another factor in depressing the social position and influence of recently important merchants. There were, of course, demands for luxury wares from the Court, wealthy officials, and Buddhist monasteries, some of which, well endowed with lands, provided beautiful places of recreation for nobles, and even developed a financial business. But such demands were now met to a far greater extent by native craftsmen, partly because they had improved their standards of work, and partly because Buddhism was weakening in China or becoming corrupted in Korea so that there was no longer the same impulse for cultural contact. Communications, in any case, had become more difficult. After the Khitan took over Manchuria and began raiding Korea, overland trade with China suffered. The Jurched also attacked Korea when they took Manchuria from the Khitan, and sea trade was affected when they began a conquest of North China. When this was completed in 1127, Korea was forced to become a tributary of Chin. It remained a tributary of Southern Sung, but was at a greater distance from their new court in Hangchow. By this time, moreover, conditions were deteriorating within Korea through renewed factionalism, loss of state revenues to greedy officials, military struggles, and peasant risings. In 1170 the palace guards massacred civil officials, and three decades of incessant civil warfare followed. It ended with dominance of the Ch'oe family, who ruled selfishly through a puppet king until the Mongols invaded Korea.

Japan, too, had a brilliant century following the Taikwa reforms and the shift of the capital to Nara, a centre of great Buddhist monasteries. These institutions of high scholarship and increasing wealth did much for the exquisite and varied cultural achievement of the Nara period (A.D. 710–84) and, following an imperial dedication of a colossal and beautiful bronze statue of the Buddha, made their faith the religion of the Court. They were far less successful, however, in overcoming the paganism of country people, because excessive scholasticism and undue concern for monastic organization or property tended to set them apart from ordinary life. Buddhism did not become really widespread until, in the twelfth century, the simple Amida creed swept the country with emphasis upon trust in the Buddha as the main requirement for rebirth in a wonderful paradise.

Nor did the Court, in spite of persistent efforts, succeed very far in promoting the Chinese politico-economic system which the reforms had envisaged, partly because it failed to create the scholar-bureaucracy of the T'ang, but largely because it was too weak for effective control over a backward country. The main trouble was the growing private ownership of tax-free land by nobles, officials, and monasteries through devices which may have been legal, but which diminished state revenue, made allocation of land to free peasants more difficult, and threw on them an increasing burden of taxation. Much the same thing, of course, had happened under the T'ang, whose equal field and militia systems could work only so long as there was spare land to redistribute. Japanese rulers attempted to meet this problem by bringing more land into cultivation through reclamation or conquest of the aboriginal Ainu; in A.D. 722, for example, they ordered that 3 million acres of new land should be brought into cultivation. Peasants were quite unable to undertake such extensive, large-scale work, so it had to be handed over to estate owners who were promised three generations of private ownership for all land reclaimed. In A.D. 743 this concession was extended to ownership in perpetuity. The new land was supposed to be subject to tax, but an exception was made in favour of Buddhist monasteries and, before long, had to be extended to nobles. There is no doubt that the cultivated area increased to match food supplies with growing population, but ownership passed, about as rapidly, to monasteries and nobles having estates of 1,000 to 10,000 acres. The process was quickened as many free peasants, in order to escape fiscal burdens, transferred their services to great landowners, or else abandoned their holdings to become vagrants or bandits. Militia service thus broke down and was replaced, under the Emperor Konin (A.D. 770–81), by enlistment in regular forces for campaigns against the Ainu.

Konin made other attempts at improving the situation by retrenchments, replacements of bad officials, and improvements to local administration and communications. Soon after his death the capital was shifted from Nara in order to free the Court from dangerous pressures by seven great Buddhist monasteries, which had come to exert a strong political influence for protecting and promoting their enormous wealth. Thus was built the great city of Heian-kyo (Kyoto), also laid out in close imitation of Ch'ang-an, and Japan's imperial capital until 1868. At the same time an edict was issued prohibiting further transfers of land to monasteries, and limiting their recruitment. The first decades of the Heian period (A.D. 794–857) saw the imperial power raised to a higher level than ever before. The Ainu were pushed back to the junction of the Kuriya and Kitakami Rivers in North Honshu, new farms were provided there for pioneer settlers, and roads and bridges were built to improve communications. Before long, however, there was a weakening of central government and a reaction against the very Chinese institutions by which it had been hoped to weld Japanese tribes into a civilized state. The allotment system broke down as taxes rose to finance increasing state expenditures, because state tenants transferred to private landowners and provincial officials favoured, rather than restrained, such a development. They were bribed or intimidated by nobles to falsify land registers, to put corvée labour at work on private estates or to use various devices for transferring crown land to private estates. Power gradually passed from the Court to a growing manorial system, under which the ordinary people sank into serfdom and the central government into administrative impotence. By the tenth century, most peasants and agricultural land had come under the tax-free estates of nobles or monasteries, state revenues had badly shrunk and central administration had atrophied. Official posts became hereditary and of only honorific importance, and legal codes lapsed into customary law, administered by military men instead of judges. Regular embassies to China ceased in A.D. 838 and when, after fifty-six years, another was proposed, it was refused on the valid ground that China had disturbed conditions.

As the T'ang dynasty was collapsing, Japan slipped into its Fujiwara Period (A.D. 857–1160), characterized by a family monopoly of key imperial offices. The large and remarkably cohesive Fujiwara clan held wealth and power as great landowners, advanced this power by marrying their daughters to emperors, and exploited it by skills in government and intrigue. They scrupulously maintained the throne, while usurping its effective authority, and did much to develop a brilliant court society with a high culture of great refinement. But they did little for provincial administration, owing to their family interest as landowners. Crown land passed more quickly into private estates under their regency, crown revenues correspondingly dwindled and central authority failed beyond the capital. Provinces became increasingly lawless and dependent for order upon the loyalty of nobles or abbots, both of whom were now recruiting armed retainers to protect or advance their interests. In these circumstances it was difficult to curb private absorption of land; only a few emperors attempted that, and none succeeded.

Nevertheless deterioration of central political institutions did not inhibit economic progress. The emerging manorial system in the provinces led to only one serious period of civil strife (A.D. 935–41), and was associated with a considerable expansion of the cultivated area. It gave enough stability, moreover, for great improvements to be effected in roads and waterways, partly in order to transport produce, in a still moneyless society, from estates to owners living in the capital. Resident landlords or estate managers grew wealthier, and so able to gratify their own tastes for luxury articles. These were supplied, not only by manufactures from the capital, but increasingly by provincial industries, e.g. iron-working, pottery, and paper-making. Mining, metal-working, and the manufacture of weapons and armour were particularly stimulated by this rise of a feudal military class on rural estates.

Foreign trade had declined as the Koreans sharply reduced sea-faring activity during the ninth century, and as the Japanese, reacting against sinification, developed national institutions and arts on the basis of previously assimilated Chinese influences. When the Sung were reviving the Chinese Empire they sent an embassy which the Japanese Court received only with reluctance; nor did it respond to further overtures after the Sung were firmly established. However, the development of shipping under the Sung led to a gradual increase of Chinese voyages to Japan, so that private trade between the two countries recovered during the twelfth century.

In the second half of that century there were social upheavals in Japan as armed retainers on estates became feudal warriors under their own leaders. Legal owners at the Court were reduced to something like rentiers, and the estates were increased by seizure or fighting under a distinctive military code. Clashes of this kind developed into large-scale disturbances, and some military cliques became strongly allied with other court families than the Fujiwara.

Two civil wars, in 1156 and 1160, thus transferred control of government from the decaying Fujiwara to Taira Kiyomori, and another, from 1183 to 1185, led to the establishment of the Kamakura Shogunate by Yoritomo, leader of the Minamoto clan. He did not abolish any court institutions but made them more formal than ever by setting up at Kamakura, away from court intrigues, simple new institutions of a feudal-military character, so as to govern the whole country on a basis of personal loyalty to himself as Shogun. There were Boards of War, Administration, and Justice at this new centre, and Bakufu protectors in the provinces and stewards on the estates, both appointed from the warrior caste and personally responsible to the Shogun. Power passed, soon after his death, to his wife's family, the Hojo, who only slightly complicated the system by ruling as Regents and making the Shogun a titular rank, usually held by an imperial prince. After putting down a serious rebellion, in 1221, the Hojo gave Japan a period of strong, efficient rule that later enabled it to repulse Kublai Khan's invasions. Notwithstanding its military basis, the Kamakura Shogunate was a period of further artistic progress and of great intellectual and religious activity. Sculpture came to a glorious flowering, and there were major advances in poetry and prose. Zen Buddhism came from China, an austere sect emphasizing meditation and strict discipline that strongly appealed to the dominant warriors, just as the new worship of the gentle Buddha Amida won peasants and humble workers.

Simpler and cruder although the Bakufu was than the T'ang model of government that had been attempted in the Nara period, it gave more effective control over Japan and greater security. There was, accordingly, considerable economic progress. Expansion of the cultivated area was such as to make demand for farm workers outrun the supply. Both mining and industrial techniques advanced rapidly and there were increasing demands, not only for weapons and armour, but also for costly houses, temples, and their equipment as growing prosperity raised incomes of wealthy nobles at the capital and of Bakufu officers at Kamakura or in the provinces. There were, accordingly, growing demands, too, for the services of architects, artists, and such skilled workers as carpenters, masons, smiths, metal-workers, and weavers. Even the position of 'base people', butchers, leather-workers, and others who offended the Buddhist prohibition against taking animal life, gradually improved.

The Shogunate's most prosperous years were those corresponding to Southern Sung (1127–1279), whose wisely benevolent rule raised South China to high economic and political levels. There was no full resumption of official relations between the two countries but a renewed Japanese interest in Chinese philosophy and art, and a great increase of commercial intercourse. As Sung ships and navigation improved, more and more of their trading vessels came to Japan, which developed harbours on western coasts to help this foreign trade. Increasing wealth, matched by increasing acquaintance with the sophisticated luxuries of Sung, made Japan's upper classes ever more desirous of Chinese silks, brocades, porcelain, perfumes, and incense. In contrast to previous periods, the greatest demands for Chinese products were now secular. Religious demands, of course, were still important, as is indicated by many exchanges of Zen monks between the two countries. One of them, Eisai, brought back tea in 1191 and recommended its consumption with the result that, during the next century, it began to be Japan's national beverage and associated with a ritual ceremony which stimulated demands for pottery. Japan paid for its imports by supplying China with timber, mercury, and such manufactures as swords, lacquerware, fans, and screens. Japanese swords, the pride of the Samurai, were also highly regarded in China; and Japanese craftsmen must have brought their fans and screens to high levels of tasteful accomplishment to find buyers among the sophisticated gentry of Sung.

A striking feature of this foreign trade was large imports of

copper coins from China. Government efforts to promote the
use of money had failed in Japan during the ninth and tenth
centuries, and the official mint had actually closed down. Now
the growing internal trade of the Kamakura period led to a
spontaneous replacement of barter by monetary transactions
using Chinese cash, especially after the discovery of gold
deposits in 1175 at Mutsu provided a sure means of importing
cash. Officials were not altogether pleased. One writer complained: 'There is a strange sickness going around the country
nowadays. It is called the money disease.'[1] But nothing could
stop the inflow of cash, especially as counterfeit coins were con-
fusing transactions. Chinese coins were made legal tender for
private transactions in 1226, when some types of barter were
forbidden. The Regent himself, in 1261, sent gold to China for
copper cash, which was soon made legal tender also for payment of taxes. Sansom says that during the thirteenth century
metal currency may have increased by as much as ten times; if
so, there was, indeed, a rapid growth of monetization and trade.

7. Srivijaya and Ankor

By the time the Sui were rebuilding the Chinese Empire, and
Soga were trying to centralize Japanese government, Funan, the
first trading empire of South-east Asia, had disintegrated. It had
made the plains of South Cambodia and Cochinchina fertile
by constructing a remarkable network of drainage and transport canals, but these were badly damaged, about the middle of
the sixth century, by catastrophic floods which forced a withdrawal from coastal regions. Never great sailors themselves, the
Khmers quickly lost much of their trade with India and China,
and so control over the portage states of the Malayan Peninsula.
In these weakened circumstances Funan was attacked by the
vassal kingdom of Chenla, which had expanded its original territory in the middle reaches of the Mekong to include most of
North Cambodia and South Laos. Its king, Bhavavarman, during the second half of the sixth century, turned against Funan,
whose conquest was completed by his nephew Isanavarman II
(A.D. 611–35). Buddhism was then replaced by Sivaism, and a
Chinese pilgrim, I-ching, complained that in Funan 'the law

[1] Quoted in Sansom, *A History of Japan*, vol. ii, p. 184.

of the Buddha prospered and spread, but now a wicked king has destroyed it completely and there are no more bonzes'.[1] Jayavarman I (A.D. *c.* 657–81) had a long and peaceful reign over territory which included Laos as well as Cambodia, but after his death the kingdom fell apart. Chinese records of the eighth century refer to a Land Chenla, in the middle of the Mekong Valley, and a Water Chenla which was divided between a number of kingdoms in South Cambodia and the Mekong Delta.

Funan's trade passed to a rising kingdom of Srivijaya, based on South-east Sumatra. Indonesians, who had long participated in trade with India, came during the fifth century to participate in trade with China. This development was connected, not only with the Sassanian ships that were coming to Ceylon for Chinese as well as Indian wares, after the land routes were disturbed by nomads, but also with a foisting of such Indonesian jungle products as benzoin, camphor, and pine resin as substitutes for frankincense and myrrh in the Chinese market. Chinese records state that a number of embassies came, during the fifth century, from 'kings of the southern islands'; from Cho-po and Ho-lo-tan in Java or Sumatra in A.D. 430, and from Kan-t'o-li in Sumatra in A.D. 441. During the following century they speak of two kingdoms in Sumatra, Mo-lo-yeou, or Malayu, at Jambi on the Batang River, and Che-li-fo-che, or Srivijaya, at Palembang on the Musi River; they also mention three kingdoms in Java. These were far from savage places, as I-ching testified; he spent six months at Srivijaya, in A.D. 671, to study Sanskrit before proceeding on his voyage to India, and returned there in A.D. 685 after a long stay at the Buddhist university of Nalanda. Srivijaya was thus commended to other pilgrims:

In the fortified city of Bhoga, Buddhist priests number more than one thousand whose minds are bent on learning and good practices. They investigate and study all the subjects that exist just as in the Middle Kingdom (China); the rules and ceremonies are not at all different. If a Chinese priest wishes to go to the west in order to hear and read he had better stay here one or two years and practise the proper rules and proceed to Central India.[2]

---

[1] Quoted in Coedès, *The Making of South East Asia*, p. 90.
[2] Quoted in Vlekke, *Nusantara: A History of Indonesia*, p. 27.

I-ching had also stayed at Malayu on his first visit to Sumatra but, on the second, found it had become incorporated in Srivijaya. A series of inscriptions in Old Malay, put up between A.D. 683 and 686, also mention the island of Banka as an appendage of Srivijaya, and show that an expedition was being prepared against Java. Srivijaya sent embassies to China between A.D. 695 and 742, but the next glimpse of its history comes from a puzzling Ligor stele of A.D. 775; the first side tells of a Mahayana sanctuary there, founded by a king of Srivijaya, and the other side of a victorious king who belonged to the Sailendra family of Java.

It seems clear that Srivijaya, although its capital was not obviously well placed for trade, being 75 miles up a winding river, was exploiting an equidistant position from the Malacca and Sunda Straits to dominate both of them by conquests in Sumatra and Malaya. These Straits were becoming more important as the Arabs began direct voyages from the Persian Gulf to Canton, and Srivijaya's conquests presumably reduced the old Malayan portage trade by controlling pirates and providing better harbour facilities for Arabian or Indian merchants. Kedah was under Srivijaya by the end of the seventh century, and other places along the Malacca Strait, or the east Sumatran coast, seem to have been kept in subjection by a Srivijayan fleet. T'ang records say that fourteen cities were under its suzerainty. Arab records do not mention the Malacca area until the mid-ninth century, but Arabian ships must have passed through the Strait somewhat earlier. Mas'udi, writing in A.D. 955, spoke admiringly about the power and wealth of the 'Maharaja of Zabag' who was 'king of the isles of the eastern sea', ruling over Kalah (Kra) and Sribuza (Srivijaya). His territories produced aloes, camphor, cardamom, cloves, cubeb, nutmeg, and sandalwood, and his trade reached far and wide. Its reach to India is confirmed by the endowment of a vihara (monastery) at Nalanda by a King of Srivijaya, about A.D. 850, and by a Srivijayan temple built at Negapatam in 1005, for whose proper maintenance the Chola king granted the revenues of a large village. Similarly, its reach to China is confirmed by entries of Srivijayan merchants on the register opened at Canton in A.D. 971 for recording foreign ships and cargoes there. The Sung court, moreover, received fairly regular embassies from Srivijaya between A.D. 960 and 1178. Besides undertaking its own voyages between India and China, Srivijaya used forceful methods to develop entrepôt trade. Chou K'u-fei reported, as late as 1178, that any foreign ship passing near the Straits was attacked if it refused to pay tolls or to enter a Srivijayan port; and Chao Ju-kua, writing a century later, said: 'If some foreign ship passing this place should not enter here, an armed party would certainly come out and kill to the last man.'[1]

Srivijaya did not obtain this commanding position over the transit trade of South-east Asia quickly or without opposition. There would have been no great difficulty about absorbing the Malayan states soon after they had become independent of Funan, and it seems likely, from the absence of any Chinese mention of kingdoms in West Java, that Srivijaya also expanded across the Sunda Strait. But there was a strong Kingdom of Mataram in Central Java, ruled by Sanjaya kings until they became vassals of the Sailendra family, who may have been connected with later Kings of Funan; they shared the same Buddhist faith and took over the same mystic title, 'kings of the mountain'. Mataram must have been a wealthy kingdom, as during the eighth century the Sailendras built the immense Borobudur, a magnificent expression of Mahayana faith and the greatest architectural achievement of Indonesian civilization. A Javanese inscription claims that King Sanjaya (A.D. 732–c. 750), the Saivite predecessor of the Sailendras, had conquered Cambodia, and a Cambodian inscription says that Lower Chenla was attacked by pirates from 'Java', which may have been loosely used here for Indonesia. From an island base off Cambodia, these pirates went on to raid Tongking in A.D. 767, and Champa in both A.D. 774 and 787; the Vietnamese Annals refer to bands from Java and the southern islands. Both Srivijaya and Mataram could have been plundering Chenla, and trying to take over Funan's trade. Java must have been involved in some way because, apart from the not very clear evidence of inscriptions, Jayavarman II certainly returned from Java in A.D. 802 to found the great line of Ankor's God-Kings, and so free Cambodia from Java's suzerainty.

The Sanjaya line appears to have regained control of Mataram about the same time. A daughter of the last Sailendra king

[1] Wheatley, *The Golden Khersonese*, p. 298.

of Java had married a Sanjayan prince who displaced her infant brother and took over the throne; according to an inscription of A.D. 832 this usurper had authority over most of Central Java. When the child became a man, he tried to recover the kingdom and another inscription of A.D. 856 describes his failure. After defeat he escaped to Srivijaya and somehow or other became its king, perhaps through a useful dynastic connection or the valuable claim he gave Srivijaya for control over Mataram. The Javanese capital, at any rate, was later shifted to East Java, perhaps, as Krom suggests, owing to fear of Srivijayan attack.[1] Chinese records attest a later struggle. A Srivijayan ambassador had returned to the Sung Court in A.D. 992 after hearing, at Champa, on his way home, bad news of Javanese attacks, and begged imperial protection for his country. But his unexpected return coincided with the arrival of a Javanese ambassador, who replied that there was chronic warfare between the two Indonesian states. Srivijaya, through good relations with China and Champa, and help from Malayan vassals, emerged the victor in c. 1006 by sacking the Javanese capital. East Java's power immediately collapsed, and Srivijaya's position seemed to have become impregnable.

So impregnable, indeed, that it tried to make its ports the entrepôt terminus for ships coming from both China and India. The first half of this ambition was easy to achieve, but the second half brought devastating conflict with the Cholas, who had similar commercial aspirations. They had resented the monopoly position built up in western trade by an alliance between Ceylon, the Pandyas, and Kerala, where Arab merchants were by now well established. Rajaraja I (A.D. 985–1014) tried to bring Malabar under his control, and eventually took the key port of Quilon. Not daring to attack the Arabs' trade directly, he then raided the Maldive Islands where they built ships and obtained timber and fibre. His biggest blow, however, against the commercial alliance was a conquest of Ceylon, during which its ancient capital, Anuradhapura, was destroyed. He sheathed the sword in 1005, after having waged northern campaigns which subdued Kalinga. But his son, Rajendra I (1014–42), after a successful campaign against the king of Bihar and Bengal, prepared a great naval expedition to attack Srivijaya.

---

[1] Quoted in Hall, *A History of South-East Asia*, pp. 52–53.

9

He began by taking the Andaman and Nicobar Islands to serve as an advanced base and, in 1025, launched a powerful attack on Srivijaya, with results that were recorded on an inscription at Tanjore six years later. Palembang was taken and its king captured; the Chola fleet then went on to seize Malayu, Pané, and Acheh in Sumatra, the island of Tumasik (Singapore), Ligor, Takkola, and Kedah, another key port for the Arabs' Far Eastern trade.

But the Cholas had no interest in permanent occupation, apparently being content with breaking Srivijaya's attempt at commercial monopoly. Friendly relations, indeed, were soon resumed, as Srivijaya was helped to subdue a Malayan vassal in 1068, and the old hostelry at Negapatam was reopened in 1090. During the next two centuries there was a gradual decline of Chola power which was quite extinguished in 1336 by the new Hindu Kingdom of Vijayanagar, whose ruler declared himself, among other glorious titles, 'Lord of the Eastern, Western and Southern Seas'. Vijayanagar, however, had no navy and so never threatened Srivijaya.

After the Chola attack, Srivijaya also lost its brief monopoly over Indonesian shipping because Airlangga (1019-49) was able to revive his father's kingdom in East Java. This took time but was accomplished by 1030, when the King of Srivijaya gave him a daughter in marriage. They must have reached some kind of agreement about their respective roles, no doubt based on common fear of another Chola attack. Srivijaya probably accepted a limitation of its sovereignty to Malaya, Sumatra, and West Java, leaving the east to Airlangga, who developed ports in the Bay of Surabaya and at Tuban. These ports not only traded actively themselves but attracted merchants from Champa, Cambodia, Thailand, Achin in North Sumatra, Ceylon, Coromandel, and Malabar. There was a confused state of affairs after Airlangga's death, resolved by the rise of a new Javanese Kingdom of Kediri which, besides developing shipping activities, reached out to control Bali, Borneo, and the Moluccas. The major reason for this expansion was not so much imperial ambition as a new interest of Arab and Indian merchants in cloves, mace, nutmeg, and other spices, an interest which benefited Srivijaya. Cloves, mace, and nutmeg were found only in the small, scattered islands of the Molucca and

Banda Seas, Ternate and Ambon being especially important for cloves and the Banda Islands for mace or nutmeg. These Spice Islands were remote from Indonesian affairs until the twelfth century but, after Kediri introduced their products to Moslem merchants, demands quickly increased in both the Caliphate and Europe.

Kediri's trade appears to have surpassed Srivijaya's by the end of the twelfth century, as Chou K'u-fei put it ahead of Srivijaya in point of wealth. Srivijaya was still prosperous through control over both sides of the Malacca Strait and the Sunda Strait, even if it had to use rather piratical methods for boosting revenue from passing ships. Chao Ju-kua described it, in the thirteenth century, as a great shipping centre whose people paid no taxes, yet whose ruler was so wealthy that he sometimes distributed his own weight of silver for the relief of poor people. Moslem trade was growing, Indonesian exports were increasing, and Sung ships were making ever more frequent voyages to southern waters. There were difficulties over controlling Malaya, where a ruler of Tambralinga (Ligor) claimed independence and was powerful enough to send two expeditions against Ceylon, which severely defeated the second. There was also to be strife with Singosari, the kingdom which a rebel established in East Java after overthrowing Kediri in 1222. But Srivijaya flourished until the Mongol invasions disturbed the whole balance of power in South-east Asia.

Meanwhile another great power had arisen in Indochina. Jayavarman II, the Cambodian prince who had returned from Java in A.D. 802, succeeded in reuniting his country. He chose, as its new centre, the region around the northern end of the Great Lake, accessible to the sea but remote enough to be defensible against further Javanese attacks. It also had the further advantage of being a junction for land routes crossing Indochina from the Gulf of Siam or the Tenasserim coast, and of access to varied natural resources; the timber, game, and jungle products of nearby forests, the enormous fish harvest of the Great Lake after its seasonal swell by the flooding Mekong River, and iron, sandstone, and clay from the Dangkrek Mountains. After experimenting with three other capitals in this region, he finally settled on Mahendraparvata (Phnom Kulen). There he used Brahminic ritual for embodying his own soul with the power of Siva in a linga which symbolized that 'the land of the Cambodians was no longer dependent on Java, and had only one ruler whose sway was universal'. Thus was inaugurated the line of God-Kings who brought Cambodia to the highest level attained by any South-east Asian civilization.

God-Kings were necessary for reuniting a people whose independence had been lost and for building, then controlling, great hydraulic works which were the basis of Ankor's remarkable prosperity. Funan had also been largely dependent on hydraulic works, and Ankor learnt from them. But its problem was different; not draining 'cesspools of soft mud held together by mangrove trees', but turning an irregular, seasonal spate of water into a controlled supply, available during the long dry season or supplementing a poor monsoon rainfall. Eventually 1¼ million acres of rice land were served by a network of irrigation canals which raised the yield to at least two harvests a year and sometimes to as many as four, thus providing an assured food supply for over a million people. The canals depended upon large barays, or artificial lakes, formed by raising dikes to contain rainwater or flows from diverted streams, and so elevated as to give gravity-feed throughout the network. Barays were associated with important towns and those at Ankor, the later capital, were as large as six square miles and had a combined capacity exceeding 13,000 million gallons. No water was wasted as it was fed, with suspended fertile mud, through canals of regularly decreasing size into ditches that reached the smallest paddy field. The canals, of course, did more than provide water for households or crops; they also served as highways and streets for moving people or goods. In particular, they facilitated transport of enormous quantities of stone for magnificent temples, and timber for palaces and other secular buildings. Much of the unskilled labour on these works and buildings was provided by slaves captured in war or recruited from primitive hill tribes.

Jayavarman's son, Indravarman I (A.D. 877–89), consolidated the new kingdom and extended its limits much beyond those of present-day Cambodia. He is notable for beginning a tradition that each God-King should carry out useful public works, above all extensions to the irrigation system, before erecting a temple-mountain which would ensure his own immortality. Indravarman shifted the capital to Phnom Kulen, building a huge baray to the north; and his son, Yasovarman (A.D. 889–900), shifted it to the Phnom Bakheng area of Ankor, where he constructed the largest of all barays, big enough to supply Ankor's requirements for two centuries. Jayavarman IV (A.D. 925–41) made another new capital at Koh Ker, which he provided with the usual irrigation system, but Rajendravarman (A.D. 944–68) returned to Ankor, where the God-Kings then stayed until their downfall in the fifteenth century. Cultivation was extended, during the reign of Suryavarman I (1010–50), to land west of Ankor, and his successor built another huge baray to meet bigger requirements for irrigation.

Not much is known about political events. There were apparently disputes over some successions and a nine years' war over that of Suryavarman I, during whose reign Khmer power was pushed into the Menam Valley of Thailand and over the Mon centre of Lavo (Lopburi). His successor had to cope with revolts in the south and in the east. There was warfare with the Chams in the next reign, but both Ankor and Champa participated, as allies of China, in an unsuccessful attack against the Dai Viet of Annam. A new dynasty came to power in 1080 and, after another succession dispute, Suryavarman II (1113–50) began a long and glorious reign. He made three campaigns against the Dai Viet by invading the Red River Valley, defeated Champa and occupied its territory for four years, and also temporarily occupied Haripunjaya (Lampun), the other Mon kingdom in Thailand. China recognized him as a great vassal of its Empire. His campaigns are partly recorded on fine bas-reliefs at Ankor Wat, the huge, magnificent funerary-temple built to ensure his 'supreme sojourn with Vishnu'.

This temple, overwhelming in size and grandeur, and once incredibly rich in graceful decoration, marks the peak both of Khmer civilization and the power developed by its God-Kings. A usurper, who seized the throne in 1165, was killed twelve years later when the Chams, after defeat on land, sailed up the Mekong and the Great Lake to sack Ankor and devastate its land. Khmer power was tottering, undermined by ruinous warfare and overstrained by heavy demands for works of lesser benefit than those constructed in earlier reigns. It was also weakened by a popular reaction against the cult of God-Kings and Hinduism. Defeat by the Chams, says Groslier, 'was bound

to appear as a divinely ordained catastrophe, and as a sign of
the overthrow of the system . . . to which men gave their
obedience only because it seemed unshakeable and ordained by
the gods themselves'.[1] Reaction took the form of increasing conversion to Buddhism—basically a democratic and pacifist
religion.

For a time, however, the situation was wonderfully redeemed
by Jayavarman VII (1181–1219), the most remarkable of all
Cambodian kings. He had to wait for the usurper's death before
rallying the country successfully against Cham invaders and
coming to the throne, at the mature age of 55. He had then to
put down internal revolts, make order out of anarchy, and repulse another attack by the Chams. Some years later he annexed
Champa, re-established Khmer rule over Laos, up to Vientiane,
most of the Menam Valley and parts of North Malaya. Even
more remarkable than this restoration of Funan's dominion
were Jayavarman's civil achievements, based on the Buddhism
which many of his people were accepting and to which he himself had become converted by two sisters, whom he married in
turn. Nothing illustrates his social policy better than the Bap-
houn, at the centre of rebuilt Ankor Thom. This imperfect, but
amazing and strangely beautiful, temple reveals Jayavarman's
personal identification with the compassionate Buddha, in a
new syncretism of the God-King cult, and its sympathetic bas-
reliefs a concern, not so much with the Hindu mythology of
Ankor Wat, as with the life of ordinary people. Manifold statues
of a Buddha-King serenely brood over the four quarters of the
kingdom, throughout which Jayavarman erected 102 hospitals
for the poor and 101 rest-houses for pilgrims or travellers. He
also restored waterworks and extended them by a new baray
east of Preah Khan. His reign, indeed, saw more building than
those of all five predecessors put together, and the last architectural or hydraulic masterpieces of the Khmers.

Ankor was already in decline when it was visited, in 1296, by
a Chinese mission, one of whose members, Chou Ta-kuan,
nevertheless gave an impressive account of Cambodian life.[2]
Sea trade had been given up since the days of Funan, and also
cultivation in the lower reaches of the Mekong. Chou Ta-kuan

[1] Groslier, *Indochina*, p. 168.
[2] Quoted in Mirsky, *The Great Chinese Travellers*, ch. 6.

wrote that even mariners had difficulty in finding the channel
where 'all that meets the eye are high rushes, dead trees, yellow
sand, and white reeds'.[1] There were, however, many boats on
the Great Lake, rivers, and canals. Large boats, made from
hàrdwood planks and shaped only by axes, were propelled by
oars. For road journeys the Khmers had carts, horses, elephants,
and palanquins borne by two or four men, but the elephants had
no howdahs and the horses no saddles. The Great Lake
abounded in fish—clams, mussels, oysters, carp, and many
others; it also contained dolphins, turtles, and crocodiles. Salt
was obtained by evaporation at coastal places, and some from
the mountains. Forests abounded in birds and animals: cor-
morants, cranes, ducks, king-fishers, parrots, and pigeons;
bears, buffaloes, deer, elephants, foxes, goats, monkeys, pan-
thers, rhinoceroses, and tigers. Buffaloes were ridden, and there
were horses, but 'very small' ones. Domesticated animals included cattle, chicken, ducks, pigs, and sheep besides geese
which, Chou Ta-kuan says, had been quite recently introduced
from China by sailors.

Only pomegranates, sugar cane, lotus flowers and roots, taro,
peaches, and bananas are common to Cambodia and China. . . .
The kinds of trees are many, the flowers even more abundant, beautiful and sweet-scented; there are a thousand kinds of aquatic flowers,
but I do not know their names. . . . Among their edible plants are
onions, mustard, leeks, egg plant, melons, pumpkins; they do not
have radishes, lettuce, chicory or spinach. They have gourds. . . . The
cotton tree grows higher than their houses; it lasts more than ten
years. There are also many vegetables whose names I do not know;
and also many edible aquatic plants.[2]

Agriculture was very flourishing.

Generally, the Cambodians harvest three or four crops a year. . . .
The cultivators calculate the exact time when the rice is ripe, the
time of the flood crest, how much land it will cover and, following
the location of their fields, they sow. They do not use buffalo to
plough. Their ploughs, sickles and hoes are the same kind as ours but
made differently. . . . To fertilize their fields, they plant legumes;
they do not use animal manure, disdaining it as impure . . . and I
think the Cambodians consider the Chinese method of fertilizing

---

[1] Mirsky, *The Great Chinese Travellers*, p. 203.

[2] ibid., pp. 224–5.

disgusting. . . . They do not use millstones to husk the rice, but mortars.[1]

The jungle itself yielded many useful products: 'The most precious articles are the feathers of the kingfisher, ivory, rhino- ceros horn and beeswax; cardamom and other jungle products are more common. . . . Cardamom is cultivated in the moun- tains by the savages. Pepper is also found occasionally.'[2]

Manufactures were not well developed. Cambodians made wine from rice, sugar, honey, and the leaves of a tree; but they did not know how to make vinegar, using instead an acid con- coction of leaves from another tree. Food was cooked in earthen- ware pots, and eaten by the poor from earthenware basins, which also served them as drinking vessels. Better-off people used Chinese plates of pottery or copper, and drank from pewter goblets. Wealthy people used silver goblets or sometimes gold ones. Only tables in the palace were covered by gold brocades which were presented to the king by foreign merchants. Cam- bodians could not produce silk wares until the Thais had introduced sericulture to Indochina from Nanchao. Their women spun and wove cotton or hemp, but had no proper spin- ning wheels or looms, and did not know the art of sewing. 'When a Cambodian tears his clothes, he hires a Thai to repair them.' South-east Asian women, however, have never had to fight for economic emancipation.

In Cambodia, women attend to trade. Even a Chinese who arrives there and takes a woman will profit greatly from her trading abili- ties. They do not have permanent stores, but simply spread a piece of mat on the ground. Everyone has her own spot. I have heard that they pay an official for the right to a location. In small transactions, one pays in rice, grain, Chinese goods, and, lastly, fabrics; in large transactions they use gold and silver.[3]

Merchants came to Cambodia from Sung China mainly for jungle products. Its manufactures were neither distinctive nor attractive, and entrepôt traffic must have dwindled to small proportions. Chou Ta-kuan did not think Cambodia produced either gold or silver. But it had keen demands for Chinese goods.

What the Cambodians value most is Chinese silver and gold, then

[1] ibid., pp. 221 and 228.   [2] ibid., pp. 222-3.   [3] ibid., pp. 223-4.

silks, lightly patterned in two-toned threads. After these items comes the pewter of Chen-chou, lacquerware from Wen-chou, the blue porcelain of Ch'uan-chou, mercury, vermilion, paper, sulphur, salt-petre, sandalwood, iris root, musk, hempcloth, umbrellas, iron pots, copper platters, sieves, wood combs and needles. That which they desire most of all is beans and wheat—but their exportation is forbidden.[1]

China was not the only source of imports: 'Even though they weave cloth in this country, the fabrics used by the nobles are imported from Thailand or Champa; those most highly prized are the gossamer pieces brought from the western sea.'[2] Indian goods were still reaching Cambodia, as they had in Funan's day, by the overland route across Lower Burma and Thailand, but now Indian ships went to Champa rather than to Cambodian ports. 'Formerly', says Chou Ta-kuan, 'this country was engaged in active trade',[3] implying that the Khmers' shift north of the Great Lake had sacrificed trade which had been a main basis of Funan's prosperity.

Ankor's prosperity came from its advanced agriculture. Chinese merchants, we are told by Chou Ta-kuan, had long praised Cambodia 'as a land rich and noble'.[4] He himself was impressed by Ankor Thom's seven miles of walls, its great bridges and gates, magnificent temples, and splendid palace whose ceremonies showed that, 'though this country is barbarous and strange, they do not fail to know what it is to be a king'.[5] Nor did they fail to know what it is to be properly governed.

In this country are counselors, generals, astronomers and so forth, and, under them, all kinds of minor officials. They differ from us only in their titles. Most of the time they choose nobles for the high positions. Otherwise, those who are appointed send their daughters to be royal concubines.[6]

Only palace women, of whom there were thousands, could deck themselves out in gold jewellery, but ordinary women, and men, annointed themselves with 'perfumes of sandalwood, musk and other scents'.[7] The people, indeed, were addicted to cleanliness: 'Cambodians are ill frequently. I think this comes from their bathing too often and their incessant washing of their

[1] ibid., p. 224. [2] ibid., p. 208. [3] ibid., p. 204.
[4] ibid., p. 206. [5] ibid., p. 233. [6] ibid., p. 208.
[7] ibid., p. 211.

heads.'[1] Their life was eased by slaves, of whom 'even those of modest means have ten or twenty';[2] and brightened by lengthy monthly festivals, paid for by officials or nobles whose largesse, according to Chou Ta-kuan, was enormous. A happy society for most Cambodians, so long as they had peace, and so long as their king was strong enough to maintain the great, essential hydraulic works.

[1] ibid., p. 219.   [2] ibid., p. 215.

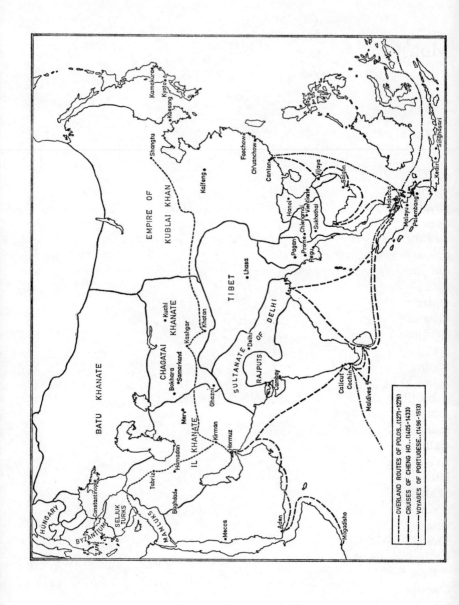

OVERLAND ROUTES OF POLOS..(1271-1295)
CRUISES OF CHENG HO..(1405-1433)
VOYAGES OF PORTUGESE..(1496-1513)

BATU KHANATE

EMPIRE OF KUBLAI KHAN

CHAGATAI KHANATE

IL KHANATE

SULTANATE OF DELHI

RAJPUTS

TIBET

BYZANTIUM

HUNGARY

SELJUK TURKS

MAMLUKS

Constantinople

Tabriz

Baghdad

Hamadan

Mecca

Aden

Mogadisho

Kirman

Hormuz

Merv

Ghazni

Bokhara

Samarkand

Kuchi

Kashgar

Khotan

Delhi

Cambay

Calicut

Cochin

Maldives

Lhasa

Kaifeng

Shangtu

Kamakura

Kyoto

Kwesng

Foochow

Ch'uanchow

Canton

Hanoi

Chiengmai

Vientiane

Sukhothai

Prome

Pegu

Pagan

Saigon

Vijaya

Malacca

Malayu

Palembang

Kediri

Singhasari

CHAPTER THREE

Mongolian conquests and their aftermath

1. *The Khanates and the landways*

The vast region from the Kansu Corridor of Jurched China to the Caspian border of the shrunken Abbasid Caliphate was, at the beginning of the thirteenth century, controlled by three main powers. A Tibetan people, the Tangut, had carved out a Kingdom of Hsi Hsia between the Ordos Loop of the Yellow River and the Tarim Basin. Most of this desert was under the Mongolian Khitan who, after their expulsion from North China by the Jurched, had moved west to make a state of Kara-Khitai (1124–1211), although Turfan and its neighbourhood remained under the Uighur Turks, now civilized by conversion to Buddhism or Nestorian Christianity. Beyond the Pamirs the Khitan competed for Fergana and Sogdia with the state of Khwarizm (1173–1220), split from the Caliphate by a governor of the Aral region, and controlling an area from the Caspian Sea to the Indus River.

By this time the Caliphate had lost Egypt to the Fatimids (909–1169), and had been taken over by Seljuk Turks who exercised authority as Sultans (1055–1194). They restored the Caliphate from Jerusalem to Kashgar, and wrested much of Asia Minor from Byzantium. But they lost Central Asia to Khwarizm and were overthrown, at the Caliph's instigation, by Shah Takash. He refused to vacate east Iran and his son, after taking the greater part of Iran, Bokhara, Samarkand, and Ghazni, was preparing to finish off the Caliphate when the Mongols came to destroy both Khwarizm and its prospective victim.

Byzantium, like its rival, was in serious decline. The organization upon which its greatness had depended for many centuries was undermined by disastrous conflicts between bureaucrats and soldiers, and by increasing fiscal extortion of peasants and subject peoples. Dangerous new foes appeared on its borders, and all South Italy was lost to the Normans as well as most of Asia Minor to the Seljuks. During the twelfth century complex wars reduced the once powerful Eastern Empire to a mere remnant around Constantinople, ruled by puppets of the Italian trading cities. There were further conflicts with Normans and Seljuks, new conflicts with Hungarians, a great insurrection of Bulgars, and attacks by Venice which disputed trading privileges granted to it, Pisa, and Genoa in return for help against the Normans. A popular reaction led to massacres of these Italian merchants, so that Venice diverted the Fourth Crusade (1202–4) to a merciless sack of Constantinople, and installed a Latin emperor. The Palaeologi expelled the Latins in 1261 and recovered some territory, but only with aid from Genoa, which had to be rewarded with such Black Sea trade as the Venetians had not already grasped.

Asian trade was far below the level of those days when T'ang controlled the Tarim basin and Abbasids the remainder of the Silk Road. It had suffered severely from the nomadic disturbances that pushed the Sung into South China and the Abbasids out of West Turkestan. Seljuks, Khwarist Turks, and Khitans, it is true, all showed an interest in trade and tried to promote it, helped here by the recovery of North China as the Jurched or Chin became sinicized. These new states, however, were to be short-lived, and trade was hindered by conflicts between the Seljuk and Khwarist Turks as well as by declining economic conditions in both the Caliphate and Byzantium. The Italian trading cities did not reap anything like the full harvest of their rapacious diplomacy until the Mongol conquests gave unparalleled security throughout the landways.

Within an amazing century the Mongols won mastery over all lands from the Carpathian Mountains to the Sea of Japan. This transformation of Asia, more remarkable and extensive than that of Alexander, came largely through the military genius and political talent of Temuchin (1162–1227), a chieftain's son who renewed his father's attempt at uniting tribes of the Mongolian steppes. All of them were brought, through persuasion or force, under his leadership by 1206 when, at a great assembly on the banks of the Kerulen River, he was proclaimed Jenghiz Khan—Universal Emperor. At this time he commanded 140,000 mounted warriors, equipped with superior bows, rigorously trained to execute rapid manoeuvres in flying columns, co-ordinated by means of various signals, and assisted by widespread espionage and the fear inspired by ruthless terrorism. He had welded an invincible fighting force, which was soon to be dreaded and cursed by Confucianists, Buddhists, Moslems, and Christians. 'I am the Scourge of God', he characteristically told the defeated townsmen of Bokhara. 'Heaven has delivered you into my hands that I may punish you for your sins.'[1] The scourge fell on other sinners than Khwarizm, and terribly; the immediate result of these barbaric conquests was slaughter and destruction that took at least decades to repair.

Audaciously, he struck first at North China. The Tanguts of Hsi Hsia had few friends, because of their interference with trade, and so were quickly reduced to vassalage in 1209. But the rich, populous empire of Chin, with its large armies and strongly fortified towns, seemed an impossible conquest for the comparatively small Mongol forces. Yet Jenghiz Khan sent 200,000 men across the Gobi to attack Chin at a time when it was embroiled with Sung. Manchuria and territory north of the Great Wall were quickly seized, and within two years the Mongols forced the passes in order to devastate Shansi, Hopei, and Shantung. The Chin court retreated to Kaifeng and, after protracted hostilities, Peking fell in 1215; its treasures were looted, its buildings burnt, and its people massacred.

Leaving a lieutenant with only 43,000 men to continue pillaging and ravaging Chin, the Khakan returned to Mongolia in order to take advantage of serious discontent among Kara-Khitai's Moslems with the harsh rule of a Naiman prince who had gained its throne through marriage. Posing as liberator of the oppressed, Jenghiz sent 20,000 men under Jebei to attack this extensive realm of many cities. Most of them welcomed deliverance and Jebei, after hunting down the king in the mountains, sent his head to the Khakan. Kara-Khitai was now a Mongol province, and Jenghiz master of the whole Tarim.

Through it he built a road, along which were regularly spaced military and post stations with requisite pastures or stores for grain. These stations served 'arrow messengers' who, having first priority for horses or passage, could travel as far as 200 miles

[1] Quoted in Prawdin, *The Mongol Empire*, p. 169.

a day. They served, too, for helping cavalry movements or
nomadic migrations across East Turkestan. But they were also
used by growing numbers of merchants, traditional travellers
of the Tarim whom all nomads appreciated in varying degree.
The Khakan especially favoured them; even before attacking
Chin he had welcomed traders to his camp, drew upon their
multifarious knowledge of Asia and held up their skill in business
affairs as a model to his followers. Immediately after annexing
Kara-Khitai, he favourably received an embassy from Moham-
med of Khwarizm, and concluded a treaty that seemed to
establish good and profitable relations between the two halves
of Turkestan. His reply said:

I am already acquainted with the size and the power of your Shah's
realm. He is the ruler of the West, just as I am the ruler of the East,
and we should do well to live together on friendly terms. Our
boundaries come into contact in Kipchak, and it would be advant-
ageous if the merchants could move freely from one country into the
other.[1]

Jenghiz Khan's interest in trade was also shown by intelligent
use of the Uighurs, a nomadic people who had become traders,
whose alphabetic script was used to codify Mongol law and
whose talents were used to develop a Mongol administration.

When the Shah launched a campaign against the Caliphate,
news reached him that a caravan which included Mongol spies
had arrived at Samarkand. All members of the caravan were
thereupon massacred by the governor and its freight seized.
The Khakan sent an embassy demanding surrender of this
governor, but the Shah insultingly killed its leader. Arrow
messengers sped throughout the steppes to summon warriors or
allies for a campaign of vengeance, and only Hsi Hsia was
foolish enough to refuse. A quarter of a million men, prepared
to the last detail, made difficult crossings over the Pamirs and
through the desert of Kizil-Kum to outflank the Shah's army
and take Bokhara, Samarkand, and Balkh. The Shah fled west,
but his brave son, Jelal ed-Din, succeeded in rallying the Moslems, whereupon the Khakan ordered a war of annihilation.
Khurasan was ravaged; fields were laid waste, irrigation works
destroyed, towns sacked, and their inhabitants massacred. At

[1] Prawdin, op. cit., p. 149.

Herat over a million people were killed, and a similar fate befell Merv, Nishapur, Urenj, Balkh, Ghazni, Talikhan, Kerduan, and Bamyan. Jelal was hunted across Afghanistan to the Indus, and the pursuing Mongols plundered districts of the Punjab. By 1222, accordingly, the Khakan was master of both West and East Turkestan, but turned back from India because of an epidemic which he interpreted as a warning from Heaven to its favourite son.

Meanwhile a force of 30,000 had been sent from the Caspian to explore westwards. In Georgia it defeated an army that was preparing to join the Crusaders, crossed the Caucasus, and ravaged Kuman territory up to the Dniester. There it was attacked by Russian forces, defeated them, rode up the steppes to their forest limit, turned east, conquered agricultural Bolgary, and also added the Lower Volga to the Mongols' north-west fief. Jenghiz Khan, more than gratified by this extraordinary success, led an army east to punish Hsi Hsia for refusing support in the campaign against Khwarizm, and to deal with resurgent Chin. He died during this terrible campaign but it was completed by his generals.

They chose his third son, Ogàtài (1229–41), to succeed him and, immediately after this election, new campaigns were launched against the remnant of Chin around Kaifeng, and against Korea. In 1231 the Mongols crossed the Yalu River, besieged Kaesong and soon forced submission of the Korean Court. But, after the invaders left, the Court moved to the island stronghold of Kanghwa to direct a stubborn resistance. During the next twenty-eight years the Mongols repeatedly despoiled Korea but could not take Kanghwa until 1258, when all resistance ended.

Ogàtài captured Kaifeng in 1234 with some help from the Sung, who were rewarded with territory in Honan. Thinking it insufficient, the Sung Emperor foolishly attacked the dangerous Mongols, with the result that Ogàtài took Szechwan and Hopei in 1236. Like previous nomadic invaders, he could make little progress against Central or South China, where mountains, lakes, rivers, paddy fields, and numerous fortified cities greatly hindered the mobility of horsemen. Hostilities went on without much result, other than destruction, until Mangu Khan (1251–9) led an army from Szechwan while his brother, Kublai, led another from Honan. Mangu died during the campaign so that Kublai became Khakan (1260–94). It took him another nineteen years to conquer South China, and so receive the Mandate of Heaven as founder of the Yuan Dynasty (1279–1368) and the first foreigner to rule the whole of China.

By this time Mongol forces had also pushed far into the west. From the Russian steppes they sent a new army which, in 1237, took Ryazan, the principality of Vladimir containing the small town of Moscow, and, in 1240, the great trading centre of Kiev. From there they turned into Poland, Silesia, and Moravia, finally defeating an army of 100,000 Magyars, Croats, Germans, and French Templars at Liegnitz (1241). This crushing victory, and its subsequent carnage, threw Europe into terrified despondency, lifted only by the Mongols' unexpected withdrawal in order to participate in choosing Ogàtài's successor. There were factional struggles, both before and after the brief reign of Kuyuk (1246–8), but they seem to have been resolved by the accession of Mangu.

Besides joining Kublai in the conquest of China, Mangu ordered his brother Hulagu 'to destroy the fortresses of the Assassins; and you must bring the Caliph under the yoke'. The fanatical sect of the Assassins had many strongholds in the Elburz Mountains of Iran, and terrorized most of the Moslem world. It took the Mongols three years to destroy these strongholds, after which Baghdad soon fell and the last Caliph was trampled to death by horses. Syria and Mesopotamia were then ravaged and subdued, but the Mamluks saved Egypt from the Mongols by inflicting a great defeat at Ain Jalut (1260).

When Kublai succeeded Mangu as Khakan the Mongol Empire comprised four huge fiefs. He chose for himself China, well satisfied with possession of by far the richest and most civilized of all the Mongol conquests. Central Asia, from the Kansu Corridor to the Oxus or Amu Darya River, was the Khanate of Chagatai, second son of Jenghiz Khan, now ruled by his descendants. Hulagu had the Il-Khanate of Persia, so called because he accepted a duty of vassalage to Kublai which the other two Khans refused, partly because they disapproved Kublai's decision to become a Chinese Emperor rather than a nomadic ruler of the steppes. The fourth Khanate was that of Kipchak, centred on the Lower Volga and stretching from Hungary to Lake Balkash, and from the region north of Moscow to the Caucasus.

The Khanate of Kipchak (1237–1391) remained basically Mongol; there the Golden Horde pastured herds over a vast area, and retained their nomadic or military organization. They skilfully exploited Russia by dividing its princes and making the Grand Duke of Vladimir chief agent for collecting taxes and enforcing discipline upon the conquered. Southern trading cities, such as Kiev and Chernigov, had been largely abandoned by their people and were now only big villages. But the Golden Horde became converted to Islam, which did much to civilize them. Their capital, New Sarai, was made a splendid city of fine buildings, and a leading centre of Moslem culture. Trade, naturally, was encouraged; Hansa wares came through Novgorod in the north, and Italian or European wares from the Venetian and Genoese merchants, who had become strongly established in Byzantium, and for whom several ports were opened in the Crimea. Asian wares reached the Golden Horde from the Il-Khanate of Persia as well as from the Khanate of Chagatai.

The Mongol conquest of West Asia had been immediately disastrous, involving great destruction of people and towns, and much damage to agriculture. In a horrifying attempt to make Mesopotamia fit only for pasture, Hulagu ordered his men to destroy the complex irrigation system of the Tigris-Euphrates region, thus permanently damaging what had long been a major farming area. But he came to appreciate, and use, Iran's great administrative tradition, and even built a famous library-observatory at Maraghah. The Il-Khanate (1260–1335) soon renounced early barbarity in order to assimilate and foster the rich civilization which it now controlled, a process which was made the more necessary by failure against Egypt and by a threatening alliance of the Mamluks with the Golden Horde. This danger induced Hulagu's successor to adopt Islam and to seek friendly relations with European powers. During the reign of the ablest Il-Khan, Ghazun Mahmud (1295–1304), there was a considerable assimilation of Persian culture and a marked revival of prosperity. He codified laws, improved administration, developed land by irrigation works, encouraged handicrafts, improved communications, and fostered towns and trade.

Ghazun did his best to restore fraternal unity between the Khanates, now threatened by the unsuccessful attack of Kaidu, Khan of Chagatai, on Kublai as a renegade who had shifted from Karakorum to Peking. The attempt succeeded, because of a recognition that strife harmed the valuable caravan trade passing through their separate dominions, and the next Il-Khan could tell Philip of France that all the Mongols were again united.

The Khanate of Chagatai (1227–1369) was the key sector for caravan trade as it embraced the two halves of Turkestan. Jenghiz Khan's immediate successors expanded, improved, and protected the road he had built there, and linked it by cuttings through passes, or bridges over rivers, to roads going through Iran or Kipchak. The Khans also enforced strict security by military pickets to suppress brigands or punish robbers, and by checks at posting stations for missing caravans. These stations, spaced at roughly thirty-mile intervals, provided both good accommodation and fresh horses. Never before nor since were the transcontinental routes more thronged with merchants, who were so well protected, according to a contemporary, that 'a maiden bearing a nugget of gold could wander safely throughout the realm'. The Mongols also fostered trade by adopting Chinese paper money in order to standardize currency payments throughout their landways. The issue was backed by silver, and drew off large amounts of this metal from China until later inflation led to cessation of further issues in 1356.

For a whole century, accordingly, the barbaric Mongols imposed a *Pax Tartarica* of wider scope than the *Pax Romana*. Nevertheless the roads carried a smaller proportion of trade to Europe than in the days of Imperial Rome. Sea transport had become relatively cheaper, and most Chinese exports to Iran and Europe now went through southern ports. Demands for Chinese silks, moreover, were not so much for the raw cloth so eagerly sought by Roman factories but for expensive patterned wares; Iran and Byzantium had long ago become silk producers and, when Norman Crusaders pillaged Byzantium, they packed off silk weavers to Palermo so that it became an important producer from which the industry spread to Valencia and Provence. Most trade from North China was to Central Asia and Iran, involving exchange of silks, tea, and miscellaneous wares, for horses, minerals, and furs. It was largely conducted by

Moslem companies of Central Asians, supported by the Mongol government which also used them as tax-farmers. Latin traders did not become active along the landways until the thirteenth century, when they helped a limited revival of overland trade in silk.

A guide to their activities was given by Pegolotti's famous commercial handbook.[1] The route he details began at the Crimean port of Tana, went to Astrakan (twenty-five days by ox-wagon or half that time by horse-wagon), to Armalee on the Ili River (forty-five days with pack asses), and then to Kanchow in Kansu (seventy days with asses). It took another eighty days to Peking so that the whole journey through West Turkestan, and along the North Tarim, took over four months to China, and seven months to its capital. Pegolotti bears witness to the *Pax Tartarica:* the whole route 'is perfectly safe, whether by day or by night', but, should a merchant die, 'everything belonging to him will become the perquisite of the lord of the land in which he dies', unless it can be given to a brother or intimate friend. He also describes the Mongols' paper money; 'Whatever silver the merchants carry with them to Cathay the lord of Cathay takes from them and puts in his treasury and gives that paper money of theirs in exchange . . . and with this money you can readily buy silk and whatever other merchandise you desire to buy.' By his day, evidently, its use was not compulsory over the whole Mongol Empire.

You may calculate that a merchant with a dragoman, and with two men servants, and with goods to the value of 25,000 golden florins, should spend on his way to Cathay from sixty to eighty sommi of silver, and not more if he manage well; and for all the road back again from Cathay to Tana, including the expenses of living and the pay of servants, and all other charges, the cost will be about 5 sommi per head of pack animals or something less. And you may reckon the somm to be worth 5 golden florins. You may reckon also that each ox-wagon will require one ox and will carry 10 cantars Genoese weight; and the camel-wagon will require three camels and will carry 30 cantars Genoese weight; and the horse-wagon will require one horse, and will commonly carry 6½ cantars of silk, at 250 Genoese pounds to the cantar. And a bale of silk may be reckoned at between 110 and 115 Genoese pounds.

[1] Reproduced in full in Yule and Cordier, *Cathay and the Way Thither*, vol. iii, pp. 143 and 171.

Transport costs thus appear to have been a surprisingly small margin of about 2 per cent on the outward freight, but this figure does not include tariffs. Pegolotti gives details of these only for some western places, together with helpful advice on bribing customs officers. The best merchandise to bring from Italy for sale in Tana or Urgenj (near the Aral coast) was linens, but the trader should exchange them only for silver, convertible into paper money in China, unless he could take 'some bales of the very finest stuffs which go in very small bulk'. Once in China, he could buy coarse silk at 20 lb. per sommo or damasked silk at 3½ lb. per sommo.

Silk, for Pegolotti, was still the most desirable purchase from China. But Italian merchants found greater profit in importing spices, perfumes, and drugs from India or through Iran. The Caliphs had somewhat restricted this trade with Europe, and it had been disturbed by the Crusaders. When the Il-Khanate threw open its roads from Syria to the Gulf of India, Italians took full advantage of the new opportunity, and growing European demands for spices in cooking soon made Genoa and Venice rich. West Europe came to seek ways round their monopoly, especially after the Il-Khanate, on conversion to Islam, so reversed its liberal trading policy that spices became much dearer.

In Kublai's reign, however, the landways were securely open to all. The first Europeans to travel over them, in 1260, via Bokhara and the Tarim to Mongol China, were two Genoese merchants named Polo. Kublai warmly welcomed them, not only because of Mongol interest in trade, but because he needed able foreigners for ruling the enormous Chinese Empire. He was doing much to deserve the Mandate of Heaven. Mongol ravages to farms, irrigation works, and towns were being repaired, and roads, waterways, ports, and shipping were being improved. State granaries were revived as an insurance against famine, charitable relief was given to the old or orphaned, and hospitals were built for the sick. The taste of his magnificent court kept up encouragement to craftsmen and artists. Kublai had also preserved the Sung system of administration—with the important omission of examinations and the exclusion of Confucianist scholars from top posts. He could not trust these mandarins, most of whom were ineradicably loyal to Sung and resented his dividing policy of tolerant support for Taoists and Buddhists. Mongols could handle military affairs, but lacked the background for administering so large and old an empire. The Polos were charged with a request to the Pope for a hundred scholars or technicians, a mere Christian handful among the Nestorian Uighurs, Moslem Turks, and Tibetan Buddhists who were being appointed to key civil positions. Foreigners also took over Chinese banking as guilds from Bokhara and Samarkand became, under Kublai's patronage, the great money merchants of the Far East. The Polos, however, returned with only young Marco, because even the two Dominicans, who were all the Pope would send in response to Kublai's request, lost heart at Lajazzo. Travelling via Balkh and Kashgar, the three Polos reached Kublai's court in 1275, and there accepted official appointments which they held for a lengthy period of seventeen years.

2. *China's maritime expansion*

Marco Polo's famous book[1] says something about the landways, but has more valuable information about China's internal trade and that of its seaports. He saw these on a journey made to Amoy, and gained more insight into sea trade during a return journey which brought him from Ch'uan-chou to Champa, Sumatra, Coromandel, Malabar, Cambay, and Ormuz. Further information was given by that great Moslem traveller, ibn-Battutah,[2] who came to China on a very leisurely journey (1325–55) along the Arab sea routes. There are, too, useful observations by such missionaries as John of Montecorvino,[3] sent to Kublai by the Pope in 1289, Odoric of Pordenone[4] who, after reaching Canton in 1324, spent three years in Peking, and John of Marignolli, a Franciscan who was in China between 1342 and 1347.

The Mongols were, of course, not seafarers themselves, and their own contribution to China's trade was restoration and extension of overland traffic. But Kublai took over the great development of maritime activity that had been promoted by

---

[1] The translation used here is *The Travels of Marco Polo*, ed. Latham.
[2] Yule and Cordier, *Cathay and the Way Thither*, vol. iv.
[3] ibid.   [4] ibid.

Sung, and showed a proper appreciation of its importance. His first interest here was, naturally enough, in purposes of war. He used a fleet for an unsuccessful attack upon Japan, in 1274, and destroyed the last Sung fleet, south-west of Canton, in 1279, but only because of defections from it. In that year he ordered ship-yards to provide 600 ships for another attempt on Japan but, in 1281, again failed to add this stubborn island kingdom to his Empire. Nor was he more successful in attempting to subdue South-east Asia by naval means. A combined fleet from Champa and Annam repulsed his forces in 1282, and again in 1287. Another Mongol expedition, as we shall see, was repulsed by Majapahit Java.

These naval misadventures at least kept up China's maritime activity, which was also encouraged by continuing and vigorous sea trade with South-east Asia, India, and Iran. Marco Polo has left a vivid account of three great ports in Yuan China. The first is Hwai-ngan-chau at the mouth of the Yellow River. It was, he said, 'a very big city, of great wealth and splendour', having 'an enormous number of ships' and importing 'enormous quantities of merchandise'. These came from other Chinese ports, and were widely distributed up the river. Salt was made here in sufficient quantity to provide exports which met the needs of more than forty cities, so that the Khan derived a huge income from this monopoly as well as from import dues collected at the port.

Sinju (I-ching), on the Yangtze, 'is of no great size but is a busy resort of ships and merchandise'. The river on which it stands, however, is the biggest in the world so that, 'in the amount of shipping it carries and the total volume and value of its traffic, it exceeds all the rivers of the Christians put together and their seas into the bargain. I give you my word that I have seen in this city fully 5,000 ships at once', ships carrying 200 to 600 tons. Kwa-chow (Caigiu), another Yangtze port, sent great quantities of rice and corn up the Grand Canal to Peking.

Kinsai or Hangchow, the capital built by Southern Sung, was a magnificent city. Polo described it as 'without doubt the finest and most splendid city in the world', a judgement shared by Odoric who said it was 'the greatest city in the world'. Wonderingly, Polo lists its 100-mile circumference, numerous bridges, 1,600,000 houses, and 12,000 workshops, each employing ten to forty men. 'As for the merchants, they are so many and so rich and handle such quantities of merchandise that no one could give a true account of the matter; it is so utterly beyond reckoning.' To take only one commodity; the city's daily consumption of pepper was forty-three cartloads of 233 lb. There were ten principal market-places, each half a mile square and frequented by 40,000 to 50,000 people, not to speak of countless local markets. One canal was lined with 'large stone buildings, in which all the merchants who came from India and elsewhere store their wares and merchandise', which included mainly spices, gems, and pearls.

The main foreign port, however, was Zaiton (Ch'uan-chou) in Fukien. It was

the port for all the ships that arrive from India laden with costly wares and precious stones of great price and big pearls of fine quality . . . so that the total amount of traffic in gems and other merchandise entering and leaving this port is a marvel to behold. I assure you that for one spice ship that goes to Alexandria or elsewhere to pick up pepper for export to Christendom, Zaiton is visited by a hundred. . . . The revenue accruing to the Great Khan from this port is something colossal . . . what with freight and the imperial tithe merchants pay half the value of what they import . . . (yet) ask nothing better than to return with another cargo.

Odoric thought Zaiton twice as big as Rome, and John of Marignolli wrote that it was 'a wondrous fine sea port and city of incredible size'. Moslems also marvelled at Zaiton and its trade. 'The harbour of Zaiton', said ibn-Battutah, 'is one of the greatest in the world—I am wrong: it is the greatest! I have seen there one hundred first-class junks together; as for small ones they were past counting.' Besides its trade, he admired the city's manufactures of satin or velvet.

Although its paganism distressed ibn-Battutah, he was as impressed by China as Marco Polo had been. He found it a beautiful country, 'the best cultivated in the world', abounding 'in all sorts of good things'. Its sugar was better than Egypt's, its plums better than Syria's, and nowhere had he seen better wheat, melons, peas, or beans. Porcelain, the finest of all pottery, was as cheap as earthenware in Arabia. Silk was in 'such abundance that it is used for clothing even by poor monks and beggars'; but one cotton dress in China was worth two or three of silk. It was generally agreed that the Chinese 'of all mankind have the greatest skill and taste in the arts'. Little wonder, then, that 'China is the safest as well as the pleasantest of all the regions on earth for a traveller'.

Ibn-Battutah gave first-hand information about conditions of Arab merchants in China.

When a Musulman trader arrives in a Chinese city, he is allowed to choose whether he will take up his quarters with one of the merchants of his own faith settled in the country, or will go to an inn. If he prefers to lodge with a merchant, they count all his money and confide it to the merchant of his choice. . . . When the guest wishes to depart his money is again counted, and the host is obliged to make good any deficiencies. If, however, the foreign trader prefers to go to an inn, his money is made over in deposit to the landlord, who then buys on his account whatever he may require.

The big junks developed by Sung continued venturing abroad. They went most frequently to South-east Asia and South India, all of whose major ports had many resident Chinese traders. Good relations between the Il-Khanate and China led to a development of voyages to the Persian Gulf so that Tabriz, now the leading market for West Asia, also had a Chinese quarter, and Kublai sent Chinese engineers to help repair Hulagu's damage to the irrigation works of the Tigris-Euphrates area. Co-operation with the Khanate of Kipchak was similarly evident in the Chinese quarter of far distant Moscow or Novgorod. Foreigners described the huge junks, such as those in the fleet sent by Kublai to take a Mongol princess to her marriage in Iran. They had double planks, watertight compartments and four to six masts; their fifty to sixty cabins accommodated a crew of 200–300 and as many passengers; their holds took up to 6,000 baskets of pepper and their decks had space for growing vegetables in tubs; they towed two to three large boats of supplies, and carried about ten small ones.

All this trade led to further useful cultural exchange. The Arabs brought the major food plant, sorghum, to Yuan China, and taught it how to refine sugar. Distillation was introduced, and the abacus came into wide use, two centuries later than in Europe. Carrots, grapefruit, pistachios, and grape wine now appeared on Chinese tables, and chaulmoogra oil came from

Thailand as a remedy for leprosy. Bowed zithers, guitars, and Byzantine reed organs were among the musical instruments brought across Central Asia. Yuan China, in return, acquainted the West with porcelain, printing, playing-cards, saltpetre, and gunpowder.

Much as foreigners admired the size and wealth of China, the Yuan period was inferior to its predecessor. The Southern Sung had about 100 million subjects but the much wider Yuan China around 60 million. These figures indicate the depopulation that resulted from the terrible campaigns waged by the Mongols and their subsequent disruption of economic life. Political life was also disrupted, and there was a serious loss of administrative efficiency through replacements of hostile Confucianist mandarins by Taoist, Buddhist, or Moslem officials, uninformed, unsympathetic, venial, or ruthless. Kublai's able successor Temur (1294–1307), had to punish no less than 18,000 of them for corruption.

After Temur's death, six weak and debauched emperors followed one another within a quarter of a century of increasing disorder which degenerated into anarchy during the long reign of Togan Temur (1333–68), a particularly scandalous voluptuary. Chinese secret societies were organized to work for the expulsion of the hated Mongols and, after 1352, revolt spread from the south. A poor peasant who had become a monk cast off his robe to gain dominance over all other adventurers. He took Nanking in 1356, Canton in 1367, and Peking a year later. There he was proclaimed the Emperor Hung-wu, made Nanking the capital of a new Ming dynasty (1368–1662), and dedicated it to the revival of T'ang and Sung glories. Peace, however, was not fully secured until the reign of Yung-lo (1403–24), who transferred the capital back to Peking.

Between them, these two great men restored the threefold administration of civil ministries, military hierarchy, and censorate, although replacing the chancellery of a prime minister by a more personal system of rule. Local government, too, was recast on T'ang lines, and the examination system for selecting officials was even more highly developed than under the Sung, whose ardent sponsorship of arts and letters the Ming also tried to emulate. In these and other ways they restored China's culture and advanced its prosperity.

They sought to revive the old system of tributary relations with foreign countries, and had far more success here than Kublai Khan. Hung-wu dispatched envoys who induced Japan, Korea, Annam, Champa, Cambodia, and Thailand to send embassies to his Court, and it subsequently received other tribute missions from Borneo, Java, Sumatra, Malayan states, and even from a few Indian princes on the Coromandel coast. There was nothing aggressive about this Ming claim to suzerainty, as there had been about Kublai's, because the main purpose was to confirm ancient boons of trade with the Celestial Empire. In Japan's case, Hung-wu also wanted suppression of piratical raids that were damaging Chinese ports; but he had no success until, near the end of his reign, the Ashikaga Shogun sent lavish tribute and a profession of dutiful loyalty. Yung-lo was thus able to reopen three Superintendencies of Merchant Shipping in the south, and to build hostels for tribute missions, including those now coming annually from Japan.

Far more important were the remarkable naval expeditions sent to establish a brief, but most impressive, Chinese hegemony over the whole Indian Ocean. In the year following his accession, Hung-wu sent a mission announcing that event to Coromandel, and another mission in 1370. Yung-lo also sent an expedition there when he ascended the throne, and two others in 1403. One of these, under Yin Ching, was intended to promote maritime trade with Iran as well as with India and Ceylon; it had the incidental effect of making friendly contact with the rising commercial power of Malacca, which was successfully competing with Majapahit but needed protection against the southward driving Thai.

Then came the seven great voyages of fleets commanded by Cheng Ho, the 'three-jewel eunuch' from inland Yunnan. Official records of these voyages were erased by disapproving mandarins, but Cheng Ho erected steles whose brief accounts can be supplemented by writings left by four members of his staff. His first fleet of sixty-three junks (the largest of which measured 444 ft. by 180 ft.), carrying 27,870 men, sailed from Foochow, in 1405, to Java, Malacca, Ceylon, and Calicut. He persuaded the Paramesvara of Malacca to send a tribute mission to the Ming court, and captured the pirate-ruler of Palembang, who was brought to Nanking. But, hearing that the King of Ceylon was hostile, Cheng Ho avoided that island and proceeded directly to Calicut.

The second expedition was prepared by Cheng Ho although he did not command it. Leaving the Yangtze in 1408 it visited Java, Aru, Achin, Kayal (in Madras), Cochin, and Calicut, where recognition was accorded a new king. Ceylon was again avoided. Immediately after its return, Cheng Ho led a third expedition of forty-eight junks and 30,000 men to Champa, Java, and Malacca, whose ruler was given the status and insignia of a client-king. After leaving Samudra, Cheng Ho stopped at the southern coast of Ceylon in order to erect a trilingual stele thanking the Buddha for safe passages, and went on to Quilon and Calicut. But on the return voyage he put into Ceylon, captured its refractory king and brought him back to China in 1411. In the following year he put to sea with a fourth expedition which ranged much further. After visiting Champa, Kelantan, Pahang, Java, Palembang, Malacca, Aru, Samudra, Achin, Ceylon, Kayal, the Maldives, Cochin, and Calicut again, it proceeded to Ormuz in the Persian Gulf. It brought back the usurper of Samudra's throne, and he was beheaded in 1415. The fifth expedition swept over the entire Indian Ocean between 1417 and 1419; besides revisiting ports in South-east Asia, India, Ceylon, and the Persian Gulf, it went to Aden where it managed to secure a giraffe which became a wonderful, auspicious curiosity of the Ming Court. The sixth expedition (1421–3) went beyond Aden to Mogadishu and Brawa on the East African coast, although Cheng Ho remained in China.

As dates are known for the various calls made by the seventh expedition (1432–3), China's last burst of maritime activity, sailing times can be computed. They are:

T'ai-p'ing Bay to Champa	15 days
Champa to Surabaya	23 days
Surabaya to Palembang	11 days
Palembang to Malacca	7 days
Malacca to Achin	10 days
Achin to Ceylon	26 days
Ceylon to Calicut	8 days
Calicut to Ormuz	34 days
Ormuz to Calicut	22 days

Calicut to Achin	17 days
Achin to Malacca	8 days
Malacca to Champa	?
Champa to Swatow	8 days

They are good times, as Willetts points out,[1] but perhaps no better than those made six centuries earlier by Arab ships; their sailing time from Masqat to Canton was 120 days, as compared with 134 days from T'ai-p'ing to Ormuz by Cheng Ho. The comparison is not exact, as the times are for voyages in opposite directions, and we cannot make a full, direct comparison because of the unknown time Cheng Ho spent at Malacca on his way home. His return journey, however, as far as Malacca, took forty-seven days as against sixty days for Abbasid merchants from Masqat to Kalah Bar.

Cheng Ho's own estimate of these remarkable voyages deserves quotation.

The Imperial Ming dynasty, in unifying the seas and continents, surpassing the three dynasties, even goes beyond the Han and T'ang Dynasties. The countries beyond the horizon and at the ends of the earth have all become subjects; and to the most western of the western or the most northern of the northern countries, however far they may be, the distances and the routes may be calculated. Thus the barbarians from beyond the seas, though their countries are truly distant, with double translation have come to audience bearing precious objects and presents.

The Emperor, approving of their loyalty and sincerity, has ordered us and others at the head of several tens of thousands of officers and flag troops to ascend more than a hundred large ships to go and confer presents on them in order to make manifest the transforming power of the Imperial Virtue and to treat distant people with kindness. From the third year of Yung-lo till now we have several times received the commission of ambassadors to the countries of the Western Ocean. . . . We have traversed more than one hundred thousand *li* of immense water spaces and have beheld in the ocean huge waves like mountains rising sky-high, and we have set eyes on barbarian regions far away hidden in a blue transparency of light vapours, while our sails, loftily unfurled like clouds, day and night continued their course, rapid like that of a star, traversing the savage waves as if we were treading a public thoroughfare.[2]

---

[1] *Journal of Southeast Asian History*, vol. 5, no. 2, p. 30.

[2] Mirsky, *The Great Chinese Travellers*, pp. 249–50.

Why then did these exciting voyages cease and their potentialities, political and economic, go untapped? Chinese merchants and migrants did follow the Ming fleets to settle in South-east Asia, but there seems to have been little attempt, as in Mongol times, to establish trading quarters further west. No official trading companies, certainly, were formed such as those of the Europeans who later penetrated the Indian Ocean. The Ming Court was far more indifferent to trade, beyond diplomatic bounds, than the Sung or Yuan, being content to derive most of its revenue from land taxes instead of customs dues. Mandarins were openly opposed to Cheng Ho's expeditions, which they criticized as a costly strain on imperial resources and as breaching tradition against voyages beyond coastal waters. After they succeeded in preventing the dispatch of an eighth expedition, by 'losing' essential sailing directions, no more were attempted. The Emperor may have become disappointed with a tribute system that required a costly navy to make it work or, especially after Annam's successful revolt for independence (1431), he may have decided to concentrate resources on campaigns against the Mongols, now regrouped under the Oirats and threatening his northern border. The final blow to maritime effort was the prohibition of sea trade in response to a dangerous renewal of Japanese piracy. And so the expertise and knowledge gained for China by Cheng Ho and his captains were thrown away, and exploitation of the Indian Ocean left open to Europeans, who were to become a far greater danger to China's traditional way of life than any nomads from the northern steppes. As Grousset sadly remarks: 'China allowed her hour of destiny, on land and on the sea, to pass her by.'[1]

3. Japanese piracy

Neither Korea nor Japan was immune from Mongol attacks. Jenghiz Khan had reduced Korea to vassal status in 1231, but subsequent resistance, directed from Kanghwa Island, continued until the assassination of the last Ch'oe dictator in 1258. Kublai Khan then annexed the northern half of Korea and kept a tight control over the remnant Koryo kingdom, as did his successors, through Mongol consorts and officials. Korea's

[1] Grousset, *The Rise and Splendour of the Chinese Empire*, p. 264.

trade had shrunk to small dimensions before its further impoverishment by the long, destructive struggle against the Mongols,
and made no real recovery afterwards, in spite of closer association with China and the Yuan policy of fostering trade; so
little, indeed, that the ceramic industry, whose fine celadons
had been admired by Sung China, gave up their production
and now made only inferior pottery. One reason for stagnation
was corrupt, oppressive government as strong bureaucratic
families again exploited royal favours or revenues. Another was
the heavy burdens imposed on Korea by Kublai's two unsuccessful invasions of Japan, and a third was the increasingly
damaging raids by Japanese pirates. These came from freebooting clans around the Inland Sea, the leaders of which were
immune from central authority and hardly distinguished
between trade and piracy. Their activities, already damaging
in the thirteenth century, had reached such proportions by the
mid-fourteenth century as to force coastal dwellers to withdraw
from some of Korea's best lands, and prevented even the transport of grain taxes by sea. Under these conditions Korea had
little hope of achieving any substantial foreign trade.

Repeated rejections of his demand for suzerainty led Kublai
to order an invasion of Japan in 1274. He had a force of 25,000
men to which Korea had to supply 5,000, as well as 900 ships
and large quantities of provisions. Although the Japanese were
not well prepared, they fought stubbornly to hold the invasion
until, during bad weather, the Mongols went to their ships,
many of which were then destroyed by a terrible storm. Kublai,
nevertheless, renewed his demands for submission, all of which
were again refused. In 1281, accordingly, he ordered a second
invasion, involving a force of 140,000 and much heavier requisitions upon Korea. This time the Japanese were well prepared,
held the invaders to a narrow bridgehead and, once more
favoured by the weather gods, saw most of the Mongol fleet
destroyed by a typhoon.

The victory, although crushing and glorious, yielded little
booty for feudal retainers of the Kamakura Shogunate. Western
clans, who had done much to cope with the Mongol invasions,
were particularly dissatisfied with the meagre rewards which
were all the Shogunate could afford. They went back to piracy
and raiding with such vigour as to terrorize the coasts of Korea

and Shantung. The Shogunate was in no position to check them, even if it had wanted to; impoverishment had weakened most of its retainers' strength or loyalty. Power passed from the centre to local leaders, who were developing into a new feudal class, later known as daimyos. Some of its members supported Go-Daigo's attack on the Shogunate in his vain attempt at restoring imperial authority. The attack quickly developed into a long period of civil war, during the earlier stages of which a renegade Kamakura general founded a new Ashikaga Shogun-ate (1336–1573). Not until the rule of the third Shogun, Yoshimitsu (1368–94), did the war end, through exhaustion, and his restoration of central government hardly extended to control over powerful or distant vassals.

Contrary to what might be expected, the six decades of civil war were a period of fairly rapid economic growth for Japan. There was little interference with peasants or workers, and a great stimulation of agriculture, handicrafts, and trade. Agricul-ture gained by a change from sole inheritance of estates to their division among a lord's sons, and by the growth of an important class of small, independent farmers; these changes made for more intensive cultivation using better methods of cropping or rotating crops, together with the adoption of a more resistant strain of rice from Champa. In many places, accordingly, yields doubled or even tripled. Handicrafts and trades gained both from growing agricultural prosperity and loosening of tradi-tional bonds. Craftsmen had been slaves or servants during the Nara or Kamakura periods, but now became independent workers, organized for mutual protection in a developing *za* system of guilds. Traders became similarly organized, and also peasants, who were often both traders of their own produce and spare-time craftsmen. All gained from the development of mar-kets and towns, which was a feature of the period and, of course, based on the remarkable growth of agriculture. This develop-ment of trade and towns was associated with a growing shift from barter to monetary transactions, largely conducted in Chinese copper cash. Trade with China, however, was severely reduced by hostile relations between Japan and the Yuan dynasty, so that there was an acute shortage of currency. This was a major reason for Yoshimitsu's anxiety to resume trade with China after the Mongols had been expelled.

11

Their expulsion assisted Korea. The Koryo Court had been obliged to help the Yuan in their struggles against Chinese rebels but, as the Mongols' position became desperate, seized the chance of regaining North Korea. There was then division about support for Yuan or Ming, and it was eventually decided to send troops against Ming forces in Manchuria. Yi Song-gye, a leading general who thought this folly, thereupon seized the capital, took the throne, and founded the exceptionally long-lived Yi dynasty (1392–1910).

The Yi were loyal to Ming and, during a brilliant first century, reshaped Korea again on Chinese lines. A sweeping land reform of the T'ang kind strengthened both the central government and the defence of border or coastal regions. It also helped production by making landlords more directly interested in their estates, and by binding peasants more tightly to the land. There were large, forced migrations to the relatively under-populated northern regions, and a considerable expansion of the area under cultivation. Administration was improved by establishing six ministries and two powerful Boards of Censors, and by a fuller institution of the Chinese examination system. This had the effect of strengthening Confucianist scholarship, and so helped a great revival of letters and fine arts, the most striking aspects of which were printing with moveable type and a scientific system of phonetic writing (Han'gul). Books were printed in great quantity, and printing flourished along with letters, both fostered by a new imperial academy; but there was little revival of Korea's great ceramic tradition.

Strong rule and reviving prosperity helped trade. Markets were set up along the Manchurian border to regulate dealings with nomads. Annual tribute missions to the Ming Court revived trade with China, and Yi established something like friendly relations with Yoshimitsu, who was persuaded to suppress the activities of Japanese pirates against Korea in return for trading privileges at the port of Pusan, later extended to other places. After this agreement Korea suffered less from pirates, but had to protest continually about some attack or other upon a town or granary. There was, indeed, such fear of predatory raids that Yi prohibited mining of gold, in spite of Ming complaints about the omission of gold from tribute.

The main base for the pirates who, it must be said, included

Koreans and Chinese, was the island of Tsushima. Until 1418 it was controlled by the So family, who were interested in friendly trade with Korea, but, in that year, came under a pirate chief. Angered by an immediate increase of marauding, the Koreans attacked this island in strength. They were defeated and pacified by the So, but alarmed the Shogun who thereafter did his best to confine pirate attacks to China. Korea suffered little from them after that, and was able to conduct a comparatively peaceful and flourishing trade with Japan. It sent mainly coins, from its own mints or China's, pottery, and textiles of cotton which it had learnt to grow and process during the fourteenth century. In exchange, Japan sent sulphur, copper, and tropical fruits or woods from the Luchu (Ryukyu) Islands. Hakata, in these islands, had become a considerable entrepôt, attracting ships from China, Korea, and Japan, and sailing its own ships, not only to these countries, but to Java, Sumatra, Malaya, Thailand, and Burma.

The first Ming Emperor was so worried by piracy that he sought to have it suppressed by making Japan a tributary. Kanenaga, Yoshimitsu's western rival, was induced to send an embassy, but that did not help relations with Kyoto. There were further attacks, which the Emperor tried to meet by defensive measures and by restricting maritime trade. Things improved when Yoshimitsu gained the upper hand in Japan. He then accepted tributary status, exchanged embassies and, in 1405, made an agreement for the suppression of piracy in return for a monopoly of official trade with China. Both sides honoured the agreement; pirates were vigorously put down and trade flourished on terms favourable to the Shogunate. It made a profit of 200–300 per cent on imports of silk, porcelain, drugs, and books, and gained so much of the copper cash, which was a main object of the agreement, that Japan's deficiency of coin was remedied. On their side, the Chinese obtained horses, armour, swords, sulphur, inkslabs, fans, lacquer chests, and bronzeware. Yoshimitsu's son continued these embassies until 1411, when they were discontinued for obscure reasons of nationalism. But official trade was resumed in 1432 by a later Shogun, and increased up to 1453 after which it declined owing to limitations imposed by Ming officials who found that the Japanese were bringing excessive supplies of copper and sulphur.

The Shogunate then allowed the official trade to pass into the hands of certain monasteries and daimyos who had largely financed its resumption. For this purpose they needed tally stub books as credentials in China and, in 1469, one of these daimyo families, the Ouchi, captured them from a returning mission, thus gaining a monopoly of official trade with China.

By this time the Ashikaga Shogunate, never strong enough for its tasks, had become weakened as increasingly powerful daimyos took over whole districts, and collapsed when the Onin War (1467–77) ushered in another, but far worse, century of civil strife. During it pirate activity went quite unchecked and became a serious problem for Ming China. When the Ouchi were themselves overthrown by vassals, in 1551, pirate activity greatly increased. The pirates moved from western ports in Japan and the Luchu Islands to a new base, Chusan Island, off the mouth of the Yangtze, and from there began raiding south of the Shantung Peninsula, the previous focus of their attacks. Between 1545 and 1563 there were almost annual raids upon Chekiang, Chihli, and Fukien, with Kwantung added from 1550. Yangtze ports were also raided and, in 1555, both Hangchow and Nanking suffered attack. Korea, too, lost its long immunity when a fleet of seventy craft attacked Quelpart Island and adjacent coastal areas in 1555. After that it was frequently attacked by both Japanese and Chinese pirates.

The Ming Court was much to blame for the situation. It had limited official trade well below the volume sought by Japanese merchants, and had tried to deal with freebooting or piracy by a complete prohibition of trade. Chinese merchants were forbidden to deal with Japanese, and Chinese sailors were forbidden to venture on the high seas. Merchants, chafing under these restrictions, began co-operating with the Japanese in various ways, and sailors, to avoid unemployment, often joined the pirates. By the opening of the seventeenth century, accordingly, Japanese ships, largely manned by Chinese sailors, and with some Koreans, were raiding or trading with ports on the weakly defended Ming coast, or making voyages to the Philippines and most of South-east Asia. Japanese merchants had secret quarters in Chekiang, Fukien, and Kwantung, where they managed to evade the prohibitions, although their trade could not yet compare with that of the pirates. Some Chinese merchants moved to Japan, often via piracy which they helped to convert into something nearer free trade. The Portuguese, too, after being banned from trade at Canton because of bad behaviour by one of their captains, seized Macao in 1557, and became carriers or brokers in the illegal trade between China and Japan.

Ming naval forces, badly shrunken since the days when Cheng Ho's great fleets had mastered the Indian Ocean, could do little to check piracy. They were driven from Namoa Island, off Kwantung, but went to Taiwan which, for more than a century, became a great lair for all kinds of pirates. Some success attended later efforts at suppression, but the main improvement occurred when the prohibitions were relaxed. Wang Chih, a leading Chinese trader among those who had gone to Japan, told a Ming embassy, which had been sent to protest about piracy, that the best way of halting it would be co-operation with those daimyos who were protecting pirates. He was induced to return to China, where he was executed, but Ming officials began to urge repeal of the prohibitions. The prohibition on Chinese voyages was soon lifted and Ming junks again sailed, in the second half of the sixteenth century, to South-east Asia in such numbers as to carry emigrants who founded the great overseas Chinese communities in the Philippines, Indonesia, and Malaya. Trade with Japan was still prohibited, but flourished. Piracy, from being general, was now limited to certain areas, such as Luzon and some parts of the South China Sea, and changed its character to something like smuggling. One good consequence was a decline of slavery, illegal but not uncommon in Japan, and supplied by captives of the pirates.

Japan, nevertheless, was indirectly responsible for the fall of Ming. Its own awful civil war ended with reunification of the country by three successive daimyos. Nobunàgà and Uyesugi Kenshin broke the military power of strong Buddhist monasteries; Hideyoshi (1537–98), after subduing central Japan and Kyushu, defeated the Hojo in Kanto and then subdued North Honshu. For the first time in two and a half centuries, Japan was under the effective control of a single master, who controlled it rigorously. But he had comparatively little economic damage to repair. The daimyos, by reducing other feudal claimants, had eased burdens on peasants, and did something to improve their status. Daimyos, moreover, were interested in developing mining or promoting handicrafts, so that industrial and agricultural outputs both increased. There was particularly good progress in mining and smelting silver and gold, helpful to the illegal trade with China. Communications had also been improved, for economic as well as military reasons, and better ships were built for the increasingly distant voyages made by pirate–merchants.

Immediately after his conquest of Japan, Hideyoshi, flushed with ambition, contemplated taking over China from the Ming. He asked the Yi Court for help in this grandiose enterprise and, when it refused, sent 160,000 men to invade Korea. The Ming, naturally enough, came to the aid of their loyal tributary, and a great Korean admiral, Yi Sun-sin, managed to disrupt Japanese supply lines. Hideyoshi withdrew his forces, but renewed the attack in 1597. Once again the Koreans and Chinese combined effectively and, on Hideyoshi's death (1598), the Japanese gave up the struggle; but not before they, and undisciplined Ming troops, had so ravaged Korea that it was economically disrupted for six whole years. The Yi dynasty never recovered from this disaster, as Korea was given over to increasing and damaging factionalism.

The Ming, for their part, were fatally weakened. Formidable tribes of Jurched, in Manchuria, had been kept divided or subdued by diplomatic bribes or strong garrisons. Decaying Ming authority and, more particularly, the deployment of forces to Korea, enabled Nurhachi to effect the union of four main tribes. He then attracted able Chinese officials and soldiers for the administration and defence of a new Manchu state, financing this effort by trade in horses and ginseng, a root which the Chinese desired because of its supposed rejuvenating powers. By 1618 he was strong enough to wrest part of Liaotung from the Ming and seven years later made Mukden his capital. He died in 1626 but able successors continued his work of building a Manchu state. Abahai attacked Korea, reduced it to vassalage, won Inner Mongolia from Ming and annexed the Amur region. He then took the remarkable step of having the Mukden Court proclaim him Emperor of China, founder of a new Ch'ing dynasty.

From Mukden Abahai watched the Ming decay, and waited

his chance. It came when discontented soldiers and peasants who were suffering from crop failures began pillaging the countryside of North China. Li Tzu-ch'eng organized them into a rebel army which captured Peking, and the last Ming Emperor hanged himself. When the news reached Wu San-kuei, a general then fighting the Manchus, he secured their co-operation for routing the insurgents and retaking Peking. There he soon found that his ally's army of 100,000 men, so far from retiring as he expected, was being reinforced by Mukden. The Manchus exploited a situation for which they had long prepared. Abahai had just died, but the Mandate of Heaven was passed to his infant nephew. By 1651 the Ch'ing ruled all China and, within a century, extended its boundaries well beyond previous or present limits.

4. *Burmese and Thai*

The Mongols did not conquer or annex Indochina. Kublai Khan tried to subdue both Dai Viet (Annam) and Champa but, after military failures, had to be content with their acceptance of nominal vassalage. He did overthrow the Burmese Kingdom of Pagan and, by conquering Nanchao, sent the Thai into Khmer territory where they were encouraged to attack Ankor. The thirteenth century, as Coedès says,[1] was one of crisis for Indochina, of disintegrating change in old political or cultural conditions.

Burmese and Thai are Mongoloid people who, long before the Christian era, were forced out of the north by Chinese pressure. They came eventually to Yunnan, where a Han governor acknowledged their fighting quality by describing them as 'ungovernable vermin'.[2] As Han power waned, the Thai, then known to the Chinese as Ailao, were able to dominate the region about Lake Tali and hence, until it was closed in A.D. 342, the caravan route going across the gorges of the Mekong and Salween rivers to Bhamo. During China's first partition they built up a Kingdom of Nanchao, from which Burmese migrated in order to escape Thai domination. Upper Burma, at that time,

---

[1] Coedès, *The Making of South-East Asia*, p. 121.

[2] Carthew, 'The History of the Thai in Yunnan', Siam Society Selected Papers, vol. iii, p. 135.

was under the Pyu, a civilized people, devoted to Buddhism. They traded with neighbouring countries and with the Arabs, who not only appreciated such natural products as aloeswood but also the Pyu's cottons, velvets, and earthenware jars. Lower Burma and Thailand were under the Mon, who had long controlled Tenasserim ports and the land routes running from this coast to Cambodia.

Nanchao was strong enough to repulse T'ang forces when they tried to regain the area in order to reopen caravan trade with Burma and, through the Mon ports, with India. King P'i-lo-ko was induced to become a T'ang vassal because of a threat to Nanchao from the rising Kingdom of Tibet, but his son made an alliance with the Tibetans and attacked China. He conquered the Pyu and advanced Nanchao's border to the Upper Irrawaddy, although the Pyu were not finally overthrown until A.D. 832. After attacking Annam, and holding it for three years, Nanchao made peace with China and became its rather nominal vassal towards the close of the ninth century. Nanchao appears to have been a fairly well-organized kingdom, military in character, as every able-bodied man had to serve when required, but organized on Chinese lines with some help by officials recruited from China. Sericulture was practised, and cotton was woven among other crafts, both Chinese and native. It is not clear whether the Thai used Chinese characters or had any form of writing, but they were probably acquainted with Buddhism.

Nanchao fell to Kublai's forces in 1253, but long before that Thai had been slowly moving down the river valleys of Indochina. Those going to Burma were called Thai Yai (Big Thai), as distinct from the Thai Noi (Little Thai) who, after crossing the Mekong, formed their own settlement at Chiengrai about A.D. 860. Other Thai continued down the Mekong to settle at Luang Prabang in Laos, or down the Red and Black rivers to Tongking. Penetration was necessarily slow because powerful rulers controlled the areas into which the Thai were moving. The migrants had more scope in Upper Burma, but Shan chiefs there had to submit to Anawrahta (1044–77), founder of the first Burmese Kingdom of Pagan (1064–1287), to which he added, by conquest, Mon Thaton in Lower Burma.

Although the Mon were never to accept Burmese sovereignty,

there was co-operation between them and Anawrahta in regard to trade and religion. They had close relations with Ceylon, which was active both in South-east Asian trade and the great centre of Theravada Buddhism. Anawrahta sent help to Ceylon in its struggle against the Cholas, and received from its king a replica of the Buddha's tooth held at Kandy. He built the Shewzigon Pagoda near Pagan to enshrine it. By the time his dynasty fell there were over 13,000 shrines or monasteries in the Pagan area, a staggering architectural expression of piety and one containing many masterpieces. But conversion of the Burmese to the Theravada faith did not prevent trouble with Ceylon over trade. Although Burmese sources have no mention of this, it appears that a fleet was sent, during Ankor's embroilment with Champa, to take over the valuable Malayan portages, to which Ceylon's access was then restricted. Protests by the Sinhalese led to the loss of their trade with Burma, as well as with the portages, so that they sent a fleet which looted Bassein. Good relations were not restored until 1174, when Buddhist monks helped peace negotiations; thereafter the Theravada faith made sweeping progress among the Burmese. Trade with China also developed after T'ang forces had subdued Yunnan and, from 1103, tribute missions were sent to the Chinese court. During the reign of the pious Nantaungmya (1210–31) the Burmese ended Nanchao's control over Upper Burma and fortified Bhamo at the Irrawaddy's extreme reach for navigation.

Pagan and Ankor had a simultaneous decay, which enabled Thai migrants to set up principalities of some importance at Mogaung and Muong Nai, in Upper Burma, and at Ahom in Assam, as well as a number of petty principalities in the upper basin of the Menam. The chiefs of two Menam principalities joined forces to attack Sukhothai, the north-west stronghold of Ankor's Empire in 1238. By capturing it they gained control over central Thailand and established a new Kingdom of Sukhothai (1238–1350), to which a great many Thai came from Yunnan after Kublai Khan took Nanchao. But Sukhothai adroitly became a full vassal of Yuan, and was encouraged to go on attacking Ankor, which Kublai naturally wished to see weakened. Pagan was less astute. It stubbornly refused vassalage, and Kublai's forces invaded the Irrawaddy Valley to inflict a crushing defeat upon the Burmese. Three Shan chiefs then took over Upper Burma, and the Mon regained the south.

Sukhothai's third king, Rama Khamheng (1275–*c.* 1317), by far its greatest, brought under his sway a large area from Ligor, in Malaya, to Chiengmai (whose king became his ally), the north-east provinces of modern Thailand and some territory in Laos between Vientiane and Luang Prabang. He even made a vassal of Wareru, the ruler of Mon Burma. But Rama Khamheng was far more than a conquering soldier; the Thai revere him as the father of their culture, who ensured absorption of the best things from Mon and Khmer civilizations. In particular, he promoted Theravada Buddhism, built great temples in the Khmer style, and adapted Mon-Khmer script to give the Thai a written language. A famous inscription in this new writing records his work, and says about its economic aspect:

In the lifetime of King Rama Khamheng this town of Sukhothai prospers. There are fish in its water and rice in its fields. The King imposes no tax on his people, who throng the roads leading cattle to trade or riding horses to sell. Whoever wishes to deal in elephants or horses can do so; whoever wishes to deal in gold or silver can do so. . . . Sukothai is full of people.[1]

As success against Ankor depended on good relations with China, Rama Khamheng led two tribute missions and sent another five. They had the usual subsidiary purpose of promoting some trade, but Rama Khamheng was also anxious to promote Chinese crafts at Sukhothai. He brought back potters who built kilns there, and they were soon producing a hard, thick stoneware, decorated with white slip under a yellowish-grey glaze, similar to the wares of T'zu Chou in Hopei, and superior to Sukhothai's previous output of a simple, Khmer-type earthenware or stoneware. The Chinese potters may have become dissatisfied with the clay at Sukhothai or, as Spinks believes likely, a second group may have arrived from Lung-ch'uan in Chekiang. New kilns, at any rate, were soon built at the neighbouring town of Sawankhalok which during the sixteenth century gained export markets in Java, Borneo, the Philippines, and, above all, Japan where tea-masters developed a taste for simple, rustic pottery.

[1] Coedès, *Les États Hindouisés d'Indochine et d'Indonésie*, pp. 345–8.

One product of Sawankhalok quickly gained an export market—a large jar, much used in Asian trade for holding water, rice, oil, sugar, and other wares. These jars had been produced in China from which they came, usually by sea, but sometimes by ass-caravan, through Bhamo to the Mon port of Martaban, which became the centre of the jar trade. Sawankhalok's jars were also found to be acceptable, and went to Martaban by elephant-caravan through the Three Pagodas Pass. The main buyers were Indian merchants, and the jars became so widely sought that when, in the eighteenth century, they were manufactured by Moslem Indians, the word 'Martaban' was often stamped on the imitation.

Rama Khamheng's son and grandson were scholarly Buddhists under whose saintly rule Sukhothai's power waned as quickly as it had risen. Lower Burma threw off Thai suzerainty and Chiengmai became completely independent. In 1350 a northern prince, who had married a daughter of the Mon ruler of U Thong, founded a new Kingdom of Ayuthia (1350–1767), taking the title of Ramadhibodi (1350–69). He soon reduced Sukhothai to vassalage, recovered the south and possibly extended his power down to Malacca. But he had to contend with the Khmers. They supported another Thai chief, Fa Ngum, who, after marrying one of their princesses, made Luang Prabang, in 1353, an independent kingdom extending from the Chinese border to the Korat Plateau, and from Vientiane to Dai Viet. It developed an export trade in gum-lac and benzoin to Ayuthia and Dai Viet, as well as to Ankor, and so tried to keep up good relations with them.

After restoring Rama Khamheng's empire, Ramadhibodi gave it a lasting system of law, based on the Indian code of Manu. His successor had many problems: struggles by Sukhothai to regain independence, intermittent wars with Chiengmai, and more serious warfare with the Khmers. Ankor was ravaged in 1352 and sacked in 1431, after which the Khmers retreated to a new capital of Phnom Penh at the south end of the Great Lake. Nevertheless Ayuthia became consolidated, and Trailok (1448–88) gave it a better administrative system than that possessed by any other South-east Asian state until recent times. Its main features were centralization, separation of civil from military functions, and ministries for agriculture, finance, the capital, and the palace, the last of which involved justice. Another durable feature was a re-allocation of land according to complex *Sakdi Na* grades which placed everyone in a royal order of merit. Compulsory military service was added in the next reign, and the kingdom was divided into military districts.

Ayuthia continued diplomatic relations with China after the fall of the Mongols. A Ming envoy came in 1386 to acknowledge tribute of 100 *piculs* (6 tons) of pepper and 100 *piculs* of sappanwood. Next year Ayuthia sent thirty elephants and, in 1389, 1,700 *piculs* of sappanwood; two years later it received standard sets of Chinese weights and measures. Besides these official exchanges, the missions would have involved some private trading which, by the fifteenth century, had become established. There is a record of a Thai merchant visiting Fukien in 1403, and a complaint was made to the Ming Court, in 1456, about Chams plundering a Thai vessel; they retorted that the attack was merely retaliation against Thai piracy. All foreign merchants were hit by the later Ming prohibition, and a Canton official was executed for trading with a Thai ship.

Trade of the Mon ports had been disturbed by Sukhothai's attacks, which forced a shift of the capital to Pegu in 1369. But, after the reign of Razadarit (1385–1423), there was little further trouble from Ayuthia, so that the ports had a long period of prosperous trade in brazil-wood, sandalwood, cotton, silks, and rubies, and this trade provided most of the royal revenue. Ludovico di Varthema, who visited Pegu before its fall to Toungoo, said it was full of palaces or fine houses, and that its king wore rubies worth more than a very large city. Pegu's trade with the north, however, was disturbed by violent conditions in Shan Ava (1364–1555) and by attacks from the Shan or the rising power of Toungoo. Disorders were such, both among the Shan and the tribes of Yunnan, as to cut off Chinese trade. The Ming finally subdued Yunnan in 1441 and, five years later, forced Ava to accept tributary status with the result that there was some revival of trade across the frontier. But new disorders came after 1482, and Chinese trade again ceased.

Shan disorder helped Toungoo, a small Burmese kingdom that had been formed in an area relatively immune from strife. When Ava fell into chaos through Shan revolts, the King of Toungoo seized the chance of adding Upper Burma to a realm which had already been expanding. His son then conquered most of Lower Burma, although the Mon put up stiff resistance until Prome was captured in 1542. After defeating a Shan coalition he had himself crowned, both at Pagan and Pegu, as king of a unified Burma. He was succeeded by Bayinnaung (1551–81), the most overwhelmingly energetic ruler of all the Toungoo dynasty (1486–1752).

His reign saw a revival of trade through the establishment of much better order. Caesar Frederick, a Venetian who came to Pegu in 1569, gave a valuable account of its exports and imports.

The Merchandizes that go out of Pegu are Gold, Silver, Rubies, Saphires, Spinelles, great store of Beniamin (benzoin), long Pepper, Lead, Lacca (lac), Rice, Wine, some Sugar, yet there might be great store of Sugar made in the Countrey, for they have abundance of Canes, but they give them to Elephants to eate, and the people consume great store of them for food.[1]

The main import was Indian textiles, all strictly examined by customs officers. There was no coinage, but goods were paid for in *ganza*, a mixture of copper and lead. Most ships came to Pegu during the brief period between the south-west and north-east monsoons around October.

Duarte Barbosa, a Portuguese who visited Pegu later, mentioned the great Martaban jars used for exporting rice to Malacca or Sumatra, and noted that Pegu's foreign trade was in the hands of Moslem Indians or Arabs. Fitch, the first English visitor, although also impressed by Pegu, regretted the gold used for decorating temples: 'If they did not consume their gold on these vanities it would bee very plentiful and good cheape in Pegu.'[2] Much of the gold he saw had come from the recent looting of Ayuthia. Bayinnaung, after putting down revolts by Mon and Shan, had seized Chiengmai and defeated a Thai coalition led by Luang Prabang. The Lao king then made an alliance with Ayuthia, against which Bayinnaung immediately struck. Ayuthia's royal family were brought as prisoners to Pegu, in 1564, and a puppet was installed under the control of a Burmese garrison. A counter-attack, five years later, obliged Bayinnaung to retake Ayuthia, which was thoroughly plundered, and to install another puppet. He had less success against Luang

---

[1] Hall, *Burma*, p. 52.　　[2] ibid., p. 54.

Prabang whose throne he could not control until 1575, and then only temporarily because of persistent Lao revolts.

These were raging at his death, but were nothing to those which faced his successor, Nandabayin (1581–1599). He coped with more or less annual revolts by the Mon, whose lands were reverting to jungle because heavy demands for military service had deprived them of labour. But disaster came when the Thai successfully revolted under the able and daring leadership of Naresuen, eldest son of the puppet king of Ayuthia. While a mere lad he had distinguished himself in fighting against the Cambodians, who had taken advantage of Ayuthia's weakness to attack it in 1575. After a period of compulsory residence and training at Pegu, he was sent back as Governor of Pitsanulok, and there organized a national struggle for independence. He began it by raiding Lower Burma and defeating two armies sent against him. Ayuthia was faced with a full-scale invasion led by Nandabayin, but Naresuen had to put down, relentlessly, another Cambodian attack before disorganizing the Burmese army and forcing its retreat. After this great victory, he was given the Thai crown.

The Burmese launched four more unsuccessful invasions, and were then overwhelmed. Naresuen secured his flank by a campaign that forced the Khmer king to seek refuge in Luang Prabang, after which Thai troops took possession of Burma's trading ports; Tavoy and Tenasserim fell in 1593, and Moulmein and Martaban soon after. Chiengmai renewed its vassalage to Ayuthia, and Naresuen attacked Pegu. He had to withdraw, but Nandabayin became the victim of a general revolt by his sorely tried subjects. The Thai secured Lower Burma south of Martaban, while rival warriors divided up the rest of Toungoo's realm. A grandson of Bayinnaung, based on Ava, managed to reunite the country down to Syriam but, when this work was completed, Ayuthia still held the important southern ports. Moreover, the shift of the Burmese capital to Ava made for the same kind of intransigent xenophobia that was to render the later Ch'ing unable to deal with European penetration, and with similar consequences for both Burma and China. Thailand, on the other hand, became responsive to outside influence, while retaining independence.

5. Majapahit and Malacca

Srivijaya, the great trading empire of Sumatra and Malaya, had become weakened by internal divisions after the great Chola raid of 1025, and fatally damaged both by Rama Khamheng's conquest of North Malaya and by Java's expansion under Kertanagara of Singosari. Kublai Khan was interested in exploiting this deterioration and, besides sending envoys to demand acknowledgment of Yuan suzerainty, required a report on conditions in the Strait of Malacca from the Chinese fleet which took a royal bride to the Il-Khanate of Persia. His first move, however, was to send, in 1292, an expedition to punish Kertanagara for an insulting refusal of tributary status. When it became known in Java that this expedition was being prepared, the Prince of Kediri rebelled and executed Kertanagara. Vijaya, Kertanagara's son-in-law, persuaded the expedition to help overthrow the usurper and, after this had been done, turned against the Mongols so successfully that they withdrew. Vijaya thus founded the Majapahit Dynasty (1293–1468), and attempted some recovery of Kertanagara's empire by ritualistic marriages to princesses of Malayu, Bali, Kalimantan, and Champa.

He and his son had their hands tied by a number of rebellions within Java, and there was no great expansion until Gaja Mada became, in 1330, chief minister to Queen Tribhuvana, a position he continued holding under her successor, Hayam Wuruk (1350–89). Grandiose claims were made by the contemporary poet, Prapanca, that Gaja Mada advanced Java's power over all Indonesia and much of Malaya. Until recently historians were inclined to accept them, but subsequent research reveals that, 'so far as the ascertainable facts go, the state of Majapahit was limited to East Java, Madura and Bali'.[1] It is likely, however, that the other places listed by Prapanca—Sumatra, West Java, Celebes, the Moluccas, Kalimantan, and Timor, were all areas with which Majapahit actively traded, as were other places said to be in friendly relations with Majapahit—Burma, Thailand, Cambodia, Champa, and Dai Viet. Nor is it hard to accept Prapanca's claim that Majapahit traded with Coromandel, Bengal, and China. Wang Ta-Yuan, who visited

[1] Hall, A History of South-East Asia, p. 83.

Majapahit in 1350, described it as prosperous, fertile, and densely peopled, 'first among the barbarians of the eastern seas'.[1] It sent embassies to China between 1369 and 1382, and, after Cheng Ho had put down the pirates of Palembang, the Ming emperor awarded this trading city to Majapahit. China traded with the Moluccas through Java, and allowed Kalimantan ports to continue trading with Majapahit after they became Ming tributaries.

By this time, moreover, Majapahit's power, however great it may have been in days of Gaja Mada, had greatly declined. The king who survived him was little more than a voluptuary and under his successor there was civil war which lost Majapahit any real control over subject states. When, therefore, Cheng Ho brought his fleets to Indonesian waters, Majapahit, so far from being in any position to challenge Ming hegemony, had to be grateful for protection against the pirates of Palembang or the claims of exuberant Malacca.

When the fifteenth century opened, Malacca was a small fishing village, used by pirates, and regarded by the Thai as a possession of little value. To it came, in 1401, Paramesvara, a noble of Penang and a rebel against Majapahit. He had first sought refuge at Tumasik (Singapore) but, after killing his host, was expelled by the Raja of Patani, a Thai vassal. With the help of a few score followers he took over Malacca, where men from Palembang and other adventurers joined him. These pirates made Malacca a market for their loot, and used the old Indonesian tactic of forcing ships to put into the port for passes. Malacca might not have survived but for Chinese protection against Sukhothai, accorded after Paramesvara sent an embassy to Ming in 1405 and made effective by Cheng Ho's cruises as well as by careful attention to good relations with the Celestial Empire. Ming protection meant little after the cruises were abandoned but by that time Malacca was a great trading centre for merchants from South India, Gujarat, Bengal, Iran, and Arabia. Most of these merchants, especially those from Gujarat, were Moslems who had shifted their Indonesian headquarters from North Sumatra, and Parameswara helped this development by adopting Islam himself. Other princely traders followed suit, so that Islam spread rapidly and peacefully

[1] Quoted in Coedès, *Les États Hindouisés d'Indochine et d'Indonésie*, p. 390.

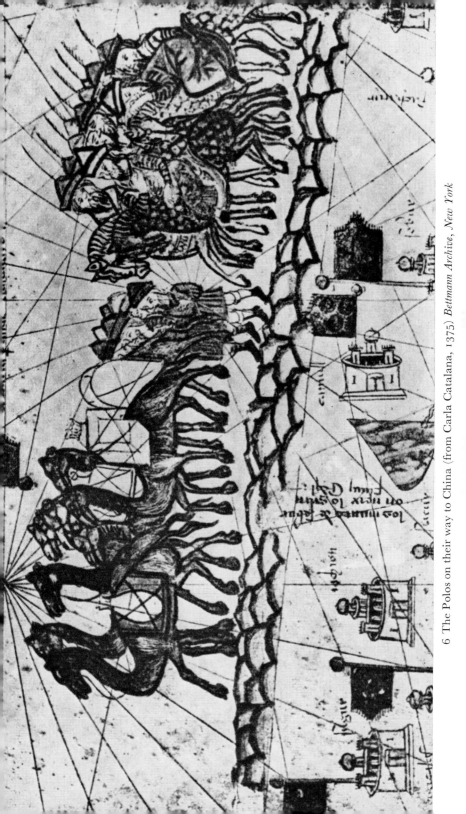

6 The Polos on their way to China (from *Carla Catalana*, 1375) *Bettmann Archive, New York*

7 Near-Eastern merchant in China
(T'ang, fifth century, A.D.)
Seattle Art Museum

8 Jayavarman VII
(from Ankor Thorn)
Editions Arthaud

throughout most of the archipelago. There was trouble, after Ming cruises ceased, with the Thai and their vassal states in the Peninsula. But Tun Perak, the chief minister of Malacca for half a century, both repelled Thai forces and waged successful campaigns against his neighbours.

By the opening of the fifteenth century Malacca had become both a political and an economic power. Its rule extended from Kedah or Trengganu to much of the Sumatran coast on the opposite side of the Strait, and its trade attracted merchants from sixty different countries. There were few Malays in Malacca, and they were mainly subsistence farmers or fishermen who produced little in the way of domestic exports. Most of the regular inhabitants were Indonesian and, more especially, Javanese; they manned the army, navy, and shipyards and provided most of the general, unskilled labour required by merchants. These merchants four came under *shahbandars* or harbour masters. One looked after ships from Java or other parts of Indonesia; a second, ships from China, Champa, Burma, and Thailand; a third, ships from Bengal, Malabar, and North Sumatra; and the fourth, ships from Gujarat. This division may roughly indicate the balance of Malacca's trade with different regions, but the largest group was the Gujarati, comprising as many as 1,000 resident merchants and 5,000 transient sailors. Chinese traders were also numerous, although more widely scattered over South-east Asia. The general throng of foreign merchants at Malacca was so great and diverse that a Malay lingua franca developed to overcome the confusion of eighty different languages or dialects.

Most of our information about Malacca at this time comes from the *Suma Oriental* of Tomé Pires, the Portuguese official who visited it in 1512–15. The main trade was with Gujarat, and so important that 'Malacca cannot live without Cambay, nor Cambay without Malacca'. He described it in some detail.

Four ships come every year from Gujarat to Malacca. The merchandise of each ship is worth fifteen, twenty or thirty thousand cruzados,[1] nothing less than fifteen thousand. And from the city of Cambay one ship comes every year; this is worth seventy or eighty thousand cruzados, without any doubt. The merchandize they bring is cloth of thirty kinds, which are of value in these parts; they also

---

[1] One *cruzado* was worth £2. 17s. od. in current gold value.

bring pachak, which is a root like rampion, and catechu, which looks like earth; they bring rosewater and opium; from Cambay and Aden they bring seeds, grains, tapestries and much incense; they bring forty kinds of merchandise. . .

The principal merchandise brought back is cloves, mace, nutmeg, sandalwood, seed pearls, some porcelain, a little musk; they carry enormous quantities of apothecary's lignaloes, and finally some benzoin; for they load up with these spices, and of the rest they take a moderate amount. And besides they take gold, enormous quantities of white silk, tin, much white damask—they take great pains to get this—coloured silks, birds from Banda for plumes. . . . These have the main Malacca trade. They pay in dues six per cent . . . they pay the Bemdara, Lasamane, Tumunguo and Xabamdar one cloth per hundred, and each one according to who he is, which the merchants regard as a great oppression.

Bengal's trade with Malacca was also considerable.

A junk goes from Bengal to Malacca once a year, and sometimes twice. Each of these carries from eighty to ninety thousand cruzados worth. They bring fine white cloths. . . . They bring steel, very rich bed canopies, with cut-cloth work in all colours and very beautiful; wall hangings like tapestry; and also sugar preserves of various kinds in great plenty. . . . They bring an abundance of strongly scented vases in dark clay, which are highly esteemed in these parts and very cheap.

These people sail four or five ships and junks to Malacca and to Pasé every year. . . . From here in Malacca they use all their money . . . and make a great profit with it, which they cannot do in Pasé, except with pepper and silk.

The chief merchandise they take to Bengal is Borneo camphor and pepper—an abundance of these two—cloves, mace, nutmeg, sandalwood, silk, seed pearls a large quantity, white porcelain in plenty, copper, tin, lead, quicksilver, large green porcelainware from the Liu Kiu, opium from Aden and some little from Bengal, white and green damasks, *enroladas* from China, caps of scarlet-in-grain and carpets; krises and swords from Java are also appreciated.

In some years Malacca could thus do as much trade with Bengal as with Gujarat, but in most years it did still more trade with South India.

The Malabars come to Pulicat to take their companies. They bring merchandise from Gujarat, and those from Choromandel bring coarse Kling cloth. There came every year in Malacca three or four ships, each one must be worth twelve to fifteen thousand cruzados and from Pulicat come two ships each worth eighty to ninety thousand cruzados, or a junk worth no less. They bring thirty kinds of cloths, rich cloths of great value. They pay in Malacca six per cent. These Klings have all the merchandise and more of the Malacca trade than any other nation.

The principal thing they take back is white sandalwoods. . . . And they take camphor from Pansur which is to the south-west . . . alum, white silk, seed pearls, pepper, a little nutmeg, a little mace and a little cloves, much copper, little tin . . . calambac, damasks, Chinese brocades, and gold. They pay six per cent entry dues and nothing on coming away. They leave here in January and come back in October.

Pires gives only scattered information about Indonesian trade with Malacca. He says something of various places in Sumatra: *Pedir*, which could supply up to 15,000 *bahars*[1] of pepper a year and benzoin, gold, and white silk; *Pasir*, which exported 8–10,000 *bahars* of pepper with some benzoin or silk; *Aru* (Darau), which had plenty of rice or foodstuffs, benzoin, edible camphor, lignaloes, pitch, rattans, honey, wax, and slaves; *Jambi*, which also produced foodstuffs, lignaloes, and gold; and *Palembang*, which sent to Malacca ten or twelve junks laden with rice, wines, vegetables, honey, wax, rattans, pitch, black benzoin, cotton, iron, and gold, buying there mainly coarse Indian cloths. These are only the leading Sumatran ports; he mentions others with like products.

There is a similar account for Java. The kingdom of *Sunda* sent up 1,000 *bahars* of fine pepper, much long pepper and 'enough tamarinds to load a thousand ships'; but its main export was rice, 'up to ten junks a year', together with other foodstuffs, coarse cloths, and slaves. The best and busiest port in Java was *Calapa* (Batavia) which attracted ships from most parts of Indonesia. (East) *Java* had 'infinite quantities of rice' and 'oxen, cows, sheep, goats, buffalos without number', a 'goodly quantity of gold', many topazes, up to 30 *bahars* of cubebs a year, long pepper, great quantities of tamarinds, cassia fistola, and some cardamoms. Both Sumatra and Java used copper cash imported from China.

Mace and nutmeg came from the *Banda Islands*, 500 *bahars* of

[1] One *bahar* was 500–600 lb.

mace and 6–7,000 *bahars* of nutmeg, but sold in a fixed proportion of 1 to 7. As these islands produced hardly any food, they
imported rice, and used sago for money. Cloves came from the
Moluccas, about 6,000 *bahars* a year, fetched by eight junks sent
from Malacca.

Malacca's commercial ascendancy does not appear to have
damaged *Pegu*. Gujarat still sent an annual ship to Martaban
loaded with 'copper, vermilion, quicksilver, opium, cloth', and
Bengal would have kept up some direct trade with Burma.
Pegu's own trade with Malacca was very large, as it sent fifteen
or sixteen junks, together with twenty to thirty smaller vessels,
bringing to Malacca, Pasé, and Pedir a great deal of provisions,
benzoin, lac, musk, rubies, and silver. Some of these goods came
from Upper Burma, which had 'the mine for precious stones'
and transmitted musk from Tibet.

Thailand used to have an even greater trade with Malacca, to
which it sent thirty junks a year, bringing similar produce—
foodstuffs, benzoin, lac, sappanwood, ivory, lead, tin, silver,
gold, vessels of copper or gold, rings of diamonds or rubies, and
'a large quantity of cheap, coarse Siamese cloth for the poor
people'. But bad relations had prevented direct trade between
Thailand and Malacca for the last twenty-two years. During
them, the Thai must have been stimulated to develop their own
foreign trading activities. In spite of Malacca's proximity and
pre-eminence, Thailand was vigorously trading with Isthmian
ports and supplying them with Gujarat cottons and Sumatran
pepper, among other products. It also provided the vent for
most of Cambodia's or Champa's exports of rice, foodstuffs,
ivory, and lac. Nor did Cochinchina send more than an
occasional junk to Malacca, as Pires says, it conducted most of
its trade with China. Thailand sent six or seven junks a year to
China, and others to Sunda and Palembang as well as to
Cambodia, Cochinchina, and Champa.

Merchants from *China*, owing to Ming suzerainty, had a
privileged position in Malacca, as they paid no dues 'except for
a present'. Pires heard that 'China has more than a thousand
junks, and each of them trades where it sees fit'; so great was the
effect of Cheng Ho's cruises. What these junks brought to Malacca may be judged from the following account.

The chief merchandise from China is raw white silk in large quantities, and loose coloured silks, many in quantity, satins of all colours, damask chequered *enrolados* in all colours, taffetas and other thin silk cloths . . . an abundance of seed pearl . . . musk in powder and in pods, plenty of this . . . camphor in large quantities, *abarute*, alum, saltpetre, sulphur, copper, iron, rhubarb, and all of it is worthless—what I have seen up to the present has been rotten when it arrived . . . vases of copper and *fuseleira*, cast iron kettles, bowls, basins, quantities of these things, boxes, fans, plenty of needles of a hundred different kinds . . . countless copper bracelets; gold and silver come and I did not see much, and many brocades of their kind, and porcelains beyond count.

A far more varied list than for any other country's exports. As for China's purchases at Malacca:

The chief merchandise is pepper—of which they will buy ten junk loads a year if as many go there—cloves, a little nutmeg, a little more pachak, catechu; they will buy a great deal of incense, elephants' tusks, tin, apothecary's lignaloes; they buy a great deal of Borneo camphor, red beads, white sandalwood, brazil, infinite quantities of the black wood that grows in Singapore; they buy a great many carnelians from Cambay, scarlet camlets, coloured woollen cloths. Pepper apart, they make little account of all the rest.

One reason for this indifference was that some of the thousand junks went directly to the sources of supply for South-east Asian or Indian products.

Malacca had serious political troubles after Tun Perak died in 1498. There were repeated attacks by Ayuthia and its vassal, Ligor, intensified when Malacca occupied Kedah and interfered with Isthmian trade. Hostilities were going on when the Portuguese arrived at Malacca, immediately after Albuquerque had seized Goa (1510). The last of a poor run of sultans made the mistake of attacking them, so that the Portuguese quickly and gladly took over 'a city that was made for merchandise, fitter than any other in the world; the end of monsoons, and the beginning of others'.[1]

6. *Moslem and Mughal India*

When Jenghiz Khan decided to withdraw from the Punjab after his raiding pursuit of the young Sultan of Khwarizm, India

[1] Pires, *Suma Oriental*, p. 286.

was spared a Mongol conquest. It was, however, already undergoing a Moslem conquest following the defeat inflicted by Muhammad of Ghur upon a great Rajput coalition at the fateful battle of Tarain (1192). This victory gave Afghans control over all North India, except Gujarat, and the slave minister who was largely responsible for the conquest became, on Muhammad's death, the first ruler of the Sultanate of Delhi (1206–1506). It was cut off from Ghur when Afghanistan was made part of the Chagatai Khanate, and suffered attacks from the Mongols. Balbàn (1266–86), nevertheless, put the Sultanate on a firm basis, and his successors both annexed Gujarat and advanced into the Deccan. Gujarat was a major gain because of its textiles and busy ports, but gains in the south proved only temporary. Hindu resurgence halted expansion beyond the Deccan, and led to the formation of a strong Kingdom of Vijayanagar (1336–1565). The Deccan itself was lost to the Sultanate when a renegade general made it into an independent Bahmani Kingdom (1347–1482). The two new kingdoms fought with each other throughout their existence for the fertile area between the Tungabhadra and Krishna Rivers and for Golkonda, but the Sultanate soon accepted Bahmani independence.

India's overland trade with Iran and China had been cut off by Jenghiz Khan's campaigns, but revived when they were completed in spite of intermittent hostilities between the Sultanate and the Khanate. The Mongol policy was to foster trade, and the Sultanate became so prosperous that ibn-Battutah could describe its capital as the most magnificent city of the Moslem world, a position derived from its commercial wealth. Sea trade had also suffered during Hulagu's savage conquest of Iran, but revived under the Il-Khanate. More important, there was a remarkable revival of Red Sea trade, which had long been inferior to Gulf trade. After the Mongols' failure to conquer Egypt, the Mamluk sultans who took over this last remnant of the Caliphate, vigorously developed it so that Alexandria's trade with growing Mediterranean markets expanded, and Aden again became an important entrepôt for Indian trade.

Revival of Red Sea trade was associated with a pacific Moslem conquest of Indian shipping. The Caliphate's annexation of Sind had established the Arabs in the two Indus ports of

Dabhol and Mansuriya, but they settled in far greater numbers at other western ports during the ninth and tenth centuries, and particularly at Quilon which became their great port of call for Chinese trade. Hindu seamen were still active, but their ports had a sound tradition, from Roman days, of welcoming foreign merchants. The Arabs were particularly welcome because they brought the horses which Indian princes required but could not properly rear or maintain, because they had wide commercial connections, and because their trade brought revenue to local rulers. After the Chola's great maritime activity Hindu seafaring declined, partly because the Hindu renaissance made it less respectable, and even sinful for Brahmans, but more because of increasing Arab competition. The fall of the Caliphate to the Mongols must have led some Arab merchants to move residence from Gulf to Indian ports, and the revival of Red Sea trade was certainly associated with an influx of Egyptian Arabs. These newcomers concentrated on Calicut in a new Malabar principality whose Zamorins made special efforts to attract foreign traders. By the time ibn-Battutah visited Calicut its trade was beginning to surpass that of Quilon, which was suffering from the decline of Arab shipping to China as Sung voyages to South-east Asia made a shorter haul more profitable. The Arabs, in any case, were busy enough taking over the trade of the western Indian Ocean. Even India's coastal trade fell into the hands of Moslems or Mappillas, the descendants of Arabs by Indian women. It should not be over-looked that many Moslems participating in this collective mono-poly of India sea trade were converts from the lower castes of Hinduism. Conversion was slow, but it would have had attrac-tions to those who were seafarers, and was helped by the spread of the pacifist, egalitarian, and mystic sect of the Sufi, far more congenial to the Hindu mind than the original form of Islam.

While Indian sea trade was expanding peacefully and con-tinuously, overland trade was again checked by the simul-taneous division of the Il-Khanate between strong Iranian families and of the Chagatai Khanate into small principalities whose contentions and exactions ruined the prosperity of Cen-tral Asia. Prosperity in West Asia was further checked by new nomadic migrations which brought some two million Turks into Asia Minor. Before long the situation was more than restored by a descendant of Jenghiz Khan, whose chosen title, Lord of the Conjunctions, indicates a burning zeal to emulate the career of his great ancestor.

Timur-the-Lame (1336–1405), this descendant, began his own career of conquest by usurping what power was left to the last Chagatai Khan, and soon took Samarkand, Herat, and Balkh to gain mastery of Central Asia. Further years of bold campaigning, accompanied by ruthless massacres, brought Iran, Mesopotamia, and Armenia under a new Timurid Empire (1369–1500). An attack by the Kipchak Khan led Timur to invade Russia, up to Moscow, and the Golden Horde was reduced to subservience. Then came his terrible raid upon the Sultanate; 100,000 Hindus were massacred, Delhi was sacked, and Samarkand gained enormous booty. Although Timur had been proclaimed king at Delhi, he had no desire to keep India. He proceeded, instead, to capture Aleppo, Damascus, and Baghdad, after which he checked the Ottoman Turks by over-running Asia Minor. Only death stopped him from campaigning next against Ming China.

These superhuman achievements, beyond those of any other single conqueror, were undertaken for glory, but Timur appreciated that trade could help him achieve glory, and make it worthwhile. By blocking the routes from the Black Sea to China he diverted trade to make Samarkand the great junction for caravans plying between Europe, India, and China. Merchants were fully protected against marauding or cheating, and attracted by favourable terms. Timur went so far as to write to all fellow sovereigns, in Europe and Asia, urging them to send merchants because 'trade makes for prosperity'. Nor did he neglect the related conditions of agriculture and industry. Cultivation was helped by irrigation works, sericulture was developed further, and orders were given for planting cotton, flax, and hemp. Textile workers were brought to Samarkand from Syria or Iran, as were many other craftsmen; armourers from Turkey, goldsmiths from Georgia, glass-blowers from Syria, and even potters from China. The vigorous cosmopolitanism of Timur's capital is reflected by its great palace, mosques, and gardens, blending the styles of Islam and Iran with influences from China and India. His brief dynasty is remembered for a renaissance of poetry and painting, and more especially for Persian miniatures that also reflect Chinese influence.

Shah Rokh (1404–47) was a strong ruler who kept up most of his father's conquests, repaired some of their damage and made Herat, Bokhara, and other towns into subsidiary centres of trade and arts. But soon after he died the Empire fell apart through frequent revolts and tribal struggles. Eventually the confusion was resolved in Iran by the ascendancy of a native, if Moslem, Safavid dynasty (1501–1736). Ismail, the founder, united the country and extended his authority from the Euphrates to Afghanistan; but there were frequent conflicts with the Turks over Mesopotamia and with the Uzbecks over Khurasan.

Afghanistan came into the hands of Babur (1483–1530) who could trace, on his two parental lines, descent from both Jenghiz Khan and Timur. He was to prove himself worthy of them. His father, who had precariously ruled Fergana, died when Babur was only twelve, yet two years later the boy took possession of Samarkand. He held it for barely 100 days because his men left on news of trouble at home, but he assembled another force to retake Samarkand. He quickly lost both Samarkand and Fergana to the Uzbecks, who hunted him, with a mere 300 followers, across the Hindu Kush. In Afghanistan he gained unexpected support and, as he wrote in his arresting memoirs, 'I obtained and subjected Kabul and Ghazni with their provinces, without effort or battle.'[1]

He tried to improve his new kingdom and its transit trade which, he noted, was mainly caravans bringing horses to India, or coming from it with slaves, cottons, sugar, candy, and spice-yielding roots. This work was disturbed by the Uzbecks who took Herat, and were threatening Kabul when they were attacked by Ismail. Babur seized another chance of taking Samarkand but again lost it when the Uzbecks defeated a half-hearted combination of his forces with those of Ismail. His ambition then turned to India.

There the Sultanate of Delhi had come, after Timur's raid, into the hands of the Afghan Lodis, who proved good, if bigoted, rulers until Ibrahim came to the throne. His arrogance provoked such opposition that the Governor of Lahore invited Babur's help in dethroning him. Owing to his ally's treachery,

[1] Quoted in Lamb, *Babur The Tiger*, p. 82.

Babur suffered defeat, but returned with a force of only 12,000 men whose skill routed a much larger army. The Sultan died in the battle, and Babur entered Delhi to found India's great Mughal Dynasty (1526–1858). He expressed little enthusiasm for his conquest.

Hindustan has few pleasant things in it. Its people are not handsome or at all friendly. . . . They have no genius or manners. . . . As for pleasant things—it is a large country and has great quantities of gold and silver. When it rains the air is fine. . . . Another good thing is that Hindustan has numberless workmen of every kind.[1]

Pleasant or not, he fought hard to hold Hindustan during the remaining few years of his life. Defeat of a Rajput coalition at Kanwaha, and a further battle, gave him control from the Punjab to Bengal. This considerable empire was held by bare force and lacked any civil administration, so that Babur's successors had much to do. The cultivated but unstable Humayun (1530–56) made a brilliant campaign into Gujarat, but could not hold it and before long was forced into exile by an Afghan rebel, Sher Shah. This capable man strengthened the empire and laid the basis for its sound administration by creating governorships and improving land taxation. A dispute over succession, and help from the Safavids, enabled Humayun to return but he died within a year, leaving the throne to Akbar (1556–1605), a boy of 13. Bariam Khan, his loyal guardian, defeated Sher contenders, made reconquests and improved the administration founded by Sher Shah. Notwithstanding this invaluable service, he was dismissed when Akbar became 18.

After two discreditable years of petticoat government, Akbar began a long, successful reign that made the Mughal Empire durable and powerful. North India had first to be thoroughly pacified, after which Gujarat was annexed, in 1573, and Bengal three years later. Akbar won support from his most dangerous subjects by diplomatic marriages to Rajput princesses and by appointing many Rajput nobles to high administrative posts on something like equal terms with Moslems, although two-thirds of such posts were held by Afghans, Iranians, and Arabs. Towards his humbler Hindu subjects he showed tolerance, and removed from them such previous discriminations as the poll-

[1] ibid., pp. 166–7.

tax on non-Moslems. Care was taken to limit the power of officials by paying them cash salaries or, if they received land grants, by insisting on surrender of an estate when its post lapsed. The Empire was divided into provinces, districts, sub-districts, and cities, each under separate military and revenue officers.

The basis of revenue was a levy of one-third of the crops from the land held by a village commune, a lower rate perhaps than the Sultans had fixed, and Akbar gave much thought to its assessment. Traditionally, each man's harvest had been divided into portions, one of which went to the king, whose revenue thus depended upon fluctuations of yields or prices and was diminished by losses in transporting perishable commodities. Akbar moved to a system under which land in each sub-district was carefully surveyed to determine its average yields of different crops, and tax value was then fixed by applying average local prices for the previous decade. By the end of his reign, this system applied to North India and had made the royal revenue much more stable. At the same time, it tended to give a more productive revenue because the peasant had some incentive to increase his harvest above the assessed level. Moreland judged that agricultural production per head was about as high in Akbar's day as it was in 1910–12, but that the peasant had to pay twice as much for his land.

Not much of this revenue was spent on agricultural improvement. Some irrigation was undertaken but mainly to improve water supplies to towns or to water the pleasure gardens of which the Mughals were so fond. It seems likely that food was usually as plentiful as in modern days, but fell drastically in terrible famines, two in Akbar's reign, the second lasting for four years, and another bad one in Shah Jahan's reign. Abdul Hamid, the official historian, wrote of this last famine in Gujarat and the Deccan:

The inhabitants of these two countries were reduced to the direst extremity. Life was offered for a loaf, but none would buy; rank was to be sold for a cake, but none cared for it. . . . Destitution at last reached such a pitch that men began to devour each other, and the flesh of a son was preferred to his love. The numbers of the dying caused obstructions on the roads.[1]

[1] Smith, *The Oxford History of India*, p. 377.

Another miserable check to population was the plague. A bubonic variety appeared in the Punjab in 1616 and spread, during the next eight years, with severe mortality over the whole north.

The Mughals did more to promote crafts and internal trade. They issued a good coinage, based on a rupee of 172.5 grams of silver, full-bodied copper *dams*, and some gold coins which went mostly into hoards. There was an accompanying reform in weights and measures; Akbar fixed the *ser* at 30 *dams*, the *maund* at 40 *sers*, equivalent to 55½ lb., and the *gaz* at 30¾ inches. Encouragement to industry was almost wholly associated with lavish expenditures of the Court and those of the relatively small class of very highly paid officials, who had no inducement to accumulate fortunes which the State would seize when they died. Jewellers, silversmiths, goldsmiths, druggists, perfumers, textile and clothing workers, furniture makers, and metal workers happily catered for such extravagant demands, and their ranks were swollen by foreign artists or craftsmen recruited to enhance Mughal splendour. Attempts were made to help internal trade by reducing local tithes or tolls, but with limited and uneven success. Not much was done to improve roads or ports, although some expenditures were made on roads to the north-west and on waterways between Delhi and Bengal. Nor was security of travel brought to a high standard, even if merchants could travel long distances without encountering serious danger. Rich merchants faced greater insecurity from the liability of their estates, like those of officials, to seizure by the Emperor; as Bernier remarked, 'Let the profit be never so great, the man by whom it has been made must still wear the garb of indigence.'[1]

The Mughals, notwithstanding their fondness for luxuries and novelties, were indifferent to foreign trade. Overland trade was naturally helped by the inclusion of Afghanistan within the Empire, and by good relations with the Safavid Empire which *was* interested in trade. But travel to Afghanistan was far from being safe. Bernard Goez, who joined a caravan of 500 men at Lahore to go to China, reported that, in spite of having 400 guards, it was so severely attacked that many merchants refused to go further than Kabul. Two agents of the English East India

[1] Moreland, *India at the Death of Akbar*, p. 47.

Company joined a caravan to Kandahar, and reported that the extortions of fortress commanders were worse than those of robbers; the caravan, moreover, split up at Kandahar because the most dangerous part of the journey to Iran was then over. North-eastern routes were little used, although Roe heard, in 1615, of an annual caravan to China, and there was a little trade with Tibet. Moreland estimated, from reports of 12,000 to 14,000 camels leaving Lahore, that the normal overland traffic from India in Akbar's day would have been 600 to 700 tons a year. This is less than one-fifth of a corresponding estimate for sea-borne traffic, which had been greatly expanded by the Moslems.

Their monopoly was now being smashed by the Portuguese, who had appeared on the Indian scene at almost the same time as the Mughals. From the middle of the fifteenth century Portugal's navigators had been searching for a sea route to India round Africa, in order to strike at the Egypto-Venetian monopoly over Europe's spice trade and, as militant Christians, to damage Islam in the ocean which furnished so much of its infidel strength. Diaz de Novaes at last rounded the Cape of Good Hope in 1487, and ten years later da Gama found at Zanzibar experienced Moslem pilots to bring his three small ships to Calicut.[1] There the Zamorin, in accordance with the ancient tradition of Malabar's coast and the successful policy of his own house, welcomed da Gama and refused to yield to a Moslem threat of taking their trade to another port if he persisted in helping the newcomers. Da Gama returned to Lisbon with a representative cargo to substantiate much useful information about Malabar trade. Portugal quickly dispatched a fleet of thirteen ships and 1,200 men under Cabral. His voyage was so erratic as to lead to the accidental discovery of Brazil, and he brought only six ships to Calicut in 1500. Cabral, too, was well received by the Zamorin, but became embroiled with the Moslems and departed after sinking a number of vessels and bombarding the citadel for two days: a first sample of the perfidious brutality which Asians were to associate with the Portuguese. At Cochin, nevertheless, Cabral was welcomed by the Raja, who was anxious to attract trade from Calicut and

[1] Pires described Calicut as 'a very famous port, and the best thing in all Malabar'.

allowed the Portuguese to establish a factory. After making a similar arrangement with the Raja of Cannanor, Cabral returned to Portugal with a cargo which paid for the whole expedition. Another fleet, sent in 1502, attacked Calicut and strengthened the bases in Cannanor and Cochin.

Portugal now decided to keep a standing fleet at Malabar and to blockade the entrance of the Red Sea. Almeida brought such a fleet in 1505, defeated a big force of Moslem ships, and withstood a long attack upon the base at Cannanor. The Zamorin, who had participated in this attack, had already sought joint action with the Sultan of Egypt. Helped by the Venetians, the Sultan quickly prepared a strong fleet which joined ships from Calicut and Gujarat to defeat the Portuguese off Chaul in 1508. Next year, however, the allied fleet was destroyed off Diu, and it became demoralizingly clear to the Moslems that no Asian ships could withstand mounted cannon on Portugal's strongly built caravels. The Portuguese had gained supremacy over the hitherto peaceful Indian Ocean, and could be challenged there only by similarly equipped European rivals.

At this time the Bahmani Kingdom of the Deccan was splitting up into four independent Sultanates, as provincial governors took advantage of a decayed court. Western ports came under the new Sultan of Bijapur about 1490, and the most important of them was Goa, the embarkation point for Deccan pilgrims to Mecca. Albuquerque, who had succeeded Almeira, seized this valuable port in 1510, and proceeded to make it the main base for the Portuguese fleet. Goa was strongly fortified, and Albuquerque attempted to make it a great commercial centre by sending out patrols which would force merchantmen to use it (the same method that had been used for developing Srivijaya and Malacca). Realizing that Malabar was not the only source of spices demanded in Europe, Albuquerque promptly captured Malacca in 1511, a blow to Islam for which the Pope gave public thanksgiving. The next blow was struck at Aden and missed. But in 1515 Albuquerque took Ormuz, the main port of the Persian Gulf, thus nearly completing a grand design for controlling the trade of the Indian Ocean by means of bases which covered all its entrances.

Control was exercised by a system of passes, which Asian ships had to obtain by paying customs at a Portuguese port or by having a resident agent there. Each pass listed the ports that a ship could visit and the commodities it was permitted to carry; spices for Europe were excluded and pepper, especially, was made a royal Portuguese monopoly. Any ship stopped by a patrol was liable to seizure if it had no pass, or was violating conditions listed on its pass. The system took time to develop and did not become really effective on India's west coast until Portugal had acquired ports in Gujarat. This opportunity came during Humayun's campaign when, in return for an empty promise of help to Gujarat's ruler, the Portuguese obtained Diu and Bassein, although they had to withstand a later attack by Egyptians and Gujarati. By similar bribery Portugal acquired the port of Daman in 1559.

Ten years later the Zamorin and the Sultans of Bijapur and Ahmadnagar joined large forces in a final, desperate attempt to expel the Portuguese, but failed. Their failure coincided with the last stages of Akbar's conquest of Gujarat, and he realized that only a fleet with strong fire-power could hope to dislodge the Portuguese. He made no attempt to build one; his only fleet was based on Dacca and used for supporting land operations against Bengal or for suppressing pirates. Having little interest in trade, he left the Portuguese in undisturbed possession of their western bases, and preferred to check their power by encouraging European rivals.

For their part the Portuguese made little attempt to interfere with the trade of Coromandel or Bengal. They did, however, complete their control of the Malabar coast by taking over more and more of Ceylon, after its discovery by a squadron sent in 1518 to intercept Moslem ships which were avoiding patrols by a detour round the Maldive Islands. A fort was soon erected at Colombo but there were many troubles with the hostile Sinhalese. Portugal improved its position by defeating two fleets which the Zamorin sent in 1538 and 1540 in support of a younger brother's claim to the throne. All the goodwill thus gained was thrown away when the Portuguese had the legitimate king killed, brutally repressed a subsequent revolt, and made a child-successor their puppet. The Sinhalese repeatedly attacked until, in 1597, they were at last forced to hand the entire island over to His Most Catholic Majesty, Philip II.

Portugal's main effect upon Indian trade was to divert it from the Moslems by means of two fleets sent each September to patrol the west coast from the Gulf of Cambay to Cape Comorin; they enforced the pass system and put down Malabar corsairs. Rather more pepper may have reached Europe as a result of Portuguese enterprise, but the only new trade was from an opening of markets in West Africa and Brazil for Indian textiles. Portugal was no more successful than Rome had been in developing sufficient Asian markets to avoid a heavy drain of gold or silver; it could, after all, add little to the western luxuries and novelties that had reached Asia from Byzantium or Venice. The Portuguese soon found, as did their successors, the Dutch, that the spice trade to Europe and bullion exchanges in Asia, lucrative though they were, could not compare with the profits from a monopoly of carrying trade in Asian waters.

Even their enterprise in Goa disappointed the initial expectations held out by Tomé Pires in a passage of his report which may have sought to moderate Albuquerque's brutality:

The Deccan used to do a great deal of trade, chiefly in Dabhol. It was a rich and honoured port of call, a good port with many ships; and Your Highness treated these ports so ill that they were destroyed. . . . Most of the horses imported into the kingdom of the Deccan were landed here . . . but now that the Captain-General has made over this trade to the civilized kingdom of Goa the kingdom of the Deccan will not be able to maintain its position much longer. The way is open for it to be lost beyond recall, or for Goa to become the greatest place in the world.[1]

But many of the horses and luxuries imported by Goa went to Vijayanagar, by all accounts a most prosperous kingdom. Conti, who came there in 1420, put the capital's circumference at 60 miles and admired both its fortifications and the royal harem of 12,000 women.[2] Paes thought the capital was as big as Rome, and very beautiful with a great palace, splendid temples, fine orchards and gardens, artificial lakes, and irrigated farms between seven enclosing walls; he was also impressed with its large bazaars and strong guilds of merchants or craftsmen.[3] Nuniz reported the army as having 600,000 men and 24,000

---

[1] *Suma Oriental*, pp. 52–53.
[2] Smith, *The Oxford History of India*, p. 310.
[3] Rawlinson, *India: A Short Cultural History*, p. 271.

9 Akbar receiving the Persian ambassador (from the *Akbarnama*)
Victoria and Albert Museum

10 Portuguese ship in Japan (early seventeenth-century Japanese Namban or South Barbarian screen) *Museu de Arte Antiga, Lisbon*

horses.[1] Albuquerque refused the King's offer of £20,000 for a monopoly of importing horses, but the Portuguese tried to keep on good terms with Vijayanagar because of its importance for their trade. Besides horses it took elephants from Ceylon and Pegu, spices from Malacca, and silk and porcelain from China; it provided exports of pepper, ginger, cinnamon, teak, sandalwood, cotton textiles, dyestuffs, coconut, sugar, and rice. Vijayanagar remained prosperous and made some gains at the expense of the new Deccan Sultanates. But they combined, in 1565, to inflict so crushing a defeat upon Vijayanagar as to ruin it. Goa then suffered a rapid and serious decline of trade with South India. Thereafter its commercial success depended heavily upon entrepôt trade, enforced by the pass system.

India, as a whole, continued with a traditional trade which was of marginal importance to the Mughal North but of real consequence to the small southern kingdoms. Horses, of course, were important for every Indian ruler, whether they came from Iran and Transoxania through Afghanistan, or from Arabia and Iran through western ports. All districts of India had a seemingly insatiable appetite for gold or silver, and most were deficient in copper, lead, mercury, tin, and zinc. But these metals were so expensive that their use was largely confined to luxury articles produced for a relatively small wealthy class, and that was even more the case for imports of amber, coral, ivory, and gems needed for artistic productions. Textiles made from imported silks, velvets, and brocades were also upper-class luxuries, as were most drugs, dyes, perfumes, and spices. The small upper class had demands, too, for a wide range of luxuries or novelties, among which Chinese pottery, European woollens and wines, and African or other slaves were the more important, but these played very little part in ordinary life. Indian merchants were anxious to sell any type of produce and usually found many buyers for cotton textiles, pepper, indigo, and other spices or dyes.

Moreland made an interesting estimate of the volume of Indian exports during Akbar's reign, based upon various figures for shipping.[2] He puts the total tonnage of sea-borne trade from Indian ports at under 60,000 tuns, equivalent to 24,000–36,000

[1] Thapar, *A History of India*, vol. i, p. 328.
[2] Moreland, *India at the Death of Akbar*, pp. 218–22.

13

modern net tons. This compares with a 1911–14 figure of 6,750,000 net tons, but the discrepancy would be much less on value figures, if these were obtainable. The estimates, admittedly very rough, show an almost equal balance between India's trade with the west and that with the east, and so match the more limited observation made by Pires about Gujarat: 'Cambay stretches out two arms; with her right arm she reaches towards Aden and with the other towards Malacca.'[1]

These estimates are summarily reproduced for the light they throw upon India's regional export markets.

WEST	*tuns*	EAST	*tuns*
Europe	6,000	Pegu, etc.	5,000
East Africa	1,000	Malacca	10,000
Red Sea		Sumatra	3,000
(a) Pilgrim ships	5,000	Java	2,000
(b) Other ships	4,000	Moluccas	1,000
Arabia and Gulf	10,000	China and Japan	3,000

They include Portuguese ships, and so reflect the diversion of European-bound exports from the Red Sea or Persian Gulf. Even so, remaining trade with these two regions appears to have been about as large as that with Malacca. Direct trade with Europe was comparatively unimportant, only one-sixth of the total, and direct exports to Europe here include nearly all Asian commodities, not merely those produced by India; Asian exports to Europe would thus be a far smaller proportion of total Asian exports. Trade between Asian countries, that is, was far larger than their trade with Europe—and remained so until the Industrial Revolution altered the world's economic balance.

[1] *Suma Oriental*, p. 42.

CHAPTER FOUR

Intrusion, withdrawal, and disintegration

1. *Portuguese and Spanish enterprise*

Portugal's impact on Indian trade was but one aspect of a widespread enterprise ranging over all the seas of Asia. Besides strategic bases at Ormuz, Goa, and Malacca, and posts around the Indian coast from Diu to Chittagong, Portugal had forts at Ternate and Amboina, trading rights from Thailand at Ayuthia, Mergui, Tenasserim, Patani or Nakhon Srithammarat, and military adventurers in Burma and Cambodia. Beyond the eastern limit of the Indian Ocean it had a base for Chinese trade at Macao, and an even more distant base at the Japanese port of Tanegashima. Had it possessed the strength and competence to exploit this whole network fully, Portugal would have co-ordinated Asian sea-borne trade from the Persian Gulf to the limits of Indonesia, and controlled also Southeast Asian trade with China and Japan. So grandiose a plan was inevitably beyond the resources of a small nation at the other end of the world, but it is remarkable how much the bold Portuguese did accomplish before the advent of European rivals.

Their domination was most complete in the western Indian Ocean, where they had quickly established naval superiority over the Moslems and were not seriously challenged by the Mughal Empire until Shah Jahan in 1632 successfully attacked Hooghly. They had to contend earlier with attacks on Goa and Chaul by Bijapur or Ahmadnagar, and attacks by 'Cunnale', the Malabar pirate-king, but more than held their own. It was here that their new system of trade was most ambitious in scope and execution, a model for the Dutch East India Company which later ousted them. Treaties were imposed on local rulers for supplying produce at prices below market levels. The pass system brought customs dues and business to Portuguese harbours, reserved trade in arms, pepper, and a few other products to Portuguese ships and excluded Indian or Moslem ships from routes to East Africa, the Spice Islands, and China and Japan. But little attempt was made at controlling purely coastal trade, and none at controlling trade in foodstuffs. Licensing, moreover, was widely breached by officials who, according to Pyrard, 'for money let everything pass'.[1] Many Indians developed privileged partnership arrangements with Portuguese officials or merchants and, for political reasons, free licences had to be granted to a number of Indian rulers. Other Indians tried routes which would enable them to evade Portuguese control. Such control became increasingly ineffective as Portugal began to suffer crippling shortages of men and money for an enterprise well beyond its strength. There were never more than 10,000 Portuguese in Asia, and many left the public service for private ventures. Capital was also short, in spite of partnership loans from foreign bankers like the Fuggers or Welsers, and became shorter still when religious intolerance led to the expulsion of Jews from Portugal.

For these and other reasons, including poor administration, Portugal was unable to develop the commercial position it had wrested in India. New markets were opened for cottons in West Africa and Brazil, but no new Indian products were brought to Europe; in 1603 the four carracks from Goa to Lisbon carried mainly pepper (1,500 tons), some textiles (5,314 small bales, 959 large bales, and 931 chests), and a little indigo (47 tons), together with gems and Chinese pottery. Nor did Portugal succeed in monopolizing the spice trade in Europe. It had an initial success from blocking routes to the Persian Gulf and the Red Sea, but need for Persian support against the Ottoman Turks led to relaxing control over Gulf trade and, in 1538, the Turks gained the Red Sea's east coast, including Aden. By 1560, according to Lane's estimate, more spices were reaching Alexandria than Lisbon and, in 1580, Philip II had no success in offering the sale of Portugal's spices to its Italian rivals.

Indonesians from the outset resisted intrusion by Portugal. It had taken Malacca and quickly secured factories at Ternate and Tidore for obtaining precious cloves and for buying the equally precious mace and nutmeg of the Banda Islands, where it was denied a foothold. But Malacca's deposed Sultan re-

[1] Moreland, *From Akbar to Aurangzeb*, p. 8.

established himself at Johore to challenge Portuguese control of the Strait, and his sea-gypsies, the Celates, harassed even Portuguese shipping. Their activities threatened Malacca's food supply, which was made more precarious by loyalty of Malayan principalities to the Sultan and hostility of other Moslem rulers in Sumatra or Java; for this reason, the Portuguese sought good relations with Hindus of East Java and with Pegu. Serious efforts were also made to undermine Malacca's entrepôt trade, so that some Moslems left this port to settle in Borneo. Johore took others, retained a certain control over exports of pepper, tin, and gold and, denied contacts with West Asia, succeeded in attracting Chinese trade. Malacca, however, had better landing facilities, accommodation, and business arrangements, which prevented Johore from getting most Indian goods, especially the textiles which were so important in South-east Asian trade. The Sultan, moreover, lost support after unsuccessful military attacks on Malacca, and Johore's trade was continally harassed by the Portuguese.

They faced a more serious threat from Acheh where a pirate sultan, after taking Pasé and Pedir, the ports of an area where pepper cultivation was rapidly increasing, also dreamed of taking over Malacca's entrepôt trade. He obtained some Indian trade, denied to Johore, by developing a new route through the Maldives, familiar to Acheh fishermen, and in using the Sunda Strait to avoid Portuguese patrols. After repulsing a Portuguese attempt on Pasé and Pedir in 1529, Acheh established relations with the Ottoman Empire which gave help for repeated attacks on Malacca and its shipping. These attacks, some powerful, continued up to 1587 when the Sultan made peace with Portugal. He might have crushed Malacca with sufficient aid from other Indonesian opponents of Portugal, but his megalomania enabled Johore to lead a coalition which defeated Acheh in 1540. Rivalry between these two states continued into the next century.

In the Spice Islands Portugal soon confronted Spain. It was their products, the cloves of Ternate, Tidore, and Amboina, and the nutmeg or mace of the Banda group for which, together with pepper, the Portuguese had come so far. As Malacca's conquest had disrupted the trade of these Spice Islands, they gave a warm welcome to the first Portuguese ships which visited them, and as Ternate and Tidore were rivals for control over neighbouring islands, they angled for Portuguese support. But the possibility of other support appeared when a ship from Magellan's expedition reached Tidore in 1522. Portugal complained that a Spanish presence infringed the Treaty of Tordesillas, which had divided their interests at the meridian passing through a point 370 leagues west of the Azores. An expert conference met but could not agree about the exact position of the Moluccas, so that Spain sent an expedition, one of whose ships reached Tidore. It was welcomed there because Portugal had just made an alliance with Ternate. The two Iberian powers competed for trade and soon came into conflict until Spain decided in 1529 to withdraw. It again intruded in 1542–5, and renewed its claims after Manila was founded in 1570.

Portugal made big profits from the spice trade but was far from being able to monopolize it and, indeed, held a limited position in the Moluccas only with difficulty. The Crown did not do particularly well, and soon came to regret a policy of allowing its subjects private trade in cloves provided one-third of purchases were delivered to government agents at a fixed price; but corruption and opposition prevented reversal. Nor could Portugal, in spite of the initial treaty with Ternate, exclude Asian traders whose ranks were rapidly swelling with men from Java. The Sultan stood firmly for free trade which had so increased exports that clove production was being organized in tidy orchards and spreading to Amboina, Ceram, and other islands. As relations deteriorated in the second half of the seventeenth century, the Portuguese concentrated more of their activities on Amboina, which was independent and produced nutmeg and mace as well as cloves. They never came anywhere near to monopolizing trade in nutmeg and mace, as the Bandanese, who were the major producers, stoutly refused Portugal any privileges, although valuing both its official and private trade. The Crown eventually left Banda trade to Asians, among whom the Javanese were again prominent. Monopoly pretensions were further weakened by the growth of spice trading at Macassar, where Malay merchants, from about 1540, developed trade between Johore and the Moluccas. Portuguese merchants were also attracted to Macassar, and were quickly followed there by the Dutch.

Religious, even more than commercial, influences led to serious troubles with Ternate whose remarkable Sultan, Hairun, undermined Portugal's position in the Moluccas. He destroyed the mission and threatened the fortress in Ternate, so that another had to be built in Amboina. There seemed to be a reconciliation, but when the Portuguese treacherously murdered Hairun, his son, after a five-year siege, destroyed the fortress at Ternate in 1574. The Portuguese were also attacked on Amboina, whose people were helped by Bandanese and Javanese, and had to abandon the fortress at Hitu for another built in territory where they had converts. In these circumstances they turned to Tidore, which allowed them to build a fortress there. No sooner were they installed than Francis Drake appeared at Ternate, which gave him so friendly a reception as to arouse English interest in the Spice Islands. There would, too, have been further trouble with Spain, now established in the Philippines, but for the union of the two crowns, in 1580, under Philip II. His instruction that Spaniards should intervene in the Moluccas only if the Portuguese asked their help strengthened Portugal in a worsening struggle for survival against Asian enemies, but soon brought disastrous conflict with Spain's enemies, the Dutch and English.

From Indonesia the Portuguese extended their commercial relations to China and Japan. They had come into contact with Chinese merchants at Malacca, from whom they learnt much about the Celestial Empire's trade and won support by more favourable treatment than the Chinese had received from the Sultan. These merchants sent complimentary reports to the Ming Court, but the Sultan wrote denouncing the newcomers as pirates and imploring redress. The first Portuguese ship reached China in 1514 and three years later Tomé Pires was sent there on a trading embassy. He had immediate difficulties with etiquette and a demand for Malacca's traditional vassalage. When a private Portuguese trader came into disgraceful conflict with Chinese authorities, Pires was imprisoned and told to advise his king that Malacca should be returned to its sultan. The Portuguese were expelled from Canton in 1522, and later from other ports at which they attempted trading. But in 1557, after helping to put down pirates, they were allowed by local authorities to rent a base at the tip of the Macao Peninsula where they built a 'Settlement of the Name of God in China'.

It quickly developed a flourishing, if very limited, trade. Chinese were anxious to have wares from Malacca, and the Ming were discouraging their subjects from venturing abroad. Moreover, as the Portuguese developed direct trade with Canton, they felt that their competitive interest required increasingly unfavourable treatment of Chinese merchants at Malacca; these merchants came to shun Malacca and gave up voyages to the Spice Islands. To compensate, they went to various ports in Malaya, Sumatra, and Java, where both Indian and Moluccan products could be obtained, as well as local tin and pepper, and still went to Timor for sandalwood, notwithstanding Portuguese opposition.

Macao was made more profitable by the trade which developed with Japan. The first Portuguese had come there as passengers on a Chinese junk which, blown off course by a typhoon, brought them in about 1542 to the island of Tane-gashima, where Kyushu warlords greatly admired, and copied, their muskets. Soon after this discovery was reported, Portugal sent ships whose trade was welcomed as a source of revenue, as providing fire-arms which altered Japanese warfare, as showing the way to big improvements in shipbuilding and navigation, and as introducing new plants like potatoes and tobacco. It was also welcomed as a further breach in the Ming proscription of foreign commerce, so that Macao quickly developed a carrying trade between China and Japan. Each spring, an official 'Captain-General of the Voyage of China and Japan' would sail in a 1,200–1,600 ton carrack from Goa with European, Indian, and Indonesian wares which would be exchanged at Macao, during the winter, mainly for silks, porcelain, and gold; on reaching Japan in the following summer he would sell mainly fire-arms or Chinese wares and take away silver. Japanese silver could be used to finance later purchases from China, and Chinese gold helped to meet the chronic European deficit of trade with India.

Spain, too, developed trade with China across the Pacific from Mexico. Colombus's expedition had been dispatched in the hope of finding an eastern route to the Spice Islands and, far from being pleased with his discovery of America, Spain found it disappointing, until silver was mined in Mexico. Magellan's expedition was the precursor of attempts to get round an unwanted continent to the source of enriching spices. But the Portuguese were already there, and it seemed politically unwise to provoke enmity by challenging them, even after Villalobos had reached the Moluccas directly from Mexico instead of going round Cape Horn. A new treaty was made, binding Spain to come no further than a meridian 17 degrees east of the Moluccas. Nevertheless, in 1564 Philip II sent a fleet to take the Philippines, which are somewhat west of Ternate, and an easy way back to Mexico was found by sailing north to the zone of prevailing westerlies. In spite of Portugal's protest, the Philippines were made a Spanish province and, in 1571, the fine harbour of Manila was captured to become the headquarters of Spain's enterprise in Asia.

Most of the population were Indonesians whose successive waves of immigration had swamped indigenous Negritos. Its trade was limited to pearls and jungle products and is not mentioned by Chinese records until the tenth century. By that time these islands were coming under the domination of Srivijaya so that there was a real development of trade. Crafts spread from the Sung Empire and new migrants came from both China and Japan. But, as Srivijaya declined and the Ming were plagued by pirates, this trade fell off. Chao Ju-kua, writing in the thirteenth century, described it as slow and difficult, conducted with a half savage people who were so lacking in government that few Chinese would venture ashore.

Soon after its foundation, Manila was strongly assaulted by a fleet of Moros from Mindanao or Palawan, and then by a more dangerous fleet of Chinese pirates. Both were repulsed and the Spanish quickly secured effective control over northern coasts without needing to attempt a conquest of the formidable Moros. Chinese pirates were a great menace, but some came to appreciate the commercial advantages of Manila, and Spain reinforced Ming efforts to suppress open piracy. Tens of thousands of Chinese settled in Manila to take advantage of the new law and order and also of new demands for Chinese goods, backed by ample silver from Mexico. There were occasional serious troubles with this large Chinese community, and with a smaller, but far more truculent, Japanese community. Mutual dependence on trade, however, proved a strong enough bond for the new colony to become secure and prosperous.

The Spanish had come to the Philippines expecting to gain a share of the lucrative spice trade. A number of expeditions were sent to help the Portuguese against Ternate but all failed, mainly because crews were stricken with disease. Before long the Dutch appeared and helped Ternate repulse a strong Spanish and Portuguese force. In 1606 Spain reversed this defeat but, as Dutch power in the area was strengthened, the two nations contended over the Moluccas for many years. Gradually the Dutch gained the upper hand, and Spain came to find the spice trade unremunerative; expenses were high because of constant warfare and because routing across Mexico to Europe was more costly than round the Cape of Good Hope. Spain, however, did not finally withdraw from the Spice Islands until the evacuation of Tidore in 1663.

It was Chinese trade which proved the colony's salvation. China had strong demands for silver, and Spain could produce it so cheaply in Peru that silk was bought on terms which more than sufficed for high costs of defence and those of the long, dangerous, and unhealthy voyage between Manila and Acapulco. Some of this silk was sold in Mexico, some transhipped at Acapulco to Peru, but most went by pack train across Mexico to Vera Cruz for shipment to Spain. Macao obtained great benefit from this new trade, but silk also reached Manila in Chinese junks, thirty to fifty of which arrived each year. They brought, in addition to silk and such other luxury wares as velvet, porcelain, jade, and bronze, local requirements for ironware, gunpowder, saltpetre, furniture, and many kinds of food.

After paying modest harbour dues of 3 per cent, they took away bullion and such quantities of the Mexican dollar to Canton, Amoy, and Ningpo that it soon became the principal currency of the China coast. In the peak year of the trade, 1597, Acapulco sent to Manila 12,000,000 pesos, a higher figure than the value of Spain's whole trans-Atlantic trade, but in more normal years the export was 3,000,000 to 5,000,000 pesos.

Spain by no means fully exploited its China trade owing to mercantile preoccupations; Peruvian silver was diverted from Spain, and Chinese textiles coming to Mexico or Peru limited those markets for Spanish producers. The trade, moreover, involved direct relations and benefits between two colonies instead of trade between a colony and the metropolis for the latter's benefit. But local and other interests were strong enough to prevent suppression, so that Madrid had to be content with limiting the Manila galleons to two per year and to a size of 300 tons. Most of these galleons were built in the Philippines by Asian craftsmen.

The northern return voyage through the zone of prevailing westerlies brought the galleons close to Japan. Authorities at Manila wished to establish relations with the Shogun in order to have a port of call as well as some Japanese trade. A first galleon which went to Hirado for shelter was well received and offered trading facilities, but goodwill was soon lost by zealous missionaries who insisted upon a passage in order to make converts; their excessive zeal provoked Japanese hostility and in 1597 the Shogun had seven of them brutally executed. Nevertheless, Japanese interest in trade was shown by an agreement, signed in 1609, for friendly treatment of Spanish ships in return for aid in shipbuilding and mining; it was also shown by the arrival of two Japanese ships in 1613 and 1616 at Acapulco where their welcome was not so friendly. Relations quickly deteriorated when the Spanish tried to reserve all trade from Manila to Japan for their own ships and forced many Japanese to leave the city. In Japan, Dutch and English agents intrigued against Spain, and its missions continued to provoke trouble. In 1624 the Shogun broke off relations with Manila and expelled all Spanish friars.

In spite of a bold start, imaginative penetration, and stout fighting, Iberian enterprise in Asia had only a limited and dwindling success as the seventeenth century opened. Goa was a secure and important base which had developed useful connections with Mughal officials and Indian merchants at most ports. It was through increasing partnership arrangements with these merchants, and use of Asian crews, that Portugal was able to keep up coasting trade and voyages to Aden. But its trade with Aden inevitably suffered from Ottoman hostility, and van der Broecke claimed, in 1621, that Portugal's coasting trade with Gujarat had been ruined. There was a fairly tight control over trade with the Persian Gulf until the loss of Ormuz in 1622, but an English report, four years before this event, claimed that imports of Portuguese spices were only one-sixth of their former level.[1] Portugal was well established on the Coromandel coast, even more important than Gujarat in providing textiles for Indonesian trade, but could not prevent Dutch newcomers from quickly gaining a share of these textiles.

The best trade seemed to be that of Macao and Manila with China and Japan, mainly becaues Peruvian silver both solved the perennial European problem of heavy deficits in Asian trade and gave a quasi-monopoly power which helped trade with Indonesia. Trade between Macao and Manila, nevertheless, was suffering from activity by Chinese merchants, and that between Macao and Japan ended abruptly in 1639, when the Portuguese were also expelled by the Shogun.

Moluccan trade had never approached the level desired, and was now hard pressed by Indonesian or European enemies. Spanish help did not enable the Portuguese to exclude the Dutch who, after capturing Amboina in 1605, rapidly took over the spice trade. Portugal, however, did retain Timor and so kept up exports of sandalwood to Malacca. Ralph Fitch and other European visitors attested that Malacca was still busy and prosperous;[2] a Dutch visitor said that 300 ships came to it a year, but that most of their cargoes were bought by Indian merchants.[3] These imports, according to a Portuguese report of 1610, amounted to some 800 tons, excluding untaxed foodstuffs which were brought in 200 boats.[4] There is other evidence, too, that the Portuguese in Malacca had become demoralized or lacking in business energy.

'Look at the Portuguese,' wrote Sir Thomas Roe, James I's ambassador to the Mughals. 'In spite of all their fine settlements they are beggared by the maintenance of military forces; and even their garrisons are only mediocre.'[5] Similar reports were reaching the Netherlands from Dutchmen who had taken service with Portugal as it became increasingly short of men for Asian enterprises. The most expert of these informants was Jan van Linschoten who, after spending some years in Portugal and Spain, served at Goa for over five years as secretary to its Archbishop. His detailed account of Portugal's Asian trade repeatedly emphasized how it had become vulnerable through corruption

---

[1] cf. Meilink-Roelofsz, *Asian Trade and European Influence*, p. 190.
[2] ibid., p. 172.   [3] ibid., p. 172.   [4] ibid., p. 170.
[5] Quoted in Hall, *A History of South-East Asia*, p. 225.

or abuses. The Dutch had better ships and navigators, and so could prevail on the high seas, but Portuguese forts in Asia were still strong. The best approach would be through the unde-fended Sunda Strait to Bantam, an important centre for pepper and for trade both with Malacca and the Spice Islands. This sound advice was quickly acted upon by fellow countrymen, who were as anxious to profit from the spice trade as they were to damage their bitter enemy, the joint king of Spain and Portugal.

2. *The Dutch and English East India companies*

A company was formed in 1595 to send four ships under Cornelius de Houtman to Java, where the Sultan of Bantam made a friendly treaty with the Dutch but soon became incensed at their bad behaviour. Although the expedition made only a meagre profit, its successful return immediately led to the forma-tion of many new companies in Dutch towns. Before 1600 over sixty ships had left for the Indies via the Cape of Good Hope or the Straits of Magellan, and visited Java, Sumatra, the Molucaas, Thailand, Cambodia, Borneo, and Canton, even sighting Japan. It became apparent almost at once that these diverse enter-prises should be concentrated in order to cope with Portuguese or Spanish opposition and to avoid damaging competition in the spice market. The States-General accordingly sum-moned a conference at which it was, with difficulty, agreed to form, in 1602, a United Netherlands Chartered East India Company (V.O.C.), having a national monopoly of trade between the Cape of Good Hope and the Straits of Magellan, and powers to make treaties, erect forts, and wage defensive wars.

The new company had many advantages. Dutch ships were lighter and more manœuvrable than those of Portugal or Spain, yet better armed and able to stay at sea for longer periods. Dutch sailors were superior navigators and tacticians, and Dutch troops well trained and disciplined. On the commercial side, the Netherlands had a long tradition of efficient trading, direct connections with all important markets in Europe and the help, too, of Portuguese Jews who, after their expulsion, brought to Amsterdam skills in Asian trading which Portugal could ill afford to lose. Nor was there to be trouble from religious zealots in Asia; the Reformed Church was much too dependent upon the Company in Indonesia to risk upsetting trade by efforts at conversion. Unlike the Spanish–Portuguese Crown, moreover, the Company was able, for a time, to discipline its men in Asia effectively enough to prevent their private activities from upsetting official trade. As compared with earlier companies it had the advantage of a permanent capital, 6,500,000 guilders, and so did not have to raise and then disburse capital for single voyages. Another financial advantage was accumulation in the Netherlands of large stocks of bullion from previous trade with Spain or from Spanish military expenditures. These metals, as has been repeatedly stressed, were essential for successful European trade with Asia, and the V.O.C., if less well placed in this respect than Spain or Portugal, was not subject like its English counterpart to harassing restrictions upon exports of bullion.

This English counterpart, founded two years earlier, was long hampered by lack of funds. It had no permanent capital and, for the first voyage, could raise only one-tenth of the V.O.C.'s capital (£68,000). England was also the enemy of Spain, and London's merchants were just as covetous as Amsterdam's for profits from spices. Drake's circumnavigation voyage had paused at the Moluccas, Fitch had returned from travels in India and Burma, and Lancaster had penetrated the Indian Ocean to Penang. Was the victory of the Armada to result merely in Dutch gains of Asia trade? London merchants petitioned the Queen and obtained in 1600 a charter to undertake voyages to the East Indies, 'for the honour of this our realm of England as for the increase of our navigation and advancement of trade of merchandise'. It said nothing about piracy, which was to characterize England's early Asian trade, but the 'Governor and Company of Merchants of London Trading into the East Indies' (E.I.C.) immediately told their seamen that prizes might be taken, provided there was no hazard to a voyage. The first voyage, under Lancaster, had four ships aggregating 1,500 tons, as against the fourteen ships sent out by the V.O.C., and reached Acheh in 1602; at Bantam it was allowed to erect a fort and bought so much pepper, thanks to capturing a Portuguese prize, that the London market became glutted. The second voyage, of 1604, returned to Bantam and went on to the Moluccas where it obtained cloves, mace, and nutmeg in spite of a powerful Dutch fleet which, by taking Amboina and Ternate, prevented the English from building a factory in the Spice Islands.

This was the first inkling of a Dutch plan not merely to expel the Portuguese and Spanish from the Moluccas but to monopolize the whole spice trade more effectively than Portugal had ever been able to manage. The V.O.C. took over from its predecessors factories at Ternate, Banda, Bantam, Gresik, Acheh, Patani, and Johore, and also a war with Goa which had unsuccessfully attacked the Dutch at Bantam. A first fleet of fifteen heavily armed ships sailed in 1602 and within two years was reinforced by twenty-three similar ships. It had orders to attack the Portuguese in their strongholds at Mozambique, Goa, and Malacca, as well as in Moluccan waters, but had success only at Amboina and Tidore. Malacca beat off the Dutch attack, and Spain destroyed the V.O.C.'s trading posts at Ternate. Yet, while this initial fighting was going on, Matelieff, who commanded the fleet in 1605, wrote a remarkably long-sighted memorandum. He argued that the V.O.C. must have Asian bases, that it should monopolize the trade in cloves, mace, and nutmeg, excluding the English therefrom, and should also monopolize trade with China and Japan. The V.O.C. should drive the English out of Indonesia by selling pepper at ruinously low prices, and should develop Coromandel trade because of the cotton goods so eagerly sought in South-east Asia.[1]

Progress was quickly made towards realizing these objectives. The Dutch gained predominance over the spice trade by taking Banda Neira and fortifying it as a twin-base to Amboina; their fleet was then able to impose treaties upon various native rulers, giving the V.O.C. monopoly rights. The Twelve Years' Truce with Spain, in 1609, recognized the Company's Asian conquests besides giving a respite in Europe. Spain still held Tidore, and Portugal found a trading refuge in Macassar under the neutral protection of its strong sultan. Timor fell to the Dutch but, disappointed with the results of the sandalwood trade, they soon withdrew and Portugal recovered this island. The English had trading rights at Macassar but were hard pressed by the Dutch in obtaining spices elsewhere. To strengthen its position, the

[1] cf. Moreland, *From Akbar to Aurangzeb*, p. 20.

V.O.C. appointed a Governor-General of the Indies, assisted by a four-member Council of India, with control over all its bases and affairs in Asia; he was instructed that first priority was to be given to the spice trade, from which all competitors should be excluded. In India the Dutch had made a treaty with the Zamorin of Calicut, established five factories at Coromandel ports, and withstood strong Portuguese attacks. By 1613 their position was secure enough, after fortifying Pulicat, for the Commercial Directorate of the Coromandel Coast to be made a Governorship, the Governor taking a seat on the Council of India.

A year later, Jan P. Coen (1586–1629), the young director of commerce at Bantam, produced an ambitious programme for the Company's guidance. He urged that the objective of monopolizing the spice trade should be vigorously pursued but that new measures were needed to make it profitable. Over the decade, 1613–23, the Company had spent 9,396,000 guilders but had obtained a return from the fifty-six ships bringing cargoes to the Netherlands of only 9,388,000 guilders, thus incurring a loss of about 1 per cent. (These figures cannot now be checked but the V.O.C., during its first seventeen years, paid but a single dividend; although this was at the high level of 162 per cent, it had to be partly distributed in spices). Coen believed that the spice trade could be made to cover its very high expenses only if both European and Asian competitors were excluded. That would require a measure of colonization, so that Dutch settlers should be established at Amboina, Banda, and Jakarta or Bantam; they would need reinforcing by migrants from Madagascar, Burma, and, above all, China, whose people were both industrious and pacific. Far greater profit, however, would come from a wider monopolization of inter-Asian trade; for this exceeded European trade in the same degree that Asia's population or production exceeded Europe's. Coen estimated that such a monopoly would yield 5,000,000 guilders, and that another 5,000,000 guilders could be gained by monopolizing trade with China. He urged the Company, accordingly, to send a fleet powerful enough to take Macao and Manila and using thousands of mercenaries from Japan, whose 'soldiers are just as good as ours'.

This plan is obviously similar to Albuquerque's grandiose

scheme for controlling all the trade of the Indian Ocean by strong fleets operating from strategic bases. It also reflects Portugal's experience of the interconnections of Asian trade and the impossibility of driving it by means of European exports. The desired spice trade of Indonesia and the silk trade of Iran required large supplies of Indian cottons, and the trade with China both cottons and spices. But India had very limited demands for European exports. The most promising means of payment, especially for the Netherlands which had no direct access to Latin American bullion, was the profit from trading goods at various Asian markets between the Persian Gulf and the Sea of Japan. Indian cottons and Indonesian spices or sandalwood could procure silks and horses from Iran or silks, porcelains, and gold from China, and Japan would readily exchange silver or copper for Chinese wares. But Coen's base had to be in Java, not at Goa or some other Indian port. From this central base the whole vast commercial enterprise would be carefully controlled and from it, each year, a few ships would leave for Europe, well laden with valuable spices. Coen did not underestimate the ability of Asian merchants, but hoped to displace them by superior naval power or the competition of Dutch settlers. He never made clear, however, the division of trade between the V.O.C. and its settlers or how settlers' trade would be controlled. In any case, the proposed monopoly could not be made complete so long as there was overland trade from India or China through Iran and Turkey; Gujarat and Ormuz long continued to export pepper and silks to the Mediterranean because the overland route, notwithstanding heavy Turkish duties, remained at least as cheap as the sea route round the Cape.

Coen's arguments were impressive enough to gain him appointment, in 1618, as Governor-General of the Indies; at a time when it took 18 to 24 months for a reply to reach Amsterdam from Java, he had a fairly free hand, limited only by the ships, men, and money the Directors saw fit to send. He complained bitterly about inadequate support, yet opponents alleged he had raised costs in Indonesia from 600,000 guilders a year to 1,600,000 guilders. Some also argued that his policy would be disastrous, as the V.O.C.'s profits depended upon a flourishing native trade rather than upon its destruction.

14

His destruction of native trade and shipping in the Spice Islands, at least, was fully supported by the Directors as the realization of an old policy. This was being thwarted by the English who, after James I's peace with Spain, refused to share attacks upon its Indonesian bases, and helped the natives to avoid Dutch pressure both by paying higher prices for cloves or nutmeg and by supplying rice or cottons more cheaply. Dutch and English frequently clashed in Moluccan waters, and also in Java, although their governments tried unsuccessfully to reach a peaceful compromise. The clashes in Java arose from competition at Bantam for pepper. Coen was intimidating Bantam when an English fleet arrived and forced his withdrawal to the Moluccas. Although its commander had been sent to protect English trade with the Spice Islands, he unwisely decided to stay at Java in order to help the ruler of Jakarta attack the new Dutch fort in which Coen had left a garrison. But the English soon quarrelled with their ally, and withdrew when the Sultan of Bantam attacked him. The garrison held out until Coen returned to capture Jakarta and build there a fortified Dutch town named Batavia. He also attacked the dispersed English fleet, which withdrew to India, leaving him master of the Java Sea. News then arrived of the Anglo-Dutch alliance made against Spain in 1619. Its stipulation that the English should have half the trade in pepper and a third of that in spices, in return for sharing the cost of operations against Spain in Asia, was so far from pleasing Coen that he did his best to make the treaty unworkable.

First, however, he proceeded to the small Banda Islands whose inhabitants had actively resisted his demand for a monopoly of their mace and nutmeg. They were crushed, many were executed or died of starvation, and the remainder were deported as slaves to Java. Their lands were then divided among Dutch settlers to work with imported slave labour. Coen's ruthlessness is said to have shocked even the Company's servants, but the Directors made only a mild rebuke. Turning to Amboina, Coen forced its chiefs to accept Dutch authority and, when Ceram showed reluctance over a similar treaty, brought it to heel by a sample of the Banda pacification. There was greater difficulty with the Moluccas, because of the Spanish base at Tidore, and Coen had to leave for Batavia before they were subdued.

Bantam and Mataram had not given up their rival claims to Batavia and both kept it under constant pressure. Coen replied by blockading Bantam so vigorously that the English had to leave; they were received as allies in Batavia but subjected to Dutch rules and asked to share the heavy cost of defensive and commercial operations. The E.I.C. was about to withdraw from Java when news came of a 'massacre' at Amboina, i.e. eight Englishmen were executed there for alleged conspiracy with Portuguese and Japanese to seize the fortress. A new agreement was patched up, but the E.I.C. had to quit the Moluccas and transferred its activities in Java to Bantam, until the Dutch took this port in 1682.

Coen lived to see a Dutch monopoly established over only mace and nutmeg, and no very profitable one as the V.O.C.'s annual deficits for Banda averaged 37,000 guilders between 1632 and 1634. These deficits may be related to the Company's estimates of 450,000 lb. of nutmeg and 180,000 lb. of mace sold in Europe about 1621, and of 200,000 lb. of nutmeg together with 30,000 lb. of mace sold in Asian markets. By this time the Moslem caliphates had greatly decayed; van Leur thought that, in their hey-day, Asian purchases must have been much higher, perhaps four times higher, but his estimate included cloves.[1] The V.O.C.'s estimates for cloves for 1621 were 490,000 lb. sold in Europe and 100,000 to 150,000 lb. sold in Asia. It did not obtain a monopoly of this spice until the fall of Macassar in 1667, but it tried to suppress cultivation at places other than Amboina, which grew enough cloves to meet all demands in Europe and Asia. This was a hopeless enterprise, as the natives of Ceram and other islands could always find new places for cultivation as old ones were destroyed, and could ship cloves to Macassar where other Europeans eagerly bought them. At this port, in 1637, the English and Danes are said to have obtained 300,000 lb. of cloves. During the 1630s the V.O.C. also had deficits for Amboina, averaging more than 80,000 guilders, and perhaps as much could be added for the cost of extirpating clove production in the Moluccas or containing the Spanish. The extirpation policy succeeded only after the conquest of Macassar; annual fleets were then sent to destroy spice trees on other islands than the Bandas or Amboina, and reduced

[1] Van Leur, *Indonesian Trade and Society*, p. 123.

production of cloves, mace, and nutmeg to about one-fourth of the previous level. This drastic reduction was made because of decreasing demand in Europe but, when demand recovered, the V.O.C. failed to obtain increased supplies. Extirpation and oppression had reduced population as well as incentives in the Spice Islands.

Pepper was the other spice which the V.O.C. sought to monopolize. In van Leur's opinion[1] most Indonesian pepper, before the advent of European ships, went to China, which may have taken 50,000 bags a year or 2,000 tons, about five-sixths of the Indonesian supply. The remainder went to Malabar which supplied most demands for pepper in West Asia and Europe. By 1600, under pressure of European demands, Indonesia's pepper supply had increased to 6,200 tons, contributed in roughly equal proportions by West Sumatra and East Sumatra, together with Malaya and Bantam. The V.O.C.'s estimate of total European purchases of pepper put these at around 4,670 tons, one-fifth of which was sold by Portugal. By this time the supply of pepper and other spices to European markets had increased so greatly that prices fell to a level which made it impossible for the Levant route to compete; the Netherlands, indeed, were already re-exporting pepper, cloves, and nutmeg to Italy before the V.O.C. was formed.

Most of the pepper from Malaya and Sumatra was controlled by the Sultan of Acheh until his defeat by the temporary alliance of Malacca, Johore, and Patani, but he kept firm control over Sumatra's western ports for another quarter-century. His hostility to the Dutch made them prosecute most of their Sumatran trade at Jambi and Palembang where they had no special privileges and competed with other traders, notably the English and Chinese. But in 1641 the Dutch finally took Malacca. In itself this was no great acquisition; trade had declined under the Portuguese and was to dwindle rapidly under the Dutch, partly because of physical damage and an exodus of traders and partly because of Batavia's promotion as a great Asian entrepôt. The V.O.C. did get some control over Malayan pepper and tin, but the chief gain from Malacca was elimination of a hostile base and consequent dominance of Indonesian waters. That dominance, and the commercial strength of Batavia, enabled

[1] Van Leur, op. cit., pp. 124-5.

the V.O.C. to gain exclusive rights of buying pepper at Jambi and Palembang in 1658. Four years later it acquired an absolute monopoly of trade with three other Sumatran ports whose rulers had rebelled against Acheh and accepted Dutch suzerainty.

Bantam, at the beginning of the seventeenth century, was the main pepper port for both European and Chinese traders. Its ruler welcomed customers but soon resisted Dutch or English attempts to dominate his market and so favoured traders from China and Gujarat. The Dutch and English found that they could exploit the situation by lending to Chinese merchants, most of whom were short of trading capital, and by making resale of pepper at fixed prices a condition of their loans. The Chinese began defaulting on these loans in 1616 and had some of their cargoes seized by the Dutch. The ruler of Bantam then forbade sales at prices below that which he himself fixed, restricted purchases by the V.O.C., and, when it stopped Chinese junks from embarking, cut off its supply. Coen blockaded the port so successfully that a dramatic fall in price reduced the crop to 7,000 or 8,000 bags, less than one-sixth of the former level. This greatly reduced output was bought mainly by English and Chinese, but some of it reached Batavia, through resident Chinese merchants, although Sumatran pepper was now far more important to the V.O.C.

Malabar was a greater source of pepper than Indonesia, and Coromandel textile centres had quickly been recognized by the V.O.C. as the 'left arm of the Moluccas'. Coen, believing that Gujarat cloth was also needed for the spice trade, had sent van den Broecke to Surat in 1616 and later opened factories at Broach, Cambay, Ahmadabad, Agra, and Burhanpur. They supplied a profitable trade in indigo as well as cloth, in spite of some trouble with the Mughals. Another factory was opened in 1627 at Bengal; it supplied, in addition to textiles, rice, and salt-petre, the opium which was sent to Java or China at great profit. Nine years later the Dutch began an annual blockade of Goa, greatly damaging its trade. But they found more difficulty in penetrating the trade of the strongly defended Malabar coast. It was not until 1661 that the V.O.C., after gaining mastery of Indonesian seas, could send a large fleet to take Quilon, Cranganore, and the Island of Vypin; another large fleet then arrived from Batavia to take Cochin.

The V.O.C. appointed a separate administration for its new Malabar possessions and interests, and attempted to take over the Portuguese pepper monopoly by exclusive contracts with rulers of the various principalities. That proved difficult because the V.O.C., shrinking from the cost of a massive naval patrol, could not prevent competition from Portuguese, English, and Gujarat traders, especially as smuggling was rife and Malabar rulers gladly accepted higher prices for pepper than the Dutch offered. Towards the end of the seventeenth century the V.O.C. was obtaining such large quantities of Indonesian pepper that it ceased buying in Malabar and so eased restrictions there. They were reimposed in 1698, but by then Asian and European traders were too well established to be ousted.

The Dutch had more success in monopolizing Ceylon's cinnamon trade. They made an agreement with Raja Sinha in 1638 to expel the Portuguese in return for exclusive rights over Ceylon's trade with European nations. Strong Portuguese resistance, quarrels between the Raja and the V.O.C., and the ten-year truce with Portugal after it broke with Spain, held up expulsion for two decades. When the last Portuguese stronghold fell, the V.O.C. had difficulty in restraining local governors from attempting a complete subjugation of Ceylon. It gained, nevertheless, direct control over a much wider area of the island than ports and cinnamon fields.

By comparison the English Company's achievement appeared meagre. The last of its few trading posts in Indonesia was lost when the Dutch took Bantam, and those which had been precariously set up in Burma, Thailand, and Cambodia were all abandoned, so that trading operations became limited to Iran and India. By 1619, it had established, against Portuguese opposition, factories only at Agra, the inland capital, at the Cambay ports of Surat, Ahmadabad, and Broach, and at the Golkonda port of Masulipatam. Three years later it acquired exemption from tolls at Bandar Abbas, together with half of this port's customs revenue, in return for helping the Shah of Iran expel the Portuguese from Ormuz. For a time, the Portuguese were strong enough to exclude both English and Dutch companies from Malabar, and the V.O.C., as well as the Portuguese, kept the E.I.C. out of Coromandel. The two companies joined after 1622 in naval operations against Portugal but, following the peace made by Charles I, England and Portugal began to co-operate against the Dutch. This co-operation enabled the E.I.C. to erect Fort St. George at Madras in 1641, from which it controlled new factories at Balasore and Hariharpur in Orissa and, before long, other factories at Hooghly, Patna, and Kasimbazar in Bengal. Cromwell's treaty of 1654 gave the E.I.C. valuable rights to free trade in Portugal's Indian possessions, particularly valuable in opening Malabar ports, and Charles II's marriage brought, as part of his Portuguese bride's dowry, the island of Bombay which was transferred to the Company in 1668.

Dutch supremacy in Indonesia forced the E.I.C. to concentrate on an Indian trade, which had become reasonably extensive before the end of the seventeenth century. From its factories in Cambay the Company obtained Indian cottons, some of which were used for procuring silks in Bandar Abbas. Indigo was the biggest initial export to England but demands were growing there for cottons and, to a lesser extent, silks. The Company was fortunate in obtaining access to Malabar pepper just as the Dutch tightened their control over Indonesian supplies. Wars in Europe were increasing demands for saltpetre, which Malabar supplied, but the Company obtained greater amounts from its Bengal factories. From these, too, it obtained sugar, silks, and cottons, although more cotton was obtained from Madras, especially when Gujarat's production was set back by the disastrous famine of 1630–1.

To India the Company brought English broadcloth, tapestries, embroideries, various minor manufactures, lead, mercury, tin, vermilion, Mediterranean coral, and African ivory, and it earned something from carrying goods for Asian merchants between Red Sea, Persian Gulf, and Indian ports. But, in the main, it was forced by the very limited Indian demands for European wares to make payment in silver. This was an important restriction as, between 1615 and 1644, the Company dispatched only forty-eight vessels to England, averaging 500 tons and bringing cargoes of about £50,000 a year, a value which was but one-half of the *profit* made by the V.O.C. on its Asian trade and a sufficient indication of the E.I.C.'s much smaller scale of operations. These would have been somewhat larger but for private business activities by its own servants, who used money borrowed in England or India to trade on their own account. Much of their trade was conducted in association with Indian merchants who obtained the benefit of cheaper freight and customs concessions on 'English' goods. The Company, after vainly trying to suppress this 'country trade', confined itself, after 1661, to direct trade between England and India and, three years later, allowed its servants direct trade in gems, ambergris, musk, civet, and some other goods. During the Civil War and under the Commonwealth, the Company suffered badly from interlopers as well as from the general economic depression in England. There were further troubles from two rival companies but they ended when Cromwell, in 1657, granted a new exclusive charter which Charles II confirmed. This enabled the Company to establish government in its own settlements and to make war against heathen rulers as well as English interlopers.

For the rest of the Stuart period the Company did very well on a new paid-up capital of £370,000 which was increased by ploughing back profits; from 1662 it distributed dividends averaging more than 20 per cent and in 1682 actually paid 50 per cent while doubling shareholders' capital by a bonus issue. By 1708 the Company's imports had risen to £500,000—ten times the 1640 level. It was, indeed, importing so many Asian textiles that an Act was passed in 1700 forbidding domestic use of silks or calicoes which had been printed or dyed. Two new imports had also become highly profitable: Arabian coffee, procured at Surat from Mocha, and Chinese tea, of which the Company sold, in 1706, 54,600 lb. in England for £45,000.

3. Japanese withdrawal and Chinese restriction

Like the Portuguese, both the Dutch and English tried, almost as soon as they came east, to reach beyond the Indies to China and Japan. They had a greater need of bullion for driving Asian trade and knew that these markets could supply it as well as valuable silks, porcelains, and lacquerware. The Ming, however, had forbidden their subjects to venture abroad and closed Chinese ports to foreign trade. It is true that these prohibitions could not be completely enforced as many Chinese either joined 'pirates' who traded illegally with the Empire or left its ports to reside as merchants in Manila, Bantam, and Malacca, among other places in South-east Asia. It is also true that the Portuguese had a firm, if unofficial, base in Macao which enabled Manila to do a thriving trade with the mainland. But the Portuguese and Spanish could defend this trade, the Ming had strong coastal forces to suppress pirates, and their officials held an unfavourable opinion of the Dutch. One wrote:

The Hollanders . . . are covetous and cunning, are very knowledgable concerning valuable merchandise, and are very clever in the pursuit of gain. They will risk their lives in search of profit, and no place is too remote for them to frequent. Their ships are very large, strong, and well-built. . . . If one falls in with them at sea, one is certain to be robbed by them.[1]

The Portuguese fostered this adverse opinion, but Coen's Asian policy was responsible for it. He had hoped to attract Chinese junks from Manila to Batavia but few came because there was no free market and they feared Dutch seizures; Coen was kidnapping Chinese to provide settlers for the new port. In 1621 he began a systematic blockade of Manila, during which many junks from Fukien were attacked, and sent Reyersz to blockade the China coast until a Portuguese fleet defeated an attempt to take Macao. Nor could the V.O.C. subdue Manila, although it imposed a heavy burden on the Spanish colony until the Treaty of Münster (1648) brought peace between Holland and Spain.

The best that the Dutch could hope for was a foothold off the China coast. They landed at the Pescadores, but were tricked by mandarins into moving to Taiwan, on the false assumption that it had an official trading centre. The Directors, nevertheless, were pleased with the beautiful island and resolved to make it a colony. Fort Zeelandia was built on the south coast, whereupon the Spanish built a fort on the north coast in order to protect their trade. They were driven out in 1642 by the Dutch who then ringed Taiwan with forts and began a ruthless exploitation from which Japanese escaped only by leaving the island.

Until then they had had a favoured position on Taiwan owing to the V.O.C.'s anxiety to promote its own trade with Japan, which had begun, in 1609, on the western island of Hirado. The

---

[1] Quoted in Boxer, *The Dutch Seaborne Empire*, p. 236.

English had also traded at this port between 1613 and 1623, helped by the strange position of an Englishman, William Adams, as a trusted adviser to the Shogun. Adams, pilot on a Dutch vessel which had to enter Kyushu because of damage in storms, was induced to help the Japanese build ships embodying western advances. He pointed out to the Shogun that the English and Dutch could give Japan the advantages of foreign trade and western technology without obliging it to accept Jesuit or other Catholic missionaries. The newcomers were accordingly welcomed and, for some years, did a thriving trade in Japan.

Ieyasu (1603–16) was the first of the Tokugawa Shoguns whose long rule gave Japan unprecedented peace and stability. He was anxious to strengthen his government by profits from foreign trade and by making western improvements to Japanese shipbuilding, mining, and weapons. Between 1604 and 1635 an average of ten licences a year was issued for voyages to places as distant as Burma, and both European and Chinese ships came to Japan. Exports comprised silver, copper, iron, sulphur, camphor, lacquerware, and other manufactures, and imports comprised raw silk, high-quality finished silks, cottons, scented woods, dyes, sugar, lead, tin, sharkskin, and deerskin. During this period many Japanese went to the Philippines, Cambodia, and Thailand.

Before long, however, Ieyasu's expansionist policy was drastically reversed. He himself approved a memorial for the expulsion of foreign missionaries and, immediately after his death, Christianity was proscribed. It had made about 300,000 converts, many of whom were now executed, sometimes cruelly, as were Catholic missionaries. The English quit Hirado in 1623 because they found Japanese trade unprofitable, and the Spanish were expelled in 1624, perhaps because they were ill-treating Japanese at Manila. Fourteen years later the Portuguese were expelled because of suspected complicity in a partly Christian rebellion. The Dutch were left as the only European traders in Japan, and they were soon forced to move to a small island in Nagasaki harbour where they were tightly confined. The Chinese also had their trade limited to the single port of Nagasaki.

The Shogunate went much further than confining foreign

traders to a narrow limit. It issued drastic regulations which prohibited Japanese from going abroad or from building ships beyond a size that was too small for ocean voyages. Previously vigorous contacts with other lands were thus abruptly ended and Japan, for more than two centuries, withdrew into a rigid isolationism. The reasons for this change are somewhat puzzling and obscure, but may be best explained by a Ming envoy, Huang Tsung-hsi, who visited Japan in 1646. He mentions fear of Christianity undermining traditional loyalties, upon which the Shogunate rested, and fear of European aggression; but the basic reason, he thought, was the Shogunate's determination to have internal peace, which foreign contacts might well endanger.

Seclusion, of course, could not be absolute. Traditional trade continued with Korea, and Japanese still went to the Ryukyu islands for Chinese goods. These were also brought to Nagasaki, along with other goods, by licenced Dutch or Chinese traders. In 1711 imports at Nagasaki were valued at about 170,000 lb. of silver, exports at 120,000 lb., and hence the deficit at 50,000 lb. This was no great sum, even if the silver output was falling off and domestic needs for currency were rising, and subsequent quotas on silver exports probably indicate isolationist prejudice against any foreign trade. They were set in 1715 at 25,000 lb. of silver for the Chinese and at half this level for the Dutch; later reductions forced these traders to take increasing quantities of dried fish as a new Japanese export, but the Shogunate made no attempt to provide other substitutes for silver.

Soon after the Ming dynasty was toppled, the V.O.C. sent an embassy to the Ch'ing court hoping that the new regime would ease restrictions on Chinese trade. This first European mission to Peking was graciously received but obtained no concession. Six years later (1661) the Dutch lost all their Chinese trade when the Ming loyalist, Cheng Ch'eng-kung (Koxinga), expelled them from Taiwan. He had inherited from his father, a pirate who became a Ming admiral, hatred of the Dutch and command of the fleet based on Amoy. After the Manchu seizure, his father led Ming forces in the south until captured and executed. Cheng continued the struggle on land for twelve years but, on being seriously threatened by Manchu armies, took his fleet to make Taiwan a new base for resistance. It fell after a six months' siege and then received thousands of refugees from Fukien and Kwantung. He and his able successor made the island prosperous by developing agriculture and trade, but a grandson weakly surrendered to a Manchu fleet in 1683. Taiwan was thus made an integral part of the Chinese Empire.

So as long as Taiwan threatened them, and Ming loyalists were active in the south, the Ch'ing had no wish to foster sea trade; for a time, indeed, they forced an evacuation of off-shore islands and ordered coastal dwellers to move ten miles inland. When China was firmly under control, restrictions were lifted. There was steady trade with Taiwan, although this was held back by serious misrule of local officials and exclusion of foreign traders from the island. Tribute missions revived official trade with Korea, the Ryukus, Annam, Thailand, Laos, and Burma, and Chinese merchants went in growing numbers to Manila, the Moluccas, Java, and Malaya. Hundreds of their trading junks, some as large as 1,000 tons, left Amoy or Canton every winter on a western route around the coasts of Indochina to Malaya, or on an eastern route to the Philippines, the Moluccas, or Java. The Ch'ing attempted to regulate this private trade by licensing certain merchant firms as brokers who were held responsible for its conformity to official regulations. There was another group of licensed merchants ('hang' or 'hong') for coastal trade to the north and a third group was later appointed to handle trade with Europeans.

Both Dutch and English were permitted to trade at Amoy, notwithstanding support given to Cheng by the E.I.C. which, for a time, had opened a factory on Taiwan and supplied him with arms. But Amoy was controlled by rapacious Manchu soldiers whose exactions made trade so unprofitable that in 1664 the English went to Canton where the Dutch soon joined them. They depended upon the connivance of local officials until 1685, when the Emperor officially broke Portugal's monopoly by opening his ports to all European traders. The English gained a bigger share of Canton trade than any rival and opened a factory in 1699. There was a rather sporadic trade at other Chinese ports until 1757, when an imperial edict confined all foreign trade to Canton; this limitation was difficult to avoid as the Ch'ing administration could enforce the monopoly of hong merchants over trade with Europeans at Canton.

China's overland trade became subject to European pressure through Russia's expansion across Siberia, an expansion which began when the Grand Dukes of Moscow had united western Russians and led them to victory over the remnants of the Golden Horde. Cossacks, strongly encouraged by merchants interested in furs or skins, pushed so rapidly across thinly peopled forests and marshes that by 1639 they had reached the Pacific coast. They had come far to the north of China's boundaries, but difficulties over food supplies, and a desire for trading contract with the great populations of East Asia, led to a descent from Fort Yakutsk, on the Lena, down the valley of the Amur. A related advance was made from Lake Baikal to the Shilka, the main tributary of the Amur, so that another trading fort was built at Nerchinsk. Further west the Russians had begun to make contact with West Mongols, who were threatening Ch'ing hegemony over East Turkestan and interfering in Tibet.

Two Russian embassies came to China, in 1656 and 1660, seeking, like the Dutch, to open trade relations, but they were refused audience because they did not come as tribute bearers to acknowledge Ch'ing suzerainty. Before long the Emperor decided to breach Chinese tradition by making a treaty with the Tsar and so accept him as an equal, a radical change which was forced by circumstances. Tribes in North Manchuria were appealing for help against the oppression of Russia's Amur forts, and a Tungus tribe had set a dangerous precedent of defecting to the newcomers. When China was sufficiently pacified, the Emperor sent adequate forces to make a systematic advance in the Amur region. The Russians were pushed from the river's lower reaches, and their fortress at Albazin was so strongly beseiged that a Russian ambassador was sent to negotiate a settlement. His cause was helped by a new Chinese anxiety over Dzungaria, where the West Mongols had defeated tribes allied to China; but negotiations were difficult and could not have succeeded without the diplomatic skill of two Jesuit priests in the Emperor's service. The Treaty of Nerchinsk (1689) secured withdrawal from the Amur and a favourable delimitation of the North Manchurian boundary, in return for which the Emperor had to agree to regular trade relations. The remainder of the vast common frontier was not delimited until the Treaty of Kiakhta (1727) which excluded the Russians from Mongolia but gave them further trading rights at the border town of Mai-mai-ch'eng opposite Kiakhta and near Lake Baikal. There the Chinese established a similar type of control to that used for foreign trade at Canton.

This border trade became more important than the caravan trade to Peking sanctioned by the Treaty of Nerchinsk. It allowed three caravans a year, each limited to 200 persons. The Russians brought furs or gold and took back mainly 'brick' tea, for which they had acquired the taste from West Mongols, and became even greater tea-drinkers than the English. Up to 1730 only twenty such caravan–missions arrived in Peking and, over the following century, only six. At Mai-mai-ch'eng, however, regular trading continued until 1860, and was supplemented, as Russia advanced into West Turkestan, by other trade with the Tarim towns of Sinkiang.

Further stimulus to overland trade was given by the extension of Ch'ing rule over Central Asia. Inner Mongolia had been subdued before the Manchus conquered China, and was carefully governed by a Superintendency of Dependencies which had resident agents in key spots. After the conquest they restored Chinese control, lost by the later Ming, over the Tarim basin. This control was later threatened by the Khan of Dzungaria who had built up an independent power strong enough to dominate the Tarim and threaten the East Mongols. K'ang-hsi (1662–1722), third and greatest of the Ch'ing emperors, personally led a force which, equipped with artillery supplied by the Portuguese, destroyed the Khan's power in 1696. Outer Mongolia and the East Tarim then came under the Superintendency but the Dzungars, aided by Tibetans, gave further trouble in the west. A final settlement was not made until 1757 when the Dzungars were almost exterminated and their territory, the Ili region, was put under a military governor who commanded strong garrisons.

Tibet, meanwhile, had also become a Chinese protectorate. The rise of its Yellow Sect of Lamaism led to a struggle for power with the established Red Sect, and spread Lamaism so widely over Mongolia as to involve its tribesmen in Tibetan politics. Mongol support enabled the head of the Yellow Sect, the Dalai Lama, to obtain theocratic power in 1642, but when he was killed by other intervening Mongols, his successor helped the Dzungars who invaded Tibet and sacked Lhasa. Three years later (1720) Ch'ing troops expelled the Dzungars, installed a new Dalai Lama and made the eastern part of the country a Chinese prefecture; another violent civil war led to further control through two imperial residents, but internal troubles did not cease until 1750, when the Ch'ing established a full protectorate. This gave better security to the old, physically difficult trade routes from Khotan to Kashmir and from Lanchow or Chengtu to Lhasa, from which two southern routes led to Khatmandu in Nepal or through Bhutan to Darjeeling. Tea became so important a drink for the Tibetans, as for the Mongols and other peoples, that the route from Chengtu to Lhasa was called the 'tea road'. But little of this overland supply reached India which, before it could grow its own crop, received tea by ships leaving Canton.

The Manchus had much difficulty in imposing, and preserving, their rule over China. Although Peking fell easily enough in 1644, and Ming resistance was quickly crushed in Nanking, Fukien, and Amoy, Prince Kuei kept up resistance in the south. He was defeated by Wu San-kuei, a Ming general who had helped the Manchus and been rewarded with the governorship of Szechwan and Yunnan, but in 1674 Wu San-kuei himself attempted a national revolt, backed by the governors of Fukien and Canton. They were all beaten, and Yunnan was finally subdued in 1681. The naval threat from Taiwan was eliminated in 1683, and the Dzungar threat to Mongolia in 1696. During the lengthy conquest, and after it, the Manchus were acutely conscious of being a small minority in a vast subject population, and took extraordinary measures to preserve their national identity, including a ban on trading by Manchus and the maintenance of separate Manchu forces or military controls.

For the rest, they interfered with the proven system of Chinese administration only to the extent of having Manchus share top posts with Confucianist mandarins in order to have effective supervision. As they had to rely heavily upon Chinese officials for imperial administration, and almost wholly for local administration, care was taken to conciliate the scholar–gentry and to disturb neither them nor ordinary Chinese by radical innovations. This conservative tendency, which became even stronger as the Manchus were assimilated to Chinese thought and life, made for strong and increasing resistance to contacts with foreign powers.

K'ang-hsi was a great enough ruler to be open-minded about such contacts. This was shown by his sensible accommodation with the Russians, and by his opening of Chinese ports to European ships or to Chinese ventures in South-east Asia. It was also shown by his intelligent use of the Jesuits who had come to Peking before the fall of the Ming. Led by Ricci, these remarkable men mastered Chinese language and classics to become influential members of the Court and, by skilful adjustment of Christian doctrines to Chinese philosophy, made some converts. To Europe they gave information about the Celestial Empire which inspired a widespread eighteenth-century enthusiasm for Chinese art, culture, and civilization. To China they gave valuable help in astronomy, mapping, medicine, gun-founding, and diplomacy. K'ang-hsi made them trusted advisers and rewarded their work for the Treaty of Nerchinsk by granting permission to preach their faith throughout his empire. They seem to have made about 300,000 converts, but conversions were soon checked by the 'Rites Controversy'; Dominicans and Franciscans who had reached Fukien from Manila disagreed with Jesuit accommodations of Christianity to Chinese institutions and, in particular, to toleration of the rite of ancestor veneration as a 'civil' practice. The controversy lasted a century and was matched by increasing Confucian opposition to Christianity. When the dispute was referred to Rome, K'ang-shi wrote a letter supporting the Jesuits' interpretation of Chinese philosophy and, when the Papal Legate contradicted him, ordered all missionaries to accept the Jesuit position or else leave China. The Pope, however, issued a bull against the Jesuit position, and K'ang-hsi was disturbed, as well as affronted, that a foreign power should claim a superior loyalty from Chinese Christians. The Jesuits were kept in their official positions at Peking, but conversion was discouraged and a semi-persecution of Christians began. This was stimulated by another Papal bull which strictly forbade Christians to practise Chinese rites. Under the next Emperor Christians were driven from some provinces, and Lord Macartney was told in 1798 that their total number had fallen to 150,000. The Catholic effort failed in China as in Japan.

Both countries, after an initial interest in European contacts, sought to limit them. Japan's policy of seclusion was the more thorough-going but China also became increasingly concerned with its own political stability and largely self-contained prosperity. For a time, both achieved much in regard to isolation. The Tokugawa shoguns succeeded in imposing centralized government over traditional feudalism and in giving Japan a strong national unity for more than two centuries. Central power was based upon the Shogun's personal domain, which was seven times larger than that of any daimyo, included the more important towns or mines and was supported by the estates of collateral Tokugawa families. It financed a large army and a central administration which comprised, beside officials to administer the Shogun's domain, censors to supervise the daimyos, commissioners to control monasteries and cities, and 'junior elders' to supervise craftsmen, public works, and the greater castles. The daimyos were responsible for local government in their own domains, but were required to adapt this to the Shogun's laws and were strictly supervised. They had to send hostages to Yedo and were themselves required to spend every second year at the capital so that, at any time, one-half of them were at the Shogun's mercy. At Yedo, moreover, they had expensive ceremonial obligations and were encouraged in a conspicuously competitive consumption which severely diminished their resources for subversive activity. Social classes were made more rigid, a Bushido code of heroic loyalty was developed for warriors, and neo-Confucianism was fostered in order to promote conservative loyalty among the upper classes.

No radical economic change could be expected under this system, especially as Japan was isolated from foreign contacts. Nevertheless, peace and national unification were associated with a remarkable expansion of agriculture, industry, and trade which led to a big increase of population and greater prosperity for both agriculturists and townsmen. Economic growth depended basically on agriculture and, during the seventeenth century, the cultivated area was almost doubled while the rice crop increased from 18 million *koku* to 25 million. As a *koku* (almost 5 bushels) represents the average annual consumption of one person, there was a corresponding growth of population and, in fact, the census of 1721 recorded 26 million people.

15

Irrigation works helped expansion of the cultivated area, especially in the great Kanto Plain, and important advances in husbandry raised yields by widely extending double cropping. Fields were given better winter drainage and treadmills were used for raising water from ditches at other times. Better fertilizers were provided by night-soil, dried fish, and oil cakes. Improved ploughs made for deeper tilling, and mechanical devices assisted threshing and other farm operations. Better seeds played a role in raising rice yields, and so in allowing land to be used for other crops. There was a rapid growth of cotton, mulberry trees for silk-worms, indigo, tobacco, oil seeds, and fruits as farming changed from a subsistence towards a commercial basis, and most peasants came to have a life of some comfort in spite of heavy taxes or feudal obligations.

Rural growth was more than matched by urban growth. Yedo, by the end of the eighteenth century, had a population of 500,000, and the next largest cities had populations ranging from 63,000 to 400,000. Some castle towns developed into trading centres and many villages into small country towns. They all participated in a growing trade in farm products which was dominated by large wholesale merchants and helped by a thriving class of exchange brokers or money-lenders. Sea transport had to be improved to cope with bulky farm products and some merchants became wealthy shipowners. The chief impetus to highway development was the great procession of daimyos to compulsory residence in Yedo, and many posting stations or hotels sprang up to cater for them. Manufacturing played a lesser part in promoting urban growth, but benefited it. There were big advances in weaving silks and cottons, and notable improvements to both the quantity and quality of porcelain and paper.

Trade was associated with further and rapid monetization of the economy. Special monopolies issued gold, silver, and copper coins in such quantities that even agricultural taxes were being paid in money. Daimyos often issued paper money which circulated locally, but commercial credit was more important; pawnshops and loan associations flourished, and commercial notes or money orders came into use for large transactions. Some money exchangers developed into considerable bankers, accepting deposits and making loans, usually at 12 per cent a year. Their main clients were daimyos, who were spending lavishly at Yedo and whose revenues were hit by monetization and inflation. As the Court and the Shogunate were also clients, many family firms, such as the Mitsui, acquired a powerful position through business interests which spread into wholesaling, manufacturing, shipping, and banking.

China, too, had a remarkable economic growth within the limits of traditional methods of production. Official censuses showed an increase of population from 64 millions in 1578 to over 143 millions in 1741 and to 432 millions in 1851. Serious defects in the censuses prevent their figures from being trustworthy but there is no doubt that Ch'ing peace and order led to a very considerable increase of population and assisted this increase by repairs or extensions to public works, especially irrigation, by promoting cultivation of new land, especially in the south or south-west, and by spreading new food crops. Some extension of cultivation proved short-sighted as it involved cutting down forests on mountainous country; later erosion damaged agriculture on the plains as well as on the hillsides. New crops, however, gave permanent and substantial benefits. Most had been introduced previously, but in Ch'ing times their cultivation greatly increased. Earlier ripening varieties of rice from Vietnam further reduced the growing period so that double cropping became common and other crops could be grown between rice harvests. Cultivation of sorghum and maize increased and, in South China, the sweet potato, which grows in sandy soil, became the main food of poor people. The ordinary potato was introduced, about 1650, from Taiwan, and the custard apple, pineapple, cayenne pepper, and cinchona also reached China at this time.

A less fortunate development was the spread of the opium poppy. It had been known in China for some centuries but most supplies had come from India and been used medicinally. Piracy and Ming restriction of foreign trade led, in the seventeenth century, to a substantial Chinese production reinforced by imports through Macao. Early in the eighteenth century the practice of smoking opium spread from Java to China, and great areas of land in Yunnan and Kweichow were put under opium cultivation. The practice spread so rapidly and deleteriously that in 1729 an imperial decree banned the sale or smoking of opium. European merchants, however, continued to exploit the new demand, so helpful to their chronic problem of foreign exchange, even after 1800 when imports of opium were also banned.

China's internal trade and handicraft production would have at least matched the very considerable growth of population and agriculture. Silk- and cotton-weaving were basically farm handicrafts which expanded with the rural population and the prosperous cities of the Empire. The Ch'ing followed the Ming in upholding traditional culture, and the scholar–gentry who cherished it, so that all the arts flourished. Great scholarly enterprises, together with the rise of novels, made considerable demands upon the printing and paper trades. Large demands for ceramics were swollen by such eager European buying that special porcelains or pottery were made for western markets.

The major export commodities, of course, were silk and tea. Europe had long been able to manufacture silk and could obtain supplies from Iran and India, but its demands were growing rapidly, raw material was always short because of difficulties in producing cocoons, and the Chinese still had superiority in the finer silks, notably in crêpes. Tea did not come into wide European demand until the second half of the seventeenth century but, during the next century, developed into a more important Chinese export than silk. By 1770 English ships were taking about 2,600,000 lb. of tea from Canton and other European ships about 3,000,000 lb.; by 1800 the total had risen to 20,000,000 lb.

If the trade which the Ch'ing limited to Canton was never more than of marginal significance to the almost self-contained Celestial Empire, it helped acquisition of silver for an increasing monetization of the Chinese economy, and wiped out the old overland trade with Europe. It has been estimated, in regard to monetization, that China obtained, up to 1830, 100 million Mexican dollars' worth of silver from Manila traders, about the same amount through the Dutch trade with Nagasaki, and perhaps 70 million worth from the two East India Companies at Canton. Sea-traffic from this port, moreover, reduced Silk Road traffic to short-distance caravans for Tibet, Siberia, and Central Asia; European travellers and merchants, except a few

Russians, now all came by ship. Canton trade became important to Europe, and especially to England. By the close of the eighteenth century tea comprised no less than one-half of the E.I.C.'s total sales of Indian or Chinese wares, and opium, mostly sold at Canton, provided 5 to 10 per cent of its Indian revenues.

4. *Indochina's relative immunity*

The kingdoms of Burma and Thailand were more powerful than those of Indonesia, could not be conquered by naval force alone, and had fewer products of interest to European traders. Neither Portugal nor Spain secured any important or durable advantages in Indochina although it was not entirely beyond the scope of their political, religious, or commercial interests. Within five years of taking Malacca the Portuguese sent envoys to Ayuthia, the Thai capital which then held the Tenasserim ports, and so established trade with Mergui, Patani, and Tenasserim as well as with Ayuthia. These were useful to the Portuguese both as sources of benzoin or lac and as halting places for ships which needed shelter from the winter monsoon on their voyages to China; Anderson reported, in 1528, that there were 300 Portuguese at Patani alone.

In Burma, Portuguese adventurers took a part in the warfare by which Toungoo kings overthrew Shan Ava to gain control of the whole country. Tabinshwehti and Bayinnaung were far too strong for the Portuguese to be more than auxiliaries, but the revolt of 1599 against Nandabayin, following his defeat by the resurgent Thai, gave the Portuguese a chance. De Brito seized the port of Syriam, with Mon help, made foreign trade pass through it, and tried to extend Portuguese control over Lower Burma. He was defeated and impaled, in 1613, by Nandabayin's grandson, Anaukpetlun, who reconquered Burma for the Toungoo dynasty. The Portuguese then helped the Thai in a successful defence of Tenasserim so that, five years later, the Dutch and English were allowed factories at Ava and Syriam; the Dutch were also allowed a factory at Pegu and the English one at Bhamo. Before long the Dutch ousted the Portuguese who could retaliate only by piratical attacks upon Indonesian shipping from bases in the Ganges delta, and until such freebooting was ended by the annexation of Chittagong to the Mughal Empire in 1666.

Spain attempted to make Cambodia a protectorate, and was even less successful. Satha I (1576–94) had to continue his predecessor's struggle against Thailand and, when Malacca refused help, appealed to Manila. Two Spanish adventurers were sent and arrived just before the Thai captured Lovek, forcing Satha to find sanctuary in Laos. Manila then dispatched a small expedition but, owing to bad weather, only one ship reached Cambodia. Its men went to the capital and attempted negotiations with the usurper who had succeeded Satha. After an attack upon their camp they sacked the palace, killed the usurper, and returned to their ships. Two of their leaders disembarked at Faifo, in Vietnam, went to Laos where they found Satha's grandson, and helped him to regain Cambodia's throne. They were trying to persuade him to make Cambodia a Spanish protectorate when insurgents massacred both them and the king. In 1603 the Thai, by placing Satha's brother on the throne as a vassal, made Cambodia their protectorate instead. Twenty years later the Dutch were allowed to open a factory at Phnom Penh and traded there until 1643; in that year Indonesian traders persuaded the king to close it down so that, during the next two centuries, Cambodia remained almost exempt from European influence.

Thailand had again become strong through Naresuen's expulsion of the Burmans and reunification of the kingdom. His brother and successor, Ekathotsarot (1605–10), more interested in finance and trade, began a lasting policy of promoting commercial and diplomatic relations with foreign powers. The major aim was revenue, which came from a new royal monopoly over imports and exports as well as from new taxes on shipping and markets. Ramadhibodi had made a treaty with Portugal in 1516 and Naresuen one with Spain in 1598, but Ekathotsarot turned much more energetically towards the Netherlands (to which he sent an embassy in 1608), England, and Japan. At his invitation the V.O.C., which had already opened a factory at Patani (1602), and the E.I.C. both opened factories at Ayuthia. Thailand attracted Europeans partly because of its direct exports of tin, lead, ivory, saltpetre, sappanwood, and areca but more because its ports, especially Patani, were frequented by Indian, Chinese, and Japanese traders from whom more valuable Asian products could be obtained; Patani soon had 400–500 European residents.

Indian or Chinese trade with Thailand went back a long way but Japanese trade was quite recent. Christian converts escaping from Hideyoshi's persecution, or soldiers who had lost employment through Ieyasu's pacification, came to Thailand as well as to other places in South-east Asia. Some became palace guards under their own captain, Yamada Nagamasa, whom Ekathotsarot made a royal confidant. Others became merchants residing in their own quarter of Ayuthia, and Ieyasu himself became interested in direct trade between the two countries, as Thailand could supply hides, tin, and, through the Europeans, fire-arms and gunpowder. Ekathotsarot responded so well to this overture that Japanese junks soon came in large numbers to Thai ports. Relations were disturbed at the beginning of the next reign when, owing to the execution of a minister who had been their patron, the Japanese attacked Ayuthia and went off to fortify a new settlement at Petchaburi. King Songtham (1610–28) suppressed this revolt, and a simultaneous Laotian advance, but came to terms with the Japanese who quickly regained their former position in Ayuthia.

The Europeans quarrelled, not with their host, but with one another. Their conflicts at Bantam and in the Moluccas spread to Ayuthia, where they became exacerbated by a Dutch agreement with the King for purchasing hides (1617) and by Coen's destruction of Jourdain's ships at Patani (1619). The E.I.C., in 1622, closed its factories at Ayuthia and Patani, for thirty-seven years, and the V.O.C. soon did the same, although it reopened the Ayuthia factory about 1629. Both companies appear to have overestimated the trade which could be obtained in competition against Indian, Chinese, and Japanese merchants, or to have underestimated the costs of dealing through Thai officials.

The Japanese withdrew for very different reasons. They had been supporters of Prasat Thong (1630–56) but turned against him when he murdered Songtham's young successor and took the throne for himself. Prasat Thong then had Yamada Nagamasa poisoned and tried to have the Japanese massacred. Most of them escaped by putting to sea, and did not return if only because of the new Tokugawa policy of seclusion. Their withdrawal gave a further advantage to the Dutch who helped and flattered the usurper in order to gain new privileges at Ayuthia. Various crises arose, however. A dispute in 1649 over V.O.C. claims led to the threat of calling in a Dutch fleet, and that to a siege of the factory; another crisis, five years later, was resolved by an actual Dutch naval demonstration.

Prasat Thong needed Dutch support against the revived Toungoo dynasty and rebellious subjects, and became more dependent upon it. Ekathotsarot had lost the Shan states to Burma, and Songtham lost both Martaban and Chiengmai while Cambodia repudiated Thai suzerainty. Prasat Thong had trouble with Patani, whose queen refused to recognize his usurpation, but a reconciliation was effected through Dutch mediation. He also succeeded in restoring suzerainty over Cambodia, without fighting, and kept up the struggle with Burma for Chiengmai. It was not retaken, however, until the reign of Narai (1657–88) who had first to defeat a Burmese invasion of Central Thailand through the Three Pagodas Pass (in 1622). His success came as a result of the confusion caused in Upper Burma by Ming loyalists. Yung-li, last of the Ming, had fled before Manchu forces to Bhamo where his followers were disarmed and he was taken to Sagaing. Other loyalists then came to attempt his rescue in such numbers that, for three years, they ravaged Upper Burma down to Pagan. The raids ceased only when the Governor of Yunnan marched into Burma to secure Yung-li's surrender in 1662.

These events and the long period of stagnation which followed them led to Dutch withdrawal from Burma. The English had left in 1657 as a result of the First Anglo-Dutch War which swept their ships from the Bay of Bengal. Nevertheless, the Dutch had been disappointed by their factories in Burma, owing to Indian competition, and might have closed them but for a fear that the English would take their place. All trade stopped during the Ming raids, but the Dutch became anxious to have a factory at Bhamo when it began to receive large Chinese caravans after the Ch'ing had pacified Yunnan. The Burmese Court, now controlled by a small group of cautious traditionalists, refused permission and obstructed foreign trade in other ways. In 1679, the V.O.C., deciding that operations in Burma were not likely to become worth while, closed its factories. The

E.I.C. was then tempted to revive trade with Burma but dropped the idea when the Court of Ava refused to consider any export except saltpetre or lead. English merchants, however, received licences from the Company for trade with Syriam so that an active trade developed between this port and Madras.

During the long and remarkable reign of King Narai, Thailand became more than ever the focus, and arena, of European interests in Indochina. He tried to reduce dependence upon the Dutch by attracting English traders and by favouring those French priests or diplomats who now came to Thailand, as well as to India, seeking for their country a major role in Asia. The French newcomers were to prove far stronger challengers to the Dutch because the E.I.C. was never able to give Narai much help. He invited it back to Ayuthia after the English factory at Lovek, re-opened in 1654, was abandoned because of the disturbances that followed Vietnamese intervention to change the Cambodian succession. The V.O.C. reacted to its rival's return by demanding new privileges and blockading the Menam River until Narai reluctantly gave the Dutch a full monopoly of the trade in hides and a virtual monopoly of Thai trade with China. This blow to the E.I.C. was accompanied by such mismanagement of its affairs at Ayuthia that the factory's business passed to interloping merchants who defied the Company's royal monopoly of English trade with Asia.

The first French arrivals in Thailand were priests of the Foreign Mission Society which had been formed, backed by Louis XIV, to carry out religious work in China or Vietnam, independently of Jesuit, Portuguese, or Spanish activity. They had intended to reach China via Bhamo but, hearing of the troubles with Ming loyalists in Upper Burma, came to Ayuthia for passages to Vietnam. News that Vietnamese were persecuting Christians, and Narai's encouragement, induced them to make Ayuthia their headquarters. Before long they were sending back enthusiastic reports which aroused so much interest at the French Court that Jesuits, Navy, and French East India Company all began co-operating with a view to bringing Thailand under French control. One of these reports gave a vivid description of Ayuthia at the peak of its entrepôt trading:

I stood frequently in admiration of the strong great city, seated upon an island round which flowed a river three times the size of the Seine.

There rode ships from France, England, Holland, China, and Japan, while innumerable boats and gilded barges rowed by sixty men plied to and fro. No less extraordinary were the camps or villages outside the walls inhabited by the different nations who came trading there, with all the wooden houses standing on posts over the water, the bulls, cows, and pigs on dry land. The streets, stretching out of sight, are alleys of clear running water. Under the great green trees and in the little houses crowd the people. Beyond these camps of the nations are the wide rice fields. The horizon is tall trees, above which are visible the sparkling towers and pyramids of the pagodas. I do not know whether I have conveyed to you the impression of a beautiful view, but certainly I myself have never seen a lovelier.[1]

The French design received extraordinary help from a for-mer employee of the E.I.C. who rose to a high position in Narai's service. The Company had been persuaded to re-open its Ayuthia factory by grants of monopoly for tin at both ends of of the portage route from Chaiya to Puket, and by other pro-mises. In 1678 it sent Richard Burnaby from Bantam to restore order in the Ayuthia business and he took with him Constant Phaulkon, an able Greek who had just left the Company's ser-vice to venture on his own account. At Ayuthia they met George White, an interloper operating from Madras, where he had been Phaulkon's patron. Burnaby persuaded White to join him in putting the Company's affairs into a condition that would benefit their own private trade. They decided that Phaulkon, who had mastered Thai in addition to other languages, should become a royal interpreter. Within four years of securing this appointment he was made Narai's Superintendent of Foreign Trade, and soon procured Burnaby the Governorship of Mer-gui. George White had returned home but his brother, Samuel, who was a captain in one of Narai's ships trading between Mer-gui and Masulipatam, became *shahbandar* (harbour-master) of Mergui. The Ayuthia factory was then handed over to a man who quarrelled with Phaulkon, and did so badly that it was again closed in 1684 after an agent from Surat had failed to secure an annual trading contract. He had made the dual mis-take of insulting Phaulkon and of demanding an end to the interloping, even piratical, activities of Burnaby and White.

Their activities did not appear illegal to Phaulkon or Narai.

[1] Quoted in Collis, *Siamese White*, p. 47.

After Thailand regained the Tenasserim ports from Burma, Moslems developed a considerable trade between these ports and Coromandel as the Thai were not themselves seafarers and, if the V.O.C. dominated the Gulf of Siam, it had little influence in the Bay of Bengal. The Moslems found that Indian goods brought over the difficult land route from Tennaserim to Ayuthia could compete there with those brought by Dutch ships from Coromandel. They found, too, that Ayuthia could supply Chinese and Japanese wares in addition to Thai products. Narai had gained so much from the Moslems' trade that he appointed them to governorships of Mergui and other towns along the overland route. At Madras the E.I.C. gained from the other end of this trade, although its servants made private profits from arrangements with interlopers, such as George White, whose trade was tolerated because it did not exceed 'coastal' limits.

Phaulkon sought to reduce Moslem influence, and to make even bigger royal profits from trade with India, by obtaining ships for Narai's service and putting them under English officers. When Samuel White was made *shahbandar* he became responsible for building ships at Mergui, staffing them, collecting taxes, and acting as the King's commercial agent. It is hard to agree that he, or others sailing under the Thai flag, were interlopers, but there is more substance in the associated charge of piracy. White was authorized to take action against Moslem interference or to make reprisals for losses inflicted by the Moslem Governor of Masulipatam, provided his men did not provoke the E.I.C. He quickly exceeded these instructions by making such attacks on Indian shipping that the trade of Madras suffered. The Company then secured a proclamation by James II forbidding English subjects to serve in ships of Asian rulers, and sent two men-of-war to Mergui in order to enforce the proclamation and to recover a claim against Narai for damages. White and his men gave in but, during a lavish feast, Thai forces killed English troops ashore and sank one of the warships. The remainder of the English made off; White returned to London with a fortune exceeding £30,000 but the E.I.C. never collected its claim for £65,000 damages, and gave up hope of trading in Thailand.

Meanwhile the French had made strong headway at Ayuthia.

Bishop Pallu returned there with a letter from Louis XIV to open relations between the two courts and Phaulkon, deciding to throw in his lot with the French, became a convert to Roman Catholicism. A large Thai embassy was sent to Versailles on a French ship which, unfortunately, was lost, but a later embassy had a brilliant reception. Louis sent a return embassy under de Chaumont, who made a secret agreement with Phaulkon for Jesuits to receive strategic positions in the Thai government. A more open agreement was drafted for French garrisons and trading concessions, so that the Dutch decided to close their own factory. In 1687 French warships brought six hundred troops as well as a number of Jesuits and commercial agents. Phaulkon helped them to occupy Mergui and Bangkok, but, at this critical juncture, Narai fell mortally ill. His regent had Phaulkon tortured and killed, gathered a large force against the French at Bangkok and, after succeeding to the throne as Pra Phetraja (1688–1703), forced the departure of the French garrisons. Remaining missionaries and traders were then badly persecuted until Desfarges, by a temporary seizure of the island of Puket, secured them better treatment.

So ended, disastrously, a bold attempt at French control over Thailand. The V.O.C. returned to Ayuthia under a new commercial agreement which restored concessions for exclusive purchases of hides and tin. These were its chief source of profit in trading with Thailand and were mainly sent, along with sappanwood, to Japan. But the Dutch position was weaker than before owing to greater suspicion of Europeans and less interest in the royal monopoly of foreign trade. Tin output fell off because of rapacious Chinese governors in the Isthmus areas, Mergui was closed to the Dutch, as to other Europeans, and from there to Puket the coast became so infested with pirates as to make normal trade impossible. Ayuthia was disturbed in 1690 by a revolt from Nakhon Nayok and Lopburi, followed by other revolts at Korat and Ligor, and trade was not helped by the depraved tyrant who succeeded Pra Phetraja. The next king had trouble with Laos and Cambodia, but gave Thailand good government, marked by beneficial works of irrigation. His successor, Boromokot (1733–58), is said to have had a 'golden reign', notable for patronage of Buddhism, new religious links with Ceylon, and good relations with Burma. Within three years of his death, however, Thailand was invaded by Alaungpaya, founder of a new Burmese dynasty. Ayuthia, the city which had once attracted hundreds of foreign merchants, was to be completely destroyed.

The same fate overtook Syriam, the Burmese port which was something of a magnet for European traders. After the V.O.C. withdrew from it in 1679, the E.I.C. at Madras had issued licences to European residents for voyages to Syriam, but responded only partly to pressure from the Ava Court for a reopening of the English factory. At first it appointed a private merchant to control other English merchants and shipwrights at Syriam, and then in 1720 established a Residency which was awarded to a private contractor. The French East India Company made similar arrangements because of a growing interest in teak for shipbuilding. Things did not go well at the English shipyard so that the E.I.C. decided to close it, just before the great Mon revolt of 1740 overthrew the Toungoo dynasty. During the struggle Burmese and Mon forces burnt all European installations at Syriam.

By this time Toungoo power had become weak through palace intrigues and dispersion of authority to feudal lords. It controlled, indeed, little beyond the river area between Syriam and Pegu, which had shrunk to a mere fraction of its former size and was now surrounded by jungle instead of prosperous villages. The Mon thus gained control over Lower Burma, but their victory was very brief. Alaungpaya (1752–60) led the Burmans in a nationalist revival which enabled him to conquer and reunify the whole country under a new Konbaung Dynasty (1752–1885). Ava was quickly recaptured and, by 1758, Lower Burma was completely subdued. The Mons sought help from the French and English. The E.I.C. decided it would be best to cultivate good relations with Alaungpaya but Dupleix, at Pondicherry, had ambitions of bringing Lower Burma under French control. De Bruno, his agent at Pegu, was soon directing Mon forces. Alarmed by such intervention, the English seized Negrais, a malaria-ridden island, and obtained from Alaungpaya both recognition of this settlement and permission for another at Bassein in return for military stores. When Alaungpaya took Syriam and Pegu in 1756, he had de Bruno slowly roasted to death and, by trickery, obtained possession of French ships that had been sent to help defend Syriam. His demands on the E.I.C. became so heavy that, now the French had been ousted, it prepared to leave Negrais and Bassein. Before the last men had been evacuated, Alaungpaya, suspicious that the English had helped a Mon attack, ordered their massacre.

By 1760, therefore, the Dutch, English, and French had all quit Burma. In Thailand and Cambodia only the Dutch remained; their position in Thailand was not strong and in Cambodia was insignificant. Laos, which had already been visited by a few Europeans, was much too remote and poor to attract their commercial interest. Nor had the Europeans achieved any real success in Vietnam.

Portugal had opened trade with Faifo, the main southern port which supplied Macao with raw silk, eaglewood, and sugar in return for porcelain and tea. Soon after their expulsion from Japan, Jesuits, often assuming the role of traders, came to open missions in Tongking and Annam, where they were later joined by competing French missionaries sent from Ayuthia. Portuguese trade was furthered to some extent by the long struggle (1620–73) between the Trinh, who took over the Court of Le, and the Nguyen, who were carving out an independent southern kingdom below the Song Gianh River. The Nguyen, seeking Dutch as well as Portuguese help, invited the V.O.C. to establish trade and it opened a factory near Faifo. Difficulties arose with the Nguyen when further Dutch factories were opened in Tongking, Hien-nam, and Ke-cho, all in Trinh territory, so that the factory at Faifo had to be closed in 1654. The English, after fruitless attempts at trading with Vietnam, also opened a factory at Hien-nam in 1672. Trinh indifference made trade so difficult that this factory was closed in 1697, and its Dutch competitor three years later. During the century of peace that followed their long war, Trinh and Nguyen ordered their kingdoms without European support and free from European influence; commercial relations, accordingly, dwindled to a sporadic trade with Macao, mainly for arms.

5. *Indonesian disintegration*

This extremely limited impact of Europeans upon East Asia or Indochina was strikingly different from their increasing domination of both Indonesia and India. If, by the end of the seventeenth century, the Dutch had been driven from Taiwan, confined to a narrow trade with Japan, and ceased trading with Indochina, except at Ayuthia, they gained political as well as commercial mastery of Indonesia. Initial suzerainty over Ternate and its many small dependencies had been quickly followed by Coen's annexation of the Banda Islands and founding of Batavia. His immediate successors had ensured control over Javanese, as well as Moluccan, waters by capturing Malacca and Ceylon. Between 1650 and 1680 the remaining major states, Acheh, Bantam, Mataram, and Macassar, were broken to give the V.O.C. control over the whole of Indonesia during a century of complete trading monopoly.

Acheh and Macassar crumbled almost simultaneously. After its defeat by forces of Portuguese Malacca, Johore, and Patani, Acheh had managed to keep firm control over the pepper trade of West Sumatra and the tin trade of Perak in Malaya. Tin interested the Dutch because of its importance for trade with India and China so that, when they took Malacca, attempts were made to secure monopolies at the Malayan tin centres. Thailand granted such monopolies at Kedah, Puket, and Bangeri, although the agreement with Kedah could not be enforced. Pressure was put upon Perak until, in 1650, the Queen of Acheh agreed to share her monopoly of its tin equally with the V.O.C., and to exclude other traders. This arrangement so damaged Perak's trade with India that attacks were made upon the Company both at Perak and Surat. A blockade of Acheh and Perak secured a new agreement, more favourable to the Company but damaging to Acheh's influence in Malaya. The Dutch took advantage of Acheh's decline by pushing further into the Sumatran pepper areas. They obliged the Sultans of Jambi and Palembang to grant monopolies for pepper-trading at eastern ports, and then penetrated Acheh's subordinate western ports, three of which granted similar monopolies to the V.O.C. in 1663, and put themselves under its protection. Forcible diplomacy thus gained the Dutch control over both coasts of Sumatra as well as a strong position in the Malayan tin trade.

Macassar, at the other extremity of the Archipelago, fell to the Dutch in 1667. This Moslem kingdom had been a major loophole in the Company's spice trade because it received

cloves, mace, and nutmegs smuggled from Amboina and the
Bandas and because it welcomed Chinese, Portuguese, English,
and Danish traders. Yet the Company long shrank from the
expense of an expedition strong enough to capture the well-
fortified town and, for a time, tried to protect its monopoly by
forcibly restricting production of cloves to Amboina and that of
nutmeg and mace to the Bandas. The rigour of this policy
caused great hardship, and so revolts. These were brutally put
down but were not completely suppressed until 1656 when the
Sultan of Ternate was made a pensioner and his people were
forced to plant rice or sago instead of cloves, and to buy additional rice from the Company at prices which completed their
impoverishment. Many took to piracy or kept up smuggling.
In 1660 the Dutch, by taking one of Macassar's forts, exacted
from the Sultan a promise that he would halt all trade with the
Spice Islands and expel the Portuguese. When it became
obvious that the promise meant nothing, the Company decided
to crush him. Speelman led twenty-one ships to the Spice
Islands and collected Indonesian recruits from Amboina and
Boni, whose people sought revenge from Macassar; further
recruits were gained at Ternate, after Speelman defeated its
rival, Tidore, which the Spanish had left in 1663 because
Manila was threatened by Chinese pirates. It took the Dutch
four months to reduce Macassar, and longer than that to enforce
the treaty which was signed in November 1667. The V.O.C. got
rid of the Sultan, took possession of his capital and all its trade,
put South Celebes under a Dutch governor, and ceded the
eastern and northern coasts to Ternate. Other Europeans were
now firmly excluded from East Indonesia, and all its princes
were dependent on the Company.

Mataram and Bantam, in Java, both lost their independence
soon afterwards. Batavia had defeated a strong attack by the
Sultan of Mataram in 1629, but did not make a formal peace
until seventeen years later. This treaty recognized the Sultan's
overlordship by stipulating that the V.O.C. should send an
annual embassy to his court, bearing gifts and such merchandise
as he had ordered, assist him against enemies, and allow his subjects to trade freely throughout Indonesia from Malacca to
Macassar. The annual gifts cost the Company about 60,000
guilders but secured for Batavia protection, a practical mono-

poly of trade, and needed supplies of rice and wood. Peaceful relations continued until a rebellion broke out in Mataram during 1674. Sultan Amangkurat, because of his completely personal rule and his check to the Islamization of Java, had made enemies who rallied round the dissident Prince of Madura and were joined by exiles from Macassar. Bantam decided that this was an opportune time for attacking Mataram's western provinces, and so for encircling Batavia whose trading monopoly it was already challenging. The Company did not act quickly enough to prevent the defeat of Amangkurat, who died while making his escape, but its forces then put down the rebels and placed Amangkurat's son on the throne. Mataram thus became a vassal state, completely dependent on the Company, which acquired trading monopolies over all important products.

Bantam was overtaken by the same fate. It, too, had attacked Batavia in the early days, and continued giving hospitality to English traders or other rivals of the Dutch. Little trouble occurred, however, until Sultan Agung came to the throne determined to restore Bantam's previous commercial strength. Hostilities broke out in 1656 and were ended, three years later, by a Dutch blockade. Agung then enlisted the help of English, French, and Danish merchants for building ships and sailing them to Macao, Manila, Bengal, and Iran. He also attracted so many Indian, Arab, and Chinese merchants after the Dutch had driven them from Malacca or Macassar that Bantam began to challenge Batavia as a port, and to demand a share of Amboina's spices or of Malaya's tin. Agung's agents intrigued with Ternate and sought alliances with Turkey and England; his soldiers attacked Dutch posts in Sumatra and, during Mataram's civil war, plundered the coast east of Batavia. But Agung's plans were ruined by his eldest son who, resenting the investiture of a brother as heir-apparent, organized a revolt and intrigued with the Dutch; they helped him, soon after Mataram had been pacified, to depose his father but obliged him to give them a complete monopoly of Bantam's foreign trade. The E.I.C., already forced out of Macassar, had now, like other European rivals of the Dutch, to leave Bantam; it went, for a last foothold in Indonesia, to the small port of Bencoolen on Sumatra's south-west coast.

Bantam's prosperity crumbled rapidly. It had rather poor
16

land and backward farmers so that nobles had depended upon trade. When all trading profit passed to the V.O.C. they were impoverished and lost interest in pepper production. The Sultan tried to augment his own diminished revenues by admitting Chinese, who became internal traders or tax-farmers over agricultural districts. These changes made for discontent so that the Sultan, and his successors, had to rely upon the V.O.C. to support their authority. A new treaty, in 1731, gave the right to build more forts which strengthened control over Bantam's trade. The Company also tightened control over Mataram by intervening in a succession dispute which involved refugees from other islands. When the campaign was over it deported thousands of Balinese, Madurese, and Macassars, gained a complete monopoly of Mataram's foreign trade, and took possession of a large part of Central Java as well as the eastern half of Madura. A later succession dispute enabled it, in 1743, to add all of Mataram's north coast and the remainder of Madura, thus bringing almost the whole of Java under Dutch rule.

Native trade and shipping declined with the power of Indonesian princes who, from primitive times, had led their people in trade or piracy as well as war. Moslem penetration might have ended long-distance voyaging by Indonesians but had stimulated their exports and helped their trading organization; some port–states, at least in Java, were founded by Moslems and many Indonesian harbours had Moslem *shahbandars*. Chinese merchants were also active at such ports as Bantam, Jambi, Palembang, and Grise, where they took over the intermediate trade in pepper and often married into higher-class Indonesian families. Local rulers made arrangements with Moslem and Chinese merchants for promoting their own trade or shipping but, except at Malacca, nobles or private Indonesian merchants took little part in foreign trade. Some Asian ships carried small-bulk luxury wares to Malacca, or to such collecting points as Bantam for pepper and Macassar for spices. Their activities are reflected in a pre-European maritime code[1] which shows that captain and crew (unless slaves) were partners in the enterprise; they received no wages but were allowed to trade on their own account after completing transactions for the owner and waiting for passenger–merchants to complete their

[1] Meilink-Roelofsz, *Asian Trade and European Influence*, pp. 46–49.

business. Most native ships, however, were engaged in carrying rice, jungle products, cheap textiles, or other bulky goods across Indonesian waters.

The Portuguese, realizing that their own interests depended upon a flourishing coastal trade, had made no attempt to suppress Indonesian shipping. The Dutch, on the other hand, ruined it. In the Molucca Sea they suppressed both foreign and native trade, and so damaged the shipping of the Spice Islands, especially when clove production was limited to Amboina and nutmeg production to the Bandas. Javanese shipping was damaged to the extent that it had brought food or clothing to the Spice Islands, and was further damaged by the decline of a similar trade with Malacca after its capture by the Dutch. Malaccan, as well as Javanese, shipping was hit by the Dutch monopolies at the tin and pepper centres, reinforced by a pass system for native ships voyaging in Indonesian waters. Ships with passports were supposed to have safe conduct, but they were so murderously attacked by the free burghers of Batavia that even Coen expressed shame. Later monopolies over the foreign trade of Mataram and Bantam completed the ruin of native merchant shipping. Speelman, writing in 1677, remarked that 'the eastern Javanese of Mataram, besides their great ignorance at sea, were now completely lacking in vessels of their own, even for necessary use'.[1] Bantam, which had made a strong effort to develop its own shipping against Dutch pressures, lost nearly all of it on becoming the Company's vassal.

The only scope for Indonesian sailors was now their ancient practice of piracy which in the eighteenth century spread over the whole Archipelago from the Sulu Islands to Timor and from New Guinea to Malaya. Most pirates came from the north-east where the former busy ports of Macassar, Ternate, and Tidore were empty of trade and stricken by poverty. The Buginese of Boni took the lead in preying upon the coasts of Java, Sumatra, and Malaya, where they overran Johore and threatened Malacca. From Tobelo, in Halmahera, other freebooters raided as far south as Timor. But the most fearsome pirates of all were Moros of the Sulu Islands, beyond the sphere of Dutch control; their fleets, often comprising more than a hundred heavily armed galleys, would attack even Dutch cruisers, and they

[1] Boxer, *The Dutch Seaborne Empire*, p. 196.

established a pirate base on the Sumatran side of the Sunda Strait.

This base helped attacks upon ships coming to Batavia on the roaring forties route which the Dutch had pioneered soon after their arrival in Indonesia. The success of the northern pirates must, indeed, be partly explained by a growing weakness of Dutch shipping. In Europe it suffered badly from participation in the War of the Spanish Succession (1701–15) and from the subsequent poverty of the States-General, which could no longer maintain a first-class fleet. Fewer ships were built and to a standard that lagged seriously behind innovations adopted in English or French yards. Private financiers, moreover, were investing in foreign funds rather than in overseas trade, and working men were more reluctant to become sailors. Between 1640 and 1743, therefore, the number of Dutch Indiamen in Asian waters declined from eighty-five to forty-eight, and without any marked increase in average size.

This decline also reflects the decay of Indonesian trade which began almost as soon as the V.O.C. reached the zenith of its power. The spice monopoly was a disappointment, expensive to maintain but hard to make profitable. There had been early difficulties because of narrow and inelastic European markets for cloves and nutmeg and, when the demand increased after 1656, the supply could not match it as the extirpation policy had been all too successful in discouraging native producers. By the end of the eighteenth century both the clove and the nutmeg had been smuggled from Macassar to India which could supply enough to make prices unprofitable for the expensively maintained Dutch control over the Moluccas. Pepper was never completely monopolized but it had formed about two-thirds of the V.O.C.'s exports to Europe; increasing competition from Malabar and the E.I.C. substantially reduced this proportion in the eighteenth century. The Company had the monopoly of European trade with Japan, but its trade was much smaller than that of Chinese merchants, and the English took the lead in trade at Canton where they could obtain Japanese as well as Chinese goods; after 1700 the V.O.C. did not find its Japanese trade very profitable. Exports of Indian textiles and other wares to Indonesia shrank through the impoverishment of its people by monopoly restrictions and the V.O.C.'s short-sighted policy of buying cheap and selling dear; as one of Coen's opponents had warned, 'There is no profit at all in an empty sea, empty countries and dead people.'[1]

The Company had obviously to find other sources of revenue. It was paying dividends of 20 to 40 per cent but had debts of 12,000,000 guilders and was obliged to ask the States-General for help in fighting wars. Its new monopoly over Ceylon's cinnamon might have helped, but costs of acquisition and maintenance were so high that the Company never broke even on the operation. Growing European demands for Chinese tea and Indian textiles did help, but the Company, far from monopolizing them, was outstripped by its English competitor. Tea became the V.O.C.'s largest single import to Europe but, like textiles, involved a new drain of bullion; this rose from 2,400,000 guilders in 1690 to about 8,000,000 guilders in the 1720s. The problem was intensified by the later popularity of coffee, as Mocha, then the only source, set a high price.

Zwaardekroon, who was Governor-General of Indonesia from 1718 to 1725, attempted to improve the Company's difficult position by introducing new products into Java. He had some success in improving the processing of indigo, developing cotton-growing, and planting sappan-wood, but his greatest achievement was the introduction of coffee. Java proved so suitable for this crop that by 1720 it was producing 50 tons and, within another twelve years, over 6,000 tons. This was too much for the Directors, who lacked the capital or inclination for large-scale exports and became uneasy about the new prosperity of Javanese district rulers. They ordered a reduction of the buying price from 50 guilders per *picul* (122 lb.) to 12 guilders, a reduction which proved so effective that the Company soon had difficulty in obtaining the limited supplies which it sought. It made coffee a monopoly article, set the annual requirement at nearly 1,800 tons and obliged district rulers in West Java to deliver set quantities at 12½ guilders per *picul* or else render such quantities as tribute. A Commissary of Native Affairs was set up to administer this system of forced cultivation which, in 1760, was extended to make obligatory yearly plantings of a specified number of trees. Any benefit that this new crop might have conferred upon the Javanese was limited by exactions of feudal

[1] Quoted in Meilink-Roelofsz, *Asian Trade and European Influence*, p. 232.

leaders on peasant labour and by growing indebtedness of these
rulers to the Company in respect of advance payments; by the
end of the century the interest on their debts exceeded payment
for the current crop. For the Company, however, coffee shipments in the latter half of the eighteenth century provided a substantial compensation for dwindling profits on other Asian trade.

There could be no offsetting the dwindling efficiency of Batavia
as an operational centre for a complex trading system. Here, in
a castle whose walls enclosed a space of less than 5 acres, resided
the Governor-General, members of his Council, a central garrison of about 1,200 men, the Company's factors, and a few
hundred clerks, all overworked and underpaid, as were another
few hundred craftsmen who trained or supervised slaves in the
Company's workshops and shipyard. Beyond the Castle's walls
a few thousand 'free burghers' lived in Dutch-style houses so
attractively set along tree-lined canals that an English sailor
described Batavia as 'one of the neatest and most beautiful
cities' in the world.[1] In spite of appearances it was far from
being a Dutch city as Europeans were swamped by about
10,000 Chinese and 20,000 Indonesians, all living in separate
areas under their own leaders. The Chinese were a particularly
important as well as sizeable element, dominating most of the
crafts, money-lending, and commerce left open by the Company.
Nor was the small minority of free burghers a solid core of Dutch
life. Few migrants came from the Netherlands, other than lower-
class and often dissolute women seeking well-off husbands, so
that free burghers were former employees of the Company who
had accumulated enough money, by infringing its regulations,
to set up as independent craftsmen, traders, money-lenders, or
tavern keepers. They usually took native wives, concubines, or
slaves and their children grew up more as Asians than as Europeans; Portuguese and Malay, not Dutch, were the daily languages of Batavia.

Officials at the Castle controlled extensive and difficult trading operations. They dispatched ships to Japan, China, the
Spice Islands, Sumatra, Malaya, Ceylon, India, and Iran in
such a way as to make the best of market conditions and mini-
mize needs for bullion. The cargoes brought back were carefully
assembled in the Castle's warehouses both for later Asian voy-

[1] Quoted in Vlekke, *Nusantara: A History of Indonesia*, p. 186.

ages and for homeward-bound Indiamen which left Batavia in December and February to sail through the Sunda Strait on their way to round Cape Horn. Outward-bound Indiamen left the Netherlands in September, December, or April and also came through the Sunda Strait; September sailings were particularly important because their European cargo reached Batavia in time for transhipment to the Persian Gulf, Bengal, or Japan at the onset of the south-west monsoon. But this cargo was a mere 4 per cent of the total cost of an outward voyage, less than the supplies brought for the consumption of the Company's servants and much less than the bullion which, always much needed, had to be sent in increasing quantities as European demands grew for tea and cottons.

The Company was obviously dependent upon the skill and honesty of distant agents but failed to pay them adequately or to supervise them effectively. In the second half of the seventeenth century, a clerk received, at most, 24 guilders a month and a senior merchant or captain only four times that sum, no more than a preacher. These men, moreover, were sent to a place of endemic malaria which, they believed, could be warded off by heavy drinking, smoking, and avoiding exposure to fresh air. Many died within a few months of arrival, and none had anything like a normal expectation of life. This became strikingly evident when the plague of 1732 took a frightful toll, and so raised the subsequent death rate that Captain Cook, who visited Batavia in 1770, wrote: 'Death means nothing here.'[1] There were other dangers, too. Hostile natives were always a threat, but even the Chinese, whom Coen had thought pacific, caused a bad crisis. Their excessive immigration led to unemployment, and this to banditry outside Batavia's walls. The Governor thus decided, in 1740, to deport all unemployed Chinese and, when they forcibly resisted, ordered a search of their compatriots for arms. During this search mobs and troops slaughtered thousands of Chinese in the city's streets. Chinese rebels then roamed over the countryside attacking various Dutch posts, sometimes with Indonesian help, and almost captured an important port at Semarang.

Men exposed themselves to such dangers or privations only if they could make fortunes by swindling the Company or evading

[1] Quoted in Vlekke, op. cit., p. 212.

its many restrictions. Most joined in a fairly open game of extortion, fraud, smuggling, or illicit private trading—directors, merchants, captains, preachers, clerks, sailors, free burghers, and Chinese merchants. Everyone knew that the Company's agent in Japan, for example, could supplement his official income by 30,000 guilders, and one agent was actually deported by Japanese authorities for contraband trading at Nagasaki. At the same time, the chief of the Hugli factory was scandalously dismissed, with a number of subordinates, for embezzlement and private trading. High officials frequently returned to the Netherlands with private fortunes much exceeding their salaries, and some published memoirs explaining their methods. Occasionally the Company took stern action; in 1722 the Governor-General executed twenty-six offenders at Batavia, and in 1731 the Directors recalled the Governor-General, together with three members of his Council, for complicity in smuggling. But the general attitude was one of tolerance or hopelessness. The Company's Advocate, Pieter van Dam, wrote that, whenever the Directors considered the remedy of higher salaries, they always decided that this 'would not lessen the covetousness of their servants nor induce them to do their bounden duty any better'.[1] Later opponents of the Company read its initials as meaning Vergaan Onder Corruptie—Collapsed Through Corruption.

The shock of the Chinese troubles led to the appointment of Governor-General van Imhoff (1743–50), a vigorous but rather impractical reformer. He tried to improve the Company's marine, and persuaded the Directors to open Java's internal trade to free burghers as well as all direct trade between Batavia and Indonesian or Indian ports, but smuggling had gone too far for this liberalization to be effective. Nor was his attempt to open a direct connection between Batavia and Mexico successful. In the political field, he involved the Company in twenty-three years of costly warfare by backing wrong claimants to the thrones of both Mataram and Bantam. His only real success was promoting cultivation by sale of waste lands to Dutch peasants, whom he induced to migrate, and by improvement to coffee deliveries. When the warfare ended, later governors built roads which did much more for deliveries of coffee and also sugar,

---

[1] Quoted in Boxer, *The Dutch Seaborne Empire*, p. 203.

an old Javanese crop for which exports were now increasing.

Nothing, however, could stop the Company's financial decay. It had done well so long as it was only a commercial enterprise and able to control its servants; dividends of 20 to 40 per cent were paid and the general balance sheet of 1700 showed an accumulated surplus of Fl. 21,000,000. But, as it became a territorial power in Indonesia and Ceylon, heavy military expenses more than absorbed trading profits which were progressively eroded by English competition, Dutch corruption, Indonesian poverty, and Moro piracy. After 1724 dividends could be maintained only by borrowing so that, by 1789, the V.O.C.'s debt reached Fl. 74,000,000. Difficulties became acute as the eighteenth century closed. Soon after Java had been subdued the Company had to pay an indemnity of £100,000, exacted by Clive in Bengal, and became involved in military operations against Kandy in Ceylon. The Anglo-Dutch War of 1780–4 was disastrous because it cost the Company ships, trade, and, at the Peace, its Indonesian monopoly; British ships could now trade freely at all the V.O.C.'s ports. Seven years after this war the Company's debt was Fl. 96,000,000 and it had exhausted its credit. Unable to raise a further badly needed loan, it appealed to the States-General. Before a special commission could do much to restore the Company's affairs, the Netherlands was invaded and made a French protectorate. British forces accordingly occupied the Cape of Good Hope and the E.I.C. took over Dutch posts in India, Ceylon, West Sumatra, Malacca, and the Banda Islands.

6. *The collapse of Mughal India*

The E.I.C. had overtaken the trade of its Dutch rival somewhat earlier; by 1780 its exports to Asia reached £909,000 as against Dutch exports of £640,000. It, too, changed from a commercial enterprise to a territorial power ruling many millions of Asians and so overstrained its resources as to require state assistance. But the E.I.C. survived these strains and gained a much more important prize than Indonesia, as control of India gave it a land revenue of £4,000,000 and exports of at least the same value. This achievement was more difficult than the conquest of Indonesia's small, divided kingdoms. The Mughal Empire had been a great one, yet within a century of Aurangzeb's extension of this Empire to its widest limits, a British Governor-General ruled the whole sub-continent, directly or indirectly, while the descendant of the Great Mughals was confined to empty state in the Red Fort at Delhi.

There was no sign of Mughal weakness during Akbar's reign and his immediate successors were very able men. Jahangir (1605–27) defeated Mewar and Ahmadnagar, checked the Portuguese, received the first English ambassador without giving him much satisfaction, and ruled firmly for twenty years. Shah Jahan (1628–58) was still more successful and a considerable patron of the arts, best remembered for noble buildings in the Indo-Persian style, and especially for the Taj Mahal which commemorates a beloved wife. He annexed Ahmadnagar and made Golkonda and Bijapur tributaries, putting them all under Aurangzeb, his son, as Viceroy of the Deccan. But Shah Jahan's reign saw the first, ultimately fatal, weakening of that tolerant partnership with the Hindus which was the cornerstone of Akbar's rule; he ordered widespread destruction of Hindu temples as well as a persecution of Christians. Nor was his viceroy-son able to wrest, as ordered, Kandahar from Iran, and Balkh was lost to the Uzbeks. There was also trouble in the Deccan owing to the resurgence of Bijapur and the raids of Sivaji, leader of the Marathas, who were gaining independence in the north-west of Bijapur.

Aurangzeb (1659–1707) came to the throne by imprisoning his father and destroying his brothers, but was an austere, devout Moslem who proved as good a ruler as more extravagant predecessors. Early in his reign, Assam was subdued, piratical Portuguese were cleared from the Brahmaputra delta and Chittagong was annexed. It took him until 1687 to subjugate the Deccan and, although he captured Sivaji's successor, he failed to crush the warlike Marathas. Aurangzeb was too shrewd to persecute the Hindus, as some allege, but he displayed intolerance and helped to alienate them by treating the Empire as an Islamic state. This policy made for conservative rather than progressive rule and the Empire was to lose vigour through the drying-up of a stream of adventurers from Central Asia or Iran who had helped Akbar's administration.

During a brief reign Bahadur Shah (1707–12), who had also

to fight his way to the throne, kept the Empire intact. His biggest task was to subdue the fierce Sikhs of the Punjab, originally a pious Hindu sect but welded by successive leaders into a militant anti-Moslem power. Thanks to a civil war among the Marathas he was able to hold them off, and to check a Rajput rebellion at Jodhpur. It was only after Bahadur Shah's death that the Mughal Empire visibly declined as weaker men succeeded to an increasingly hard-pressed throne.

Some pressures were to come from the European companies trading in India but in Aurangzeb's day they appeared to be weak, partly because of their own rivalries. Cromwell's treaty of 1654 had damaged Portugal by opening its settlements to the free trade of English merchants. The E.I.C. was in no position to attempt monopolization of trade at Surat, Bombay, or Madras and was co-operating, to some extent, with the Portuguese against the Dutch, who had become dominant on the Malabar coast after taking Cochin and Cannanor in 1663. All three were interested in Bengal but Aurangzeb had expelled Portuguese pirates from the Brahmaputra delta and the English from Bengal when they attempted to take Chittagong in a foolish reprisal against the Grand Mughal. He also besieged the English factory at Surat until the E.I.C. made a humiliating submission in 1690, and paid a large compensation. It did not return to Bengal until six years later when Fort William was built at Calcutta. The Danish East India Company had a small settlement at Tranquebar (1620), and the French East India Company one at Pondicherry (1673), as well as posts at Surat and Bengal. But the fiasco in Thailand affected French enterprise in India until Dupleix reanimated it with large imperial vision a century later.

Distintegration of the Mughal Empire began with the succession disputes which followed Bahadur Shah's death. Officers in the Deccan, Oudh, and Bengal soon became independent and the Afghans made new depredations by seizing a tract north of the Ganges. The Marathas, under fresh leadership, became 'land Vikings'. They swept through Gujarat, Malwa, and Bundelkhand to attack Delhi before turning south to invade the Deccan and force the cession of Malwa; before long they advanced their power to Orissa, and far to the south. Delhi had only a brief respite before a devastating attack made by Nadir

Shah (1736–47), the Turk who had become master of Iran. In 1739 he advanced through Ghazni, Kabul, and Lahore to defeat a Mughal army at Karnal; thousands more were slain in Delhi before Nadir Shah departed with an enormous loot which included Shah Jahan's famous peacock throne. By annexing all territory north of the Indus he cut off India from Afghanistan which, after his death, came under a chief named Ahmad Shah Durrani. He, too, descended upon the Punjab and subjected Delhi to another massacre and pillage in 1757 before retiring to Afghanistan. But, when the Marathas moved into the Punjab, Ahmad Shah returned to re-occupy it and crushingly defeated the Marathas at the third battle of Panipat where they are said to have lost 300,000 men. The Mughal Empire now lay within the Shah's grasp, but his troops mutinied, as had those of Alexander 2,000 years before, demanding immediate return to Afghanistan. Mughal power had collapsed and, as neither Marathas or Afghans could take it over, North India, during the next four decades, was exposed to struggles between various adventurers; Sikhs in the Punjab, various Maratha chiefs across Central India from Gujarat to Orissa and from Delhi to the Godvari River, the Nizam, descendant of the last Mughal Governor of the Deccan, and Hindu rulers in the petty kingdoms of the far south.

One of these kingdoms was responsible for ousting the Dutch from Malabar trade which, after taking Cochin, they had attempted to monopolize in the Portuguese manner by exclusive treaties with rulers and by a naval patrol of the coast. Travancore, between 1731 and 1763, gained control of territory from Cape Comorin to Cranganore, and organized a complete state monopoly over pepper and other products so as to finance the building of strong forts along the coast or across the northern boundary. Producers had to deliver pepper, tobacco, cassia, and areca nuts to state warehouses at prices fixed by royal proclamation, and the goods were sold at much higher prices to wholesale or retail merchants, including the European companies. So tight was the control that it was said district officers would note the loss of a single bunch of pepper, even if it were blown from the vine during the night,[1] and so successful was the policy that, between 1722 and 1754, the price of pepper doubled at

[1] Das Gupta, *Malabar in Asian Trade*, p. 50.

Calicut. The Dutch, finding that their procurements at the lower treaty prices suffered through diversion of supplies to Coromandel, clashed with Travancore forces and were beaten. The E.I.C., with great reluctance, had to accept an end of its own trade with private merchants and buy from Travancore officials at fixed prices. The V.O.C. tried to continue buying at lower prices and in 1753 reached an agreement to receive at least 75 tons at half the market price, in return for supporting Travancore's territorial expansion. By 1758 this had absorbed Cochin, and Dutch procurements fell off at the very head-quarters of their Malabar Council. They tried to get deliveries of pepper on agreed terms but failed as Travancore diverted supplies to more profitable Coromandel ports, exempt from the Dutch blockade. Travancore later defied this blockade by developing Allepey as a new Malabar port and obliging the Dutch to exempt royal trade from Cochin's control. The Dutch port then declined so rapidly that in 1793 the V.O.C. gave up all trading on the Malabar coast.

Long before this Dutch departure the E.I.C. had emerged as the greatest European trader in India, with a briskly rising commerce organized from separate Presidencies of Bombay, Fort St. George in Madras, and Fort William in Calcutta. The French, however, after reorganizing Pondicherry and subordinate factories at Chandernagar in Bengal, Masulipatum in Coromandel, and Calicut in Malabar, became strong competitors. Between 1720 and 1740 their trade increased ten-fold to reach almost half the English total of £880,000. During the War of the Austrian succession (1740–8) and the later Seven Years' War (1756–63) France and England projected their hostilities into the power vacuum of India, with results which were fatal to its independence. Not much happened during the first of these wars; Madras was captured in 1746, Pondicherry was unsuccessfully attacked two years later, and the peace treaty restored Madras to England. But Dupleix, as Governor of Pondicherry, conceived the ambitious idea of using his own diplomatic skill and excellent French artillery to gain his country a South Indian Empire.

The opportunity came through two disputants for the Nizam's throne. Skilful intervention in complex circumstances enabled Dupleix to install his own man and make him dependent on the

French. The only obstacles then to French control over South India were the British in Madras and their ally, Muhammad Aly, in Trichinopoly. French forces were moving against him when Clive, by taking and holding Arcot, made a diversion which enabled allies to reach Muhammad Aly. Dupleix was repulsed but continued the struggle until 1754 when he was recalled, and his successor made peace. The French resumed the attack during the Seven Years' War and, despite initial successes, were finally swept out of Pondicherry itself. Although they re-covered it through the peace treaty, they were never again a significant influence on Indian affairs.

The English faced another crisis in Bengal where they had developed a large trade in cottons, silks, sugar, and saltpetre, and had made Calcutta a city of about 400,000 people. Bengal's Mughal governor was a practically independent nawab through the collapse of central power, and relations between him and the E.I.C. were never good. His son, Sira-ud-daulah was even more suspicious of the English and, when they began to fortify their settlement against the French, drove out the Company's men. Clive was sent from Madras with an expedition which recaptured Calcutta. Seeing a chance to emulate Dupleix's policy of territorial control, he defeated the Nawab at the Battle of Plassey (1760) and replaced him by an elderly general who fully confirmed the Company's privileges and paid it an indemnity of £1,500,000. This proved beyond the new Nawab's means so that he had to deplete provincial treasuries; he quarrelled with local Hindu officials, and became more dependent upon the English. Clive also eliminated Dutch influence in Bengal by defeating the V.O.C.'s weak attempt at intervention and exacting heavy compensation.

The Calcutta Council now had Bengal at its mercy and, after Clive's departure from India, badly abused this power by plundering native revenues, exempting the personal trade of Company servants from any duties, and using military force to push their trade into the interior. Bengali merchants could not compete and their trade was ruined. The result was conflict with the Nawab, his successor, and forces from Delhi and Oudh. London sent Clive back to restore the situation. He quickly obtained from Delhi an imperial grant of Bengal's and Bihar's revenues, and also secured for the Company control over justice. An attempt was made to stamp out private trading by the Company's servants but, after his final departure, the position became so bad that the Company's revenues dwindled far below the cost of greatly increased expenditures. It might well have suffered a similar fate to the V.O.C. but for Warren Hastings and the Regulating Act of 1774.

Hastings was sent to reform Bengal and, in two and a half years' vigorous administration before the Act was passed, put revenue collection on a sounder basis by setting up a Board of Revenue in Calcutta and replacing native district collectors by English agents. He again abolished private trading by Company servants, and stimulated port trade by reducing most duties to a low and uniform level of 2½ per cent. The Regulating Act confirmed the prohibition of private trading and forbade Company officials to accept presents or bribes. More significantly, it provided for British administration of Bengal through a governor-general and council, to whom Bombay and Madras were also made subject. During his thirteen years' tenure of the governor-generalship, Hastings had to cope with difficult situations, largely caused by insubordinate officials at the other two Presidencies and aggravated by jealous or misguided interference by his own Council or Directors in London. Bombay became involved in a Maratha succession dispute and lost an army before a force, sent from Bengal, completed a brilliant march across Central India; the war dragged on for three years until Hastings could negotiate a peaceful settlement which conceded Salsette and Elephanta to Bombay. The Madras Council's foolish behaviour led to an unlikely coalition between the Marathas, the Nizam, and Haidar Ali, the adventurer who had taken over Mysore. His forces overran the Carnatic strip of the Coromandel coast, defeated two British armies, and threatened Fort St. George. England, because of the American War of Independence, could not send reinforcements, but Hastings did not hesitate to send all possible troops from Bengal. They restored the military situation while his own diplomacy broke up the hostile coalition. Madras was thus able to repulse a French naval attack, after which Hastings annexed Pondicherry and Mahé. The French encouraged Haidar Ali to make another attack, which was also defeated, but his son Tipu continued warring until French aid was withdrawn in 1784.

Although Hastings had shown that the Company's affairs in India could be controlled from Calcutta and that its territories could be defended without help from England against any combination of Indian rulers, he had to face lengthy impeachment on returning to London where there was much anxiety about the Company's activities. Even before the impeachment began Parliament had passed Pitt's India Act (1784); this forbade the Company to interfere in Indian affairs beyond its own territories and set up, for those territories, a clumsy system of double government by which a parliamentary Board of Control supervised the Company's administration. Cornwallis, Hastings's successor, purged, reformed, and developed the administration. Appalled by the corruption which had again developed, he dismissed many offenders and made a rigid separation between revenue or judicial officers and mercantile officers. Men who joined the political branch were paid a good salary but could not trade, thus becoming forerunners of the Indian Civil Service. Believing that Indians were hopelessly corrupt, Cornwallis excluded them from posts paying more than £500 a year, but ensured the rule of law by making all government officers amenable to new civil or criminal courts for acts performed in their official as well as their private capacities.

His most difficult and contentious measure was the 'permanent settlement' of Bengal's land revenue. Roughly speaking, Akbar's revenue had been collected by zamindars, who were his feudal agents with police and magisterial powers over peasants, and collected from them, under the supervision of ganungos, the King's watchdogs. Peasants, like zamindars, had traditional rights and were seldom dispossessed. But there were many types or levels of zamindars with diverse origins and rights, and many types of peasants whose varying rights were also hard to understand or define. The English were further puzzled to know how much the land could be safely taxed, a secret jealously guarded by zamindars and ganungos, now allies, because their own income depended upon it. The zamindars were treated as landlords, paying nine-tenths of fixed revenue assessments to British collectors, and lesser landholders, the taluqdars, paid their assessments to sub-collectors. Peasants were to have security of tenure, so long as they paid proper dues to zamindars, and were to be protected by the courts or by the

British collectors. But few peasants were in a position to defend their often shadowy and complex rights before the courts, and almost all became tenants-at-will of zamindars, to whom they were usually in debt. The first assessments were fixed so high that many zamindars could not avoid becoming debtors of the Company which then auctioned estates and allowed them to pass into the hands of Calcutta speculators. As absentee land-lords were worse than the old zamindars, the peasants became an exploited rural proletariat. On the credit side, Cornwallis gave country districts effective law and order, enforced by a new police system and upheld by British judges sitting with Indian assistants. This security enabled a large margin of waste land to be brought into cultivation, with increase of production and population, but higher rents swelled the income only of zamindars because their assessments were fixed by the permanent settlement.

When Cornwallis left, the reformed E.I.C. was the strongest power in a badly divided India but controlled only a minor fraction of its territory. Within a further amazing half-century it became master of the whole sub-continent, excluding the Punjab, Sind, and Kashmir. In 1784 a force from Madras easily took Ceylon from a demoralized Dutch garrison, and the Nizam of Hyderabad made the first 'subsidiary treaty' by which he gained protection against the Marathas in return for payment of a Company garrison and transfer of control over external affairs to a British resident. In the following year a last war with Tipu led to the annexation of half Mysore, the Carnatic, and half of Oudh, while Bombay absorbed the Mughal port of Surat. The key Maratha state based on Poona was induced to make a subsidiary treaty by Wellesley (1798–1805) who had then to fight other outraged Maratha chiefs. Because of the Napoleonic Wars London ordered a halt to this campaign, and no further British advances were made in India until military strains eased in Europe. Moira (1813–23) was then given a relatively free hand. He began by checking the Gurkas of Nepal and proceeded to exterminate the Pindari robber bands of the Deccan, an operation which involved some fighting with Marathas and breaking their hold over Rajisthan. British armies were completely victorious by 1818, when both Marathas and Rajputs quickly made subsidiary treaties. The United Company

17

of Merchants of England Trading to the East Indies had gained an empire greater than that of the Mauryas, Guptas, or Mughals.

This empire, notwithstanding stimulus to trade and acquisition of territorial revenue, proved most expensive. During the first half of the eighteenth century, when it was still a trader, the Company's exports and imports had doubled to exceed £1,000,000 each a year, so that it paid dividends of 7 to 10 per cent on a capital of £3,200,000 which did not have to be increased, in spite of new loans and gifts to the state amounting to £1,200,000. As it acquired an empire the Company had to increase capital to £6,000,000 and obtain a loan of £1,400,000 from the state, which then began to supervise its activities. Trade again doubled over the second half of the century, and Bengal added a territorial revenue of £4,000,000 a year. But Bengal was the only Presidency to yield a surplus, £2,000,000 in 1808, because Madras and Bombay had heavy deficits; so heavy that, although the Company's total Indian revenue rose from £8,000,000 to £15,500,000, between 1797 and 1805, there was an overall deficit of £2,500,000. Military operations, interest burdens, and shipping losses involved the Company in increasing debt so that, in 1805–6, the state had to pay it £2,000,000 towards the cost of its empire.

There was, of course, a brighter side. By the decade 1801–11 the Company's sales were about £6,000,000 a year and the corresponding costs, inclusive of freight and customs duties, were around £4,000,000, leaving a handsome trading surplus from which the Company paid a constant dividend of 8 per cent on capital. Exports of silver, moreover, had dwindled as a proportion of total exports from three-quarters in the first half of the century to less than one-third, partly because of freight-earnings on inter-Asian trade but also because of growing merchandise exports, especially woollens to Canton which was taking nearly £1,000,000 worth, nine-tenths of its total purchases from the Company. With the proceeds the Company bought mainly tea, which comprised half its sales and, in 1812, gave the state a revenue from duties amounting to £5,000,000, rather more than the Company's own receipts from tea. Cotton piece-goods, the great Indian import, now accounted for only one quarter of the Company's sales, and raw silks from China or Bengal for only one-fifteenth; the remainder was made up of indigo, saltpetre, sugar, coffee, opium, and Chinese pottery.

The Company, however, had lost its practical monopoly of Asian trade with England, and was about to lose its legal monopoly in respect of Indian trade. A major factor in this development was the growth of 'country trade' which came to be associated with 'clandestine trade'. Country trade was inter-Asian trade conducted by private individuals, tolerated by the Company as a useful supplement to its 'official' trade and favoured by its servants as a means to great private wealth. They, like the servants of the V.O.C., had come east in the hope of making fortunes and found that Europeans were no match for Asians in most traditional business activities of the countries into which they had intruded. Yet some acquired personal capital from high salaries, perquisites, or corrupt practices and sought to invest it at Indian rates of interest or profit. Besides lending to the bankers or merchants who became increasingly active around the Company's settlements, they entered into various partnership arrangements based not so much on personal investment as on ability to attract savings from other officials, to obtain European business or to secure advantages from the Company. These arrangements flourished most in the related fields of shipping and marine insurance, from which Indians were soon largely ousted. The reason was not so much the superiority of English ships, as Indians quickly adapted traditional methods of building to make ships resembling the Company's Indiamen and teak was a better material than oak. It was rather that, in order to make these ships effective in dealing with pirates, European officers were needed to direct lascar crews. Captains or mates in the Company's service were well qualified because, in addition to their maritime skill, they had experience of eastern trade through the privilege of private commerce which was their main reward from the Company. Most, however, were reluctant to work for Indians and so either joined European and partly European firms or set up on their own account. As coastal and inter-Asian trade grew, other private shippers or merchants came to India directly from England and Scotland. In all these ways, there grew up European, or partly European, shipping firms and 'agency' houses which, besides conducting their own trade and accepting monies for investment, handled ships, cargoes, warehouses, insurance, and sales on a commission basis.

The country trade's most important branch, in the early eighteenth century, was voyaging between Surat or Bombay and the Persian Gulf or Red Sea. 'At Surat', Grose reported, 'they excel in the art of shipbuilding. If their models were as fine as those of the English, of whom especially they prefer the imitation, there would be no exaggeration in averring that they build incomparably the best ships in the world for duration, and of any size.'[1] Wadia, a Parsee shipbuilder of this port, advised the Company about the dockyard which it established at Bombay in 1754, and was supplied with teak for building cruisers and auxiliary craft. The business was continued by his sons, who employed 1,000 workers, and later descendants took to trade as well as to shipbuilding. Bombay thus acquired an important industry, producing ships of 600 to 1,000 tons, on English models but using Indian craftsmen and materials. They were manned by lascar crews, officered by English seamen, and owned by English or Parsee firms. The Company maintained a Bombay marine (the origin of the present Indian Navy), mainly to protect its own ships from the Marathas' attacks, but also to protect convoys, which included private ships, to Persian or Arabian ports. This branch of trade was extensive and remained largely in Indian hands.

Bombay had another large coasting trade with Goa, Cochin, Calicut, Madras, and Calcutta. The Bengal trade had been particularly lucrative until it was constricted by increasing exports of silk and sugar from Java to Bombay. Bengal then substituted raw cotton in its greatly diminishing exports to Bombay and set out to develop trade with China. Bombay joined in and, by the end of the century, had a bigger trade with South-east Asia and China than with Iran and Arabia. Country ships in the eastern trade would leave Bombay towards the beginning of May loaded with raw cotton, gems, ivory, pepper, sandalwood, and sharks' fins for Canton, and with piece-goods which were exchanged in the Strait of Malacca for pepper, tin, and jungle products. All these cargoes reached Canton late in September, and the ships would return to Bombay with tea, silk, pottery, camphor, sugar-candy, mercury, and teak.

[1] Quoted in Parkinson, *Trade in the Eastern Seas*, p. 327.

After Bengal was annexed by the Company, Calcutta became a more important shipbuilding centre than Bombay. At the end of the century it had twice as many country ships, seventy-seven aggregating 16,327 tons, although they were about 200 tons smaller because of the Hooghly's shallow draft. They were owned by twenty-four British, twenty-one Indian, twelve Armenian, and six Portuguese firms, and most had been built at Calcutta or Pegu. Some were designed for carrying rice to Madras, which was far from self-sufficient in food and had less valuable exports—cardamoms, coir, cotton, cowries, pepper, salt, and timber. By 1789, however, most of Calcutta's country trade was with South-east Asia and China; Lambert estimated that this eastern trade involved £300,000 in piece-goods, silk, fire-arms, salt-petre, and grain, and £500,000 in opium, about three-fifths of which went to Canton and the remainder to Indonesia or Malaya.[1]

Opium, long used in China and Indonesia as a drug, was not smoked until the use of tobacco spread to Asia in the seventeenth century. The demand for opium then began to increase so rapidly that the Company took steps to monopolize the Indian supply and to foster an export trade from Bengal. Goa had developed the first Indian exports of opium from neighbouring Malwa, and the V.O.C. had obtained a yearly supply of about 45 tons from the Ganges area for its Indonesian monopoly. But the Dutch were expelled and the E.I.C. later took steps to obtain the Malwa crop. It fostered opium cultivation in Bengal and the crop became a Company monopoly which provided nearly one-sixth of the province's revenue. But, as China was the major market and the Emperor had forbidden the sale of opium, the Company could not include the drug in official trade with Canton. Instead it sold the processed crop to private merchants, and their exports became so considerable that Calcutta built ships having special compartments for a cargo which, in spite of wrapping in poppy leaves and packing in chests covered with hides, could easily be ruined by heat or damp. Exports doubled in 1799, and doubled again within the next six years.

This opium trade was to have most serious consequences for China and brought the Company into a sharp conflict of interest with private merchants. The country trade had the advantage

[1] Quoted in Furber, *John Company at Work*, pp. 182–3.

over the Company of assembling at Bombay, Calcutta, and Madras some of the Asian products which it alone could legally export to England, and the further advantage of reducing its silver exports as private merchants remitted profits from country trade by purchasing Company bills drawn on Calcutta or London. By the end of the century such bills exceeded £1,000,000 and, in the second half of the century, the Company was able to reduce bullion shipments from three-quarters to a quarter of its total exports. As, moreover, the opium trade grew, private merchants obtained Chinese silver which they sold to the Company for bills on Calcutta, the source of opium, and this silver was used to redress the heavy adverse balance of the Company's China trade. In effect, therefore, it came to finance an increasingly valuable import of tea by selling opium to country merchants who drove a contraband trade at Canton.

But monopoly provokes opposition from private interests. English merchants had early challenged the Company's control over Asian trade and during the Civil War interlopers had a fair run until Cromwell restored the monopoly. There was more trouble as a result of the Glorious Revolution, after which the Company had to pay a heavy price for another exclusive charter and to ask, later, for powers to seize both interlopers and British subjects in the service of foreign rivals. These rivals comprised, in addition to the Dutch, Danes, and French, new companies formed in Flanders, Sweden, and Prussia for trade with Asia. The most notable was the Ostend Company (1718–32) which quickly developed a profitable trade with Bengal and China and fostered smuggling into England. British pressure led to suppression of this company but some of its resources went to the Danish company which, partly because of Denmark's neutrality, was able to make the old settlement at Tranquebar an active centre of contraband trade in India. Towards the end of the century there were also a number of ships from Hamburg, Trieste, Genoa, and Spain trading over various parts of the Indian Ocean.

The most significant advent was that of fast-sailing Baltimore clippers, evolved during the American War of Independence. They came first to the French Mascarenhas Islands off Madagascar, in order to obtain spices or other Asian wares and to attack English shipping. Immediately after the war one of these clippers arrived at Canton and an American consul was promptly installed there to assist a new trade which was to grow very rapidly to rival that of the E.I.C. American clippers naturally wished to use Calcutta on voyages between New England and China, and were encouraged by the British Government which, in 1788, ordered 'most favoured nation' treatment for them. Six years later an Anglo-American treaty was signed allowing American ships to trade in India on payment of moderate duties, provided that Indian purchases were exported only to the United States. Similar privileges were then given to allies or neutrals during the struggle with France.

From these changes there developed what was called 'the Clandestine Trade', described by Joseph Cotton as 'a great commercial arrangement and combination . . . between houses in Copenhagen, or Hamburg, London, Philadelphia and India'.[1] It began as foreign ships reaching Bengal or Madras, instead of using specie, as they were supposed to for purchasing Indian goods, borrowed money from English merchants or officials by tendering bills on Europe. With the proceeds goods were bought in India and China for export to Europe or the United States, sales there enabling bills to be met. The result was a valuable indirect way for country merchants to trade with Europe, as many had vainly demanded, and foreign bills were the more popular in that the Company was limited in regard to the sterling bills which it could sell, and some merchants or officials had reasons for concealing their business. The Company made attempts to check such clandestine trade but devices were found for evading controls. As early as 1783 it was estimated that bills purchased from foreigners amounted to £1,000,000 a year, almost the same figure as for the Company's bills, and, a little later, that British funds were providing three-quarters of foreign trading capital in Asia. During the decade of peace from 1783, most illegal remittances came through the Danish Company or private Danish traders, involving fifty-five voyages and imports of £3,000,000 of Asian goods, two-thirds of which may have been financed by English capital. Revived activity from Ostend accounted for another £1,000,000 to £1,800,000 of illegal remittances from India, and lesser sums through the Portuguese at Goa. Americans were just beginning

[1] Quoted in Parkinson, *Trade in the Eastern Seas*, p. 358.

to participate in the clandestine trade so that not much would have been sent through them, although they soon became the largest transmitters of English funds from India.

Breaches of the Company's monopoly by and through foreigners stimulated demands for its abolition. London merchants pressed for Indian trade to be thrown open to them, while Liverpool and Glasgow urged complete free trade. Merchants in India joined the campaign but soon made demands that the Company's monopoly should be broken only for their benefit and to the exclusion of London, Liverpool, and Glasgow. The Act of 1793, accordingly, made a compromise concession which required the Company to provide a limited amount of space for private cargoes on its ships. Merchants' appetites were whetted by this concession, and they complained about obstruction by the Company or its high freight charges. Wellesley, who favoured Indian shipbuilding and was impressed by forcible arguments of Calcutta's merchant firms, licensed a few local ships to carry exports to London; their fast voyages and quick turnround alarmed the Company as much as their high charges for freight angered its English opponents. Pressures continued to build up until, in 1813, the new *laissez-faire* movement achieved its first triumph with the abolition of the Company's monopoly over Indian trade. If India was acquiring political stability through extension of British rule, it was to be left unshielded against the devastating impact of an industrial revolution which soon gave England an unprecedented ability to compete with India's traditional handicrafts.

CHAPTER FIVE

The passing of traditional trade

1. *The historical constant*[1]

Preceding chapters have described the trading connections which, over almost two millennia, linked the major parts of Asia with one another and, directly or indirectly, with Europe. These connections, notwithstanding many changes over so long a time-span and wide an area, were sufficiently distinctive and durable to be called a traditional system of Asian trade. Its character changed remarkably little from the days when the Han, Kushan, Parthian, and Roman empires safeguarded immense landways for traffic in localized natural products or handicraft wares, when Graeco–Egyptians developed monsoon sailing to India, and when Indians or Indonesians made fairly regular voyages between their own ports and those of South China.

There were, of course, considerable fluctuations in the quantity of such trade, and swings of traffic between the landways and the seaways. When the ancient empires succumbed to nomadic attacks, Asian trade over long distances greatly declined. Land trade then revived as Byzantines, Sassanians, and Guptas restored the roads between Europe and India, and sea trade rapidly grew as Persian and Arab sailors began voyaging over the whole Indian Ocean up to China. Land trade further revived when the Caliphates and the T'ang Empire fully restored the landways, but again suffered when the Sung lost North China to the marauding Chin. Sea trade compensatingly increased as the Sung developed Chinese shipping, and had been earlier helped by the rise of considerable trading empires in Indonesia and Indochina. Jenghiz Khan's amazing conquests led to the fullest development of land traffic, as the Mongol Khanates gave extraordinary security and encouragement to merchants' caravans plying between Lanchow and Baghdad.

[1] Van Leur's term, op. cit., pp. 87–88.

That security withered soon after Kublai's death so that the seaways became increasingly predominant. Ming China acquired a brief hegemony over the routes between China and India, or even further west, but, like the Cholas four centuries earlier, abruptly gave up seafaring. As, moreover, the Cambodian Empire was badly damaged by invading Thai and as the Javanese empire of Majapahit lost trade and power to up-start Malacca, long-distance Asian trade came under Moslem domination, until this was broken by the Portuguese, Dutch, and English.

Long after their intrusion Asian trade remained substantially what it had always been—exchanges between Asian countries themselves conducted by Asian merchants. Trade with Europe, until the late eighteenth century, was comparatively unimportant to Asia. It sought little from Europe beyond precious metals or slaves; some amber, coral, and glass, a few linens or woollens, minor novelties, and, after the fifteenth century, increasing quantities of fire-arms. Indian textiles, Frederick List observed, 'had not only the advantage of cheaper labour and raw material, but also the experience, the skill, and the practice of centuries'.[1] As for the Chinese: what could they need from the West when, as Robert Hart said, they 'have the best food in the world, rice; the best drink, tea; and the best clothing, cotton, silk, fur'?[2] He might well have added 'the best pottery, porcelain'. Both the Portuguese and Dutch quickly found that the Indonesian spices which had drawn them to Asia were to be had only in exchange for cheap Indian cottons which clothed peasants or the Chinese manufactures which nobles valued.

Europe, indeed, had few exports to match the unique gems, aromatics, and spices it sought from Asia nor, until the industrial revolution, could it compete with Asian textiles and other craft wares in quality or cheapness. There was a heavy adverse balance which had to be settled in gold or silver. Pliny's complaint about Rome being drained of bullion for exotic luxuries and women's finery was echoed, sixteen centuries later, by Defoe, who said the E.I.C. 'carried away the treasure of Europe to enrich the heathen'.[3] In these long-prevailing cir-

---

[1] Quoted in Dutt, *The Economic History of India*, vol. i, p. 215.
[2] Quoted in Greenberg, *British Trade and the Opening of China*, p. 5.
[3] Quoted in Heaton, *Economic History of Europe*, p. 321.

cumstances, although Asian trade had a world scope, it was largely confined to Asia. Coen accurately observed that the V.O.C. could make far larger profits from inter-Asian trade than from Asian trade with Europe but, even when the Dutch mastered Indonesian waters, their shipping, according to van Leur's estimates, was no more than one-seventh of the Asian total. Moreland had similarly estimated Portuguese shipping as about one-sixth of the total leaving Indian ports, and, even so, carrying South-east Asian or Chinese products as well as Indian wares. There had been earlier European participation in Asian trade but Alexander's Greek colonies soon melted into West Asian populations, Roman voyages to India declined as nomads attacked imperial frontiers, and the Italians who used Mongol landways were little seen in Asia after the Khanates crumbled.

Asian trade, then, flowed mostly between Asian countries themselves, and had a triply triangular character. The oldest triangle involved India, Iran, and Arabia which were linked by caravan routes across Afghanistan and the Iranian Plateau, or by sea lanes from India's west coast to the Persian Gulf and Red Sea, bringing India such imports as horses, carpets, fruits, and incense in exchange for textiles, gems, and spices. India and China were linked both by land across Central Asia and by sea through South-east Asia. The land triangle had early been important in bringing India and China Bactrian camels, Ferganan horses, Siberian gold and furs, and Khotan jade. But its importance dwindled as the South-east Asian triangle was developed by Moslem shipping. In the great days of the Malacca entrepôt South-east Asia was a major supplier of spices or precious woods and a major vent for Indian cottons or re-exports from Iran and Arabia, as well as for Chinese silks, porcelain, and metal wares. The importance of the South-east Asian triangle is indicated by Moreland's estimate of Indian shipping to South-east Asia and China during Akbar's reign; 24,000 tuns as against 14,000 to the Persian Gulf and the Red Sea.

The traditional character of trade was maintained both by modes of transport and methods of production. So long as goods had to be carried by pack animals or sailing ships, long-distance trade was restricted to wares of high value and small weight or bulk, although there was, as we have seen, a good deal of short-distance trade in cheap or bulky wares such as animals and foodstuffs. The capacity or speed of caravans depended on the condition of roads and bridges and on security against raiders. Facilities and protection were never better than under the Mongol Khanates when, according to Pegolotti, a journey from the Black Sea to China took over four months. It would not have taken much longer under the Han and Roman empires; for Fa-hsien, travelling in the disturbed times of the Chin, was on the road little more than three months between Ch'ang-an and Kashgar, far the more difficult half of the Silk Road. Nor were there great changes in the capacity of ships. The biggest Indian ship Pliny heard of was 75 tons, but the Romans built much larger vessels up to the unwieldy *Syracosia* of 4,200 tons. The biggest British East Indiaman was less than half that size and no bigger than an Indian ship seen by Middleton at Surat in 1616; Cheng Ho's junks were probably a good deal larger. But these were exceptions. The average size of ships in the Indian Ocean during the seventeenth century was about 200 tons, approximately the same size as contemporary Chinese junks which, in all likelihood, had not changed over centuries. Even in the first half of the nineteenth century the average size of European ships entering the ports of British India was not more than 300 tons. Speed also changed little as the opium-carriers of the early nineteenth century took two to three months for the voyage from Calcutta to Canton, not a much shorter time than that taken in the ninth century by Arab ships plying from Malabar to Canton.

The traditional handicrafts of India and China were the twin pillars of Asian trade. Not only did Europe, from Roman times, demand cottons and silks, but these, together with pottery and metal wares (kettles, knives, mirrors, needles, tools, swords, and other weapons), were the chief means of procuring Southeast Asian spices or the minerals, furs, and livestock of Central Asia. It was silk and porcelain which, in the ninth century, drew thousands of Arab or Iranian merchants to Canton, and Indian cottons which attracted them to a peaceful domination over the ports of Gujarat and Malabar. As European demands for spices increased, Islam penetrated Malaya–Indonesia because Moslems had the trade in cottons which were the only satisfactory clothing for ordinary people. Malacca also became the main entrepôt for Chinese silks and porcelain sought by wealthy Asians. Handicrafts, moreover, were transmitted to smaller countries; at various times Ceylon, Burma, Thailand, Cambodia, Java, Korea, and Japan exported some textiles, pottery, bronzeware, copperware, iron or steel products, lacquerware, leather goods, paper products, and jewellery. And such manufactures, both in the major and minor countries, gave rise to considerable trade in raw materials: raw cotton from the Punjab; raw silk from China or, later, Iran and Bengal; dyestuffs such as indigo from Gujarat or sappanwood from Southeast Asia; hides from Central Asia or Indochina; lac from South-east Asia; copper, lead, mercury, and zinc from China, Iran, and Japan; sulphur from Japan; tin from Malaya; ivory from Indochina; gems, gold, and silver from a number of sources.

It would thus be wrong to think of Asian trade as involving only luxuries. They predominated, no doubt, in long-distance trade which catered mainly for the exotic splendour of oriental courts and the associated taste of nobles, officials, or wealthy merchants. Darius, Chandragupta, Justinian, Hsuan Tsung, Harun al-Raschid, Kublai Khan, Jayavarman, Akbar, and K'ang-hsi all kept a magnificent state which dazzled more than their contemporaries, drew merchants' caravans or ships from distant parts, and absorbed the quality products of divers craftsmen in many lands. Such demands extended far beyond fine cottons, carpets, silks, porcelains, and weapons. They included all sorts of gems, precious substances, aromatics, drugs, and spices: carnelians and diamonds from India; chrysoberyls, garnets, and moonstones from Ceylon; ivory, rubies, and sapphires from Indochina; jade and gold from East Turkestan; lapis lazuli from Afghanistan; turquoise from Iran; incense and tortoiseshell from Arabia; ginger and pepper from Malabar; cinnamon from Ceylon; cardamoms, cloves, lignaloes, mace, and nutmeg from Indonesia; camphor from Borneo; sandalwood from Timor; rhubarb from China; and ginseng from Manchuria and Korea. Asian courts also required many elephants and horses for military, administrative, or sporting purposes.

But just as ordinary people needed cheap textiles and simpler types of metal wares or pottery, so they had demands for jewellery, aromatics, drugs, and spices. Indian women have long used gold jewellery as a means of hoarding modest wealth, incense is much used by devotees of Hinduism or Buddhism, and condiments play an important role even in ordinary Asian cooking. Chinese tea, moreover, became a popular beverage not merely among the townsmen of East Asia but among the tribesmen of Mongolia and Tibet. Merchants as well as nobles required horses and elephants which, with oxen and camels, carried goods along the caravan routes or across the portages. Shipbuilders, especially in Iran or Arabia, had considerable demands for teak from India or Burma and for coir from Malabar or Ceylon.

Nor was short-distance trade unimportant and here necessities did come to predominate over luxuries. Some parts of Malaya and Indonesia needed fairly regular imports of rice which would also move, if harvests were deficient, from South India to Ceylon, from Burma to Bengal, or from Vietnam to South China. Short-distance trade included other common foods such as dates, dried fish, fruits, vegetables, and vegetable oils. More exotic foods—candied fruits, honey, sugar, sharks' fins, and wine—went mainly to the wealthy but would not be beyond the occasional reach of more ordinary people.

There can be little doubt, however, that the general benefits conferred by Asian trade were far more indirect than direct. It was through trade that Indian agricultural practices, irrigation, crafts, religion, and culture early spread to South-east Asia, and also through trade that Chinese civilization contributed to the cultural and economic development of Korea, Japan, Manchuria, Mongolia, Tibet, and Indochina. Buddhism swept along the caravan routes of East Asia to enrich Chinese culture and to give it an even stronger appeal in Korea and Japan. Islamic culture, much later, penetrated Malaya and Indonesia through the activities of Moslem traders, far more peacefully than in North and Central India, which were invaded by Turkish converts.

Over the many centuries when peasants were four-fifths of the population the great economic benefit conferred by trade was the spread of useful plants and animals. The Achaemenians introduced rice to Mesopotamia and sesame to Egypt, while enabling India to obtain the almond, grape, and walnut. Their Sassanian successors imported from China the apricot, peach, sugar-cane, and the silk-worm, giving in return the almond, broad bean, chive, coriander, cucumber, date, fig, flax, garden pea, jasmine, lucerne, onion, pomegranate, safflower, saffron, sesame, vine—and backgammon, chess, and polo. In Han days China had obtained from Central Asia camels, donkeys, mules, and those fine horses so loved by the Son of Heaven, Wu-ti. It may also be noticed that Buddhist monks, concerned to have material support for spiritual activity, introduced the pawnshop from India. In the Mongol period China further obtained the carrot, pistachio, and sorghum, and, in the seventeenth or eighteenth century, cayenne pepper, the cinchona tree, custard apple, Irish potato, and, a far more damaging plant, the opium poppy. From the New World European intruders brought maize, the peanut, the pineapple, and the sweet potato, all of which became valuable Asian crops, but also the scourge disease of syphilis. In return they obtained from China such flowers as the azalea, chrysanthemum, peony, primrose or tea-rose, and the sweet orange which the Portuguese took to Brazil.

China's main economic transmissions were sericulture, which spread from Khotan to Iran, Byzantium, and Italy, and a whole range of mechanical techniques and appliances. Needham lists more than twenty-five of these, the most important being the wheelbarrow, breast-strap and collar for draught animals, and the cross-bow, canal lock-gate, chain-pump, draw-loom, cast iron, piston-bellows, rotary fan, gunpowder, the stern-post rudder, the magnetic compass, paper, printing, and porcelain. He remarks that 'Chinese technological inventions poured into Europe in a continuous stream during the first thirteen centuries of the Christian era, just as later the technological current flowed the other way'.[1] Technological contributions from the rest of Asia were meagre; the windmill from Iran and the flume-beamed swape, perhaps also the noria, from India.

One of the more important and durable features of traditional Asian trade was its political character. There were markets and competing merchants, but their activities were allowed to have only peripheral effects upon Asian societies ruled by despots who were concerned to control trade for their own benefit, or to prevent it from disrupting traditional ways of life. Merchants had usually to band together for protection, both along

[1] *Science and Civilization in China*, vol. i, p. 239.

trade routes where marauding was a danger and in foreign towns where their trade depended upon arbitrary dictates and where they were often isolated in assigned quarters.

The Hellenic kings of Greece, Egypt, and Iran were all great merchants, the Ptolemies and the Seleucids, in particular, developing powerful state monopolies over the more important branches of production or trade. The Byzantine Court, similarly, was the greatest business in Constantinople, monopolizing silk production and trade, and engaging in many other concerns down to poultry farming. Sassanian rulers exceeded their Seleucid predecessors in strict control over Iran's trade and organization of state monopolies. The Mauryan kings had at least as tight a control over the economic life of North India, with commissions to regulate industry, trade, foreigners and taxes, and with state mines, textile factories, and workshops making military supplies. Such controls appear to have been eased by the Guptas, and there was certainly much loosening in West Asia under the Caliphates, which brought about a remarkable expansion of mercantile activity over both the caravan routes and the sea lanes. But, as the original austerity and fraternity of Islam became transformed into oriental despotism, merchants had much to fear; the Abbasids arbitrarily plundered their wealthy subjects and, in Mughal India, we may recall Roe's observation that 'the King is every man's heir, which maketh him rich and the country evil builded'.[1]

So it had always been in Imperial China from the days when Han Wu-ti revived the Ch'ing system of government monopolies on minting, salt, iron, and liquor, and instituted state warehouses for holding large stocks of consumable goods in order to promote stability of prices. Throughout most of China's history the merchant was held in low esteem, subjected to official monopolies or licence systems, and dominated by officials whose power to 'squeeze' made capital accumulation precarious. His best hope of security was to become a quasi-official himself as a tax-collector or as head of a guild. There was, it is true, a commercial revolution under the Sung when trade grew spectacularly to break out of old official markets and to create big commercial cities, especially in the ports which had an unpre-

[1] Quoted in Woodruff, *The Men Who Ruled India*, vol. i, p. 35.

11 Batavia (from Valenjin, *Oud en Niew Oost Indien*, 1721-6). *Tropical Museum, Amsterdam.*

cedented increase of foreign shipping and voyaging. But the Ming, after halting Cheng Ho's great voyages, tried to prohibit sea trade and the Manchu emperors, after an initial period of relaxation, confined it to Canton and refused all requests by European embassies for an extension. As for trade with Asians, the Ch'ing tried to keep up the ancient political system of tribute missions from Central and South-east Asia. None came to the Ch'ing Court from Japan because the Tokugawa Shoguns, after an equally spectacular increase of Japan's maritime trade, had imposed even more isolationist restrictions.

Remarkably durable though it had been, and rich in widespread achievements, the traditional trade of Asia was showing signs of decay before the brutal intrusion of European powers. Moslem monopoly of Asian shipping had become more embracing when the Ming officially restricted Chinese junks to home waters. But Moslem political power was badly damaged, in the early sixteenth century, by conflicts of the Ottoman Turks with the Mamluk dynasty (1250–1517) of Egypt, heir of the Caliphate, and with the new Safavid dynasty (1500–1736) of Iran, culminating in the Ottoman conquest of Egypt and Syria. Moslem India, too, had become weak, ripe for conquest by the Mughals. Timur's damaging raid split North India between Afghan Lodis and Hindu Rajputs; the Deccan was divided between five sultanates who fought with one another as well as with the resurgent Hindus of Vijayanagar. Indonesia, after the decline of the Majapahit Empire, had dissolved into small principalities lacking either individual strength or collective interest. In Indochina, the Khmer Empire had been smashed by invading Thai, and Burma, after the Mongols overthrew the Toungoo dynasty, also split into weak states.

No Asian navy, therefore, could block the Portuguese from the Indian Ocean. Such resistance as they initially met came from the ruler of little Calicut, ineffectively supported in 1509 by a fleet from the decaying Sultanate of Egypt. Sulayman the Magnificent (1520–66) tried to reopen the Moslem spice trade from India to Alexandria and the Levant but, as the Ottomans' main military and naval effort had to be put into the Mediterranean, they neglected Egypt and the Red Sea. The Mughals restored Moslem power in India but were little interested in either trade or maritime activity. The fleets of three
18

12 East Indiamen at Calcutta (water-colour by J. Baillie-Fraser from 'Views of Calcutta and its Environments', 1820). *India Office Library.*

comparatively small European powers were thus able to contend with one another, thousands of miles from their homelands, for mastery of the seas of Asia.

Military power lasted longer. Mughal armies conquered the whole Indian peninsula and Ch'ing armies extended Chinese power to its widest limits in Central Asia. The Mughals, however, lost all influence in Central Asia after Nadir Shah's great raid of 1739, which was followed by the independence of Afghanistan. Ch'ing power became threatened by Russia's expansion eastward and, soon after the final subjugation of East Turkestan and Tibet, corruption and demoralization began to undermine both China's armies and its civil service.

More important, perhaps, was an exhaustion of the great impulses which had shaped the various manifestations of Asian civilization, and given them a certain cultural unity. Hindu civilization had decayed in India by the eleventh century when 'the last of the poets had disappeared . . . (and) the great names in science and learning were also a memory of the past'.[1] Moslem civilization, badly shaken by the Mongols, succumbed to the culturally sterile rule of the Ottoman Turks. The Mughals attempted a vigorous blending of Indian with Iranian and Moslem culture, but their 'abortive aristocratic civilization did not penetrate deep enough into the Indian soil to enable it to withstand the storms which tore down the overshadowing imperial umbrella'.[2] The alien Ch'ing, from respect and interest, did succeed in conserving the remarkably durable civilization of China, but made it so rigid that it was unable to adjust to an explosive impact of the new scientific civilization of Western Europe.

2. Agents of change

The first important manifestation of that science in Asia was fire-arms. Gunpowder, of course, was a Chinese invention, and the Sung had checked invading Chin by hurling grenades or bombs from catapults. But cannon were first developed in Europe, as a result of casting large bells for churches, and came into use there during the fourteenth century. They were quickly

[1] Quoted in Dutt, *Later Hindu Civilization*, p. 185.
[2] Quoted in Spear, *A History of India*, vol. ii, p. 70.

taken up by the Turks, who used 19-ton cannon to capture Constantinople, and from whom they spread to the Mongols. China, at any rate, cast its first iron bombard in 1346, and the Ming used many for their assault on Peking. Turks also supplied the cannon which were first used in India by both the Bahmani Kingdom and Vijayanagar during the ferocious reign of Muhammad Shah (1358–73); and when Babur conquered Hindustan his forces included a Turkish battery of artillery. Akbar manufactured cannon at an Imperial Arms Factory where he himself made improvements in casting barrels. Jesuits helped the Ming and the Ch'ing to develop gun-foundries in China, although both dynasties purchased fire-arms from the Portuguese. Iron-casting spread from China to Pegu and Thailand, which supplied most of the 3,000 small pieces of artillery captured by the Portuguese when they took Malacca; but there were a few larger bronze cannon supplied by the Zamorin of Calicut who had been able to start a gun foundry with help from two Portuguese deserters.

Asians had thus learnt to make and use cannon for land warfare before the Portuguese arrived. But they had not learnt how to build ships strong enough for mounting cannon, and it was here that the Portuguese held a decisive advantage. Their caravels had four heavy and six light cannon besides ten guns on swivels and a twin gun at the poop. The fleet sent against them by the Zamorin of Calicut suffered so badly that he had to seek help from the Sultan of Egypt, who sent a naval force equipped with cannon. It was defeated at Diu, and thereafter the Portuguese had no effective opposition in the Indian Ocean until the arrival of the Dutch and English, especially as the caravels were supported by the firepower of forts built at various places along the coasts. Portuguese commanders or adventurers used their mastery of fire-arms to help or to exploit warring princes in India and Indochina, and so developed a trade in fire-arms which was of some importance in Indonesia and extended up to Japan. There the muskets brought by the first Portuguese castaways so greatly impressed the Ikko leaders that they developed arsenals which produced muskets and ammunition. These were used in major battles of the sixteenth century but the cannon made in Japan were too small to be efficient; the first Tokugawa Shoguns, accordingly, obtained artillery from Dutch and English traders. Nor was the new trade entirely one-sided. As the E.I.C. became well established it obtained large quantities of saltpetre from Bengal (nearly 1,400 tons by 1837), and this helped to give the English navy that superiority in gunpower which made it strong against the French.

The major impact, however, of European fire-arms was to cripple Asian shipping. It was the superior armament of their ships which enabled the Portuguese to close western trade to Moslems or the Dutch to oust Indonesian shipping from home waters. Guns gave power to impose monopoly controls. They also gave European ships a solid competitive advantage in coping effectively with the pirates who long plagued Asian sea lanes. This advantage, later connected with marine insurance of cargoes, helped English firms at Bombay, Madras, and Calcutta to take over India's ocean shipping and some of its coastal shipping too. The tendency was pushed, as British dominion spread, by various discriminatory regulations, notably those issued between 1800 and 1813, for heavier duties upon goods brought to India on non-British ships.

It was not until an alteration of the British Tonnage Laws in 1836 that European vessels developed any great advantage over Indian or Chinese ships purely as carriers. These laws, by reason of a peculiar definition of tonnage, had encouraged the building of excessively deep and flat-bottomed vessels. An altered definition of strict cubic capacity gave British shipyards freedom to build larger standard vessels of around 1,200 tons. These carried twice as much cargo per ton as their predecessors and were also safer, more economical, and faster. Equipped with steam winches and other labour-saving devices, they could be manned by only one-third of the previous crew; and, helped by the better knowledge that became available about winds and currents, could cut sailing times by one-quarter. Further improvements of speed followed the abolition of the E.I.C.'s last monopoly over the China trade in 1833. Intense competition then developed in delivering Bengal opium to Canton or Chinese tea to London. Opium had been carried in ships of 500 to 800 tons, built at Indian yards, and both unhandy and slow as they could not beat against the monsoon. Jardine and Matheson led the new way by having the *Red Rover* built at Calcutta as a 254-ton copy of an American clipper; instead of two round trips a year it did three. Before long tea-clippers of about 1,000 tons were racing their cargoes to London; in 1866 two of them tied with a common time of ninety-nine days from Canton. These striking gains of speed, however, owed less to improvements in design than to 'carrying more sail, and caring less about splitting it';[1] there was a new motive rather than a new capability for speed.

Although European shipping had largely displaced Asian shipping before the industrial revolution, it had little effect upon the character of Asian trade until the advent of the steamship, and the steamship was a good deal longer in dominating the Indian Ocean than the Atlantic. Relatively inefficient engines, with consequent need for excessive coal space or costly bunkering facilities, limited earlier steamships to short hauls. Their first significant use in Asia was for carrying mail and passengers between Bombay and Suez. A monthly service began in 1835 when an E.I.C. steamer linked Bombay with Suez and Admiralty steamers linked Alexandria with London. Muhammad Ali immediately proposed a railway from Alexandria to Suez but the British were not willing to help finance it; (the line was not opened until 1866). The Peninsular and Oriental Steam Navigation Company was awarded a charter in 1840 for another steamer service from Calcutta to Suez via Ceylon, where its branch steamers had to link the mail service to Penang, Singapore, Hong Kong, and also Bombay. Before long it was operating a duplicate serivce from Bombay to Suez, and had added branch services from Singapore to Batavia and from Hong Kong to Shanghai. In this way a comprehensive mail and passenger service developed between England and the major ports of Asia by 1854, and quadrupled the speed of such communication. The Company had twenty-five steamers, ranging from the new *Himalaya* of 3,500 tons and 750 horse-power to small river boats on the Nile.

Sailing ships, nevertheless, had almost the whole rapidly expanding trade of the Indian Ocean. During 1868 those leaving British ports for India and the Far East aggregated over a million tons, more than ten times van Leur's rough estimate of total Asian shipping in the seventeenth century. Only an occasional steamer came to pick up cotton or tea, as sailing ships

[1] Parkinson, *Trade in the Eastern Seas*, p. 163.

were still unbeatable, on long voyages, for cheapness or speed in carrying goods.

The situation changed dramatically after 1869 when the Suez Canal was opened. This halved the steaming distance between India and England and reduced the largest gap between coaling stations from 5,000 to 2,000 miles. At the same time big improvements were making steamers far more efficient; compound engines reduced fuel consumption by up to 60 per cent, surface condensers provided fresh water which left little deposit on boilers and, thanks to Bessemer steel, boilers could be made to withstand much greater steam pressures. The first cargo steamer came to China in 1863 and, within a decade, clippers were ousted from their great preserve. Suez brought them no advantage because of the Red Sea's bad winds or dangerous reefs and the prohibitive cost of towing. There was now a strong impetus to build large and fast steamers for the cream of the Asian carrying trade—cotton, tea, spices, oil seeds, indigo, and hides. By 1884 over 85 per cent of British–Indian trade was going by steamers through Suez, and British shipyards were building twice as many tons of steamers as of sailing-ships. For some time yet, however, sailing-ships had a near monopoly of the Indo-china rice trade, and also survived by carrying other bulky, cheap goods such as jute, iron, coal, and fertilizer.

Asian textiles, like Asian shipping, were damaged before the advent of steam power, and not only by European action. The Ch'ing government, besides confining sea-borne trade to Canton, restricted the export of some commodities, notably silk, of which no ship could take more than 100 pieces; this restriction hit particularly the weavers of Nanking who had become dependent on foreign trade. In India cotton textiles suffered, along with other handicrafts, from the diminution, over years of turmoil and encroaching alien rule, of many princely courts. These had provided a big part of the market for finer craft wares, and cheaper textiles also suffered as disturbances or banditry impoverished ordinary people.

Both silk and cotton exports were further damaged by import restrictions in the future home of free trade. The E.I.C's imports of calicoes, chintzes, and silks had reached so high a level during the reign of William and Mary that English manufacturers of woollens and silks became alarmed. They obtained, in 1700, a prohibition on domestic imports of Asian silks or printed cottons, although the E.I.C. could still bring them in for re-exporting to Europe, America, and Africa. Some London firms then acquired from Holland the Indian art of printing calicoes, and the E.I.C's imports of plain calicoes greatly increased. Spitalfield weavers again protested and obtained a new prohibition on the use of any imported calico. Lancashire cotton firms thus gained complete protection against Indian competition until this Act was repealed in 1774; but heavy duties were then substituted, amounting to 72 per cent on calicoes and 27 per cent on other Indian cottons. In spite of growing markets in America and Africa (connected with the slave trade) the E.I.C's imports of calicoes stagnated and its imports of wrought silks markedly declined; between 1700 and 1760 its imports of white calicoes hardly changed from 951,109 to 988,709 pieces and those of Bengal wrought silks fell from 116,455 to 51,108 pieces.

Nor was Indian weaving assisted by the E.I.C's methods of procuring its requirements. As the Company's control extended over India its agents used harsher methods to obtain more oppressive contracts with weavers for specified deliveries and rates. Weavers who became indebted to the Company through advance payments had little bargaining power, especially as they were prohibited from selling their output or their labour to anyone else, and extraordinary methods were sometimes used to put weavers into bondage debt. One merchant, William Bolts, commented in 1772:

The English, with their *Banyans* and black *Gomastahs*, arbitrarily decide what quantities of goods each manufacturer shall deliver and the prices he shall receive for them. . . . The assent of the poor weaver is in general not deemed necessary; for the *Gomastahs*, when employed on the Company's investment, frequently make them sign what they please; and upon the weavers refusing to take the money offered, it has been known they have it tied in their girdles, and they have been sent away with a flogging. . . . The roguery practised in this department is beyond imagination; but all terminates in the defrauding of the poor weaver.[1]

Asian handicrafts, nevertheless, were not badly disrupted until the industrial revolution gave Britain an unprecedented

[1] Quoted in Dutt, *The Economic History of India*, vol. i, pp. 18–19.

ability to produce those very goods in which India and China had so long held the superiority. They lost, first, export markets for craft wares in Asia as well as Europe, and then much of their own domestic markets. The biggest change came in cotton textiles. In the earlier part of the eighteenth century cotton was a relatively new industry in Britain, handicapped both by a shortage of thread and its inferiority as warp. Hargreave's jenny, Arkwright's water-frame, and Crompton's mule then increased a British spinner's output by a factor of 200, while metal rollers improved the quality of thread. Steam power was applied to both spinning and weaving machines quite early in the nineteenth century and gave British textiles a further overwhelming advantage. Britain's exports of cottons thus soared from £306,000 in 1780 to £5,851,000 in 1800 and to £28,300,000 in 1850; those to Asia increased from a mere £156 in 1794 or £19,575 in 1800 to about £6,000,000 in 1850. British exports of silk goods had a less dramatic but still considerable rise from £400,000 in 1820 to £1,300,000 in 1850.

India, by 1858, was importing £4,783,000 of cotton goods and exporting only £810,000; its imports of silk goods were £108,000 and its exports £158,000, but these had fallen from £442,000 in 1850. From its age-old predominance in Asian markets the Indian cotton industry was reduced to supplying coarse products of village looms for domestic consumption, and a few high quality products of urban specialists. The Chinese cotton industry fared better as, although they sold to some wealthy Chinese, Manchester goods could not compete with the harder wearing and cheaper domestic cloth used by ordinary people. Nor were the superior Chinese silks much affected in their own market; but their export fell, by 1867 to a mere 3 per cent of China's total exports.

Other traditional manufactures were damaged by Birmingham, Sheffield, and Staffordshire. India lost iron-smelting, glass-making, paper-making, and much of its shipbuilding. China lost most of its export trade in kettles, knives, needles, and implements to South-east Asia. Throughout Asia imports of crockery, enamelware, and tinware badly hit domestic manufacturers of brassware, bronzeware, lacquerware, and pottery. China's great ceramic industry which, in the eighteenth century, had exported special wares for avid European markets, now lost both them and its more important Asian markets; in the 1850s, moreover, it was so crippled by the Taiping rebellion that it could not recover its former domestic position.

Asian trade, nevertheless, grew very rapidly during the nineteenth century on a new basis of exporting foodstuffs or raw materials for imports of industrial manufactures. Steam transportation greatly increased markets for bulky agricultural or pastoral products, and Europe's expanding industries created new or extended uses for them. Indochina thus became a great exporter of rice and timber; Malaya–Indonesia a great exporter of vegetable oils and rubber; India a great exporter of raw cotton, jute, hides, and tea; and China a greater exporter of raw silk, skins, and furs as well as a new exporter of bean and egg products and vegetable oils. Minerals, too, became far more important so that mines were extended or opened in Malaya and Indonesia for tin, in Indonesia, Burma, and Iran for petroleum, in Burma for lead and silver, and in India for manganese. India and China both acquired, later in the nineteenth century, modern textile industries which partly compensated for the loss of traditional ones, and India even recovered in this way some export markets for cotton goods. Japan, after abrupt arousal from Tokugawa isolationism, set about modernizing its economy to such effect that, by 1913, its exports were nearly one-half of India's and two-fifths of them comprised industrial manufactures.

These changes were causally intermingled with the spread of western imperialism across Asia. The Netherlands subjugated the whole of Indonesia; Britain completed its dominion over India and Ceylon and extended this to Burma, Malaya, and North Borneo; France, after 1862, took over Vietnam, Cambodia, and Laos; the United States, in 1898, ousted Spain from the Philippines; and various western powers, led by Britain, forced China to open ports and to cede territory or leases in order to promote commercial or military interests. Much of this imperialism was harmful as well as hurtful to Asia. But it had amazing economic effects. By pacification and policing it enabled Asia's population to increase by one-half within a century, —from 602 millions in 1800 to 937 millions in 1900 according to Carr-Saunders's estimate. By developing steamships, plantations, and mines it led to big migrations of Asian people; millions of

Table 1

Asian Countries: Growth of Population and Trade in the Nineteenth Century

(Population in millions; trade in £ millions)

Countries	1800	1825	1850	1875	1900	1914
BRITISH INDIA						
Population		130[1]	150	256	285	302
Trade[a]		7[b]	32	102	142	293
CEYLON						
Population		0·8	1·6	2·4	3·6	4[2]
Trade[a]		0·5	4	10	14	26
INDONESIA						
Population[c]		6	10	20[3]	29	32
Trade[d]		3	8	27[3]	34	88
MALAYA						
Population		0·4			1·3	3
Trade[e]		4	8	24	39	88
THAILAND						
Population		2–3	5–6			8[2]
Trade			1·3	3	6	16
CHINA						
Population	(350)		(430)			(450)
Trade[f]		(15)		45	59	114
JAPAN						
Population	25			35	45	51
Trade[g]				5[4]	51[4]	151

Notes

[a] Includes treasure	[1] 1835
[b] Bombay, Madras, and Bengal only	[2] 1911
[c] Java and Mildura only	[3] 1880
[d] Private trade and government consignments	[4] Centred five-year average
[e] Straits Settlements only	
[f] Seaborne trade only	
[g] Valued at 1897 parity of yen	

Sources:
Statistical Abstracts for British India
Dutt, *The Economic History of India*
Ceylon Annual Almanac and Register
Statistical Abstracts of the Colonial and Other Possessions of the United Kingdom
Furnival, *Netherlands India*
Ingram, *Economic Change in Thailand since 1850*
Cowan (ed.), *The Economic Development of South-East Asia*
Wright, *Hart and the Chinese Customs*
Carr-Saunders, *World Population*
Allen, *A Short Economic History of Modern Japan*

Indians went to Ceylon, Burma, or Malaya and millions of Chinese to Hong Kong, the Philippines, Borneo, Indonesia, Malaya, or Thailand. This increase and redistribution of population played a large part not only in developing exports of minerals or plantation products to Europe but also in promoting exports of rice, other foodstuffs, and textiles within Asia. Production may not have kept up with this huge increase of numbers, but trade, as Table 1 shows, far outstripped it.

Notwithstanding its rapid growth, Asian trade became a minor part of world trade; Asian exports in 1913 were only 11 per cent of world exports and Asian imports only 10 per cent of world imports. There were other drastic changes, too. Asian countries came to do most of their trade with Europe and America instead of with one another. India, for example, sent 80 per cent of its exports to western countries in 1913 and obtained from them 88 per cent of its imports. Indonesia, in 1920, sent 46 per cent of its exports directly to western countries and obtained from them 66 per cent of its imports. China, again in 1913, did one-tenth of its trade with India, the same proportion as with the United Kingdom, but one-third of it with the rising industrial power of Japan. Among the smaller countries, Ceylon did more than one-third of its trade with the United Kingdom alone, and Malaya nearly the same proportion. Only the new, rice-exporting countries of Indochina continued to have a substantial Asian trade; Burma, in 1913, sent three-fifths of its exports to Asia and drew one-half of its imports from other Asian countries.

The remaining change is in the character of Asian exports. Food, agricultural materials, and mineral outputs constituted 78 per cent of Asian exports in 1913 or, if Japan is excluded, 83 per cent. India was a bit below this Asian average with 77 per cent and China just above it with 85 per cent. These two great areas of traditional crafts had clearly become exporters very largely of primary products. India, it is true, was developing a modern textile industry and gaining some overseas markets for its output. But the major industrial country of Asia was already Japan, previously little more than a cultural and commercial satellite of the splendid Chinese Empire.

3. *China eroded*

Free traders completed their victory over the East India Company in 1834 when it lost the remaining monopoly of British trade with China. This monopoly had already been invaded not so much by licensed 'country' voyages between India and China as by those private traders who established residence at Canton or Macao, alongside the Company's supercargoes, mainly through securing nominal appointments, not recognized by the Chinese authorities, as consular agents for foreign governments. Their real function was to act as commercial agents for important firms in India or Britain from which they received powerful support against the Company's efforts to dislodge them. It had, in the end, to accept private merchants at Canton because of their role in promoting 'country trade' upon which it relied for sales by its Bengal opium monopoly in order to purchase Chinese tea, now the mainstay of its profits. Canton's imports rose by one-half between 1817 and 1833, but those supplied by private merchants more than doubled.

A select committee of the House of Commons found out something about the structure of this trade. In 1827, the Company brought £350,000 worth of English woollens to Canton together with £470,000 worth of raw cotton, and purchased there £1,700,000 worth of tea. Private merchants brought £700,000 worth of raw cotton and £2,200,000 worth of opium; as their purchases of raw silk, the main commodity, were only £230,000, they obtained £1,200,000 worth of silver, more than enough to meet the Company's deficit of £800,000, by purchasing from its Canton Treasury bills on Bengal, or, to a much smaller extent, on London. Although private traders became most active in the illegal opium trade, they pushed other Asian commodities at Canton. Parsee intermediaries supplied them with incense, myrrh, or other specialties of the Red Sea–Persian Gulf area; they brought raw cotton, piece-goods, or rice from India, pearls or ivory from Ceylon, and tin, pepper, sandalwood, rice, betel-nuts, birds' nests, tortoiseshell, or rattan from Malaya and Indonesia. Such trade was limited, as was the return trade in silk, sugar-candy, chinaware, lacquerware, camphor, alum, mercury, and zinc, and the Southeast Asian portion was largely conducted by Chinese junks. Raw cotton was by far the biggest legal export to China, but the demand for it depended upon the vagaries of the Nanking crop and became quite depressed in the 1830s. Demand for rice was equally uncertain although during the same decade some merchants (including Jardine and Matheson) developed a considerable rice trade with Manila and Java.

Opium was the one product which had a sure market in China. During the first two decades of the nineteenth century sales were fairly steady at around 4,500 chests a year, partly because of difficulties with the Portuguese at Macao and partly because of attempts by Chinese officials to enforce prohibition of a trade damaging to the Empire's health, discipline, and treasure. In 1821 enforcement measures were so vigorous that opium vessels had to leave Whampoa, the sea port of Canton. Private merchants then established their headquarters at Lintin Island, in the centre of the great Bay of Canton, from which their ships cruised north to other anchorages, such as Namoa Island in the Bay of Swatow. There they could meet Chinese smugglers, relatively immune from interference by the Canton authorities. Opium shipments began a rapid rise to 12,434 chests in 1824 and 16,257 chests in 1829, by which time fast ships of private firms were ranging far up the China coast. Further stimulus was given to the trade by a reversal of the Company's policy of restricting the Bengal supply. Growing access to the Malwa supply, which was increasingly popular in China, led the Company to attempt its control also, but this was such a fiasco that, in 1831, all restrictions were given up. Merchants thus obtained greatly increased supplies of opium and, by 1838, were exporting 40,200 chests to China.

Serious trouble developed with the Chinese authorities. In spite of corruption among officials and merchants at Canton, the imperial government had repeatedly forbidden the sale or smoking of opium, and sporadically tried to enforce prohibition at this distant port. It had also refused any extension of legitimate trade beyond Canton or the hong merchants. Lord Macartney, in 1793, led a well-prepared mission which was graciously received but could obtain neither diplomatic relations with Peking nor easing of levies and restrictions on English merchants. The Celestial Empire, possessing all things in prolific abundance, had not the slightest wish for manufactures of western countries but, benevolently recognizing their needs for tea, silks, and porcelain, had granted the boon of trade, a boon which had to conform to the Empire's traditions and could not be extended. Two years later another Dutch embassy had a similar refusal and in 1816 Lord Amherst's mission was not even given audience.

Shortly before the Company's monopoly expired, the Viceroy of Canton, through the Co-hong, asked the Directors to appoint a chief merchant to manage English trade in the usual way. The British government, instead, sent Lord Napier as its Superintendent of Trade. The Viceroy refused to recognize a foreign official on Chinese soil and, when Napier tried to insist upon such recognition, ordered his expulsion. This was effected by stopping trade and blockading the river so as to neutralize two British frigates which Napier had ordered to reach Whampoa. He was forced to retire to Macao, where he immediately died of fever, and where his successors had little influence upon the resumed trade of Canton. But the system was falling apart; Company control had given way to competing private merchants some of whom, the opium dealers, were pushing an expanding trade from Lintin with widespread smugglers. Chinese authorities became increasingly concerned with this lawless development, especially as it was associated with a heavy drain of silver. Some put this at as much as one-half of Peking's revenues; the actual figures are, for the period 1830–3, £3,360,000, offset by American supplies of £760,000.

The Emperor appointed Lin Tse-hsu, who had stamped out opium smoking in the province of Hu Kuang, as Imperial Commissioner to eradicate the opium traffic at Canton. Foreign merchants were quickly astounded by an order to hand over all their stocks and to make a bond never to bring further supplies of opium to China. They complied after Lin exerted strong pressure and Elliott, their Superintendent, promised compensation for surrendered chests. The British withdrew first to Macao and then to Hong Kong where, notwithstanding their bond, they resumed trading in opium. Lin cut off food and water but lost control when Elliott ordered a damaging attack upon patrolling junks. Jardine, a leading opium merchant, was then in London and had no great difficulty in urging Palmerston to send a naval expedition in order to force open Chinese ports to British trade; sixteen men-of-war and four thousand troops were dispatched from India. They blockaded the Yangtze and, after abortive negotiations at Canton followed by reinforcements which brought the expedition to ten thousand men, seized positions along the coast from Amoy to Shanghai and successfully attacked Nanking.

The once mighty Chinese Empire yielded to this small, modern force and, in August 1842, had to agree to a treaty which overthrew its traditional control of foreign trade. Britain gained Hong Kong island, rights of free trade, residence, consular representation, and consular jurisdiction at Canton, Amoy, Foochow, Ningpo, and Shanghai, as well as an indemnity of £4,200,000; a supplementary treaty clarified some of these matters and established a fixed tariff for British goods. Similar rights were quickly secured by France and the United States without conflict, partly because the Chinese government sought to offset its now evident weakness by playing one barbarian nation against another. But, in fact, all combined to take advantage of the stricken giant. As Lord Macartney had earlier forseen:

The Empire of China is an old, crazy, First-rate man of war, which a fortunate succession of able and vigilant officers have continued to keep afloat for these 150 years past, and to overawe their neighbours merely by her bulk and appearance, but whenever an insufficient man happens to have the command upon deck, adieu to the discipline and safety of the ship . . . she can never the rebuilt on the old bottom.[1]

There were no great captains of this ship after Ch'ien-lung (1736–95), although the rapid growth of population under the Ch'ing dynasty made increasing demands upon the apex of a despotic system of imperial government. About 1,500 district magistrates were supposed to rule over 350 million people, and were so handicapped by inadequate allowances that they had to depend upon unofficial exactions or fees. The proceeds were shared through a chain of higher authorities and the whole system of government became entangled in a web of corruption which prevented efficient administration. Ordinary people, who had never been reconciled to Manchu rule over China, were

[1] Quoted in Cranmer-Byng (ed.), *An Embassy to China*, pp. 212–13.

further alienated. Their discontent was strongly shown by the White Lotus Rebellion of 1796 in Hupei, Szechwan, and Shensi; it began as a revolt against the exactions of tax-collectors but quickly assumed a violently anti-Manchu character. Imperial forces took nine years to suppress this rebellion and, although they ultimately succeeded, it was obvious to the Chinese that Manchu power had decayed. The Ch'ing still kept an army of 160,000 bannermen but many of them were demoralized by corruption; no good cannon had been cast since the days of the Jesuits in Peking, and powder was of the lowest quality. Various secret societies were thus encouraged to exploit rural discontent, caused by pressure of population on a now stagnant agriculture, to fan Chinese patriotism, and to take advantage of Manchu weakness. The army was able to cope with northern societies but had less success against an increasingly powerful Triad Society in the south.

Naval power had never interested the Manchus. Their ships were limited to a size of only 300 tons, and coastal governors could use them as little more than an offshore police force. Pirates had much bigger vessels which, from the late eighteenth century, preyed upon southern shipping and in 1806 even attacked Taiwan. The British drew the obvious conclusion that a few of their own men-of-war could easily deal with the whole Ch'ing navy, as Jardine and other merchants had urged in the interests of free trade. A contributor to the *Chinese Repository* of 1836 went so far as to write:

Powerless beyond the power of description to ridicule or portray, yet set forth with all the braggadocio and pretence for which the Chinese are so famous, the marine of this vast empire presents a state of things unparalleled among even the most savage states or islands that we know of; we query much whether a couple of New Zealand war canoes would not be an overmatch for all that could be brought against them.[1]

And so, almost, it proved. After capitulating to the small British naval expedition at Nanking the Chinese authorities virtually abandoned control over their own waters. European shipping was no longer interfered with and action against pirates passed largely to the British navy which, from 1849, took vigor-

[1] Quoted in Collis, *Foreign Mud*, pp. 189–90.

13 Chinese–English naval clash in Anson's Bay, 7 January 1841
Radio Times–Hulton

14 Coffee plantation in Ceylon (engraving after C. O'Brian, 1864)
Ceylon Tea Centre, London

ous action around Hong Kong, although it was many years before the China Sea was freed from these pests. In the treaty ports Chinese hired European ships to protect junks or fishing fleets, and soon began to charter or use European ships for carrying goods along the coast. This practice was fostered by new insurance companies which refused cover for junk-borne cargoes, and it was estimated that by 1863 70 per cent of British ships at Shanghai were engaged in coastal trade.

As soon as the treaty ports were opened an extravagant surge of imports glutted the China market, especially in cotton piece-goods. A select committee of the Commons considered this slump and recommended promotion of Manchester goods by lowering the English tea-duty so as to increase China's import capacity. Nothing came of this proposal, but China's exports soon increased; tea shipments rose from 66 million lb. in 1845 to 109 million lb. in 1855, and silk exports from the two ports of Canton and Shanghai rose from 11,750 bales in 1850 to over 62,000 bales in 1855. The corresponding recovery in imports was largely confined to opium which increased from 31,000 chests in 1845 to over 43,000 chests in 1850 and, later in the decade, to 60,000. Manchester's hopes were disappointed by the poverty of a people who found their own rough cottons cheaper or more durable, although business improved after imported cottons were adapted to the taste of wealthier Chinese. There were more bizarre disappointments, such as that of the Sheffield firm which sent large quantities of knives and forks to a people who had good reason for preferring chopsticks, or that of the London firm which dispatched many pianos in the expectation of at least a million Chinese ladies wishing to acquire a Victorian accomplishment.

Nor did Hong Kong come up to Pottinger's expectation that 'within six months . . . it will be a vast emporium of commerce and wealth'.[1] The initial population of about 4,000 was raised to nearly 24,000 in 1845, mainly by migration of Hakkas. A visiting bishop described the 600 Europeans as hated for their 'moral improprieties and insolent behaviour', but also described the Chinese immigrants as 'the lowest dregs of Chinese society', attracted by 'the hope of gain or plunder'.[2] No leading Chinese merchant, certainly, then thought it worthwhile moving from

[1] Quoted in Endacott, *A History of Hong Kong*, p. 72.   [2] ibid., p. 71.

19

Canton. Attempts to develop entrepôt trade at Hong Kong were hindered by piracy, by availability of Chinese products at the open ports, and by the greater cheapness or safety of importing British or Asian wares from Singapore to these ports. In spite, therefore, of an initial attempt to discourage the opium trade, Hong Kong became its great centre with eighty clippers which went to many a smuggling rendezvous. Other illegal trade also helped Hong Kong; Chinese used the island as a means of avoiding the imperial salt monopoly and lorchas brought tea which had evaded Chinese customs houses. By 1854 Hong Kong was used by 1,100 ocean-going ships, aggregating 443,000 tons, and had a considerable junk trade with the mainland.

Canton, much the busiest port, was rapidly being overtaken by Shanghai which was close to the big producing areas for tea and silk and on the great internal waterway of Central China. It soon overshadowed the neighbouring treaty port of Ningpo. Foochow was a disappointment until tea traders began using it when rebel activity blocked transport to Canton in 1854. Amoy was both a main resort of opium smugglers and an exporter of sugar, Taiwan tea, or coolie labour for work in South-east Asia.

Trade, during the 1850s and later, was retarded by a major convulsion of the Empire, far more damaging to the Ch'ing than the humiliating intrusion of foreigners into Chinese ports, but connected with it. Between 1850 and 1855 three rebellions broke out in the south and north-east, and were not finally put down until 1868. The most serious rebellion was that of the Taiping (Heavenly Kingdom of Great Peace), a sect founded in Kwangsi by Hung Hsiu-ch'uan, the frustrated scholar and mystic who claimed the Mandate of Heaven as second son of the Christian God. He attracted support from Hakkas, the Triad Society, poor peasants, bandits, and pirates. Their revolt began in 1850, spread rapidly, and was welded into an effective military force by the able strategist, Yang Hsiu-ching, who led them to capture Nanking in 1853. A northern advance failed and, because of poor arrangements for defence and administration, the Taiping were unable to hold the south. But for some years they controlled a large area of Central China from Nanking.

Almost simultaneously another rebellion broke out in the southern part of the North China Plain where, in 1852, the

Yellow River, owing to neglect of dikes, broke its banks to begin a disastrous shift northwards of the Shantung Peninsula. Peasants suffered badly and government broke down under strains of famine and banditry. Nien, or gangs having some connection with the White Lotus Society, joined forces in 1853 under Chang Lo-hsing to control an area of 100,000 square miles, within which they made effective arrangements for food, taxes, and militia. In spite of Chang's assumption of the title, Great Han Heavenly-Mandated King, these arrangements were largely decentralized and no attempt was made to capture big cities or to expand the movement on a national scale. But he removed almost three provinces from Ch'ing rule, made plundering cavalry attacks upon adjacent provinces, and often co-operated with the more dangerous Taiping. The Ch'ing also lost control over Yunnan, the most southern and Moslem province, where Ma Te-hsin, an influential *imam*, led a rebellion which set up an independent Moslem state at Tali, the old capital of Thai Nanchao. Miao tribesmen took over Kweichow in the same year, 1855, and were not suppressed until 1881.

Loyal support from the traditional scholar-bureaucrats, and the success of Tseng Kuo-fan in building up an army based on Hunan, enabled the imperial government to contain the Taiping and also to keep control over most southern or coastal provinces. But here it had to face a further attack from western powers intent upon extending trading privileges which had already been won by force. By 1856 Britain and France, frustrated by the new Emperor's refusal to negotiate due revisions of the first treaties, resolved upon another expedition. Palmerston found a *casus belli* when the Canton police arrested the crew of a Hong Kong lorcha on a charge of piracy, and Napoleon III found a pretext for co-operation when a French missionary was executed at Kwangsi. A British bombardment of Canton failed, and an expeditionary force had to be diverted to India because of the Mutiny. Canton, however, was occupied in 1858 and Lord Elgin with Baron Gros then took an allied force to Tientsin. There they engineered sweeping changes: legalization of the opium trade; opening of eleven more ports including Tientsin, Hankow, Nanking, Chinkiang, Swatow, and Taipei; uniform tariffs to be administered by a foreign inspectorate at Shanghai; and indemnities to be paid from customs duties. The right was also secured to have resident ministers at Peking but, when these arrived, they were refused passage from Tientsin, and four British gunboats were sunk in an attempt to force a passage. Elgin and Gros returned with a stronger expedition of 10,500 men, defeated a Manchu army, occupied Peking, looted it, and destroyed the marvellous Summer Palace which Jesuits had built for Emperor K'ang-hsi. The Treaty of Tientsin was then ratified, indemnities were increased to £5,600,000, and the Kowloon Peninsula was added to the Colony of Hong Kong. The Americans quickly secured the same general benefits for their own trade.

The Russians secured even more. Although the caravans allowed by the Treaty of Nerchinsk had long ceased arriving at Peking, Russia's eastward advance had engulfed West Turkestan, just as China's ports were being forced open by Europeans, and a treaty was signed for regulating trade at the border mart of Kiakhta. About the same time the Russians again advanced down the Amur and, in 1858, forced China to cede the river's north bank. At Tientsin they obtained the same commercial advantages as had the western powers but in 1860 also obtained Manchuria's east coast for their new port of Vladivostok. Thus began the dismemberment of the Chinese Empire.

Until the close of the century, however, western powers gave the Ch'ing enough support to regain and keep control over the rebellious empire. A boy emperor had come to the throne in 1861 and his mother, Tzu-hsi, together with his uncle, Kung, effectively revived imperial authority. They gave first priority to suppressing the rebels, and extended full support to Tseng Kuo-fan for this purpose. His new Anhwei Army took Shanghai in 1862 and then used customs revenues, together with other revenues, for building modern arsenals and steamships. It was helped by a mercenary force, financed by Shanghai merchants and led by Major Charles Gordon, to capture Soochow in 1863, while a similar Franco-Chinese force helped to capture Hangchow. When Nanking fell in the following year the Taiping kingdom was finally crushed. It took another four years to crush the Nien, and much longer to suppress Moslems and Miao in the far south-west. The traditional Chinese Empire nonetheless seemed to have been preserved—except for the new, western-imposed system of foreign trading.

This had completely broken the traditional system of tribute missions and tight imperial control over boons of trade with the Middle Kingdom. Between 1762 and 1860 it received 254 embassies from Korea, the Ryukyu Islands, Vietnam, Thailand, Burma, Laos, and the Sulu Islands; but Thailand sent its last embassy in 1853 and after the 1860s only Mongolia and Nepal continued them. The system, it is true, was loose in that foreigners had long been admitted to trade at Canton, and Chinese merchant junks had long gone to South-east Asia. But official guild or hong merchants had been appointed for ensuring conformity of both types of trade to regulations and, to the extent that the Emperor could exact obedience from his subjects or keep out pirates, foreign trade was both limited and controlled. There were, of course, breaches by corrupt officials, smugglers, and pirates, but the system broke down completely only when western powers exacted unrestricted rights of free trade with any Chinese merchant at a wide range of open ports. The official monopoly of the hong merchants then followed that of the East India companies into oblivion, and the more or less arbitrary demands of the mandarins were replaced by a fixed tariff of 5 per cent, later administered by a foreign Inspectorate of Maritime Customs.

Hong merchants had given much help to foreigners in bridging linguistic, legal, and cultural differences. Such help was still needed and was soon provided by a new class of compradors, men who could put up substantial guarantees to western firms for work done on a commission basis in regard to local purchases, sales, credit arrangements, market information, or recruitment of staff. They included both former members of the hong and other traders or partners in Chinese mercantile concerns which distributed imports internally, and gained not only profitable trading connections with western firms but experience of modern business methods. There was, indeed, a considerable development of Chinese business in the treaty ports after conditions became secure, and especially at Shanghai, where an International Settlement had been obtained and was well policed by the western powers. Some of these firms became at least as wealthy as western firms in China and, at the end of the century, a Chinese member of Hong Kong's Legislative Council asserted that they made just as much profit from the import trade

There was also a beneficial relation between the Maritime Customs Service and the Ch'ing government. The Service had its beginning in the period of the Taiping threat to Shanghai, when the imperial customs house had to close and foreign consuls appointed collectors for passing receipts to Peking. Impressed by their honesty, the government appointed an English assessor who became the first Inspector-General of the Service under the provisions of the Treaty of Tientsin. Robert Hart succeeded to the office in 1863, and, with great sympathy, tact, and skill, made the Service a remarkably effective instrument of Chinese interests. It paid off the indemnities, provided security for domestic loans raised by Chinese authorities, helped suppress large-scale smuggling of opium, charted the coast, built lighthouses, improved navigation on the Yangtze, managed the ports, published useful reports and statistics, mediated between treaty rights and imperial privileges, helped to develop both a post office and a diplomatic service, and provided a splendid training ground for many Chinese as modern civil servants or as modern businessmen. Most important of all, it gave China honest administration of a customs revenue which grew from about £1,000,000 before 1850 or £2,000,000 in 1864 to £3,000,000 in 1910, or from one-tenth to one-third of imperial receipts.

Yet trade increased far too slowly after the opening of new ports to justify western assaults on the traditional system. Exports rose from £19 million in 1864 to £25 million in 1872, and imports correspondingly, but their sterling value hardly changed over the next fifteen years in spite of a heavy depreciation of the tael from 6s. 8d. to 4s. 10d. as a result of bigger world supplies of silver. A rising trend did not become evident until the 1890s when steamer transportation and Japan's industrialization were the main factors in increasing the value of China's exports and imports from a combined total of £51 million in 1895 to £136 million in 1914.

Tea continued to provide about one-half of total exports until 1884 but thereafter declined rapidly to a proportion of only one-tenth in 1914, because of expanding output from new plantations in India or Ceylon. These captured most of the British market, and China's export would have slumped even further but for increasing Russian demands for brick tea. Silk exports continued in second place at around one-third of the total throughout the nineteenth century and wrought silks accounted for about one-eighth of all silk exports. Towards the end of the century, however, these exports began to decline because of improvements to both cultivation and processing in Japan, France, and Italy and, although China began machine-reeling, Japan became the leading exporter of raw white silk. There was a sudden boom in raw cotton from the Yangtze area during the American Civil War, but the export quickly dropped from 30,000 tons in 1864 to 2,000 tons in 1867 and did not revive until Japan's textile industry developed a new demand for Chinese raw cotton which reached 58,000 tons by 1902.

There was, between 1884 and 1914, a trebling of China's export receipts but a fall in the joint contribution made by tea and silk from four-fifths to one-third. How, then, did export receipts increase? The humiliating answer is through 'muck and truck' goods: beans, bristles, eggs, feathers, hides, matting, oil-seeds, straw braid, and other miscellaneous products of low unit value or considerable bulk. Straw braid was exported from Chefoo as soon as this port was opened to trade, and exports of pigs' bristles or tung oil began in the 1870s when mechanical pressing cheapened consignment of hides. But there was no considerable export of vegetable oils, soyabean products, or egg products until the 1890s. By that time the new steamer services were leading to a rapid growth of all muck and truck goods so that their contribution to total exports rose from one-tenth in 1867 to nearly three-fifths in 1904. China had, indeed, ceased to be Asia's major source of manufactures and, like the rest of Asia, was reduced to exporting foodstuffs or raw materials, no very important ones at that.

Foreign traders had been particularly disappointed by the slow growth of China's imports. Opium continued its brisk rise after the Treaty of Tientsin to a peak of 87,000 chests in 1879, more than double the 1839 level. Thereafter increasing domestic supplies reduced its contribution from nearly one-half of total imports in 1867 to less than one-tenth in 1904. Imports of raw cotton, formerly considerable, had become of little consequence at the mid-century, again because of replacement by domestic supplies. Cotton manufactures rose from one-fifth of total imports to more than one-third but the major increase was in yarns

TABLE 2

CHINA: TRADE AND SHIPPING, 1867–1914

	Unit	1867	1884	1894	1904	1914
EXPORTS*a*	£ million	19	19	22	32	60
Silk	per cent	33	34	33	33	24
Tea		60	46	24	12	10
Skins and furs		—	2	2	6	6
Bean and egg products		—	—	2	5	14
Vegetable oils		—	—	1	2	4
Other		7	18	38	41	42
IMPORTS*a*	£ million	23	21	29	54	76
Opium	per cent	46	34	18	10	6
Cottons		21	32	32	40	36
Kerosene		—	—	4	5	19
Machinery		—	—	1	3	3
Other		3	34	45	42	36
SHIPPING	million tons	7	19	30	73*b*	
British	per cent	43	63	68	48*b*	
Chinese		—	16	18	23*b*	
Japanese		—	1	1	8*b*	
American		40	11	—	2*b*	
Other		—	9	13	25*b*	
Value of Haikan Tael.	Stg. pence	80	67	38	34	33

a From 1884 centred quinquennial averages
b 1905

Sources :
Allen and Donnithorne, *Western Enterprise in Far Eastern Economic Development*
Morse, *The Trade and Administration of the Chinese Empire*
Wright, *Hart and the Chinese Customs*

coming from India and, later, Japan. These imports crippled the Chinese spinning industry but domestic weaving long continued as a major peasant handicraft. Demands for other western imports were hard to stimulate until the last quarter of the century when a big market developed for kerosene and lesser markets for such other consumer goods as metal wares, soap, cigarettes, and matches. On the other hand, imports of sugar and foodstuffs from South-east Asia or Japan rose from less than £500,000 in the 1860s to nearly £1,800,000 in 1905. Imports of machinery were comparatively unimportant, reflecting Ch'ing failure to adapt China's economy to modern methods of production.

Shipping grew more vigorously than trade. The tonnage entering or leaving Chinese ports rose from 6,600,000 in 1864 to

18,800,000 in 1884 and then quadrupled up to 1904. This increase was largely associated with the spread and improvement of steamer services which, besides displacing clippers on transoceanic routes, took over most of the junk trade to South-east Asia by 1870. Coastal traffic had already largely gone to better protected and exclusively insured western ships but steamers carried the process further through their greater efficiency. They also led to a considerable expansion of coastal shipping in order to link other ports to Hong Kong or Shanghai, because transoceanic shippers tended to confine their services to these two centres. Steamers, moreover, proved superior to junks on the fast-flowing Yangtze, although it was not until 1884 that smaller vessels were successfully built for the shallower waters above Hankow.

If the west destroyed China's traditional shipping as well as its trade, the Chinese obtained some share in what replaced it. Singapore Chinese owned a steamship line from Penang to Amoy, another Chinese company had nearly half the emigrant traffic to Bangkok and, in 1908, Chinese and Thai interests combined to provide a service from Bangkok to Swatow. Similar developments in coastal shipping were discouraged by the unfortunate experience of the China Merchants' Steam Navigation Company whose records were scrutinized by imperial officials in order to 'squeeze' those who were foolish enough to consign goods on Chinese ships. But Chinese merchants held a good many shares in foreign companies operating in coastal waters, and a few had seats on their boards. Crews were wholly Chinese and officers wholly European.

Hong Kong's development was closely allied to shipping. Soon after the treaty ports were opened it handled about one-seventh of the modern shipping in Chinese waters, maintained this share until the 1880s, and then doubled it as steamers progressed in number and size. The Maritime Customs return for 1880 showed Hong Kong as handling 21 per cent of China's exports and 37 per cent of its imports. The colony had quite exceptional advantages for entrepôt trade; the only deep-water harbour between Shanghai and Singapore, a duty-free port made safe from pirates, and an oasis of British security at times when China's internal order was disturbed by rebellion. Foreign and Chinese merchants were attracted in such numbers that

Hong Kong's population rose from 56,000 in 1854 to 126,000 in 1866, and again doubled by the end of the century. Hong Kong also became the main centre for both Chinese migration and coastal shipping. Departures for overseas rose from 5,116 in 1866 to 70,625 in 1881 and returns from 9,253 to 52,983; the growing Chinese communities in South-east Asia, America, and Australia helped commodity trade as they retained traditional tastes and obtained from Hong Kong supplies of tea, silk, and other Chinese wares in order to gratify such tastes. Many leading firms in coastal shipping established their headquarters in Hong Kong; the Canton and Macao Steamship Company (1865), the China Navigation Company (1872), the Indo-China Steam Navigation Company (1881), and the Douglas Steamship Company (1883).

Junk traffic was also important as it accounted for one-third more cargo tonnage than modern shipping in 1867, bringing to the Colony cattle, pigs, vegetables, fruits, and firewood and taking away opium, cottons, salt, fish, rice, lime, and granite. For a few years after 1872 this junk traffic was depressed by a 'blockade' or customs check imposed by the Canton authorities in an attempt at curbing evasion of Chinese duties on opium. Junk traffic more than recovered during the 1880s, but increased far less rapidly than modern shipping so that, by 1914, it had become relatively insignificant at Hong Kong.

China's whole foreign trade, over the nineteenth century, had a much slower growth than that of most other Asian countries and, in 1914, accounted for less than one-fifth of Asian trade. A century earlier the proportion was above one-third, judging from what estimates are available and from general considerations, too. In particular, China's trade fell from near equality with India's at the beginning of the century to one-half at its close and to one-third in 1914. Among the reasons for this slower growth are the switch of tea production and exporting to India, the development there of other plantation crops and a somewhat greater development of modern mining and industry. China, that is, clung more to traditional ways and thereby suffered an eclipse of its former commanding position in Asian trade.

TABLE 3

HONG KONG: POPULATION AND SHIPPING, 1847–1913

	Unit	1847	1866	1881	1891	1913
Population	thousand	24	126	160	(210)	457
Ships	number	694	1,896	3,214	8,707	21,867
	thous. tons	229	950	2,853	10,280	22,900
Junks	number		20,768[a]	24,339	29,466	
	thous. tons		1,354[a]	1,620	1,814	

[a] 1867

Source :
Endacott, *A History of Hong Kong*

4. *India transformed*

The cost to India of its commercial progress was complete subjection to alien rule and undermining of traditional culture. When the E.I.C. lost the monopoly of British trade with China it gained renewal of a charter to control much the greater part of India under a government shared with the British Crown. By 1856 the British had completed their conquest of India and begun its transformation along western lines. Sind was annexed in 1843 and the Punjab in 1849; then came Dalhousie's (Governor-General, 1848–56) seizure of principalities whose rulers failed to leave natural heirs, and his annexations of Lower Bengal and Oudh. He also followed the westernizing policy begun by Bentinck (1828–35), who had suppressed suttee and thuggery, codified public law, and fostered schools and colleges for the propagation of European learning. Dalhousie, besides developing schools, roads, and irrigation canals, introduced a uniform postal system, telegraphs, railways, and the steamer service to Egypt's overland route.

Annexations, reforms, and innovations angered the dispossessed and made traditionalists apprehensive. Their exasperation culminated in that series of military revolts and agrarian risings which are called the Great Mutiny of 1857. But they did not have widespread or energetic support, even in the Ganges Valley to which they were largely confined, so that comparatively small forces were able to put down the Mutiny within little more than a year. The British government then abolished the E.I.C., together with the last feeble remnant of Mughal power, and assumed undivided responsibility for ruling an Indian

Empire more extensive than the Mughals had ever possessed, even if Afghanistan had become independent.

At this time it contained about 180 million people, most of whom were so desperately poor that India's average income was barely Rs. 18, or less than £2 a year—not one-tenth that of contemporary Britain. Mughal despotism had been replaced by British justice, subsequent anarchy by stable order, and rapacious officials by an honest civil service active in developing education, transport, and irrigation. But the economic gains from better government were largely absorbed by a rapid growth of population which, between 1835 and 1860, increased by 50 millions or something like two-fifths. Not all aspects of British rule, however, were economically favourable to India.

At least three-quarters of the people were directly dependent upon agriculture, and land revenues were the major component of government income, three-fifths of it in the mid-1850s. In Bengal, Benares, and much of Madras a permanent zamindari settlement had been made whereby those with feudal rights to land were given confirmed titles in return for fixed payments, amounting to 90 per cent of the fixed revenue assessments made for their land by British officials, and peasants were given security so long as they paid customary or proper dues to landlords. Dutt regarded the permanent settlement of 1793 as 'the wisest and most successful measure which the British nation has ever adopted in India'[1], because the incentive it gave to agricultural improvement and saving prevented subsequent famines in Bengal. He was more critical of the other two land systems introduced by the E.I.C. The ryotwari system was applied to the newer territories of Madras which had few zamindars; there the Company's agents set rents for lands and leased them directly to ryots or peasants on an annual basis. These peasants lacked security because neither rents nor tenures were fixed, and the level of rents was one-third of net produce as against the more usual one-quarter in Bengal. In Dutt's judgement, the ryotwari system made Madras 'a scene of depression and agricultural distress unparalleled even in India in that age'.[2] The third system was the mahalwari settlement made in North India; revenue collectors granted leases of mahals or estates to land-

---

[1] Dutt, *The Economic History of India*, vol. i, p. 290.
[2] ibid., vol. ii, p. 50.

lords and village communities, and so adjusted rent as to keep a landlord's profit down to one-fifth of his assessment. This system was so harshly applied that it had to be modified. Bentinck gave some relief by reducing the Company's share of the net rent from 83 to 66 per cent and by fixing settlements for thirty years. Even this was too much, as had to be officially recognized in 1855 when the state's proportion was lowered to one-half, a proportion which became standard for land settlements in the Central Provinces, Oudh, and the Punjab and, after 1864, was applied to Madras and Bombay where peasants paid rents directly to the government.

Outside Bengal, then, land tax bore heavily upon both peasants and landlords in the first half of the nineteenth century, offsetting gains from suppression of banditry or warfare and from resumed cultivation of lands which had been abandoned. The E.I.C. certainly spent a good deal on irrigation works. In the 1820s it restored the fourteenth-century West Jumna Canal, and in the 1830s both the seventeenth-century East Jumna Canal and the ancient Coleroon Works in Madras. In the final decade of its existence the Company also undertook important new works: the Godavari and Krishna Works in Madras and the Ganges Canal in the United Provinces. Altogether these schemes irrigated about 4 million acres and brought striking benefits. The Coleroon Works, for example, were said to have made Tanjore permanently prosperous and the West Jumna Canal to have saved crops worth £1,500,000 during the famine of 1837. But the Company's investment on irrigation was a very small proportion of its land revenue, and rents were promptly raised in the irrigated areas to give a handsome return on this investment.

The most damaging accompaniment of British rule was the partial destruction of Indian handicrafts. Bentinck, in 1829, had noted the sympathy of the Court of Directors with a report by its Board of Trade, 'exhibiting the gloomy picture of the effects of a commercial revolution productive of so much present suffering to numerous classes in India'.[1] Further evidence was provided by various witnesses to the Select Committee which reported on renewal of the Company's charter. Larpent claimed that 'we have destroyed the manufactures of India', and pleaded

[1] The following quotations are from Dutt, op. cit., vol. ii, ch. 7.

for remission of the British duty of silk in order to help 'the last of the expiring manufactures of India'. Trevelyan spoke of British cottons displacing Indian weaving; 'Dacca which was the Manchester of India has fallen from a very flourishing town to a very poor and small one'. Martin pointed to 'the decay and destruction of Surat, of Dacca, of Murshedabad, and other places where native manufactures have been carried on'. Sym remarked that many craftsmen had lost their livelihood through imports of textiles, glassware, tools, implements, and brassware, and had turned chiefly to agriculture.

Cotton goods, by 1850, were 39 per cent of India's imports but only 4 per cent of exports, and silk goods were only 2 per cent of exports. Much the biggest export item was opium, a Company monopoly, which provided more than one-third of export receipts. It was followed by raw cotton which provided one-fifth and then by indigo and sugar which, between them, provided the same proportion. These four items thus accounted for about nine-tenths of India's exports and other primary commodities, such as jute, hides, and skins, for much of the small remainder. Textiles, however, accounted for nearly one-half of India's imports.

There were other drastic changes in its traditional trade by the middle of the century. Less than one-tenth of India's exports now went to Arabia, Iran, and Malaya and most of the one-third which went to China comprised opium. The United Kingdom, however, took almost one-half of India's exports and furnished nearly three-quarters of its imports. There was a corresponding shift to western shipping, as 957,000 tons of European vessels entered Indian ports in 1850 but only 84,000 tons of Asian vessels. Shipbuilding was entirely given up in Calcutta, although some continued at Bombay, handicapped by non-recognition of Indian ships as British in countries which had signed reciprocity treaties with Britain.

Over the next half century India's foreign trade more than quadrupled in sterling value and also in volume, judging from tonnage figures for ships at Indian ports. Opium's contribution to export receipts greatly declined and four other primary commodities became just as important; raw cotton, raw jute, grain, and hides. Tea also became an important export item, as did two types of modern manufactures, cotton goods and jute goods.

Cotton textiles, nevertheless, kept their place as the leading import and new industrial imports appeared in the form of machinery or railway equipment. Two old imports, salt and metals, dwindled and imports generally became diversified.

This extraordinarily rapid growth in trade and the changes in its composition were caused by a variety of influences, some of them interconnected. Most important, perhaps, was the development of modern transportation. Internally this came from railway construction and externally from improvements to steamships and the opening of the Suez Canal. By 1900 steamships carried about 4 million tons of goods from Indian ports and railway goods traffic reached 43 million tons, far more than in any other Asian country, if only one-tenth of the corresponding British traffic.

Indian railway development began in 1849 when agreements were signed with two private companies; by the time of the Mutiny one of them had constructed 121 miles of track from Calcutta to Raniganj and the other 91 miles from Bombay to Kalyan and beyond. Four years previously Dalhousie had outlined a general scheme for a unified trunk railway system, to be built by private companies under state supervision and with state aid obtained partly by loans raised in Britain. The benefits, he said, were incalculable:

Great tracts are teeming with produce they cannot dispose of. Others are scantily bearing what they could carry in abundance if only it could be conveyed whither it is needed. . . . Ships from every part of the world crowd our ports in search of produce which we have, or could obtain, in the interior, but which at present we cannot profitably fetch to them.[1]

Contracts accordingly were negotiated in 1859 with eight companies for 5,000 miles of railways and, by 1869, they had built 4,255 miles at a cost of £8,900,000. But costs proved unexpectedly high, and the system of guarantees did not encourage strenuous efforts at economy. When the Government of India had to pay nearly £14,000,000 to meet guaranteed interest on railway capital, this system of railway development became discredited.

[1] Quoted in Knowles, *Economic Development of the British Overseas Empire*, pp. 334–5.

During the next decade the Government itself borrowed in the London money market to build new lines, unfortunately on a 3 ft. 3 in. gauge instead of the 5 ft. 6 in. gauge previously used; lines in the Indus Valley and the Punjab had later to be reconstructed when frontier wars and famine showed the narrow gauge to be inadequate. Some 4,225 miles of track were added in this decade but the Government still found the financial burden heavy, especially as the rupee began to depreciate. It could not slow down construction, if only because the Famine Commission of 1880 stressed the urgent need for more railways. The method of company construction was accordingly revived under less onerous terms to the state. From 1880 to 1900 railways were built by the state and the companies at a rapid rate of 744 miles a year, so that the system gained another 14,000 miles of broad track together with 10,000 miles of narrow track. India thus completed a reasonably extensive and well developed railway system, although a complex one as it came under no less than thirty-three different authorities.

How far did it realize Lord Dalhousie's great expectations? The first benefits came from the transport of textile fibres. General Briggs had told the select committee on cotton (1848) that India could produce enough of this fibre to meet the demands of the whole world but its exports were hampered by inadequate transport, a deficiency which was also stressed by a director of the E.I.C. A more important factor was the superiority of American cotton which had ten times the Indian share of the British market. But when American supplies were cut by the Civil War, the Indian export leapt from £4 million in 1859 to nearly £38 million in 1864. The export then declined to £20 million in 1870 and to £10 million in 1880, remaining around this level until the turn of the century. Jute exports were also helped by a war. They had begun in 1791 but were restricted by technical difficulties in bleaching or dyeing the fibre. When the difficulties were overcome, in 1838, Dundee developed a jute manufacturing industry which boomed as the Crimean War cut off supplies of Russian hemp. India's export of raw jute accordingly rose from a mere £83,000 in 1850 to £329,000 in 1856. Unlike the cotton export, it kept on rising after the wartime disruption was over, reaching a peak of £4 million in 1872. It fell during the Long Depression and did not regain the

£4 million level until 1882, after which it grew fairly steadily to £11 million in 1900, and to twice that figure in 1914. Railways in Bengal aided the big expansion of jute exports, just as railways in the north-west and south aided the expansion of cotton exports.

These gains were partly offset by declining exports of sugar and, later, indigo. Sugar was widely grown in both North India and various parts of the Deccan, but domestic consumption was so large that it was a somewhat marginal export, checked by high British duties and superior competition from the West Indies. In 1836, however, the duty on Indian sugar was lowered to the same level as for the West Indies, and the abolition of slavery led to an immediate decline in the West Indian output. India's sugar export rose to nearly £2 million in 1850, but thereafter dwindled increasingly until only £176,000 worth was exported in 1900. The export of indigo was boosted by the sack of Santo Domingo, much the largest supplier, during the Wars of the French Revolution. India doubled its export between 1800 and 1830 and by 1850 was receiving £2 million for the dyestuff. Growth was then slowed down by the development of chemical dyes following Perkins's discovery of analine in 1857, but the export reached a peak of £4,600,000 in 1896. A year earlier the Germans had invented synthetic indigo, so that the Indian export fell from 9,000 tons to only 1,000 tons in 1913.

When slavery was abolished in the West Indies the E.I.C., for the first time, allowed European planters in India. They could not establish themselves as sugar producers but the Company helped them, often by loans, to set up as indigo planters in Bengal. They were, however, zamindars rather than planters as they sublet land to peasants on contracts which specified the indigo crop and the price for its delivery to the planter's factory. Seasonal labour for such a factory was partly supplied by hill-coolies. These English planters treated tenants so harshly that there were sufficiently bad riots or disturbances in Bengal for the House of Commons to set up a committee of inquiry in 1860. But little came of this and indigo planting shifted from Bengal to the United Provinces and Tirhut.

The new planters had more success with coffee. Although this plant had been introduced to India during the sixteenth century, it was not cultivated on any considerable scale until the 1830s.

Most coffee plantations were in Mysore and adjacent parts of South India, and flourished up to 1862 when their export reached 19 million lb. or £340,000. In that year borer beetle and leaf blight began to inflict great damage, and some coffee planters switched to tea or cinchona. Exports, nevertheless, kept rising to £1,500,000 in 1880, and maintained this level until 1913, in spite of powerful competition from Brazil.

Tea, of course, is India's leading plantation industry. Wild tea plants had been recognized in Assam before the improving Bentinck sent officials to China in order to obtain seeds and labour for government tea plantations. These were sold, in 1839, to the private Assam Tea Company which found that neither the Chinese tree nor its hybrid did nearly so well as local varieties. It succeeded in exporting Assam leaf about 1850, after which many other planters took up tea, not only in Assam, but in Bengal, South India, and Ceylon. Tea planting, indeed, went ahead so fast that there was a crisis in 1866 through overspeculation. But the industry's export rose from £309,000 to £4,420,000 in 1888, when it overtook Chinese exports to the British market, and to £6,120,000 in 1900, when Britain took 137 million pounds of Indian tea as against 24 million pounds of Chinese tea. The popularity of Indian or Ceylon tea quickly spread to other Anglo-Saxon markets in North America and Australasia. As Indians, at this time, drank little tea, 96 per cent of the crop was exported.

Railways and steamers also made possible a large export of grain. The industrial revolution had increased Britain's need for food imports, and the land tax forced the Indian peasants to surrender a large part of their crops. Before the opening of the Suez Canal India was already exporting considerable quantities of rice, 8 million tons in 1833 and more than twice that amount before the Irish famine of 1845–6 pushed the export even higher. Wheat, however, was not exported until the Canal was opened, and then became as important an export as rice. Combined grain exports rose from less that £5 million in 1870 to £15 million in 1890, with some dips because of harvest variations, in particular the famine of 1877. The more serious famine of 1897–1900 reduced grain exports to under £10 million but they later trebled to reach £31 million in 1914. India was then exporting one-tenth of its rice and one-seventh of its wheat. New steamers

and the Canal had a similar repercussion on the export of oil-
seeds—castor oil, groundnut, linseed, mustard, rape, and
sesame. This export rose from £2 million just before the Canal
was opened to around £10 million in the 1880s and 1890s. In
Europe it met requirements for lubrication, lamp oil or candles,
soap, cosmetics, paints, dyeing, dressing hides, and linoleum,
but in India the oil-seeds were also used for edible purposes.

How were such large exports of cereals or other foodstuffs
obtained from a poor country whose own population doubled
between 1850 and 1914? There must have been a sufficient
increase in the area of land brought under cultivation. The
earliest estimate here is that made by the Famine Commission
of 1880 which put the sown area of British India at 188 million
acres. Later official statistics show the same cultivated area in
1891, an increase of over 5 per cent up to 1901, and a further
increase of 11 per cent up to 1913. The overall increase of 17 per
cent was not far short of the corresponding growth of population
between 1880 and 1913. It would seem likely that, if the cultivated area expanded to match population growth in the later
part of the nineteenth century, it would have kept pace with
population earlier.

In 1913, however, one-fifth of the cultivated area was under
irrigation, but only one-eighth in 1890 and a much smaller proportion before that. We have already noted that the E.I.C. had
restored or built canals, which may have irrigated an area of
4 million acres, and made handsome profits from this activity.
Private companies, not surprisingly, were inspired to take up
canal building when the E.I.C. was dissolved. An East India
Irrigation Company, formed in 1858, planned a series of canals
in Orissa, Midnapur, and Bengal but spent its whole capital
before the Orissa and Midnapur canals were completed or the
Son Canals in Bengal were begun. The state had to take over all
these works in 1866 and, in 1888, the great canal system between
the Kistna and Tungabhadra Rivers largely built by the
Madras Irrigation Company at a loss of £2 million.

Irrigation canals, after that, became entirely a matter of state
enterprise and were financed, like the railway programme, by
sterling loans. The Sind desert canals were begun in 1873,
greatly extending earlier valuable work by Jacob in the 1850s,
and the Lower Swat Canal was begun in 1876 to help pacify

Table 4

INDIA: KEY STATISTICS, 1835–1914

	Unit	1835	1840	1850	1860	1870	1880	1890	1900	1910	1914
POPULATION	millions		130	150	181	224	257	277	285	299	304[a]
REAL INCOME PER HEAD	Rs 1948/9				169	172	197	204	199	220	241[a]
LIFE EXPECTANCY	years						25	25	24	23	20
MERCHANDISE EXPORTS	£ million	11	11	18	33	55	62	75	69	108	163
MERCHANDISE IMPORTS	"	5	6	12	24	35	44	54	64	89	128
NET IMPORTS OF TREASURE	"	2	1	3	10	3	6	15	8	15	12
COMPOSITION OF EXPORTS	per cent										
Opium				36	34	20	18	9	9	6	1
Raw Cotton				20	24	37	17	17	9	15	17
Cotton Goods				4	3	3	4	10	6	6	5
Raw Jute				1	1	1	5	8	10	8	13
Jute Goods							1	3	7	9	12
Indigo				11	6	6	5	3	2			
Grains				5	10	8	12	20	12	19	19
Sugar				10	4	3	1	1			
Coffee					1	1	1	2	1	1	1
Hides and Skins				2	2	1	2	5	11	7	7
Tea						2	5	6	9	6	7
Other				11	15	18	26	16	24	23	18
COMPOSITION OF IMPORTS	per cent										
Cottons				39	47	54	49	41	38	35	38
Silk and Silk Goods				3	3	4	5	3	3	3	2
Woollens				2	1	2	3	2	3	3	2
Salt				6	1	2	1	1	1		
Metals				15	11	8	7	8	9	12	12
Machinery					4	5	2	2	3	4	4
Railway Stores, etc.					8	17	5	3	5	3	6
Liquors				5	4	3	3	2	2	1	1
Other				30	21	5	25	38	36	39	35

DIRECTION OF TRADE	per cent									
Arabia and Iran: Exports		6[b]	4	4	3	3	2	2	1	1
Imports		7[b]	5	2	2	1	2	1	1	1
Malaya: Exports		12[b]	4	4	4	7	6	4	3	3
Imports		7[b]	3	3	3	3	3	3	2	2
China: Exports		16[b]	34	38	22	20	12	7	10	6
Imports		16[b]	8	5	4	4	3	3	2	1
United Kingdom: Exports		52[b]	45	47	54	42	33	29	25	23
Imports		60[b]	71	84	81	82	78	66	63	63
Japan: Exports		—	—	—	—	—	1	2	7	9
Imports		—	—	—	—	—	1	1	3	3
SHIPPING (ENTERED)										
European: Vessels	number	1,390[b]	2,462[c]	3,314	3,614[d]	4,304	3,777	3,263	2,417	2,444
Tonnage	thous. tons	459[b]	957[b]	1,456	2,228[d]	3,199	3,779	4,166	5,916	6,199
Non-European: Vessels	number		1,383[c]	1,723	795[d]	1,901	1,713	969	1,362	1,096
Tonnage	thous. tons		84[c]	121	75[d]	101	84	59	233	216
RAILWAYS										
Track open	miles		20[e]	838	4,711	8,996	16,404	24,752	32,099	34,656
Goods	m. tons				4	10	23	43	66	82
Passengers	million				19	49	114	176	372	458
TELEGRAPH LINES	miles		32[e]	11,093	13,534	20,346	37,070	55,055	74,828	81,593
COAL OUTPUT	m. tons					1.0	2.2	6.1	12.0	16.2
IRRIGATED AREA	m. acres						27[f]	33	41	47
Ratio of Cultivated Area	per cent						12[f]	16	21	21
FOOD CROPS	Index							100	96	99
COMMERCIAL CROPS	Index							100	105	126
Ratio of Food to Non-Food crops	per cent							78	76	72
WHOLESALE PRICES	Index				72	91	78	100	128	154
COST OF LIVING (Cities)	Index				92	98	100	126	132	165
RUPEE/STERLING VALUE	pence	24	24	24	24	20	18	16	16	16

a 1915   b 1841   c 1851   d 1871   e 1853   f 1892

Sources:
Financial and Commercial Statistics of British India
Statistical Abstracts for British India
Davis, *The Population of India and Pakistan*
Singh (ed.), *Economic History of India Since 1857*

the north-west frontier region above Peshawar. The arid Punjab was colonized by a number of big irrigation schemes. After the Bari Doab network came the Sirhind Canal to tap the waters of the Sutlej in 1882. The Lower Chenab Canal (1892) and the Jhelum Canal (1901) were both associated with large colonization schemes. By the end of the century Punjab works were irrigating 3,500,000 acres and had greatly added to Karachi's wheat exports. Here, as Woodruff says, irrigation 'meant that a desert suddenly blossomed, that where a few nomad tribes had grazed their goats and camels towns and villages sprang up and good wheat was grown'.[1]

In the United Provinces no deserts had to be brought into bloom, but irrigation could offset the vagaries of monsoons in order to prevent famines. The E.I.C's Eastern Jumna and Ganges Canals were supplemented by the Agra Canal in 1875, the Lower Ganga Canal in 1880, the Betwar Canal in 1893, and the Ken Canal in 1909. Before this last work some 2,740,000 acres were under irrigation in Agra and Oudh, and the Ken Canal eventually added another 140,000 acres. Extensions were also made to the irrigation system of Madras which, by the end of the century, watered 3,500,000 acres. In Bengal the Orissa, Midnapur, and Son Canals, projected by the East India Irrigation Company and completed by the state, watered 840,000 acres.

Many held that government money would have been far better spent on irrigation, which cost £24 million up to 1902 and was profitable, than on railways, which cost £226 million and had large deficits. Cotton, the great builder of Madras canals, told a parliamentary committee of 1872 that irrigation, besides making direct provision against famine, was superior to railways as a means of transport.

My great point is this, that what India wants is water carriage; that the railways have completely failed; they cannot carry at the price required; they cannot carry the quantities; and they cost the country three millions a year, and increasing, to support them. The steamboat canals would not have cost more than one-eighth that of the railways; would carry any quantities at nominal prices and at any speed; would require no support from the Treasury; and would be combined with irrigation.[2]

[1] *The Men Who Ruled India*, vol. ii, p. 112.
[2] Quoted in Dutt, *The Economic History of India*, vol. ii, p. 270.

Sir John Trevelyan took up this last point: 'Irrigation is every-thing in India, water is more valuable than land, because when water is applied to land it increases its productiveness at least sixfold.'[1] Support for this argument also came from Lawrence, a former Viceroy, among others who knew India.

Whatever the merits of irrigation canals over railways in pro-viding transport and safeguarding against famine, it is certain that India needed far more irrigation to increase food produc-tion, and that old and close association with agriculture made irrigation fit more easily than railways into a traditional eco-nomy. But that is precisely why some have favoured railways, and recalled Karl Marx's observations on this subject.

When you have once introduced machinery into locomotion of a country, which possesses iron and coals, you are unable to withhold it from its fabrication. You cannot maintain a net of railways over an immense country without introducing all those industrial processes necessary to meet the immediate and current wants of railway loco-motion, and out of which there must grow the application of mach-inery to those branches of industry not immediately connected with railways. The railway system will therefore become, in India, truly the forerunner of modern industry.[2]

There was not much support for this thesis from the occu-pational censuses; that for 1911 showed 72 per cent of the work-ing population in agriculture, 11 per cent in industry, 6 per cent in trade, 1·5 per cent in transport, and less than 0·2 per cent in mining. Coal-mining dates from 1815 when a seam was dis-covered at Raniganj in Bengal and its output sold to steam-boats plying inland waters. Other coalfields were discovered before the middle of the century, just in time to help the rail-ways which became much the biggest customer. Output grew from 285,000 tons in 1860 to 12,000,000 tons in 1910, and India even developed a small export to Ceylon and Malaya. No iron industry emerged until 1875 when the Bengal Iron and Steel Company began operations at Barakar, but it did not attempt steel-making until 1903 and lost heavily on the venture. In 1900 India's production of iron ore was only 50,000 tons, and there was no real iron and steel industry until the Tata Company began large-scale operations at Sakchi in 1911. The one mining

[1] ibid.
[2] Quoted in Singh (ed.), *Economic History of India Since* 1857, p. 334.

development which catered for an export market was extraction of manganese from rich deposits in the Central Provinces; operations began here in 1892 and made India, by 1907, the world's largest exporter of manganese with a shipment of 902,291 tons. But manganese was not important enough for this shipment to add more than a trifling percentage to India's total export receipts.

Industrialization made a significant beginning, not through railways to heavy industry as Marx had predicted, but through textiles in light industry. Two small Parsee cotton mills began at Bombay in the mid-1850s and their success attracted some merchants who did well out of the cotton boom of the early 1860s. The boom, however, was followed by financial crisis and depression in Bombay so that development was slow. It did not quicken until J. N. Tata opened his large Empress Mill at Nagpur in 1887, an example which led to a trebling in the number of cotton mills by 1900. India then had 191 mills, equipped with nearly 5,000,000 spindles and over 40,000 looms, and employing more than 156,000 workers. There was further growth between 1900 and 1914 to 6,600,000 spindles, 97,000 looms, and 260,000 workers so that India's mill production reached 650,000,000 pounds of cotton yarn or twist and over 1,000,000 yards of piece-goods. The industry was heavily concentrated in Bombay and Ahmadabad which together had four-fifths of the looms, three-fifths of the spindles, and two-thirds of the workers; but cotton mills operated in other provinces from Bengal to the Punjab or to Madras and Pondicherry.

The scale and expansion of India's modernized cotton industry reflects its ability to compete in the domestic market, as does the fall of Manchester goods from 54 per cent of total imports in 1870 to 38 per cent in 1900, a proportion to which they were held. More than that, India was able to revive exports of yarn and cloth to China and South-east Asia and to supply yarn to the new Japanese cotton industry. By 1890 these exports had reached £7,000,000, one-tenth of India's total export receipts and one-third of its own imports of cotton goods. This hopeful progress, however, was soon checked by the vigorous expansion of Japan's cotton industry. By the turn of the century Japan could meet domestic requirements for yarn or twist and had begun exporting both yarn and cloth to China and other Asian countries. The result was that, although India's export of cotton goods rose in value to over £8,000,000 in 1914, it fell, as a proportion of total exports, to 6 per cent in 1900 and to 5 per cent in 1914.

By that time a new jute textile industry was contributing over twice as much to exports as the cotton industry, and employing almost as many people. It began soon after the Crimean War had brought a boom in raw jute; the first spinning mill was set up in 1855, and, four years later, the first power loom came into use near Calcutta. Progress was slow for some time because Calcutta's gunny cloth was so inferior as to obtain markets only in Bengal or neighbouring Burma and, up to 1873, there were no more than five mills having a total of 1,250 looms. The big impetus to the industry's development came from the Suez Canal and the improved steamships which rapidly increased exports of bulky goods packed in gunny bags or bales. Jute goods began to make such a significant contribution to India's export receipts that Calcutta, by 1894, was using more raw jute than Dundee, although less efficient processing kept its output below Dundee's level until 1908. Expansion, indeed, was so rapid that a Jute Mills' Association was formed, in 1884, to regulate competition by restricting output. For ten years it limited the increase of mills from twenty-four to twenty-nine and the number of looms from 6,926 to 10,048. But the need for such restrictions passed as the Long Depression lifted in Europe and rising prices caused a further upsurge of world trade. Calcutta's looms then increased to 15,340 in 1900 and to 36,050 in 1913, when jute goods became India's third most important export, after grain and oil-seeds.

Many have wondered, and some have speculated, about the economic effect of British rule upon India and, in particular, about the way living standards were affected by the rapid growth of foreign trade, the great improvements in transport, the irrigation works, and the beginnings of modern industrialization. The question is both inevitable and important, but the means of answering it are scant and treacherous. There was certainly a huge increase of population, put by the least imperfect estimate at a change from 150 million in 1850 to 304 million in 1915 and, as we have seen, a corresponding growth of food production and a still more rapid growth of cash crops for expanding world markets. Railways, irrigation, and the Famine Code, moreover, reduced the terrible effects of monsoon failures and, although there were twenty-one years of famine between 1850 and 1914, the very meaning of the word changed. In Mughal days famine meant widespread death by starvation but, by the end of Queen Victoria's reign, it meant relief works for drought-stricken peasants and priority deliveries of grain by railways to deficient areas so that direct deaths from starvation became quite rare.

These were great and beneficial achievements. But they are not reflected in the admittedly poor demographic statistics, which show a rise in the estimated death rate from 41·3 in 1881–91 to 48·6 in 1911–21, and a corresponding fall in the expectation of life at birth from 25 to 20 years. To some extent these changes resulted from monsoon failures, irrigation, and urbanization. For if starvation was now prevented, plague continued to increase with drought conditions, and claimed over 5 million dead in the decade 1901–10. Irrigation improved food supplies but it also provided breeding ponds for mosquitoes, and malaria was the greatest single cause of death in India. The huge growth of population and trade, moreover, crowded millions into large towns where, owing to bad housing and sanitation, death rates much exceeded those in country areas.

Such demographic evidence does not, of course, rule out the possibility that Indians experienced some rise in average real income. The most careful estimate here is that made by Mukerji, whose figures show a rise, from a pitifully low level, of nearly 43 per cent between 1860 and 1914. This, if true, would mean about the same rate of improvement as occurred in British real income per head; for Indian income per head, in both 1860 and 1914, was close to one-twelfth of the corresponding British figure. Here, perhaps, is an argument for international trade as an agent of economic growth for underdeveloped countries, at least in Queen Victoria's Golden Age. But who can be sure when the author of these income estimates warns that 'information on this topic is not available in India in any reliable form'?[1]

---

[1] Quoted in Singh, *Economic History of India Since 1857*, ch. 25, p. 661.

5. *Plantations and mines*

A plantation is an agricultural enterprise which exploits a fairly large area by modern or scientific methods of cultivation, employs native workers under foreign direction, and produces mainly for an export market. This, at least, is Robequain's definition and he observes that plantations have nowhere else had such great success as in Malaya, Indonesia, and the Philippines. To these Asian countries we should join Ceylon, the plantation economy *par excellence*. Gourou rightly emphasizes the foreign character of plantations; their very plants have usually been introduced by foreign enterprise, methods of cultivation are non-traditional, products and profits both go largely to western countries, and 'the plantation is an enclave of another form of civilization'. It is foreign, too, in a further sense; much of the non-European labour employed is provided by migrants, attracted from other Asian countries by the work offered or brought from them by planters in order to remedy local scarcities of labour. Hence arose problems both of economic 'dualism' and of social 'pluralism'—of glaring difference between the efficiency of western enterprises and contiguous traditional activities, and of social division between large groups of immigrant Asians and the peoples among whom they lived.

Although plantations had early developed in the West Indies and tropical America on the basis of imported African slave labour, they did not appear in Asia before the nineteenth century. The *encomienda* system introduced from Mexico to the Philippines stopped far short of plantation agriculture. It involved feudal grants of estates to Spanish colonists who collected taxes and rents from tenants farming on traditional lines, and there were no important exports of agricultural products until quite late in the eighteenth century, by which time *encomienda* had disappeared. The Spanish, however, may be said to have laid partial foundations for a plantation system by substituting private for communal ownership of village lands, which came to be held by the Catholic Church and Filipino chiefs or *caciques*, and by introducing many plants. Governor-General Vargas (1778–87) was particularly active in fostering all kinds of cultivation: cinnamon, coffee, hemp, indigo, opium, pepper, silk, sugar, and tea. His efforts were helped by the Royal Company of the Philippines (1785–1834) which invested considerable sums in trying to develop indigo, pepper, silk, and sugar. Vargas also created a state tobacco monopoly, which was so successful in making peasants cultivate this plant that a large export developed. Hemp and sugar became important exports under private enterprise but, up to the close of Spanish rule, cultivation was on a *métayer* system. True plantations developed in the Philippines only after American annexation in 1898.

Nor did Ceylon acquire more than a single plantation during the period that it was under the Dutch. Their export monopoly of cinnamon had depended upon supplies obtained by the Chiliya caste from the jungle. Most wild cinnamon trees were in the territory of the independent King of Kandy, who gave the Dutch a good deal of trouble. Governor Franck, therefore, decided to establish a cinnamon plantation at Colombo and encouraged smallholders to cultivate trees in their own gardens. The British took over the plantation when they annexed Ceylon, and Douglas noted that its output of 400,000 lb. 'may easily be rendered sufficient to answer the consumption of the world'. Governor North, however, stopped cultivation by smallholders and official plantations became so overstripped of bark that recourse had again to be made to the Kandyan jungles. Stocks, nevertheless, accumulated because the government tried to keep up the price, now threatened by inferior varieties such as cassia grown in South India, South China, and the Philippines. The monopoly was abolished in 1833, after which a few European plantations were established near Colombo but were forced out, in the 1850s, by a continued decline of price. Sinhalese were more adaptable as they switched to the inferior varieties which, in 1867, brought this export to a peak value of £134,269.

Private planting in Ceylon began with coffee which, at the time of the British annexation, was fairly widely grown as a peasant crop for sale to Moslem merchants. Sir Edward Barnes (1820–31), an autocratic and able governor, took steps to promote European planting. These included abolition of export duties on coffee, taxes on coffee estates, and traditional labour services from their workers; road-building into the Kandyan country whose hills were most suitable for growing coffee; transfer of the Royal Botanical Gardens from Colombo to Peradeniya (near Kandy) and encouragement of its staff to work on problems of growing coffee. He even started a plantation of his own, opposite the Botanical Gardens, about the same time as George Bird developed one at Sinnapitiya, in Gompala. Few immediately followed their example as, up to 1835, less than 4,000 acres of Crown lands had been sold and coffee remained predominantly a peasant export of around 2,000 tons. In that year the British duty on Ceylon coffee was lowered from 9*d*. to 6*d*. a pound, the same level as for West Indian coffee. Over the next decade the price trebled and there was feverish activity as officials, soldiers, and other Europeans took up 250,000 acres of Crown Land and pushed coffee exports to 20,000 tons.

Planters had some difficulties. Clear titles were hard to obtain because most peasants in the Kandyan country held land by service tenures and all had customary grazing rights in forest areas. Mackenzie, taking the view that the Kandyan King's land had been ceded to the British Crown, unsuccessfully pressed the Colonial Office for power to dispossess peasants who could not prove individual ownership. Campbell, the next governor, obtained such power in respect of forest lands but the Kandyans did not protest because they were only too anxious to sell their rights at inflating prices. On the other hand, they were not tempted to perform more than casual labour, partly because most early plantations had a reputation for treating workers unfairly. Tamils, however, could be recruited from South India under an indenture system involving advances to agents known as *kanganis*, who brought the immigrants by boat to Jaffna and then trekked them hundreds of miles to contracting plantations. Such migration appears to have reached a peak of 74,000 in 1844 after which it fell to 32,000 in 1848, no doubt because of the appalling difficulties Tamils had to face on both directions of the journey. The third problem was transport, said by some to be almost as difficult as the growing of coffee because Barnes's military roads were not designed for bullock waggons carrying thousands of tons to Colombo. More roads were built, in spite of the abolition of *corvée* labour, but planters had to pay high tolls for expensive maintenance. The cost of transport worked out at around 3*d*. a mile, and further costs were incurred at Colombo for drying and picking over beans which had been frequently exposed to rain along the route.

Large gains, nevertheless, were made from cultivation and

fantastic gains from speculation in coffee lands, until a British financial crisis tumbled the price from 45*s*. a hundredweight in 1845 to 17*s*. in 1849. Governor Tennant reported: 'The consternation thus produced in Ceylon was proportionate to the extravagance of the hopes that were blasted; estates were forced into the market, and madly sold off for a twentieth part of the outlay incurred in forming them.'[1] Officials had been prohibited from acquiring estates in 1846. Now small investors were forced out, too; those planters who survived were stronger men, backed by British banks or financial agencies in Ceylon.

The depression led to political as well as to economic troubles. Ceylon's maritime provinces had been taken over almost peacefully from the Dutch, but the Kandyan Kingdom had repulsed British forces which attacked it in 1803. Ten years later the British struck again, deposed the royal family, and annexed the kingdom; but they had then to contend with a two-year revolt of feudal chiefs who, when it was put down, lost most of their influence. Now came another Kandyan rebellion as the government levied a new poll tax and a new tax on fire-arms, in order to meet a sudden budget deficit. The rebellion was localized, quite ineffectual but so savagely repressed that the House of Commons held a select committee of inquiry. Tennant's evidence stressed fear or resentment of European encroachment: 'The causes . . . are in a great degree to be traced to the operations of coffee planting and the introduction not only of Europeans as settlers in the midst of their hills and forests, but likewise to that which has given them much greater offence, viz: the introduction of Malabar coolies.'[2]

Little resulted from the inquiry beyond dismissal of Tennant and another senior member of the Ceylon Civil Service, but the trouble was soon forgotten as coffee prices recovered and planters expanded production to make coffee the colony's major export. Development was fairly steady, helped by shelters provided for transient Tamil coolies, by improvements to roads, and by construction of a railway from Colombo to Kandy. By 1870 coffee plantations extended over 176,000 acres, involved a capital of £12 million, and provided two-thirds of Ceylon's exports.

Thirty years later their contribution had become negligible,

---

[1] Quoted in Bailey, *Ceylon*, p. 114.   [2] ibid., p. 111.

owing to the ravages of coffee rust, first noticed in 1869 at Galloola. It quickly spread to every coffee-growing district and halved the average yield, but returns were buoyed up by a rising world price and the area devoted to coffee went on increasing to 275,000 acres in 1879 so that its contribution to export receipts was maintained for another decade. Thereafter decline was rapid; from a peak of 50,000 tons in 1870 shipments fell to 5,000 tons in 1890, and to insignificant quantities later.

Some planters switched to cinchona trees, propagated from cuttings by the Botanical Gardens. The first commercial export was sent in 1868 to the London market which paid a premium for it over supplies from India or Java. There was a boom between 1878 and 1883 which brought cultivation to 64,000 acres and exports to 3,350 tons or £449,000. After that the price fell, through overproduction, from 10s. an ounce to 1s. in 1892, and cinchona became hopelessly unprofitable.

Planters found their real salvation in tea. Assam seedlings had reached the Botanical Gardens as early as 1839, and experiments were also made with Chinese varieties which have contributed to Ceylon's hybrids. It was not until 1872 that James Taylor, the famous superintendent of the Loolecondera estate and the local pioneer of cinchona cultivation, manufactured tea for sale in Ceylon—at twice the price obtainable in London. Within eleven years Mincing Lane recognized Ceylon tea as having distinctive qualities from either Indian or Chinese varieties, and planters took up tea-growing so enthusiastically that they uprooted coffee or cinchona trees and felled huge areas of virgin forest with scant regard to problems of erosion. By 1900 tea plantations covered 384,000 acres, exported 67,000 tons, and provided almost three-fifths of the colony's export receipts.

Tea, at this date, had become practically the only plantation crop. After the opening of the Suez Canal, Ceylon, like other tropical countries, gained from increasing world demand for oil-seeds with the result that coconut products contributed about one-tenth of export receipts. A few long-resident British families had coconut plantations, as had some wealthier Sinhalese, because coconuts require little labour or equipment. But most of the output was a subsidiary crop from small village gardens in the maritime provinces, supplying local rather than export markets. Sinhalese, too, supplied the cinnamon which still contributed a modest 2–3 per cent of export receipts.

The next great development in plantation agriculture was the cultivation of rubber. Soon after Kew received *Hevea* seeds from Brazil it sent a few of the resulting plants to Ceylon, where the Botanical Gardens experimented with seeds and terrain. Cultivation was unremunerative until the cycle and automobile industries suddenly increased demands for rubber. Ceylon had less than 1,000 acres under rubber in 1896 but 217,000 acres by 1912. Its export receipts, accordingly, rose from £6,300,000 to £15,000,000 between 1900 and 1914, and rubber contributed one-half of the increase. Most of the remainder came from tea, whose export rose from £3,700,000 to £6,300,000.

By 1914 tea and rubber plantations were providing 70 per cent of the colony's export receipts, and it had become highly dependent upon their peculiar combination of British capital and Tamil labour. Tamils were one-quarter of the population, and Ceylon was so densely populated, and had devoted so much land to export crops, as to require big imports of rice in order to feed its people. It also depended substantially upon imported cottons in order to clothe them. No other Asian country, except Malaya, underwent such a change from traditional economic life. But the Sinhalese gained only a limited share of the benefits. Plantations were mostly under European control and worked with Tamil labour. British banks and commercial houses handled the larger-scale finance and trade, while Indians predominated in money-lending and retail trade. There was a fairly numerous, western-educated Sinhalese middle class comprising coconut planters, merchants, civil servants, lawyers, doctors, teachers, and clerks but the vast majority of Sinhalese were illiterate peasants working tiny holdings to grow rice, coconuts, or other export sidelines such as cinnamon, cinchona, cloves, hemp, kapok, and tobacco. Ceylon's national income was probably at a considerably higher *per caput* level than India's, but the disparity would be much less for peasant incomes.

Plantations developed more slowly in Indonesia owing to an early concern about undue alienation of native land and to official export monopolies involving levies of produce, land, or labour in place of taxes. These barriers to private planting underwent some modifications or temporary reversals but remained generally effective until the switch from the Culture System to the Liberal System.

Private planters appeared only sporadically in the days of the V.O.C. Some wealthy Chinese had acquired estates from needy regents in the eighteenth century, and used the labour which went with estates for cultivating sugar; but, after the troubles of 1741, this industry was taken over by the Company. Van Imhoff, besides fostering coffee-growing, had tried to encourage Dutch farmers to settle on waste lands. Their contribution, however, was insignificant alongside the system of 'contingents and forced deliveries' of coffee and other crops.

A period of some confusion followed the winding up of the V.O.C., as this occurred during the Napoleonic Wars. Holland itself was taken over, in 1806, by the French who installed Louis Napoleon as king. He sent Daendels to Java in order to reorganize administration and strengthen defences against the British, who had already taken over Malacca, Amboina, the Bandas, and Dutch posts in West Sumatra. This energetic Governor quickly purged the island's corrupt administration and improved its defence by measures which included a road of 1,000 kilometres from Anjer on the west coast to Panarukan on the east. In order to provide finance he extended the system of forced deliveries until the number of coffee trees nearly trebled, promoted cotton-growing on the plains and made even rice an internal state monopoly. He could not, however, sell coffee or other exports to any but a few American merchants because the British tightened their blockade of Java and prepared to invade it. Forced loans and paper issues proving inadequate, Daendels resorted to the sale of large tracts of land around Batavia, including the whole regency of Prabalingga for which a Chinese paid £250,000. He also abolished the careful restrictions imposed by the V.O.C. on rights of private planters to the bonded labour which went with their estates. Before the expected British assault was launched Napoleon annexed Holland to France and recalled Daendels to serve in Europe.

Lord Minto's expedition of 12,000 men occupied Batavia without being resisted and secured, within six weeks, the surrender of Java, Palembang, Timor, and Macassar. After issuing a proclamation which promised to abolish the system of

21

Table 5
Plantation and Mining Economies: Key Statistics, 1825–1913

	Unit	1825	1850	1870	1880	1890	1900	1913
POPULATION	million							
Ceylon		0·8	1·6	2·1	2·6	3·0[1]	3·6[2]	4·1[3]
Java and Madura		6	10		20	24	29	32
Indonesia		11						43
Straits Settlements		0·1	0·3	0·3	0·4	0·4[1]	0·6[2]	0·7[3]
Malaya		0·4				1·4[4]		2·7[3]
Philippines		2·5			6		7	8
EXPORTS	£ million							
Ceylon		0·2	0·3	1·2	5	4	6	15
Indonesia		1·3	5	10	15	15	22	56
Straits Settlements		(2·0)[b]	(3·8)[b]	9	13	19	26	39
Philippines						4		11
COMPOSITION OF EXPORTS	p.c. of country total							
Ceylon Coffee		54[b]	34	66	64	11	1	—
Tea						45	57	42
Vegetable Oils		12[b]		4	9	9	7	6
Rubber						—		27
Indonesia Coffee			34	41	43	23	15	3
Sugar			30	31	34	33	32	25
Indigo			7	3				
Tea				1	1	1	2	4
Tobacco					12	21	14	15
Vegetable Oils					—	1	4	8
Tin					7	6	10	6
Petroleum				1	1	1	2	16
Malaya Tin								29
Vegetable Oils								6
Rubber								20

		total							
Philippines	Coffee						8		
	Sugar						33		18
	Tobacco						12		
	Vegetable Oils								22
	Fibres						41		46
IMPORTS		£ million							
Ceylon			0·3	1·5	4·6	5	6	8	12
Indonesia[a]			1·2	2·4	4·4	12	12	15	37
Straits Settlements			(2·0)[b]	(3·8)[b]	10	14	25	31	46
Philippines							2		12
COMPOSITION OF IMPORTS		p.c. of country total							
Ceylon	Cottons				21	15	9	6	6
	Rice				33	42	34	31	26
Indonesia	Cottons		13	41	36	24	25	20	22
	Rice				1	16	9	10	13
	Fertilizers				—	—	1	3	3
	Iron and Steel				4	2	3	6	8
	Machinery				1	2	3	6	8
Philippines	Cottons						52		25
SHIPPING: (CLEARED AND ENTERED)		million tons							
Ceylon			0·1	0·5	1·4	2·9	5	6	12
Indonesia—at Batavia						1·8[6]		5	
Straits Settlements					1·7	4·8	9	13	23
RAILWAYS		miles open							
Ceylon						139	192	297	672
Indonesia					157	157	2,180	3,020	3,259
									822

[1] 1891 [2] 1901 [3] 1911 [4] 1881 [5] 1830 [6] 1875 [7] 1867

a Private trade but includes government trade through the Nederlandsche Handelmaatschapij (N.H.M.), etc.

b One-half of total trade

Sources:

Carr-Saunders, *World Population*

Cowan, *The Economic Development of South-East Asia*

Ceylon Blue Books

Mills, *British Malaya, 1824–1867*

Report of the Philippines Commission (1901), vol. iv

Lamartine Yates, *Forty Years of Foreign Trade*

Statistical Abstract of the Colonial and Other Possessions of the United Kingdom

Furnivall, *Netherlands India*

Gullick, *Malaya*

contingents and forced deliveries, and appointing the young Stamford Raffles as Lieutenant-Governor of Java, Minto returned to India. Raffles had the advantage both of his own expert knowledge of the Malay world, acquired as assistant secretary at Penang, and the help of an able Dutch official, Muntinghe, who combined valuable experience of Indonesia with reforming zeal. Raffles was unable to do much about Sumatra beyond forcing the Sultan of Palembang to cede Britain the islands of Billiton and Banka and improving their mining of tin. Nor could he do more for the outer islands than ease controls over spices in the Moluccas or over Indonesian shipping, although he tried to suppress the Buginese slave trade.

In Java, however, Raffles 'opened windows and doors so that the wind could blow through the old house' of tired Dutch colonialism. Two of his reforms, it is true, were little more than a continuation of Daendels's policy; he broke the remaining power of Java's princes and, displacing native regents, put residencies or prefectures entirely under the control of European officials. But he made at least one novel and lasting change in administration. The basic unit became the village, under an elective headman approved by the government; villages were grouped into divisions and these into residencies. He also abolished numerous tolls which hampered internal trade, but was less sensible in regard to judicial reforms which included an attempt to impose the peculiarly British system of trial by jury.

Forced deliveries had to be retained in the Preanger districts and in forest lands because financial burdens were unduly swollen by Minto's promise to redeem Daendels's paper money in silver. Elsewhere in Java Raffles substituted a rent from one-quarter to one-half of the land's gross yield, paid in money or rice. In the first year collections were made through village headmen and produced a surprisingly good revenue, but it fell by more than one-half when Raffles too quickly tried direct contracts with individual peasants. Further financial difficulty arose from Napoleon's continental blockade and the British-American war, both of which cut off buyers of coffee and other exports. Raffles was then driven, like Daendels, to raise funds by selling land; 2,000,000 acres, later known as the *particuliere landerijen*, were auctioned to European or Chinese capitalists.

The Court of the E.I.C. had no liking for the heavy demands Raffles made upon its Calcutta treasury, especially as the Directors knew that the British Government intended to restore Java to the Dutch. Hastings, who succeeded Minto in India, was dissatisfied both with Raffles's administration and with his restless scheming for another British empire in South-east Asia. In 1816, accordingly, Raffles was recalled and, a few months later, the Dutch resumed control of their Indonesian possessions. These did not include Bencoolen, a Sumatran port which had long been a British trading post and to which Raffles returned, in 1818, as Lieutenant-Governor. There he seized Palembang and a village on the Sunda Strait, but was obliged by his superiors to hand them back, and he had no more success with plans for retaking Malacca or seizing West Borneo. Hastings, however, did authorize him to establish a British port on some island at the eastern end of the Malacca Strait in order to assure free passage of commerce in case the Dutch renewed attempts at restriction. On 28 January 1819 the expedition reached Singapore where Raffles quickly obtained its cession by the claimant who was to succeed to the Sultanate of Johore, fortified the island before the Dutch could assert their own claims to it, and began developing, as a free port, a little village of sea-gypsies into the great entrepôt of South-east Asia.

This action angered the Dutch and hence embarrassed the British in their negotiations for a general settlement of affairs in Asia. But Hastings effectively supported Raffles as did others who could appreciate the new settlement's potential. Eventually an Anglo-Dutch treaty was concluded, in 1824, whereby the British ceded their posts in Sumatra and undertook never to make settlements on, or treaties with rulers in, Sumatra or any islands south of Singapore. For their part, the Dutch gave up their factories in India, ceded Malacca and withdrew objections to the British occupation of Singapore. Both sides agreed not to attempt monopolies or unfair commercial discrimination, except that the Dutch could keep their monopoly of Moluccan spices which Britain now obtained from transplantings in India.

The Dutch resumed control of Java with so little enthusiasm that, by a Fundamental Law of 1814, colonies were vested in the Crown. William VI declared Indonesian trade open to all nations and sent three commissioners to Batavia one of whom, van der Capellan, was to remain as Governor-General. They revived the dual system of indirect rule through native regents but retained Raffles's administrative divisions, his land-rent system based on the village, forced coffee-growing in the Preanger, and serfdom in the teak forests. When van der Capellan assumed full office he excluded Europeans or Chinese from trading in the Preanger, and then prohibited all tenancy contracts which gave rights to the labour of peasants. These were not the only measures which showed a genuine concern for Indonesians' welfare. A Public Works Administration vigorously improved roads and a new Department of Agriculture, Arts, and Education was set up under Professor Reinwardt; his remarkable work included the Botanic Garden of Buitenzorg, a battle against smallpox by means of mass innoculations, and the beginning of popular education, albeit in Dutch as the language of instruction.

Restoration and development were supported by a revival of trade which, in 1823, brought exports to over £1,000,000, land revenue to £650,000, and total revenue to £2,300,000. Coffee production had sextupled since 1818 and there were big increases for sugar, tobacco, and indigo. But the government's expenditures rose even more rapidly than its revenues so that debt increased by £2,400,000. This naturally disturbed the authorities in Holland where liberals were criticizing van der Capellan for a 'reactionary' policy against European planters, and businessmen were upset both by the predominance of English or American shipping at Batavia and by the high proportion of Manchester goods in Indonesia's imports. The situation was aggravated by a slump in coffee prices and then by the outbreak of the costly Java War of 1825–30, caused by unrest over cancellation of land contracts and exactions of Chinese toll-farmers. Van der Capellan was replaced by Du Bus, whose four years of office had to be largely directed to crushing the rebels; it was estimated that 15,000 troops were killed and that 200,000 Javanese died through cholera, famine, or warfare.

William VI, meanwhile, had taken the lead in forming a Nederlandsche Handelmaatschapij (N.H.M.), a trading company in which he was the chief shareholder and for which he guaranteed a 4½ per cent dividend from the privy purse; its object was to recover a bigger share of Indonesian trade from the British, whose new port at Singapore further threatened Dutch commercial interests. Du Bus, himself a capitalist, set out to encourage European planting by restoring tenancy arrangements and by introducing new crops: cinnamon, cochineal, opium, silk, and tea. Little came of these attempts. Few took up the new crops, outputs of coffee and tobacco declined because of the war, and both sugar and indigo were hit by falling prices. His most durable economic achievement was the foundation, in 1828, of the Java Bank to which the Colonial Government and the N.H.M. jointly subscribed a capital of £100,000 but its success, like that of the N.H.M., lay in the future. Exports declined while imports rose, the colonial debt was mounting and Du Bus even had to mortgage Dutch possessions in Asia to a Calcutta firm. No sooner was the Java War ended, moreover, than the Belgians began a revolt against William which completed the ruin of the Dutch Treasury.

Conditions were also worsening for the Javanese, and not only because of war, plague, and famine. The new system of land taxation was plunging them into increasing debt to Chinese or Arab money-lenders and so diminished the authority of their own regents or headmen that indolence and crime were increasing. As Furnivall remarks, 'Although Raffles claimed for his system that it was based on native custom and would enrich the people, in application it impoverished them, broke down their customs and undermined their social order.'[1] These tendencies were aggravated, too, by the decline of native crafts through the growth of new industrial imports from Britain and other western countries.

All this was clearly perceived by van den Bosch, a soldier with Indonesian experience who, turning social reformer, was concerned to improve both the lot of the Dutch unemployed and conditions in Java. William sent him to Indonesia for an investigation of possible reforms, and was so impressed by a report which promised to restore Indonesian prosperity with great benefit to the Netherlands that he made the reformer Governor-General (1830–33). Van den Bosch had an almost completely free hand to develop that remarkable 'Culture System' of compulsion and monopoly under which 'Java poured forth riches

[1] Furnivall, *Netherlands India*, p. 108.

upon riches upon the homeland as if by a magician's wand'.[1]

The elements of compulsion were a revival of the old produce or labour rents so designed as to make much of Java, in effect, a vast government plantation. Only land which was surplus to requirements for subsistence crops could be used for this purpose and it was impossible to exclude private planters who were already established. But Javanese villages were required to set apart one-fifth of their cultivated area for providing designated export crops and further grants of land to private planters were forbidden. These planters also found increasing difficulty in obtaining labour or transport because villages had to provide the government with labour for growing a designated crop, for transporting it to factories and, if free labour were insufficient, for work in the factories.

Unlike private planters, the government did not have to pay for labour and directed it only in a general way. Van den Bosch appreciated the value of working as much as possible through native institutions or customs, and restored hereditary rights and rank to the regents; subject to government demands for produce or labour being met, they were left fairly free to administer their provinces through *wedenos* or district chiefs and village headmen. Government interests in the provinces were served by Dutch controllers who were particularly concerned with agricultural requirements, but also kept an eye on the administration of the regents or their subordinates and controlled 'foreign Asians' as well as Europeans. From 1848 there was a dual system of monthly conferences of each resident or controller with their subordinate officials at the district level, and the controller was expected to attend the regent's conferences often enough to keep in touch with native affairs. In this way the Dutch developed a system which became responsive to government requirements and sensitive to Javanese difficulties.

In restoring compulsory deliveries van der Bosch had tried to give some protection and incentive to the villages which provided them. They were to work under their own chiefs and loss from an unavoidable crop failure was to be borne by the government; export crops were to require no more labour than would rice grown on the same area and, if these crops realized more than an assessed 40 per cent of the equivalent rice crop, the surplus

[1] de Waal, quoted in Furnivall, op. cit., p. 127.

should go to the village. A new Directorate of Cultures was to ensure that villages were assigned appropriate crops, avoiding such mistakes as growing coffee on the plains, and to encourage construction of irrigation works as well as roads. But abuses soon developed. As forced labour proved much less productive than free labour on private plantations, regents and controllers were given bonuses proportionate to the production for which they were responsible. Van den Bosch's maximum of sixty-six days' compulsory labour was thus exceeded, reaching in some districts more than two hundred days and generally damaging provision for subsistence. There was, for this reason, widespread famine in Central Java between 1848 and 1850. In spite, too, of his prohibition of land rent this came to be collected nearly everywhere as an additional exaction to compulsory allocations of land and labour.

Further abuses came from the employment of labour by factories. Coffee and pepper could be exported as delivered but other crops had to be processed. The government ran factories for processing indigo, cinnamon, or cochineal and used private contractors for processing sugar or the minor crops of tea and tobacco. Few Dutch and no Javanese took up contracting so that the government relied upon English, French, Chinese, or even Bengalis, to whom it usually made advances for building a factory and for the first three years of operation. Contractors paid the government a set price for the mature crop and had to pay villagers for reaping and transporting it to the factory. The output was then sold to the government at a fixed low price up to an amount sufficient for repaying the loan, and at the market price for the remainder. Villagers were paid for labour in accordance with contracts made between officials and headmen, but bargaining power was unequal, officials or headmen could be corrupted and wages were wretchedly low while contractors made up to £5,000 a year profit. To the extortions of Chinese tax-farmers were added those of the contractors.

The monopoly elements of the Culture System went far beyond discouraging private planting or sale of export crops. All government exports were delivered to the N.H.M. for consignment to the Netherlands in Dutch ships. As the company gave advances against consignments the government came to make nearly all its payments by overdrafts on the N.H.M. and to import through it specie, military stores, or such trade goods as cotton textiles. By 1840 the N.H.M. was handling two-thirds of Java's exports and had a growing business with private planters or wholesale firms in Indonesia. Besides lending to the government it made advances to sugar contractors and private planters, becoming the first of the 'culture banks'. Its progress was helped by the associated Java Bank, although this was hampered by a maximum limit on a note issue which, in 1845, had to be made inconvertible because smuggled copper coin drove silver from circulation. Dutch shipping gained so much from the monopoly of transporting Indonesian exports, and from the double (12 per cent) tariff put on imports brought in foreign ships, that it became the world's third largest mercantile marine.

The Culture System thus involved interlocking interests for exploiting Indonesia's agricultural potential. Regents and officials were given a personal interest in exacting land or labour for export crops, European and Chinese contractors grew rich from processing these crops, the Colonial Government acquired large revenues from their sale, the N.H.M. throve on their consignment or finance, and Dutch shipping depended upon their carriage. The Netherlands gained substantial public revenue from the *batig saldo* or surplus remitted by the Colonial Government, amounting to about £1,800,000 a year or nearly one-third of budgetary expenditures. Gains also accrued to firms which handled Indonesian exports in Europe or which sent Dutch goods as imports to Indonesia. The largely state enterprise of the Culture System was far more successful than the largely private enterprise of the V.O.C.

Indonesian exports rose from £1,300,000 in 1830 to £9,900,000 in 1860. Coffee, mostly from government lands in the Preanger, gave a fairly steady one-third of exports and sugar, mostly from government contractors, increased from 8 to 32 per cent of exports. Indigo provided another 7 per cent in 1850, although its share fell to 4 per cent in 1860. As yet the government had little success from experiments with new crops of cinchona, cinnamon, oil palms, and tobacco but there was, for a time, a considerable increase in rice exports. Private plantations were mostly under rice and characterized by absentee landlords or rack-renting; but some one hundred of them, on government lands, grew coffee and another 150, on native lands, grew sugar or indigo under 'free agreements'. Cotton was produced in significant quantity for export only at Palembang. The Netherland's share of export consignments rose from little more than one-half to almost three-quarters but its share of imports, far more exposed to competitive trade, declined from one-half in 1830 to one-third in both 1840 and 1850 before partially recovering to two-fifths in 1860. Cotton goods, largely supplied by Manchester, were nearly one-half of total imports and European wines or foods, at 7 per cent, cost more than any other group in a wide range of imports.

In Furnivall's expert judgement, the Culture System had reached its limits about 1840 as the land became overworked and the people overburdened. Neither the value nor the volume of exports increased much in the following decade although they again rose appreciably during the 1850s when English, French, and German merchants reported that Javanese were relatively prosperous and contented. Population, certainly, had increased by one-half and rice exports had risen. But a falling import of cottons pointed to declining real income of peasants and the famines of the 1850s to excess demands for export crops. Rice exports had to fall and cassava was introduced from America as a secondary, but inferior, food crop. The limits of the Culture System could, of course, have been extended by adequate investment, but there was no import of capital and the *batig saldo* was pushed so high that little of the colonial revenues was spent on improving methods of production or the welfare of the Indonesian people, in spite of some good early work by the Director of Cultures in planting or irrigation and valuable experiments by the Buitenzorg Botanical Institute.

Notwithstanding, therefore, the Culture System's financial success in extinguishing both colonial and national debt, and in paying for the Dutch railway system, it came under strong criticism from the Liberal Party in the Netherlands. Criticism began as a result of the famines in Java, but could secure little more in a new East India Government Act of 1854 than vague promises to protect Indonesians against evils of forced labour, to promote their education, and to lease uncultivated land to private planters. A cabinet memorandum explained that the accepted principles of colonial administration were those which gave the greatest guarantees that in the first place the Netherlands authority shall be able to maintain itself in that conquered territory by pacific means, and that secondly, preserving the welfare of the native population, that conquered territory shall continue to furnish the Netherlands the material advantages which were the object of that conquest.[1]

Neither Liberals nor Conservatives questioned contributions from poor Indonesians to the economic development of Holland. Both professed a concern, within the limits of nineteenth-century views, for the welfare of colonial peoples as for that of Dutch peasants or workers. Their fundamental difference was over the roles of state and private enterprise as the Liberals, supported increasingly by business interests, wished to apply the apparently successful principles of political economy to Indonesia as well as to the Netherlands. Even humanitarian missionaries who, like van Hoevell, protested about wrongs done to Indonesians, or critical officials like Dekker, who exposed abuses of the culture system in the powerful novel *Max Havelaar*, tended to associate evils with state enterprise and to assume that both could be removed together.

The Liberals made slow progress in reshaping colonial policy. Slavery and debtor-bondage were abolished in 1860 and the state gave up, between 1862 and 1866, unprofitable cultures of pepper, cloves, nutmeg, indigo, cinnamon, cochineal, tea, and tobacco. At the same time there was a renewed limitation of export cultivation to one-fifth of village lands and European officials were deprived of commissions on export crops. Decisive changes did not come until 1870 when two key laws were passed. The Sugar Law permitted free export sales in Java and announced progressive withdrawal of the government from sugar production after 1878. The Agrarian Law, and a following Rent Ordinance, allowed capitalists to lease from the government hereditary concessions of up to thirty acres of land not held by Indonesians, or to rent from Indonesians land for a period up to twenty years, subject to official safeguards.

The next decade seemed to provide a triumphant vindication of economic liberalism as exports nearly doubled in value and the contribution of private plantations rose from two-fifths to three-quarters. Coffee remained a government culture but private

[1] Vandenbosch, *The Dutch East Indies*, p. 60.

planters doubled their share of its export to one-fifth. They also acquired one-third of the area under sugar and raised its yield. Tobacco, abandoned by the government as an unprofitable culture in 1866, was lifted to one-eighth of total exports. Imports rose even more steeply than exports as capital began flowing to finance plantations and other private enterprises in Indonesia.

Export prices, however, almost halved between 1873 and 1895, and planters had to contend with diseases which afflicted both sugar and coffee; export receipts, accordingly, declined from a peak of £18 million in 1877 to £15 million in 1890. Low prices and disease halved coffee exports but sugar exports were maintained, in spite of new competition in Europe from beet, and tobacco exports rose in value by over two-thirds. Exports, moreover, were partly sustained by tin production. The Banka output remained fairly steady at under 5,000 tons but was equalled by that of new mines developed on Billiton by a private company which had begun successful operations in 1861 with labour recruited from China. Thousands of Chinese also came as labourers to the tobacco plantations which were opened in East Sumatra, especially after a Coolie Ordinance of 1880 gave planters effective legal control over immigrant labour.

Planters were kept going only by new 'culture banks' which had been attracted to Indonesia during the boom of the seventies, and by forming themselves into limited companies. There were five such banks, in 1884, financing between them ninety-seven coffee plantations, seventy-six sugar plantations, and seventy other enterprises. One of these banks failed, another had to be helped in order to survive and there were a number of reconstructions which brought a further £3,000,000 of banking capital to Indonesia. The culture banks thus gained more control over plantations, and used it to ensure improvements and common sales policies. Sugar producers imported fertilizer to double yields, equipped their factories with expensive modern plant and formed a General Syndicate of Sugar Manufacturers in order to promote collective interests. Coffee producers met their difficulty over disease by switching from *Coffea arabica* to *Coffea liberica* and, when this was also afflicted, to *Coffea robusta* from the Congo. Government cultivation of coffee fell by two-thirds, but private plantations nearly doubled their output in spite of the disease. Tobacco production also doubled.

By 1900, these three major crops provided three-fifths of Indonesia's export receipts and tin another one-tenth with an output of almost 16,000 tons. Useful contributions were now being made by a number of other exports. Cinchona, which had been brought to the Buitenzorg Gardens in 1852 from South America, but takes fifteen years to yield bark, was tried by private planters in the seventies and, in the early nineties, brought in £85,000; a decade later Indonesia was becoming the world's leading producer of chinchona with an export of over £440,000. Tea production had been given up by the government and was not seriously attempted by private planters until coffee prices fell late in the century. It was only when Assam plants were tried, instead of the Chinese variety, and Indian methods of cultivation and processing were used, that tea became firmly established in Indonesia contributing, by 1900, 2 per cent to export receipts. Copra exports were slower to develop, after the opening of Suez, in Indonesia than Ceylon and, as in that island, were largely a peasant export to which plantations contributed a minor supply. In 1900, however, copra exports were £830,000, more than twice tea exports, and peasants further gained from a few more minor crops such as kapok, tapioca, and other cassava products.

Indonesia weathered the Long Depression fairly well. It had made a successful change from state to private cultivation of export crops and developed some new crops, as well as an important tin mine at Billiton. A precarious beginning had also been made with the more important mining of petroleum. Zijlker, a Sumatran planter, began drilling in 1884 and, after proving success, sold his concesssion to the Royal Dutch Company which, by 1896, had fourteen wells in production and a refinery at Pankalan Brandad. There were technical and financial difficulties from which the Company was rescued by Deterding, an agent of the N.H.M., followed by damaging competition from Rockefeller's Standard Oil Company. Progress came, however, from the acquisition of other petroleum companies in Sumatra, the discovery of rich new mines in East Borneo and an amalgamation, in 1907, with the Shell Transport and Trading Company of London which had previously bought a valuable concession in Borneo. For a few years Royal Dutch Shell had a monopoly of Indonesian petroleum and, in 1913, was providing 16 per cent of a greatly increased value of total exports. Rubber, which was to become an even more important export than petroleum, had made only a modest beginning in 1913, when it contributed 4 per cent to total exports.

Between them, petroleum and rubber accounted for one-quarter of the remarkable expansion of Indonesia's exports from £22,000,000 in 1900 to £56,000,000 in 1913. World prices for foodstuffs rose by about one-fifth but most of the remaining increase of Indonesia's exports in these years came from a trebling of tea and copra outputs and a doubling of sugar and tobacco outputs. The production of tin rose by one-third but that of coffee fell by two-fifths. Such gains of production would not have been possible but for the expansion of Dutch colonization into Sumatra and the Outer Islands. In 1880 they had provided only one-fifth of Indonesia's exports but tin, copra, tobacco, petroleum, and rubber doubled this proportion. Java, however, remained almost the sole source of sugar, tea, cinchona, and cassava.

Under the Liberal System much continued to be done in building or improving roads, still mainly by forced labour. There were two small private ventures in railway construction during the sixties but no great progress was made until the government was authorized to build railways in 1875. By 1913 it had given Java a fairly complete network of nearly 1,300 miles and had built 150 miles in Sumatra, including a link to the oil field at Ombilin from Padang and a military line in Achin. Private enterprise concentrated mainly on tramways—light secondary lines to sugar factories or to plantations. Development of the Outer Islands depended largely upon shipping and by 1880 they were well served as small steamers, mostly under the part-British Netherlands Steamship Company, thronged the archipelago and connected it with Singapore.

Raffles's settlement, as early as 1825, had as much trade as Java, and nearly twice as much as Penang and Malacca together. Because of the Culture System, and a certain indifference of British authorities in the Straits Settlements to cultivating good relations with Indonesian sultans, Singapore's trade with Indonesia, up to 1850, was less than one-fifth of its total trade and not much greater than its trade with other Malayan ports. But it was fulfilling magnificently the description given by the London Times: 'the centre and citadel of British power in the Eastern Seas, and the great house of call between Britain and China'.[1] For in 1850 one-half of its total trade was conducted with Britain, India, and China, and in roughly equal proportions between these three countries.

Singapore's trade was almost wholly entrepôt. From Britain came cotton or woollen piece-goods, fire-arms, iron wares, copper, lead, and bullion for distribution to Malaya, Indonesia, Indochina, and China. From India came a variety of commodities but mainly opium and cotton goods; cottons tended to diminish under Manchester's competition but opium was long important for trade with South-east Asia and China. Most of Singapore's shipments to Britain comprised such Straits produce as tin, pepper, rattans, shells for buttons, skins of crocodiles, lizards, and snakes, ebony, ivory, tortoiseshell, betel-nuts, and a variety of gums. Straits produce, including bêche-de-mer, birds' nests, camphor, pearls, sandalwood, and sea-weeds, was also carried away by the Chinese junks which were quickly attracted to Singapore as a free port; at Batavia, their only permitted port in Java, they were obliged to pay trading dues. To Singapore these junks carried immigrants, who sought better opportunities in Malaya, and Chinese products for those who had already found them there. It was the most important destination for Thai junks which brought sugar, rice, gamboge, ivory, or sappanwood and took away textiles, metal wares, copper, opium, tea, paper, or rattans. There was a similar but quite small trade with Cambodia and Cochinchina.

In spite of Dutch resentment at a British free port within five hundred miles of Batavia, prohibition of foreign ships in Indonesian coastal waters and attempts to open rival free ports at Riau, Borneo, Macassar, Amboina, Banda, and Ternate, Singapore had a flourishing trade with Indonesia. Straits produce came to it from all parts of the archipelago in return for cottons, silks, cordage, gunny bags, opium, saltpetre, crockery, metal wares, copper, fire-arms, or bullion. In addition Java sent rice, indigo, and tobacco. Sumatra sent benzoin, betel-nuts, pepper, ivory, and rhinoceros horn, and Bali sent rice or tobacco as well as contraband coffee from Java.

[1] Quoted in Swettenham, *British Malaya*, p. 102.

Penang had, up to the mid-century, a greater trade with Sumatra owing to its connection with Acheh, the main producing area for pepper, but was something less of an entrepôt in being the outlet for Perak's tin mines. As Malaya produced rather more than Indonesia during the 1850s, tin may have accounted for at least one-half of Penang's exports. Much of its trade, nevertheless, was secondary to that of Singapore to which it dispatched tin, pepper, and jungle products, and from which it obtained British or Indian manufactures for its own requirements and transhipment to Sumatran or smaller West Malayan ports. Malacca, although a free port like Singapore and Penang, was powerless to recover its former proud position as the greatest South-east Asian entrepôt. In 1850 its trade was moribund at £400,000, one-quarter of Penang's total and barely 8 per cent that of Singapore. Governor Fullerton appreciated, as early as 1828, that Malacca had little future in trade and tried to develop its agricultural resources, unsuccessfully because of confusion and fraud over Dutch claims to land there and British mistakes in dealing with the problem. Further mistakes led to the unprofitable Naning War of 1831–2, which made this territory part of Malacca.

The three settlements had been brought, in 1825, under a single governor who was made directly responsible to Calcutta. He was instructed to keep them as profitable trading stations and to avoid any interference with Malay sultanates. Something, of course, had to be done about pirates; their suppression was helped by armed steamers after 1837 and did not involve political troubles although many pirates came under the protection of some chief. The chronic unrest of the Malay states, however, made trading difficult. Even Calcutta could not ignore the threat from a Thai invasion of Kedah and Perak, upon which Penang depended for food and tin. John Crawfurd was sent to Bangkok in 1822 to discusss this problem but had to return with only a comforting impression that Thai military power was not formidable. Further trouble led, four years later, to Burney's dispatch on a similar mission; he secured a renunciation of claims to Perak but it took a British show of force to make the Thai garrison leave. In return, the Governor had to help Thai forces suppress a revolt in Kedah, after which the British became involved in other Malay quarrels if only to prevent

22

disruption of trade or tin-mining. Local dissatisfaction with Calcutta grew, especially in Singapore, and in 1867 the Straits Settlements were made a separate colony.

Then began an extension of British power over the disturbed sultanates. The first step was taken in Perak where thousands of Chinese tin-miners were divided between two hostile societies which added to the lawlessness caused by Malay quarrels. Clarke persuaded all warring factions to accept his arbitration and, in 1874, negotiated the Pangkor Engagement whereby British protection was guaranteed to the new sultan and he accepted a British Resident 'whose advice must be asked and acted upon in all questions other than those touching Malay religion and custom'.[1] In the same year Selangor and Sungei Ujang also accepted British protection and Residents, as did Pahang in 1888. Seven years later the Minangkabau states were persuaded to make a confederation of Negri Sembilan under British protection and control. The Resident system led to great improvements in law and order but some difficulties arose through lack of uniformity in matters of justice, land settlement, and taxation. Swettenham, the Resident of Perak, accordingly devised a plan for a federation and, after persuading the Colonial Office of its merits, induced the four sultans to conclude a treaty in 1895. He himself became the first Resident-General of the Federation at Kuala Lumpur, under the control of the Governor of the Straits Settlements, and began a vigorous period of financial reform, forest conservation, railway construction, agricultural improvement, and education.

The forward movement of the British in Malaya coincided with the extension of Dutch rule over Sumatra and with a change of policy to the Liberal System. Between 1870 and 1900, accordingly, the trade of the Straits Settlements rose from £19,000,000 to £58,000,000 and, after the Federation, to £85,000,000 in 1914, equal in value to the foreign trade of Indonesia. Malaya thus obtained great benefits from the economic liberalization of its great neighbour, and entrepôt trade was also helped by suppression of piracy in the Straits.

Some part of this growth in trade, however, came from economic developments within Malaya. Tin output grew from 6,500 tons in the fifties to 19,600 tons in the eighties as a result

[1] Clause 6 of the Pangkor Agreement.

of a rich discovery at Larut, in Perak, associated with a big inflow of Chinese immigrants. In 1880 another new mining area was opened at Kinta, also in Perak. So far tin mining had been exclusively a Chinese venture but in 1884 a French company began operations at Kinta. British and Australian interests followed the French into Malayan tin areas although in 1913 Chinese miners were still providing three-quarters of the output, now increased to 51,400 tons. Their traditional methods were not easily replaced by western technology, as Swettenham noted:

European mining is done by companies. . . . Machinery is bought, houses are built . . . and then—if things ever get so far—some Chinese are employed. . . . After possibly a series of great hardships to the staff and disasters to the company, it is found that the tin raised is infinitesimal in value when compared with the rate of expenditure . . . usually . . . when the paid-up capital is all but exhausted. The company is wound up and the State gets a bad name with investors, and the only people who really enjoy themselves are the neighbouring Chinese miners who buy the mine and plant for an old song and make several fortunes out of working on their own ridiculous and primitive methods.[1]

The Chinese, however, improved their methods by using small steam engines and centrifugal pumps, and adopted hydraulic jets for 'gravel pump' mining. They were not displaced until dredges were introduced, in 1912, to work deeper or less productive deposits under swampy soil. Europeans were more successful in regard to smelting as Chinese charcoal blast furnaces could not compete with large-scale mechanized plant. Sword and Muhlinghaus opened a big smelting works at Singapore in 1888 but the first really modern smelter was that opened at Penang in 1902, after which the Singapore works were fitted with regenerative gas-fired reverberatory furnaces.

Swettenham paid tribute to the contribution made by Chinese to Malaya's economic development.

Their energy and enterprise have made the Malay states what they are today. . . . They were already the miners and the traders, and in some instances the planters and the fishermen, before the white man had found his way to the Peninsula. In all the early days it was

[1] Quoted in Allen and Donnithorne, *Western Enterprise in Indonesia and Malaya*, p. 151.

Chinese energy and industry which supplied the funds to begin the construction of roads and other public works . . . as contractors they constructed nearly all the Government buildings, most of the roads and bridges, railways and waterworks. They brought all the capital into the country when Europeans feared to take the risk; they were the traders and shopkeepers, and it was their steamers which first opened regular communication between the ports of the colony and the ports of the Malay States. They introduced tens of thousands of their countrymen when the one great need was labour to develop the hidden riches of an almost unknown and jungle-covered country, and it is their work . . . which has provided something like nine-tenths of the revenue.[1]

This reference to Chinese as the first planters would be to those who tried spices and gambier on Singapore soon after its foundation. Some Europeans followed this example and also tried sugar at Penang, Province Wellesley, and Malacca. None of these ventures was very successful. Chinese contractors had cleared land for sugar but there were crippling difficulties in getting plantation labour, as Malays, like their Indonesian cousins, were averse to such regular work. During the eighties some planters brought indentured Tamil labour but were unable to compete with the Java sugar industry so that the last sugar factory was closed in 1913, when indentured labour was abolished.

As disease hit Ceylon's coffee plantations some Europeans came to plant coffee in Malaya. In the last two decades of the nineteenth century *Coffea liberica* was planted on estates in Perak, Selangor, and Negri Sembilan but, after a favourable start, they were set back by Brazilian competition and then by pests which seriously damaged the trees. At the peak of production, however, in 1905, Malaya exported nearly 6,000 tons of coffee or one-seventh of the Indonesian output.

Planters were saved by rubber seedlings sent from Kew to the Singapore Botanical Gardens in 1877. No great interest was taken in them until Ridley, the director, found a method of tapping which was practicable on large plantations. Under his energetic persuasion estates began interplanting rubber with coffee or coconuts but only £500 worth of rubber was exported by Malaya in 1904. The price then soared from 4s. a pound to 12s.

[1] *British Malaya*, p. 232.

in 1910, and both European estates and smallholders took up rubber enthusiastically. By 1912 Malaya exported more than £3,500,000, equal to 8 per cent of total export receipts as compared with 30 per cent from tin or 5 per cent from coconuts.

Rubber also became the mainstay of exports for North Borneo, in which Britain took an increasing interest from the time that James Brooke became Raja of Sarawak and persuaded the British government, in 1846, to accept the cession of Labuan Island in Brunei Bay. This island was later handed over to a chartered British North Borneo Company which had begun to acquire Sabah from the Sultan of Brunei and, in 1888, the Sultan accepted British protection and a Resident. The Company extended its trade from birds' nests and jungle produce to timber when Hong Kong needed sleepers for its railway, and began the successful cultivation of tobacco, whose export reached a peak of over £250,000 in 1902 as against nearly £50,000 from timber in a total export of £460,000. After that there was a rush to plant rubber which, by 1917, covered 34,838 acres yielding 2,440 tons, or about 1 per cent of the Malayan output. Chinese, again, provided most of the labour required for these exports.

Plantations and mines profoundly changed both Indonesia and Malaya. The population of Malaya rose from around 400, 000 in 1835 to 2,653,000 in 1911, and most of the increase came from migrations of Indonesians, Chinese, or Indians; Chinese were no less than one-third of the population in 1911 and Indians, who came mainly to work on rubber plantations, were one-tenth. Indonesia's population rose from 11 million in 1825 to 38 million in 1905, but Chinese were less than 1 per cent of the total and Indians a negligible proportion because most estate labour was Javanese. Yet, if the Chinese were a relatively small proportion, they had a key role as economic intermediaries between Europeans and Indonesians. Both Indonesians and Malayans clung to traditional agriculture, lost traditional crafts without participating in modern industry, and played only a small part in trade or finance. Their gains from the economic transformation of the two countries were mainly indirect, and traditionally absorbed by growth of numbers. Java, once an important rice exporter, came to rely upon imports to feed its burgeoning population. Increasing numbers on restricted land meant growing poverty and Deventer estimated that, in 1900, the average Javanese family had an income of only £7 a year, one-fifth of which had to be paid in taxes. Queen Wilhelmina thereupon set up an inquiry into 'the diminishing welfare of the people of Java', after which the Dutch Government began applying a new 'Ethical Policy' marked by a grant of £3,500,000 for ameliorating conditions in Java although the *batig saldo* was not definitely abolished until 1912.

6. *The rice trade of Indochina*

In striking contrast to the plantation economies, Burma, Thailand, Cambodia, and Vietnam became involved in the rapidly expanding trade of the nineteenth century mainly through a development of traditional peasant exports of rice. By 1913 their combined rice shipments were around £30 million and, again in contrast to the plantation economies, most of this export went, not to Europe, but to other Asian countries; more than two-fifths to the now food-deficient plantation economies and more than another fifth to India, China, and Japan. Much the biggest rice exporter was Burma with a shipment of £16 million, followed by Thailand with one of nearly £7 million, and then by Cambodia and Vietnam which together gave French Indochina a shipment of nearly £8 million. For all these countries, moreover, rice supplied over two-thirds of total exports.

The development of Burma's great rice export was, as an official report of 1916–17 put it, 'almost entirely the work of the Burmese'.[1] Yet this work did not begin until the British, by annexing Lower Burma in 1852, freed peasants from the onerous exactions or controls of the Konbaung despots, gave security for effort or accumulation, and provided new incentives by spreading money as a means of exchange and by introducing a tempting range of cheap imports. King Bodawpaya (1781–1819), indeed, had forbidden all exports of rice because of economic exhaustion on Mon lands in the Irrawaddy Delta and chronic shortages in Upper Burma, both caused by his grandiose military and building projects.

This son of Alaungpaya had begun a long reign by annexing, easily enough, Tenasserim and Arakan. He then launched

[1] Quoted in Furnivall, *Colonial Policy and Practice*, p. 84.

a four-pronged attack on Thailand in continuation of the campaigns waged by his father and brother, Hsinbyushin (1763–76), who had destroyed Ayuthia and taken Chiengmai. But the northern campaigns brought Hsinbyushin into trouble with the Chinese, who attempted a number of invasions. They failed but enabled the Thai, under P'ya Taksin, to recover national strength, regain Ayuthia, and wipe out Burmese garrisons. The avenging Thai disastrously repelled Bodawpaya's armies and, although there were further campaigns in the north, finally expelled the Burmans in 1802 from Laos and Chiengmai. So heavy were the exactions to finance both these campaigns and Bodawpaya's obsessive construction of temples that the Mon and Arakanese were driven first to revolt and then to flight. Thousands of Mon abandoned their Delta lands in order to escape to Thailand; the Arakanese crossed to Chittagong in British India, from which they later launched attacks on Burma. Symes, an official who came to Ava in 1795 to negotiate trading concessions, noted the devastated condition of Lower Burma and, seven years later, reported that Upper Burma had also become impoverished by excessive levies or taxes and by the banditry which followed Bodawpaya's neglect of kingly duties.

Troubles between the E.I.C. and Burma had been caused by Arakanese rebels operating from Chittagong, and became serious in 1811 after a major raid. The Burmans thereafter interfered in Assam, Cachar, and Manipur. Bagyidaw (1819–38), immediately he succeeded to the throne, launched an invasion of Assam. Before he attacked Chittagong the E.I.C. sent an expedition which took Rangoon in 1824, but could not advance towards Amarapura, the new capital, until 1826. The Treaty of Yandabo was then signed, by which Burma evacuated Assam and Manipur, paid an indemnity of £1,000,000, and ceded Arakan and Tenasserim. That finished the military power of the Konbaung Dynasty and so freed Thailand, as well as North-east India, from a chronic threat of Burmese invasion.

The E.I.C's new provinces were not remunerative. Maingy, the first administrator of Tenasserim, was a firm believer in free trade but had to curb its practice when rice exports threatened to absorb the people's sustenance and even their seed grain. British merchants were much less responsive, as they failed to take up land which was offered on easy terms and showed no disposition to realize Maingy's hope of Moulmein becoming a considerable entrepôt. Nor were they satisfactory licensees of teak concessions, which were ruthlessly exploited by Burmese agents and from which three-quarters of the timber fraudulently escaped duty. There was some development of saw-milling and Moulmein had a shipbuilding industry, but progress was held back by a scanty population whose main reinforcement came from Indian convicts or immigrants. Timber and rice were exported in about equal values, most of the rice going to Burma in return for native piece-goods and 'sundries', but Tenasserim's exports in 1833 were only £80,000.

The treaty had provided for a British Resident at the Court of Ava, to which the E.I.C. sent John Crawfurd, a man who had given good service in Java and Singapore besides conducting a mission to the Courts of Thailand and Cochinchina. At Bangkok he had succeeded in reopening British trade but failed to get concessions because the E.I.C. refused to allow Thai vessels the right to buy arms in India or to hand over the Sultan of Kedah who had taken refuge in Penang. Nor was Crawfurd more successful at the Court of Ava. The commercial treaty he obtained was almost worthless and, finding himself badly obstructed in other ways, he quit the capital after advising the E.I.C. not to appoint a permanent Resident. In 1830, however, Henry Burney was given the appointment owing to his skill in reaching a settlement with the Raja of Ligor and in negotiating another commercial treaty with Bangkok during the first Anglo-Burmese War. This treaty was no improvement on Crawfurd's but Burney succeeded in cultivating good relations with the Court.

Shortly before he left, because of poor health, the now insane King Bagyidaw was deposed by his brother, Tharawaddy Min (1838–46), who promptly denounced the Treaty of Yandabo and ignored Burney's successor, Benson. He, too, had to leave because of sickness as did McLeod, the fourth Resident, after which the E.I.C. severed diplomatic relations with a court which had made them a mockery. Pagan Min (1846–53), the murderous tyrant who succeeded Tharawaddy, continued provocations until Dalhousie decided to maintain British prestige by sending two warships to Rangoon. When a demand for redress was refused, the warships blockaded the port. So began the Second Anglo-Burmese War, conducted far more skilfully than the first, and resulting in the annexation of all territory south of the Myédé River. Pagan Min had been deposed and his successor, the good Buddhist, Mindon (1853–78), refused to continue hostilities; but former officials organized a stubborn resistance in Lower Burma which was not pacified until 1855.

Although Dalhousie had thought Lower Burma held out a fair promise of trade, and had emphasized the importance of building roads, the British were slow to develop their new province. As late as 1869 the Chief Commissioner complained:

> Beyond the existence of a police, most inadequately paid, there is hardly anything in the length and breadth of the Province to testify the presence of any rule superior to the one from which it has been wrested. . . . Of barracks, of gaols, of court-houses we have not a few, but as for Public Works in the true sense of the word, they are only now being called into existence.[1]

Five incomplete roads were about the total in a territory of 90,000 square miles. But roads were not urgent in a country with good waterways, and government steamers joined country boats over much of the Delta and up the Irrawaddy as far as Mandalay. Attempts to attract planters again failed as European enterprise was still attracted only by timber.

The Burmans, however, made rice a more important export than timber. Now freed from compulsory services as well as from restrictions on movement or disposal of produce, they had security and the incentive of cheap western imports. And so, on the vast, thinly populated deltaic plain of swamp and jungle, where the Mon had abandoned cultivation, Burmans began to develop the production of rice. It was, in the first stage, subsistence farming with an elastic fringe of export production. When there was little export demand much of the crop was left unharvested but, if scarcity created a ready market in Upper Burma, India, or China, then peasants could easily clear jungle to take advantage of an opportunity for acquiring textiles, metal wares, or other useful, although dispensable, supplements to a traditional standard of living.

The development was helped by rising prices which benefited fishermen, salt-boilers, potters, and boat-builders in addition to farmers. There had been an exodus to Upper Burma but, when

---

[1] Quoted in Furnivall, op. cit., p. 49.

the Indian Mutiny created a sudden demand for rice, the flow
was quickly reversed and Burmans began to spread over the
Delta, although demand was still too precarious for peasants to
become dependent on it. They could adjust readily to a fluctua-
tion of exports from 470,000 tons in 1864 to 248,000 in 1866 and
during the 1860s cultivation rose from 1,610,000 to 1,960,000
acres, less than proportionately to the increase of population.

Upper Burma, under Mindon's rule, also prospered. Religious fervour, culminating in the meeting of the Fifth Buddhist
Council at Rangoon in 1871, did not prevent him from seeking
to improve material conditions by reforms or borrowings from
the West. He altered taxation by imposing a moderate levy on
houses and by extending royal monopolies over trade; began to
modernize administration by putting officials on fixed salaries
and by sending missions and students to Europe; introduced a
coinage and a telegraph system; built a fleet of river steamers;
and tried to establish modern factories, sometimes under European management, for manufacturing textiles, sugar, cutch, and
lac. Much was done to foster, as well as to control, exports of
raw cotton, wheat, and palm sugar, and royal agents in Lower
Burma purchased rice and Manchester goods. Mindon was on
friendly terms with Williams, the first British Agent at Mandalay, who helped to negotiate a treaty in 1862 for reciprocal
rights to trade along the Irrawaddy, and for free trade on both
sides of the frontier subject to certain reservations on Mindon's
part. He also sent embassies to India and Iran in the hope of
promoting trade, tried to open relations with France, Spain,
and Italy, and, above all, tried to foster trade with China
through Yunnan.

Chinese trade was a great magnet for both the British and the
French. Crawfurd's 1827 estimate that Burma exported
£228,000 worth of goods to China led Mandalay to dispatch a
few expeditions through Upper Burma. McLeod went by
elephant up the Salween route and in 1835 Hannay reached
Bhamo from Bengal. Manchester, feeling the pinch of American
and other competition in Chinese ports, urged the British
Government to develop an overland route; Williams obtained
Mindon' s reluctant permission for a survey of the Irrawaddy
up to Bhamo and in 1868 a British Agent was posted to this
ancient border mart. There was further pressure from British

merchants or Mandalay officials for overland trade with China, but the Government of India was cool to their suggestion for a highway to Yunnan and still more to that of enthusiasts for a railway from Rangoon to Shanghai.

British merchants were doing fairly well from trade with Burma. By 1868 sea-borne exports were £3,200,000, nearly two-thirds of which came from rice and little more than one-fifth from forest products; the corresponding imports were £2,200,000, one-half of which were textiles. This trade excluded transactions with Upper Burma, which received exports of rice and re-exports of piece-goods, crockery, tinned provisions, glass lamps, matches, and other petty luxuries, amounting to about £1,350,000 in return for shipments of cotton, wheat, and sugar. Trade with Upper Burma more than doubled in the sixties, but the growth only fostered expectations of greater gain from bringing the whole country under British control. A commercial treaty had been negotiated in 1867 whereby Mindon agreed to reduce all customs duties to a uniform 5 per cent and to give up royal monopolies, except those over earth-oil (or petroleum), rubies, and timber. Rangoon merchants, nevertheless, continued to deplore Mindon's 'vicious system of monopolies'[1] because the king had to exert strong pressures in order to satisfy those external creditors who had helped finance costly, and not always successful, attempts at modernization. As well as this, most piece-goods for Upper Burma were bought by royal agents who could press for low prices, and who also eliminated middlemen's profits on rice by buying directly from peasants in the Delta. In spite of such grievances, trade with Upper Burma trebled between 1867 and 1878.

On their side, Burmans were vexed by British refusal of applications to import rifles. Further friction arose from activities of the Karens, whose independence Britain had promised to respect. They had a flourishing slave trade with Thailand and were encouraged by the Burmese Court to make raids into the British province. In 1873 Mindon went much further by making a forcible claim to suzerainty over West Karenni, and abandoned it only under strong British pressure. Relations were then broken off owing to a stupid instruction to the Resident at

[1] *Annual Report of the Administration of Burma, 1877–8*, p. 49; quoted in Furnivall, *Colonial Policy and Practice*, p. 66.

Mandalay that he should henceforth refuse to take off his shoes before having audience with Mindon. In 1879, following the bloody accession of Thibaw (1878–85) and some anti-British incidents, the Residency was closed.

Demands for annexation grew because of deteriorating government under Thibaw and his hostility to the British; dacoits were rife, both Karens and Shan were in revolt, the Court of Ava was an arena for devious intrigues and palace massacres, and Thibaw had sent a mission to Paris for a commercial treaty which threatened British interests. The French, influenced by momentary reverses in Vietnam, quickly backed out but Thibaw persisted in an attempt to transfer a teak contract from the Bombay-Burmah Trading Corporation to a French syndicate. The corporation was fined £180,000 for over-extracting logs and underpaying Burmans, whereupon the British demanded arbitration of the case. When Thibaw's reply was judged to be a refusal, they occupied Mandalay, abolished the Burmese kingship, and, on 1 January 1886, completely annexed the country. It took five years, however, to crush widespread guerrilla warfare, to put down a new revolt in Lower Burma, and to establish British rule over a people who showed a strong preference for their own despotism or anarchy.

Meanwhile, economic changes were coming over the Delta because of steamships, the Suez Canal, Chettyar money-lenders, Indian labourers, and Rangoon rice millers. They transformed the comfortable period of rice exports as an optional fringe on subsistence farming to such an increasingly commercial scramble for export production that 'the deltaic plain became in effect a factory without chimneys'.[1] The British provided steamships, developed Rangoon and other ports, built railways from Rangoon to Lashio and from Bassein to Moulmein, and, through the Irrawaddy Flotilla Company, brought steam transport to all inland waters. They also built steam-powered mills at the ports after much-reduced sailing times made it possible to ship unhusked rice to growing markets in Europe. With Indian labour they began, in the sixties, to erect great protective embankments against the Irrawaddy's seasonal floods.

But, in the main, Lower Burma's spectacular development of rice production from under 1,000,000 acres in 1855 to nearly

[1] Furnivall, op. cit., p. 90.

8,300,000 acres in 1915 resulted from an effective, if unhappy, combination of traditional Asian enterprises. Experienced farmers from Upper Burma, damaged by a clumsy official land survey, thronged into the Delta, as did landless Burmans and many whose livelihoods were destroyed by western imports or by the competition of Indian and Chinese immigrants for urban jobs. Land could be acquired by squatting, subject to payment of land-tax for twelve years, or by taking up small grants which were free of tax over the years required for bringing jungle-clad land into cultivation (but such grants led to difficulties from competing claimants or occupation by squatters). Competition for land soon became so intense that a settler was driven to acquire immediately as much land as he would need, and so had to hire labour for clearing or diking and to borrow capital until the new farm came into full production.

In the earlier stage, hired labour was supplied by Burmans who contracted to work for a full year on all types of farm work and who could then hope to save enough from their wages within two or three years to make a start as landholders. Before long, however, there was a growing migrant labour force comprising people who came from Upper Burma only for harvesting and Indians who, coming for seasonal employment in rice mills, found that by arriving earlier they could also obtain work as reapers.

Cultivation to meet local requirements gradually changed into the system of industrialized agriculture organized for the export market which prevails today. . . . In the more developed areas the earthwork, ploughing, planting, reaping, threshing, etc., are all separate functions performed by different people, and the division of function has been pushed almost as far as is possible in agriculture.[1]

Capital for farming the Delta was mostly provided by Indian money-lenders of the Chettyar caste, first active in Southeast Asia at Malacca (where they had bought up salary claims from impecunious Portuguese officials). They came to Burma soon after the British but did not send out agents to villages until about 1880. Few cultivators were then in debt, but before long many borrowed more than was needed for developing land

[1] Report of the Indian Statutory Commission (1930), XI, 18; quoted in Furnivall, *Colonial Policy and Practice*, p. 90.

and spent the surplus on imports. Most of the Chettyars' funds came from accumulated profits of generations of money-lending, but they also obtained advances from European banks in India and accepted deposits. Their loans were carefully made on good security at rates from 25 to 40 per cent, not excessive by Asian standards, and the Chettyars often showed consideration for debtors. But few cultivators could make their farms pay quickly enough to cover debt obligations, and money-lenders then took over land for resale to new cultivators on mortgage. As early as 1895 a British official could remark that land in Lower Burma changed hands about as readily as shares in London. It was passing, moreover, from cultivators to rice traders who wished to ensure supplies of paddy from tenants, and to Indian or Chinese merchants who sought a profitable investment. These shopkeepers themselves became rural money-lenders, together with some Burmans, just as Chettyars, through collections of harvest loans, became direct shippers of rice to India.

Although, then, the Delta trebled Burma's rice exports between 1880 and 1900 and made it the world's largest supplier of this cereal, peasants in Lower Burma gained little from the later stage of the development. Peasant proprietorship, the old tradition and the British aim, collapsed because of growing rural debts and sharpening techniques of land-grabbing by those who could violently dispossess squatters or outsmart them in the law courts. Cultivators could have little real security, as a report of 1911 noted, when they were 'dependent for their subsistence during the working season on loans at high rates of interest which were barely covered by the produce obtained by them at harvest'.[1] Labourers were also driven into debt by inability to find work for one-half of the year, so that an increasing number took to robbery. A later report pointed to a further source of impoverishment; 'as the public waste lands became converted into cultivation, as fisheries were declared the property of Government and as home weaving became unprofitable, the small proprietors, like the tenants, were increasingly obliged to find money for needs which they could formerly supply themselves'.[2]

The rural proletariat was swollen by those displaced from

---

[1] Quoted in Furnivall, op. cit., p. 91.   [2] ibid., p. 103.

traditional industries. Manual rice mills gave way to steam-mills employing Indian coolies; Burmese boatmen were reduced by the new steamers; and, except at Moulmein, the wharves were also taken over by Indian labour. By 1901 Indians formed 6 per cent of the population and Chinese another 1 per cent. Between them they engrossed the more profitable fields of employment as the Administration Report of 1884–5 noticed:

The moneylending business of the country is in the hands of the Madrassi banking caste of Chetties; the retail piece-goods trade is chiefly in the hands of Suratis, natives of India, and Chinamen; the retail liquor trade is almost exclusively in the hands of Chinamen. The natives of India have also driven the Burman out of the field where hard manual labour is required; the coolies employed by the Public Works Department are almost exclusively Indian, the gharry drivers are chiefly Madrassis, the coolies on the wharves and at the railway stations are also natives of India, and natives of India are here and there settling down to permanent rice cultivation.[1]

These changes so accelerated that in 1918, with the arrival of 300,000 Indian coolies, Rangoon was second only to New York as a port of immigration, and later surpassed it.

Upper Burma was much less exposed to alien penetration and, until 1910, was probably better off under British rule. There were bigger export markets for such old crops as cotton or such new crops as groundnuts, but these were still a fringe on a carefully preserved traditional agriculture somewhat improved by modern irrigation works. Europeans gladly extended their enterprise to the teak forests of Upper Burma and erected mills for processing cotton and groundnuts, but their main new interest was mineral production. The famous ruby mines of Mogok were a strong attraction, although they did not prove very profitable to the company which obtained the concession. Far more success attended the Burma Oil Company, formed in 1886 to exploit the Yenangyaung field; after driving American kerosene out of the local market it began exporting, in the nineties, to India and Malaya from an output which was rapidly climbing above 20 million gallons. During the same decade Europeans began to exploit lead and silver mines in the Shan States, especially the old Chinese workings at Bawdwin, above Lashio, but no great progress was made until 1920 when

[1] ibid., p. 118.

the various concessions were taken over by the Burma Corporation. Tin was extracted by traditional methods in Tennasserim, where Chinese miners were prominent and European interest was slight until the discovery, in 1909, that these mines would also yield wolfram. Up to 1903 western or modern enterprise contributed not more than one-fifth of Burma's exports, and this contribution had then become fairly evenly divided between timber and petroleum products with a small supplement from other minerals.

The development of large rice exports from the Mekong Delta was also, in the main, a result of Asian enterprise following European rule and hydraulic works in a sparsely populated region. Just as migrants from Upper Burma colonized the Irrawaddy Delta, so migrants from Annam helped to create rice farms in Cochinchina, although to a smaller extent and as sharecroppers rather than as landholders. Whereas tenant farming in Lower Burma developed from rural indebtedness, much of the new land opened below the Bassac River was, from the start, sold to Europeans or wealthy Vietnamese who thus acquired estates of up to 2,500 acres and let them to tenants. These estates were called 'plantations' but their owners did little to introduce new methods of cultivation, and most were akin to traditional landlords in using tenants to whom they made loans at rates which often brought in as big an income as the rents, and these were about 40 per cent of the harvest. Estates, it is true, occupied less than half the land in the Transbassac provinces, and were a small proportion of Vietnam's rice lands. But there was the same problem of peasant debt as in Burma; Chettyar and Annamite money-lenders operated in a similar way, and Chinese middlemen themselves advanced loans or acquired estates. Tenants became restless or unstable through burdens of debt, as did other peasant farmers.

Unwittingly and contrary to its own interest French colonization (has) led to the increase of a so-called 'proletariat' class in Indochina . . . defined as including all those people who either own no land or have too little for their livelihood. And to this criterion of insufficient real property should be added that of uprootedness or 'detribalization'.[1]

[1] Robequain, *The Economic Development of French Indo-China*, p. 85. See also Masson, *Histoire du Vietnam*, p. 99.

INDOCHINA: KEY STATISTICS 1830–1913

	Unit	1830	1850	1868	1870	1875	1880	1885	1890	1895	1900	1905	1910	1913
POPULATION	millions													
Burma		4		6							11			
Thailand		3	6										8	
French Indochina		5									16			
RICE ACREAGE	m. acres													
Burma								4·0		5·8		10·0		10·1
Thailand			2·3									3·7		5·4
French Cochinchina							1·3				2·7			5·6[a]
RICE EXPORTS	m. tons													
Burma			0·2								1·4		1·8	2·7
Thailand					0·3	0·4	0·5	0·4	0·8	0·8	0·6	0·9	1·0	1·0
French Indochina							0·3				0·7			1·1
RICE-TEXTILES TERMS OF TRADE (Thailand)				1·7	3·5	3·4	3·6	4·1	n.a.	4·2	6·9	4·3	4·0	3·7
EXPORT RECEIPTS	£ millions													
Burma												14[b]		24
Thailand			0·7	1·0[c]	1·4	1·8	2·0	1·5	3·2	2·6	3·1 (5)	6·3	8·4	7·8
French Indochina				3·2								5·8	8·3	11
COMPOSITION OF EXPORTS	p.c. of country total													
Rice														
Burma				61								73[b]		68
Thailand									70				78	70[d]
French Indochina				41								69		68
Timber														
Burma				20					6					6
Thailand												8[b]		6
Minerals or Oil														
Burma				16								10[b]		14
Thailand									11			11		16[d]
RAILWAYS	km										264	932		
Thailand														

[a] av. 1915–19 [b] 1903–4 [c] 1867 [d] 1915–16

Sources:
Cowan (ed.), *The Economic Development of South-east Asia*
Ingram, *Economic Change in Thailand since 1850*
Furnivall, *Colonial Policy and Practice*
Robequain, *The Economic Development of French Indo-China*
Wickizer and Bennett, *The Rice Economy of Monsoon Asia*

France acquired Vietnam, Cambodia, and Laos through the activities of its missionaries and admirals. Missionaries seemed to have gained a strong position after Bishop de Béhaine had given extraordinary help to Prince Nguyen-Anh, first in recovering southern Vietnam from rebels who had slain the rest of his family and then, as the Emperor Gia-Long (1802–20), in reuniting the whole country. But France was too preoccupied with Napoleonic Wars to take advantage of this development and, soon after their termination, a new sovereign came to the Vietnamese throne. Minh-Mang (1820–41) rejected three French attempts at negotiating commercial treaties, as he did Crawfurd's British–Indian mission, broke off diplomatic relations with France, and resumed persecution of Christians. Britain's First Opium War with China made him reconsider this anti-European policy, but it was blindly intensified by his successors. After missionary appeals for help from French warships in the area, the French government authorized them to give it. Threatening appearances in the Bay of Tourane (Da Nang) forced Thieu-Tri (1841–8) to release imprisoned missionaries on a number of occasions, but matters did not come to a head until Louis Napoleon set about creating the Second Empire.

Tu-Duc (1848–83), a pious Confucian, ordered Christians to be branded and their lands to be confiscated. Tourane was bombarded after two French priests were executed and, in 1858, Louis Napoleon ordered an expedition against Tourane following the execution of the Bishop of Tonking. A Franco-Spanish force occupied the port but could not hold it owing to muddles, disease, and Vietnamese denial of supplies. Admiral de Genouilly, in an attempt to salvage something from the disaster, shifted the expedition to Saigon although the missions had few interests in the south. The port was easily captured but further progress was delayed because of the Anglo-French expedition against Peking. It was not until 1861 that a strong squadron could relieve the siege of Saigon and master Lower Cochinchina. Tu-Duc then negotiated a peace which gave France the three eastern provinces of Cochinchina, opened Tourane, Balat, and Kuang-an to French trade, paid a heavy indemnity, and promised toleration of Catholicism. In this blundering way France's admirals began to develop an empire in Indochina.

The development was resisted by a people whose attitude was declared in a proclamation of 1862:

Your country belongs to the western seas, ours to the eastern seas . . . we differ in speech, writing and customs. . . . If you persist in carrying sword and fire through our land there will be prolonged disorder but we shall be acting in accord with the dictates of Heaven. . . . We swear to fight you incessantly and without respite. When all is lacking we shall take branches from trees in order to make banners and staffs for our troops.[1]

Admiral La Grandière thus faced difficulties in pacifying the new colony and dangers from the western provinces which gave aid to rebels. In 1866 he occupied these provinces and so brought the whole of Cochinchina under French rule.

Three years previously he had succeeded in making Cambodia a French protectorate. This withered remnant of the Khmer Empire, after losing the basins of the Menam and Upper Mekong to invading Thai, had been forced, by nearly a century of war with the newcomers, to abandon Ankor in 1434. Transfer of the court to Phnom Penh, however, was soon followed by repeated civil disorders and dynastic squabbles which gave the Thai, and later the Vietnamese, opportunities for energetic intervention. By the end of the eighteenth century the Nguyen had occupied Cochinchina, and Thailand had annexed Battambang together with Siem Reap. The unfortunate kings of Cambodia had now to receive their crown from Bangkok and pay tribute to Hué. This did not prevent further palace intrigues or conflicting interventions by Cambodia's neighbours so that Ang Duong (1845–59) came to fear they would partition his kingdom at the Mekong. He appealed to France for help and Napoleon III responded by sending a mission which, owing to its leader's incompetence, failed to negotiate a treaty of alliance. The next king, Norodom (1859–1904), after gaining his throne through Thai support, was immediately pressed by the French authorities in Cochinchina to accept their protection in place of that formerly claimed by the Nguyen. Norodom had to agree, in spite of Bangkok's demands for acknowledgement of Thai suzerainty. France, in 1867, compensated Thailand by formally ceding the Cambodian provinces of Battambang, Siem Reap, and Sisophon.

[1] Masson, op. cit., pp. 80–1.

French interest in Cambodia had been stimulated by the publication of *Tour du Monde* (1863), Henri Mouhot's graphic account of the great ruins of Ankor. After crossing Cambodia Mouhot came to Bangkok and obtained permission for a journey to Luang Prabang, the 'delightful little town' which was the capital of Laos. He had wished to cross the northern mountains to visit China but, because of his fragile collections of insects, decided to return down the Mekong. He died of fever soon after leaving Luang Prabang, but other Frenchmen were now interested in exploring the Mekong with a view to finding an overland trade route to China. Garnier and de Lagrée led a small expedition up the river between 1866 and 1868; they reached Luang Prabang and, ignoring the King's dissuasions, followed the river's course into China as far as Tali. There Garnier was courteously turned back, but he had discovered both that the Mekong was useless as a trade route between Saigon and Yunnan, owing to the rapids of its wild upper reaches, and that the Red River (Song Koi) was a more feasible route to China from Tongking. This route was quickly tested by Dupuis, a merchant whom Garnier had met at Hangkow and who had contracts with Chinese generals in Yunnan. In 1871 Dupuis left Yunnan-fu to strike the Red River at Mang-hao, south of the provincial capital, and then came down to Hanoi with a cargo of tin and copper. He returned up the river to Yunnan with a cargo of arms, and again made the downstream journey to Hanoi.

When he tried to buy salt there for another return cargo the mandarins arrested him for infringing an official monopoly. Dupré, the Governor of Cochinchina, then sent Garnier with two hundred men to Hanoi in order to make a settlement of some kind. Tongking was much disturbed by Taiping rebels, who, having escaped from China, were pillaging the province, as were Cantonese troops who had been sent, at Hué's request, to deal with them. Garnier and Dupuis were thus able, with help from Christian villages, to make a bold coup which gave them temporary control over Hanoi and Lower Tongking, although Garnier was killed during a sortie against a Chinese band which came to aid Hanoi's mandarins. Tu Duc accepted a treaty which, besides recognizing French sovereignty over all Cochinchina, opened the Red River to trade in return for evacuation of forts held by French forces in Tongking. The new concession, however, was made useless by Chinese bands along the Red River. Tu Duc encouraged them and also sought to evade the danger of French control by reviving Peking's suzerainty. Reacting from the humiliation of the Franco-Prussian War, and spurred by the British annexation of Upper Burma, Paris sent an expedition in 1881 to clear the Red River of Chinese obstruction. Its leader was killed after seizing Hanoi, and a stronger expedition was then sent in order to subdue the whole of Vietnam, now further weakened by a dynastic crisis following the death of Tu Duc. The Hué Court quickly agreed to a French protectorate over both Tongking and Annam but it was not until 1885, and after a French blockade of Taiwan, that China accepted French claims over Vietnam and agreed to evacuate forces from Tongking.

France could not regard its new acquisition with much satisfaction. Tongking was in revolt and only in Cochinchina was French administration effective. Up to 1897 Vietnam cost Paris more than £30,000,000 and very little of that could be spared for economic development. Difficulties over pacification and administration were aggravated by a strong anti-imperialist movement in France, yet the admirals, before their rule was ended, succeeded in adding Laos to the *Union Indochinoise*.

Lan Xang, after the death of the able Souligna Vongsa (1673–94), had been split by a dynastic crisis, into the three kingdoms of Vientiane, Luang Prabang, and Champassac. The ruler of Vientiane acknowledged vassal status to Annam, which had given him decisive military aid, but the Thai, after capturing Vientiane in 1778, established suzerainty over both it and Luang Prabang. Chao Anou (1804–28) sought Vietnamese help to restore Vientiane's independence, suffered defeat and had his kingdom brutally incorporated by Thailand, which also made Champassac a vassal. For some years the Thai Court was content with remote control over Luang Prabang and Champassac. The situation was changed by depredations of Chinese bandits in Laos, as well as in Tongking, and by French expansion up the Mekong. Thai armies were sent to put down the bandits and eventually succeeded, although France demanded a boundary commission and obtained the right to have a vice-consul at Luang Prabang. It appointed Auguste

Pavie, a man who had intimate knowledge of Laos and deep sympathy for its culture. At the same time he was the advocate of French control over the Mekong's right bank, and worked effectively to achieve this. A series of incidents culminated in a movement of French columns up the Mekong and in a naval blockade of Bangkok. The Thai government was thus forced, in 1893, to cede Laos. A subsequent Anglo-French treaty guaranteed the independence of the Menam valley but in 1904 Thailand had to yield claims over the Malayan sultanates of Kelantan, Trengganu, Kedah, and Perlis and, in 1907, to restore Battambang and Siem Reap to Cambodia.

France gained little materially from Laos, which added one-half to the *Union*'s territory but only one-twentieth to its population and had hardly any exploitable resources. The thinly scattered population was almost entirely self-sufficient, either in small villages along the valleys or as groups of shifting cultivators on plateaux and mountain slopes. They produced nothing for export beyond forest products, of which benzoin, sticklac, and a little teak were the most important. The French introduced small coffee plantations on the Boloven Plateau and opened a tin mine in the Nam Patané basin; but coffee exports never exceeded 1,500 tons nor tin output 15 tons a year. Few, indeed, of the French who came to Laos kept up any wish to develop it; the seductive charm of a leisurely and harmonious way of life soon undermined ambition to disturb this Asian arcady.

Frenchmen also had a sympathetic interest in Cambodia, whose great medieval civilization was rediscovered by savants of the *Ecole Française d'Extrême Orient*, founded at Hanoi in 1898. The protectorate began mildly enough but, during Ferry's premiership (1883–5), King Norodom was stripped of all but ceremonial functions as real government passed to the *Résident Supérieur* at Phnom Penh. The change caused a widespread revolt, led by a royal prince and discreetly fostered by the king; it took two years of costly warfare to suppress it. The French then restored much of the royal authority and the *Résident Supérieur*, together with his four subordinate residents in Cambodia, were instructed to respect the country's religion or customs and to avoid interference witn native affairs. Some good roads were built, a number of towns were pleasantly developed and equipped with schools or hospitals, but no industries of any consequence were established as Cambodia's only minerals were sapphires at Bokeo and Pailin (iron was not mined until the 1930s). Nor did plantations develop, as Cambodia had only forty acres under rubber in 1921 and only a single, disastrous attempt was made at a cotton plantation. The major economic change was the opening of a big rice export through Saigon, aided by improvements in Cambodia to irrigation and transport. A policy of protecting Cambodian peasants prevented the development of rice estates, but Chinese acquired a formidable grip as millers, traders, and usurers besides dominating a good deal of ordinary retail trade.

Tongking and Annam, also nominally protectorates, were reduced by Doumer (1897–1902), the first civilian governor, to much the same colonial position as Cochinchina. These homelands of the Vietnamese were only one-tenth of the *Union*'s territory but held three-quarters of its population, and settlement in the Red River's delta was as dense as in Bengal or Java. The French could do little to change an intensive cultivation of very small rice-fields by hard-working peasants. Engineers did something to improve the Red River's embankments, to tap secondary rivers, and to build roads and bridges, but efforts to develop plantations failed. European rice estates, in a coastal area abandoned because of pirates, soon reverted to native ownership. Those who tried tea-planting gave it up to become processers of the crop which peasants had long produced for local markets. A few coffee plantations were established west of Hanoi or east of Phu Ly, and a few rubber plantations in South Annam; but difficulties over climate and manuring kept coffee output to an insignificant level in Tongking and its rubber plantations produced but a small fraction of the *Union*'s output. Mining was the only significant field of French enterprise in northern Vietnam, and did not begin until the 1900s when companies set about exploiting deposits of anthracite, tin, and zinc. Up to 1913, however, minerals contributed a mere $3\frac{1}{2}$ per cent of the *Union*'s exports, or less than dried fish; coal for Hong Kong or China was the most important mineral export.

Although the Red River delta was much the biggest rice producing area, Tongking and Annam normally had little to export and, in bad years, had to import rice from Saigon. The *Union*'s export surplus came mostly from the less densely settled Mekong delta which in 1900 provided about nine-tenths of total rice shipments. Over the preceding two decades this southern export had almost trebled to 747,000 tons, while Cochinchina's cultivated area doubled and its population rose from 1,679,000 to 2,937,000. Canals had been built in the Mekong delta from the distant days of Funan and the Vietnamese were active in this respect, yet a large part of Cochinchina was half-wild when the French took it over. The admirals appreciated the importance of waterways in a low, marshy land which made road-building difficult, and used some of their scanty funds for improving or extending canals by manual labour. After 1893 Doumer's new Public Works Service let out contracts for five- or ten-year programmes to firms which used mechanical equipment, so that the annual amount of earth dredged rose from 140,000 cubic metres in 1893 to over 6,000,000 cubic metres in 1913. The canals, however, were built primarily for transportation and even in 1937 the majority of rice estates and most peasant proprietors relied upon rainfall or the Mekong's flood to water their land. European estates, moreover, accounted for only one-tenth of Cochinchina's cultivated area.

France contributed indirectly to the impressive growth of rice exports from Cochinchina and Cambodia by improving security and transportation. The direct increase of production came from the activities of traditional cultivators, whether debt-laden peasant proprietors or exploited sharecroppers. Finance, processing, and marketing were largely provided by Chinese merchants whose junks went throughout the delta to bring paddy to their mills at Cholon. French mines and rubber plantations were later to supply one-seventh of the *Union*'s export receipts but, up to 1913, the principal exports, after rice, were mostly peasant outputs—dried fish, maize, hides, pepper, and various jungle products. Only one-fifth of these traditional exports went to France but, under the mercantilist policy initiated by Doumer, France supplied three-tenths of the *Union*'s imports in 1913, and the proportion was later to double.

Thailand, the only South-east Asian country which maintained political independence, had a happier economic development because two able kings used their powers as oriental despots for making a controlled adjustment, both to the western imperialism which engulfed all neighbouring states and to the forces which were transforming Asian trade. It is tempting, if useless, to speculate how Burma might have developed had Mindon come to its throne a generation earlier and been followed by a worthy successor, or how Cambodia and Vietnam might have developed under rulers as able as Thailand's Mongkut and Chulalongkorn.

Little adjustment occurred during the first three reigns of the new Chakri dynasty because the Thai, remembering the dangerous troubles of Narai's reign, were reluctant to become involved with western powers. Rama I (1782–1809), after establishing the capital at Bangkok, nearer the Menam's mouth, successfully defended the country against Burmese aggressions, restored Thai suzerainty over Cambodia, and did much to revive royal authority and national life; his only official contact with the West was the admission of an ineffectual Portuguese consul. Rama II (1809–24) had also to repel the Burmans, and counteracted Vietnamese influence in Cambodia, but is chiefly remembered as promoting Thai culture, more especially a wonderful literary revival. It was during his reign that Crawfurd came to Bangkok for unsuccessful negotiations on behalf of the E.I.C. Rama III (1824–51) fully shared his predecessors' concern to strengthen Thailand but had to engage in cautious relations with western powers for that purpose. Hoping to recover Tennasserim, he gave military support to the British operations which culminated in annexation of Lower Burma. He dared not then refuse minimum concessions over Malay sultanates in a vague treaty which Burney negotiated in 1826, but would accord no trading privileges which went beyond Thai custom. In order to counter British influence, moreover, he took the initiative for a treaty with the United States, according most-favoured nation treatment, moderation of port dues, and admission of Protestant missionaries (they introduced a printing press in 1835 which had a remarkable effect in stimulating Thai prose works). Towards the close of his reign both British and American embassies tried to obtain better conditions for their merchants, but had to report that only martial pressure was likely to secure real concessions.

Although European traders had been virtually excluded from Thailand since Narai's death, active trade continued with China and South-east Asia. Crawfurd estimated that eighty junks a year, carrying 31,000 tons of cargo, went to the southern ports of China, and conjectured that another 4,000 tons went to Malaya or Singapore, while about 1,000 tons could be allowed, in each case, for Thailand's trade with British India, Batavia, Saigon, and the United States, making a total trade of nearly 42,000 tons. The Chinese provided junks and crews both for their own direct share of this trade and for that of the Thai king who sent two official junks a year to Canton, besides triennial tribute missions to Peking, largely monopolized trade with Malaya, and sent occasional junks to Bengal. Most of the junks were built at Bangkok, and all Chinese junks were exempt from port dues, as were royal junks at Canton. Import duties of 8 per cent were applied to somewhat arbitrary valuations of cargo made by Thai officials, and similar duties were levied on exports. The king exercised a right of pre-emption over all imports, and neither Thai nor Chinese merchants could sell export commodities until royal supplies had been disposed of. All this was thoroughly traditional, and the kingdom's revenues came mostly from royal profits or taxes on foreign trade. One estimate puts Thai exports, about 1850, at £700,000 as against imports of £540,000. The main exports were sugar (£89,000), hides (£63,000), cotton (£56,000), sappanwood (£44,000), tin and lac (each £32,000), cotton goods and dried fish (each £26,000), iron and ironware (£23,000), birds' nests (£22,000), and rice (£19,000). They obviously comprised a wide variety of small items, partly because Thailand was still an entrepôt for goods moving between South-east Asia and China. The main imports from China, according to Crawfurd, were 'manufactured silks, common earthenware in large quantity, with a little fine porcelain, tea, paper, toys and certain articles of wearing apparel'.[1]

Rama III was succeeded by his half-brother, Mongkut (1851–68), who had been a monk for almost thirty years, during which he had gained an extraordinary knowledge of the king-

[1] Crawfurd, *Journal of an Embassy to the Courts of Siam and Cochin-China*, p. 114.

dom through pilgrimages and other contacts with his people
and had extended his studies from Buddhist scripture to Latin,
English, astronomy, and world affairs, helped by French and
American missionaries. He was, accordingly, better equipped
than any other Asian ruler to adjust his country to modern
realities, and to appreciate the need for such adjustment following China's humiliation by western powers. The need appeared
urgent after Britain annexed Lower Burma, so that Mongkut
boldly decided to appease the new imperialists by opening
Thailand to foreign merchants and abandoning royal monopolies.

In 1855 a revolutionary commercial treaty was negotiated
with Britain, helped by an acceptable envoy, Bowring, and
perhaps stimulated by a British gunboat firing salutes in the
Menam. The main terms were free access of British merchants
to Thai ports, rights of residence and consular jurisdiction, a
maximum duty of 3 per cent on imports and a uniform agreed
duty on exports; a supplementary treaty freed exports of gold
and rice and abolished a royal monopoly on coconut oil. Similar
treaties were quickly made with the United States and France
and, by 1868, with Denmark, the Hanseatic cities, Portugal,
the Netherlands, Prussia, Belgium, Italy, Norway, and Sweden.
Britain, nevertheless, gained most from this open door; the
Bombay-Burmah Corporation dominated the teak industry,
British merchants replaced Chinese as Bangkok's leading
foreign traders, and both Singapore and Hong Kong expanded
trade with Thailand. During Mongkut's reign Thai exports and
imports doubled in value, and rice shipments rose to about
£800,000 or one-half of total exports.

Growth of trade must have compensated a good deal for
reduction of import duties and loss of royal export monopolies,
but Mongkut had to find other sources of revenue. There had
long been various land taxes and internal transit dues taking, in
each case, about one-tenth of the produce. These were now
tightened and concessions were farmed to Chinese for gambling,
lotteries, spirits, and opium (although its use was forbidden to
Thai). Mongkut used part of the proceeds for building canals
and ships, teaching foreign languages, sending princes abroad
as ambassadors or students, and modernizing the administration by appointments of foreign advisers. He realized that

Thailand's ability to survive British or French encroachment depended upon 'our mouths and our hearts, so constituted as to be full of sense and wisdom for the better protection of ourselves'.[1]

Mongkut, however, was able only to set a general course for modernization and to reach a modest way along it. When he died, Thailand still lacked fixed laws, general education, public health measures, a proper system of state finance, posts, telegraphs, or railways, and had few roads. These defects were remedied during the long reign of his son Chulalongkorn (1868–1910) who also ended slavery and forced labour services, improved provincial as well as central administration, and began modern irrigation. Extended use was made of foreign advisers, most of whom, including the Financial Adviser, were British; but the General Adviser was a Belgian, the chief advisers for posts, telegraphs, and railways were Germans, those for the army, navy, and police were Danes, and the leading irrigation expert was a Dutchman. Great care was taken to limit Europeans to an advisory role as the developing civil service was regularly staffed by Thai nationals and headed by western-trained members of the large royal family or the nobility.

Economic conditions favoured such reforms, and enabled Thailand to strengthen its independence by avoiding external debt. During Chulalongkorn's reign exports rose from £1,350,000 to £7,800,000, almost nine-tenths of this increase coming from rice and most of the remainder from teak or tin. An expanding world market and a doubling of price, both in money and real terms, stimulated peasants to increase rice exports to seven times their 1870 volume. Land was abundant and clearing for cultivation was encouraged by the old, liberal custom of allowing anyone free occupation of up to ten acres, by gradual elimination of *corvée* labour or slavery, and, after 1867, by waiving land tax for the first few years. Land tax, in any case, was low, and the government aimed at preserving a nation of small, independent farmers by checking acquisition of large estates through the requirement that any uncultivated land revert to the state. Nor did Chinese become rice farmers although their immigration was encouraged in order to provide

[1] Quoted in Busch, *Thailand*, p. 68.

wage-labour for public works and other activities. As elsewhere, they soon engrossed milling and marketing of rice, partly because four-fifths of Thailand's rice surplus went to Singapore, Hong Kong, and China. They also became money-lenders, as did Thai landlords, but the great majority of farmers remained peasant proprietors, not seriously burdened with debt.

All this contrasted favourably with Burma, even if exports were only half the Burmese level and railways or roads were much less developed. Thailand's exports, in any case, were at least as great as those of French Indochina. The Thai peasant may not have had a higher standard of material consumption than his Burmese or Vietnamese counterpart, but he had much greater economic security, unbroken continuity of traditional life, and freedom from alien officials who could make other Asians feel themselves to be foreigners in their own land.

7. The modernization of Japan

One other country used institutions of oriental depotism for making a successful adjustment to the dangerous expansion of western power. In Japan the Meiji Emperor (1868–1912) had a reign which almost coincided with that of Chulalongkorn and was comparable in that both their countries, after reviving foreign trade under western pressure, set about modernizing key administrative or economic activities in order to resist further encroachment. Japan, however, swung from a collapsing feudalism to a national restoration of imperial authority for pushing through sweeping reforms. The reforms were so radical and gave such wide scope for indigenous abilities that, after 1885, Japan quickly developed from a small, isolated, traditional economy into a major industrial power.

The Tokugawa Shogunate, after a first century of successful rule, during which external trade was confined to an annual Dutch voyage to Nagasaki or a few Chinese merchants at the same port, encountered increasing difficulties. By 1695 extravagance, expenses from fires in the capital or other disasters, peculating officials, diminishing yields from silver mines, and loss of profit from foreign trade had so weakened the Bakufu's finances that it debased the currency. This, of course, gave only temporary relief and, when poor harvests decreased tax revenue,

Yoshimune (1716–45) both raised the collection from 40 to 50 per cent of the crop and attempted other durable remedies; severe retrenchment, currency reform, and bringing more land into cultivation. They had some success until the great famine of 1732–3 during which two million people died and rice revenues slumped. There was a further currency debasement in 1736, and further pressures by tax-collectors. But the Bakufu's tax receipts declined from a peak of 1,800,000 *koku* of rice in 1744 to 1,100,000 *koku* in 1770, and population, after moderately increasing, became stationary at between 25 or 26 million for the rest of the century. The major cause, in both cases, was a sequence of famines and epidemics, notably the plague of 1773, the Temmei famine of 1783–7, and then the Tempo famine of 1832–6, none of which could be relieved by importing food. A secondary cause of population decline was the growth of abortion and infanticide during a long period of rural distress.

Peasants suffered from tax-gatherers and rent-collectors as well as from natural disasters; so much, indeed, that a Tokugawa councillor, could write:

The exactions from the peasant eat up 50% to 70% of his produce. There are countless other taxes—such as a tax on the field, a tax on doors, a tax on windows. . . . The nominal tax is a *koku* of rice and a *katori* of silk but actually it is increased threefold through bribery and extortion . . . and other forms of exaction and tyranny are countless.[1]

In northern and eastern Japan large areas were abandoned because they could not produce enough to meet such demands and, in other places, there was a paradoxical situation of peasants being bribed to take over good lands which were excessively taxed. Everywhere poverty obliged peasants to pledge land or sell it, with the result that villages became divided into a few well-to-do farmers, who found ways of evading levies, and tenants, who had to supplement meagre incomes by working at cottage industries or as labourers. Throughout the eighteenth century rural discontent led to frequent peasant riots, and there were also riots in the towns as workmen, already oppressed by guilds, suffered from food shortages, the Bakufu's debasements or its sporadic attempts to help depressed *Samurai* by making rice dearer.

[1] Quoted in Norman, *Japan's Emergence as a Modern State*, p. 23.

(All figures are centred quinquennial averages; values at 1897–1914 parity of yen)

	Unit	1870	1877	1880	1887	1890	1897	1900	1907	1912	1915
POPULATION	million	(35)	36		39		42		48	51	
RICE PRODUCTION	million *koku*				37		39		48	51	
NATIONAL INCOME	£ million				98		206		326	431	
from Primary Industries	per cent			64		53		47			36
Secondary Industries				11		16		21			27
Tertiary Industries				26		31		32			38
Exports				5	6		8		13	15	
to Capital Formation					11		14		14		
WHOLESALE PRICES	Index		48		47		70		96	100	
PRODUCTION	Index										
Food					57		67		85	100	
Materials					(22)		48		78	100	
Manufacturing							(37)		69	100	
Textiles							41		70	100	
Metals and Machinery							25		61	100	
TRANSPORT	thousands ton										
Rail freight					2		24		68	100	
Modern shipping					19		38		78	100	
EXPORTS	£ million	1·7		3·2		8·1	17		43	65	
Food	per cent	25		37		23	14		12	11	
Materials		23		12		11	11		9	8	
Semi-manufactures		41		40		46	46		45	50	
Manufactures		2		7		16	26		32	30	
Other		9		4		4	3		2	1	
Agricultural		93		84		69		50			
IMPORTS	£ million	2·4		3·5		7·7	21		48	68	
Food	per cent	29		15		21	23		17	12	
Materials		4		4		12	26		36	49	
Semi-manufactures		20		30		26	18		19	18	
Manufactures		45		49		40	32		27	20	
Others		2		3		1	1		1	1	

Sources:
Allen, *A Short Economic History of Modern Japan*
Lockwood, *The Economic Development of Japan*
Allen (ed.), *The State and Economic Enterprise in Japan*

All this tended to disrupt the harmony of rural life but may have helped to create pre-conditions for later economic growth. Poorer peasants became accustomed to sending their children to work in the towns, and themselves emerged from feudal rigours not only as more efficient producers of food but, according to one authority, with 'the sturdy virtue of industry, a remarkable capacity for discipline and with a secure though diminutive holding in land'.[1] Wealthy peasants used their means for various rural enterprises, such as processing silk or other crops, and for educating their families, thus preparing one stream of potential entrepreneurs to modernize Japan.

The main stream of entrepreneurs, however, was to come from the generally educated *Samurai* class which formed about 7 per cent of the whole population. These privileged retainers of the Bakufu or daimyos lost their military functions during the long years of peace, and many became impoverished through the diminishing value of allowances paid in rice. This value diminished, not only through retrenchments forced upon the Bakufu or daimyos by mounting debts, but also through collusive buying of rice merchants at Yedo or Osaka and debasements which inflated other prices more than that of rice. Many *Samurai* became functionless pensioners living in towns, where poverty obliged them to take up previously despised trades or to sell *Samurai* status by adopting merchants' sons. Peace and impoverishment, accordingly, sapped military virtues of loyalty to superiors or followers, corroded pride in an increasingly parasitic status and weakened feudal class divisions.

More fortunate *Samurai* took over administrative duties in the Bakufu or fiefs becoming, apparently, the counterpart of China's scholar-gentry, and the similarity promised to be greater when Sung neo-Confucianism was made Japan's official philosophy. This weakened Buddhism but failed, in the end, to foster sentiments of supreme loyalty to the Shogun, as the Bakufu had hoped, or to produce that pacifist and isolationist complacency which characterized Chinese mandarins. Weakening of Buddhism assisted a revival of Shintoism, the old religion based on nature worship, which attributed a divine origin and assigned a sacerdotal role to Japan's emperors. Confucianists helped this trend by emphasizing historical studies and Fujiwara, a most

[1] Asakawa quoted in Sansom, *Japan: A Short Cultural History*, p. 523.

influential teacher, even declared that 'Shinto and Confucianism are the same truth'[1]; Hayashi Razan went a little further with the statement that 'Shinto is Odo (loyalty to the Sovereign) and Odo is Confucianism'.[2] Thought along these lines led influential *Samurai* to see Japan more in terms of national unity than of feudal division, and to ask whether primary loyalty was not to the Emperor rather than to the Shogun. National interest, moreover, seemed to require a resumption of the old tradition of cultural borrowing from abroad, but now from the Dutch who provided the only chink of light from the dazzling science of the west. Scholars, in spite of obstructions and dangers, began to study, with the help of Dutch at Nagasaki, astronomy, geography, botany, medicine, and other specialist fields. Considerable impetus was given to these studies by a lifting of the ban on importing foreign books in 1720, and then by the promotion of Konyo, the leading exponent of *Rangaku* or Dutch learning, to the Bakufu's post of chief librarian. Wider enthusiasm developed through the work of Gennai and his associates for *Bussangaku*, the application of science to farming and other branches of production.

Developments within the Bakufu and at the Court gave increasing point to these intellectual currents among the *Samurai*. The far-sighted Ieyasu had founded the Shogunate in such a way as to protect it against incompetent successors, and Iemitsu, the third Shogun, had strengthened it further, notably by the policy of isolation from the outside world. There were, indeed, few able men among later Shoguns, who had to rely heavily upon counsellors and entrust them with much executive power. By the close of the eighteenth century, accordingly, the Bakufu had degenerated into a flabby and somewhat divided bureaucracy, facing critical problems with which it was unable to cope. Relations between it and the Court had also begun to deteriorate following a dispute, in 1798, about honours for a retiring emperor. Some *kuge*, or court aristocrats, whom the Tokugawa had reduced to impotence, were encouraged by growing loyalty to the Throne, and by the Bakufu's difficulties, to foster dissent, and later made compacts with powerful daimyos who came into sharp opposition to the Bakufu.

The Tokugawa political system depended upon control over

[1] Quoted in ibid., p. 512.   [2] ibid., p. 512.

some 260 daimyos who ruled their own fiefs under a type of clan government. Most fiefs were small enough for the Bakufu to treat as it pleased, but eleven of them were fairly large, ruled by families which were the last to acknowledge Tokugawa suzerainty, and at the periphery in North Honshu or in the South-west. The main control over these, and other fiefs, was the obligation of daimyos to reside at Yedo every second year. Such residence involved heavy monetary expenditures, and these soared as debasements, over the two centuries of the Shogunate, reduced the purchasing power of the standard coin to one-eighth. Revenues, on the other hand, were received mainly in rice which had to be sold for what the merchants of Yedo or Osaka would pay. No exactions upon peasants or reductions of *Samurai*'s allowances proved sufficient to prevent fiefs from becoming heavily indebted to merchants or money-lenders.

Monetization and debasement thus undermined the economic basis of feudalism, and created another pre-condition for modernization by transferring more and more of the agricultural surplus from aristocratic spending to mercantile accumulation. The immediate consequence was that nobles came under a new subjection, humiliating in itself and damaging to feudal loyal-ties. As one contemporary put it: 'The anger of the wealthy merchants of Osaka has the power of striking terror into the hearts of the daimyo.'[1] Merchants, nevertheless, also had reasons for discontent. The Tokugawa had deprived them of foreign trade and imposed degrading restrictions upon their status or social behaviour. It is true that merchants flourished, that some lived like princes, in spite of the restrictions, and that so many educated their families as to make for a gay and colour-ful blossoming of bourgeois culture in the brief *Genroku* era (1688–1704). But this withered under the Bakufu's disapproval of what it took to be a decadent manifestation of upstart ebul-lience and after 1760 it began exacting some of the merchants' gains by irregular, yet increasingly frequent, levies of forced loans. More damaging to merchants, and quite disruptive of credit conditions, were the decrees of 1831 and 1843 which abolished every type of guild. And so, when the time was ripe, great merchants financed those daimyos who overthrew the Shogunate; especially the Mitsui, whose official record states,

---

[1] Allen, *A Short Economic History of Modern Japan*, p. 21.

'The loans required for the military operations of the Imperial forces were largely furnished by the House of Mitsui.'[1]

The leaders of this revolt came from the Choshu fief, along the western entrance of the Inland Sea, and from the Satsuma fief at the southern end of Kyushu. Choshu was a large producer of rice, with subsidiary revenue from salt and indigo, and had a clan fund for marketing the commodities and those of other fiefs using its berths or warehouses along the Inland Sea. Satsuma produced twice as much rice as Choshu, and conducted a profitable trade, mainly in sugar, with the Luchu (Ryukyu) Islands; its leaders were particularly outward-looking as they made their capital an important centre for western studies. These advantages did not prevent either fief from incurring the common burden of heavy debt, but both managed to shrug it off. Satsuma, after exhausting its credit in the 1820s, simply repudiated the whole of its debt to merchants, and carried on without further credit by enlarging trade with the southern islands to include a good deal of smuggling activity. Choshu managed to profit from an inflation which reduced the real value of past debts while increasing that of the clan fund's investments. This fortunate development did not occur until the Tempo Reform of 1840, which involved sale of clan monopolies over cotton, salt, saké, and other products to merchant guilds in order to strengthen the clan fund. Productive loans were then made for farming, trade, and transport facilities, and care was taken to ship goods so as to profit from market fluctuations at Osaka.

Both fiefs used their economic power for increasing the size and quality of their armed forces. They began modernizing these forces by establishing metal industries and shipyards. During the 1850s Satsuma built two reverberatory furnaces, an iron smelter, a factory to bore cannon, and yards to build steamships. Choshu built an iron foundry in 1854 and, three years later, had a yard for equipping ships with cannon. Nor were they the only pioneers of such strategic industry. Two other south-western clans, Hizen and Mito, also set up furnaces, foundries, and shipyards. The Bakufu itself saw a need for such activity as it built a steamship in 1857, an iron foundry in 1861,

---

[1] Quoted in Norman, op. cit., p. 49.

and completed, with French help, the Yokosuka foundry and dockyards in 1865.

All this was a slight and belated response to new western activity around Japan. Envoys from Catherine the Great had appeared, in 1742 and 1804, with requests for negotiations about trade; these were refused but Rezanov, the second envoy, frightened the Bakufu by unauthorized raids on Japanese settlements in Sakhalin. Then came a number of visits from British ships seeking provisions, beginning with a fruitless quest of H.M.S. Phaeton to Nagasaki for a Dutch prize. The Bakufu, in 1825, ordered ports to drive off foreign ships or to execute any crew who succeeded in landing. Fear of reprisals prevented vigorous enforcement of this order but it was not relaxed until 1842, when the Bakufu became most alarmed at forcible opening of China's ports by the British navy.

It was the United States, however, which took the lead in forcing the Shogunate to abandon its key policy of exclusion. American whalers and clippers were making considerable use of the great circle route near Japan, and seemed to prove that 'manifest destiny' would bring their nation, not merely to the coast of the Pacific, but across that great ocean to the markets of the Far East. Commodore Perry was sent, in 1853, to demand facilities for navigation and returned for an answer, in the following year, with eight warships. The Bakufu, unable to withstand threats of bombarding Yedo or cutting off food shipped from Osaka, reluctantly agreed to open Shimoda and Hakodate as ports of refuge and provisioning. Britain, Russia, and the Netherlands promptly obtained similar agreements, quite unacceptable to their mercantile interests. Harris, the first American consul in Japan, and Curtius, the Dutch minister at Nagasaki, skilfully played upon the Bakufu's fear of western aggression to secure real concessions. In 1858, accordingly, the United States, the Netherlands, Britain, Russia, and also France obtained 'unequal treaties' which fully opened Shimoda, Hakodate, Kanagawa, and Nagasaki to trade, gave rights of foreign residence with extra territorial privileges at Yedo and Osaka, and bound Japan to moderate duties of around 20 per cent on imports or exports; two other ports, Niigata and Hyogo (Kobe), were to be similarly opened by 1863. But even before the new treaties came into force, westerners swarmed into the fishing village of Yokohama, near Kanagawa, and quickly developed it as the chief port for foreign trade.

Before yielding to Perry's demands the Bakufu took the unprecedented step of consulting all daimyos in an attempt to gain national support, and also sought the Throne's advice. Both daimyos and Court displayed a strong anti-foreign sentiment but the Bakufu had no real alternative to accepting the demands, although it took the precaution of obtaining imperial consent to the first treaties. Power then shifted within the Bakufu to Ii Naosuke, leader of a group which favoured both foreign contacts and strengthening the Shogun's power. Ii forced a reluctant Emperor to sanction the wider treaties of 1858, disciplined Mito and other opposing daimyos, and sternly repressed *Samurai* agitation. But he was soon assasinated by a group of *Samurai* from Mito, and the Bakufu came under wide attack from those raising the cry '*Sonno Joi*', 'Revere (the Emperor) and Expel (the Barbarians)'. The weakened Bakufu tried a conciliatory policy, including a fatal relaxation of compulsory residence at Yedo. The daimyos retired to their fiefs and those in the west, especially, came into more or less open revolt against the Bakufu, helped by rich merchants from Yedo or Osaka and encouraged by growing hostility of the Court to Bakufu policies.

Choshu and Satsuma now began jostling for national leadership. Choshu obtained a controlling position at the Court where it fostered anti-western policies, but overreached itself by attacking foreign ships in the Inland Sea. A combined fleet of American, British, Dutch, and French warships demolished Choshu forts in 1865; and obliged Japan to reduce its tariff to a mere 5 per cent level, as well as exacting other trade concessions. Satsuma also attacked British ships until they nearly demolished Kagoshima, the clan capital, and levied an indemnity. Choshu suffered a further defeat when it attempted, in 1864, to 'rescue' the Emperor by seizing Kyoto. Satsuma joined the Bakufu forces which inflicted this defeat but exerted powerful influence to secure lenient terms for its rival. It refused to join a second expedition sent by the Bakufu against Choshu when this fief was taken over by the clan's best troops. They defeated the Bakufu's forces and so dealt a shattering blow to its prestige. Satsuma and Choshu then agreed to co-operate for full restoration of imperial authority. Aided by other daimyos they attacked in January 1868, obtained the Shogun's surrender in May, and overcame the last Tokugawa resisters a year later. The Court moved from ceremonial Kyoto to executive Yedo, and Choshu, Satsuma, Tosa, and Hizen set all daimyos a compelling example by surrendering fiefs to the Throne. Their memorial stated: 'Now that imperial power is restored, how can we retain possession of land that belongs to the Emperor and govern people who are his subjects? We therefore reverently offer up all our feudal possessions . . . so that a uniform rule may prevail throughout the Empire.'[1]

So began the Meiji restoration, under a boy-emperor, by men who seemed to look back to the system of centralized government which Japan had long ago borrowed from T'ang China. They did remove the feudal institutions which had replaced that old system. Daimyos were made governors of the fiefs which they had surrendered, at salaries one-tenth of their former revenues but relieved of debts and allowances for *Samurai*. In 1871 fiefs were abolished, clan forces were merged into a new Imperial Army based on universal conscription, and the country was divided into prefectures and garrison districts. Feudal restrictions were lifted from agricultural land in the following year, and ownership was vested in those who actually paid imperial land tax. The final move came in 1876 when incomes of both diamyos and *Samurai* were commuted into state bonds, and when *Samurai* were forbidden to wear the swords which had been badges as well as weapons of feudal privilege. Many *Samurai* violently opposed these changes, but the new imperial forces crushed all revolts, including a last formidable rebellion of Satsuma men in 1877.

How did the daimyos, who had overthrown the Bakufu, come to yield feudal rights so quickly and easily to a Court which, for centuries, had been little more than a ceremonial puppet show? Most fiefs, as has been said, were small, half of them were in direct vassalage to the discredited Tokugawa, and all daimyos gained from the Court's assumption of clan debts and maintenance of feudal retainers as well as from generous compensation for loss of feudal revenues. No more than four clans were really powerful and had become so because of able

[1] Quoted in Storry, *A History of Modern Japan*, p. 105.

Samurai who emerged as effective administrators or military leaders. Choshu, Satsuma, Tosa, and Hizen had improved their economic position, begun modern industries, and strengthened their military forces through the direction or guidance of clan bureaucrats. It was these *Samurai* who effected the alliances which restored imperial authority and it was only they, and a few court nobles, who had clear ideas or bold visions about the use of this authority for lifting Japan to a strong position in the modern world. Their prospects, moreover, were far better in a strong national government than in backward fiefs.

They served at first as junior councillors to higher bodies of court nobles and daimyos, or as assistants to the great officers of a government which remained traditional in form. But, as a coherent *élite*, they made it execute radical policies by swaying formal superiors with the deferential skills which had been acquired in manipulating their own daimyos. So indispensable did these young and relatively lowborn *Samurai* prove that, after 1873, they usually headed the new ministries of Home Affairs, Justice, Finance, Army, Navy, and Foreign Affairs. They were then in a stronger position to speed Japan's transition from a feudal to a capitalist economy.

The main necessity here was to create a proper financial system. During its first four years the new government had to spend £148 million but, owing to initial difficulties in collecting land taxes or rents formerly accruing to the Shogun or daimyos, received only £50 million in ordinary revenue. Loans of £23 million were raised from merchants, and nearly £4 million from England for a railway between Tokyo and Yokohama. The remainder had to be financed by issuing inconvertible paper notes which added to the currency confusion of local paper issues by fiefs and variously debased coins issued by the Bakufu. The coinage was reformed in 1871 under a law which made a yen of defined gold content the standard coin, and all local issues were taken over by the government in the following year when its paper notes reached Y103 million. Government debt also rose to Y33 million with the assumption of clan debts, and expenditure nearly trebled to reach Y58 million in 1872, partly because of pensions for *Samurai* and indemnities for a now disestablished Buddhist church. Ordinary revenue, however, rose from one-third to three-fifths of government expenditure and the large issues did not cause price inflation as there was greater monetization of the economy, increased production, and an excess of imports.

Further increases of revenue, monetization, and production came from the reformed land tax of 1873. This changed the whole basis of collection by requiring *proprietors* to pay a *money tax* on *land values*, assessed at average yields and produce prices over the previous quinquennium in such a way as to give the state about one-third of gross produce. At the same time numerous petty taxes were abolished, including feudal levies which had hindered the development of national markets. There were still indirect taxes on *saké*, beverages, tobacco, sugar, textiles, and other important commodities, low customs duties fixed by the treaties at 5 per cent, and direct taxes on houses, inheritances, and personal or business incomes. Land tax, however, accounted for four-fifths of ordinary revenue in 1879, although this proportion fell through rising agricultural yields or prices and the more rapid growth of industry and trade. Government debt, nevertheless, rose from Y33 million in 1872 to Y240 million in 1877 because expenditures rose far more rapidly than receipts. The main factors were the cost of the Satsuma rebellion and the commutation of pensions for daimyos and *Samurai* to interest-bearing bonds, whose issue came to Y174 million.

These bonds had a remarkable effect upon private banking. The old merchant firms had been badly hit by a loss of rice business with daimyos or *Samurai*, and could not adapt to the kind of exchange banking which was required by the new conditions of foreign trade. At the same time there was a need for circulating capital to help industrial as well as commercial development. Regulations were therefore made in 1872 for national banks on the American pattern; these could issue their own notes up to the limit of holdings of special bonds, acquired from the Treasury by surrendering government notes, but bank notes had to be convertible into gold. Only four banks were incorporated under these regulations and none did well because of the wide discrepancy between a market interest rate of 13 per cent and the 6 per cent paid on the special bonds. Banks, moreover, lost gold because their notes were used by merchants for effecting foreign payments rather than government notes, which were at a market discount. It was obvious that the regulations would have to be changed in order to make better provision for the country's banking needs, and simultaneously obvious that something would have to be done to provide a productive outlet for the huge amount of commutation bonds just issued to daimyos and *Samurai*. A joint solution was sought by making new regulations which allowed national banks holding 80 per cent of their capital as government bonds to issue their own notes, up to a combined maximum of Y34 million, against reserves of government notes instead of gold. Daimyos and *Samurai* took enthusiastic advantage of this opportunity to enter business without loss of face and, indeed, to render patriotic service by helping the government modernize Japan. They provided three-quarters of the capital for 193 national banks, as against only one-seventh from merchants. Bank issues rose so rapidly that they reached the legal maximum by 1879, when combined issues of government and bank notes were more than one-half above the 1876 level. The result was a sharp inflation of prices which swelled profits of many industrial enterprises and reduced the burden of land tax. But it led to a corresponding fall in the real value of government revenues, to an excess of imports, associated with a heavy drain of specie, and to a marked depreciation of government bonds or rise of interest rates.

The situation was corrected by the financial reforms and severe deflation which followed Matsukata's appointment, in 1881, as Minister of Finance. He quickly improved the collection of land tax, raised taxes on various commodities, halted new expenditures on public works or grants to private enterprises, and began selling unprofitable state enterprises. Government spending was held to a fairly constant level up to 1893, some debt was redeemed, and interest charges were reduced by a conversion issue at 5 per cent. These remarkable fiscal improvements depended upon a major banking reform. Matsukata, in 1885, established the Bank of Japan to replace all previous issues by notes which would be convertible into gold or silver. National banks had to transfer reserves to the Bank and make annual payments for redeeming old issues; government notes, similarly, were retired by using budget surpluses for purchases of specie or foreign exchange. By the end of the century no government notes and only a few notes of national banks were still in circulation, and these banks had become ordinary commercial banks. Foreign exchange business, however, was largely handled and controlled by the Yokohama Specie Bank. Founded in 1880 as a quasi-government concern, Matsukata made it the Treasury's agent for dealings in foreign bills but, in 1890, replaced Treasury finance for such operations by a permanent loan of Y20 million from the Bank of Japan, which also discounted the Specie Bank's bills at a favourable rate. Other specialist banks were later added as important instruments of national economic policy; the Hypothec Bank (1896) as the central organ of agricultural and industrial banks in the prefectures, the Industrial Bank of Japan (1900) for large-scale finance of private or public enterprises, and then colonial banks in Taiwan (1899) and Korea (1909).

Matsukata's reforms brought Japan across the bridge of transitional adjustment to the brink of modern economic growth; for, during the next two decades, there was steady application of private and government saving, at a comparatively high ratio of 12–13 per cent of national income, to the development of the economy by techniques and equipment copied or imported from industrialized nations. Between 1885 and 1905 agriculture's share of the labour force dropped from four-fifths to two-thirds, and the contribution of factory industry rose from 4 to 9 per cent. Exports rose from 4 to 10 per cent of national output, and finished manufactures accounted for one-third of exports in 1907. Over the same period the share of finished manufactures in Japan's imports fell from nearly one-half to little more than one-quarter. Real national income almost doubled and, as population rose by one-quarter, real income per head increased by nearly one-half. It was still a low income —only £7 a head in 1907—but increasing at a rate of 1·3 per cent a year because of a solid development of modern industry and trade.

There was, in the favourable conditions of the late nineteenth century, a remarkably close interconnection between Japan's industrialization and its foreign trade. As one authority puts it:

For Japan herself foreign commerce proved to be the key unlocking the door of economic opportunity. Initially it provided a highway over which new impulses and a new technology came in to revolutionize much of her economic life. Later it enabled her to draw increasingly on the world's industrial resources to compensate for her own basic deficiencies. As a result she came to acquire a degree of dependence on the world economy exceeded by that of few other nations in modern times.[1]

During the transitional phase (1868–85) the development of trade was not quantitatively impressive. Exports, in the first quinquennium of the Meiji Restoration, were around £2,000,000 a year and imports somewhat above this figure; by the early eighties neither had reached £4,00,000, about Thailand's level and below that of Ceylon. Various factors held them down. Japanese merchants had lost experience of foreign trading and were slow to gain the skills required by new world markets; British firms thus dominated Japan's external trade and, as late as 1885, less than one-tenth of it was conducted by Japanese, and only one-fifth of the tonnage entering ports was domestically owned. Monetary difficulties further impeded trade as the exchange was unsettled and financial facilities inadequate until Matsukata's reforms were complete. In some ways, too, the government retarded trade by restricting exports of rice or copper on strategic grounds and, far more important, by discouraging foreign investment or borrowing. The major limitations, however, were Japan's backwardness and lack of such natural resources as had made for rapid development of trade in other Asian countries; already densely populated, it had only small export surpluses of foodstuffs or timber, presented no advantages for plantation crops, and had only copper and coal as important minerals.

Exports were thus few and for the most part thoroughly traditional when Japan commenced modern development. It had the good luck to find strong demands for raw silk and silkworm eggs, owing to a bad outbreak of silkworm disease in Europe, and was able to maintain a competitive position, thanks to the Suez Canal, after the French industry recovered. Raw silk accounted for two-fifths of Japan's exports up to 1893. There was also a strong initial demand for tea, but this soon became fairly constant at around 20,000 tons and declined, as a proportion of total exports, from 30 per cent in 1871–5 to 18 per cent in 1881–5 and later to less than 5 per cent in 1896–1900.

[1] Quoted in Lockwood, *The Economic Development of Japan*, p. 306.

Other early exports were individually small; some rice, fish, seaweed, copper, coal, sulphur, and camphor to China and neighbouring countries; and straw braids, mats, pottery, fans, lacquerware, and bronzeware to curio shops in Europe or the United States. Finished manufactures rose from 2 to 7 per cent of Japan's exports but came mostly from traditional crafts or cottage industries.

Imports were held down by both poverty and lack of foreign exchange. Much the biggest category was cheap Manchester goods, which made severe inroads into domestic markets for hand-woven fabrics or home-spun yarn; textile fabrics (including woollens) and textile materials were three-fifths of Japan's imports in 1871-5, and were still one-fifth a decade later. Sugar accounted for a fairly steady 10 per cent of imports and kerosene for another 5 per cent. Remaining items covered a wide range of consumer goods and industrial requirements but, even in 1881-5, neither machinery and vessels nor metals and ores accounted, as a group, for more than 6 per cent of the total.

The major impact of foreign trade during this transitional period was upon Japanese minds. Curiosity about the west, appreciation of its practical achievements and a desire to emulate them, already felt by a number of *Samurai* in the Tokugawa era, greatly intensified and became far more widespread. Hundreds of foreigners came to Japan as traders, sailors, experts in government employ, teachers, or missionaries. Britons came to build pilot plants, develop nagigational facilities, or train the Imperial Navy; Germans came to staff medical schools or to advise on constitutional matters; French lawyers helped to develop the criminal code and Americans to improve agriculture or mining. Many Japanese were sent abroad to study a wide variety of things, and returned to help their country's modernization. Imports of fine Manchester goods aroused enthusiasm in consumers, and imports of steam boilers opened the eyes of producers to the possibilities of power applied to industry or transport. Slight though their commercial value was, imports of books or scientific instruments also had a catalytic effect upon tastes and techniques. Small industries quickly grew up to provide soap, toothpaste, matches, shoes, umbrellas, and other western articles. According to an official report, 'The foreign mania spread everywhere, and everything was manufactured in imitation of foreign articles.'[1] The mania embraced fads, some of them rather odd. Western attire became *de rigueur* at the Court, in the armed services, and in government offices; a western haircut was the mark of a progressive man, and wealthier families had their daughters instructed in ball-room dancing as well as in foreign languages. Was there an element, in all this, of appeal to sympathetic magic, such as had, many centuries earlier, made South-east Asians adopt Hindu culture or, later, made some of them adopt the religion of successful Moslem traders?

The mania waned to some extent as traditional values recovered, but it served to put Japan on the path of modern economic growth. That had been the consistent aim of the Meiji government which helped, in some way, to promote every important modern industry Japan acquired in the nineteenth century. It took over and developed the iron foundries, armament or munitions works, and shipyards begun by the Bakufu and western daimyos. Alarmed at discovering that imports were supplying three-fifths of Japan's cottons, it built and operated, with help from western experts, cotton mills in Aichi and Hiroshima; and, seeking to diversify exports, established modern silk-reeling factories at Maebashi and Tomoika. A woollen mill supplied the armed forces, and model factories produced paper, glass, tiles, cement, sodium sulphate, and bleaching powder. Mineral output was expanded by nine state mines extracting coal, copper, iron-ore, gold, and silver. By 1880, moreover, the state had built seventy-five miles of railway, had linked the main towns by telegraph and begun to supply them with gas or tramways, had acquired fifty-one merchant steamships, and was operating three modern shipbuilding yards.

But the Meiji leaders were mercantilists without desire for collectivism. They sought to blaze industrial trails for private enterprise, to create conditions for it to be effective in developing the nation's economic strength, and to give help as well as direction to that end. Favourable conditions included, as we have seen, sweeping away feudal restrictions, opening Japan to foreign trade and western technology, and building a strong, diversified financial system to facilitate transactions or to mobilize savings for productive investment. They also included

[1] Quoted in Lockwood, op. cit., p. 326.

promoting efficiency in the largest traditional sector of Japan's economy. Realizing that most initial exports, most initial savings for industrial development, and much of the labour for modern factories would have to come from agriculture, the government paid considerable attention to this basic activity. At first it tried to encourage mechanized techniques through British or American experts but they had little success except in the northern island of Hokkaido, Japan's only large agricultural frontier. For the vast remainder of minutely divided paddy fields it soon turned to German agro-chemical methods and, in 1878, began a system of 'agricultural correspondence' to disseminate information about fertilizers, soil analysis, pesticides, and seed selection. More reliance, however, was placed upon the spread of best indigenous farming practices by appointing experienced men as practical instructors in each region.

The desired surge of private enterprise came after 1885 to complete, over the next two decades, Japan's first phase of modern economic growth. Some of the new entrepreneurs were merchants, and others came from wealthier farming families. But the great majority were *Samurai*, the educated as well as the military *élite* of Tokugawa society, now having some capital through commutation of their allowances to take a lead in every field of modern enterprise. They were helped, too, by Matsukata's policy of handing over state factories at low prices or on generous terms, as well as by government contracts or subsidies for various activities. The output of Japan's factories trebled between 1895 and 1905, rising from 4 to 9 per cent of a real national output which was itself growing by 2·4 per cent a year. Railway freight also trebled, and shipping freight more than doubled.

Here we can consider only the effects of this remarkable phase of growth upon Japan's foreign trade. Exports, between 1885–9 and 1900–4, soared from £5,500,000 to over £26,000,000 and imports from £4,700,000 to nearly £30,000,000. Raw silk was still the main export, as its output greatly increased through improvements in raising cocoons, the addition of a summer-autumn crop, and the substitution of machine-reeling for hand-reeling. But an increasing part of this output was being processed so that, by the end of the century, silk fabrics provided 11 per cent of export receipts. Other agricultural exports, owing to population growth, became much less significant; tea, rice, and fish now provided only 8 per cent of export receipts. To some extent this relative fall was made good by shipments of coal or copper, which rose to provide 13 per cent of these receipts. More significant were emerging shipments of such new manufactures as matches (3 per cent) and cotton textiles (2 per cent).

For the Manchester goods which had displaced Japan's traditional cotton industry were themselves displaced, in its domestic market, by a vigorous, modern cotton textile industry, which was soon to penetrate other Asian markets. By the end of the century, Japan had reduced textile fabrics to 12 per cent of total imports (as against 44 per cent in 1875) and was even a net exporter of cotton yarn. The industry, however, depended almost entirely upon foreign cotton, in spite of government efforts to introduce two kinds of American plants, so that raw and semi-processed textile materials (including some wool) were 27 per cent of total imports. Industrialization meant growing imports of ores and metals, principally iron, as well as growing imports of machinery; these two categories rose to 7 and 9 per cent of the total. It also involved Japan in becoming a net importer of food as cereals rose to 12 per cent of total imports and sugar remained at 10 per cent notwithstanding efforts to increase domestic production of this commodity. More success attended import-diversification in regard to shipping. The government had helped the Mitsubishi Company to develop a steamship business in coastal waters and, later, small shipping firms to combine as a rival company. In 1885, however, both companies were obliged to pool their shipping interests as the Nippon Yusen Kaisha, the nation's leading shipping line, although it soon had a strong competitor in the Osaka Shosen Kaisha. By 1900 Japan's mercantile marine was carrying not only coastal trade but one-third of foreign trade.

Far more significant, Japan had also built a navy which soon made it a major power in East Asia. The first demonstration of strength came in 1895 when Japan broke China's suzerainty over Korea, captured Weiheiwei, and acquired, by treaty, both Taiwan and the Liao-tung Peninsula, not to mention a tribute of £33,000,000 which facilitated adoption of the gold standard. Ten years later Japan astounded Asia by defeating the fleet of a great European power, Russia, and gained thereby the southern half of Sakhalin, full control over Korea, and Russian evacuation of Manchuria. With Taiwan to supply sugar, Korea to supply rice, some access to Manchurian coal or iron, and full access to China's ports, Japan entered upon a second phase of economic growth.

Long before this was completed, Japan acquired a similar pattern of Asian trade to that of western nations. By 1913 it was already conducting one-half of its external trade with Asian countries, and on the basis of exporting finished manufactures against imports of materials or foodstuffs. The main difference was a heavier concentration upon East Asia; Korea, Manchuria, China, Taiwan, and Hong Kong took more than two-fifths of Japan's exports, mainly cheap textiles, and supplied one-fifth of its imports—raw cotton, coking coal, iron, salt, soyabeans, rice, sugar, and fruit. India, as a major source of raw cotton and jute, supplied another fifth of Japan's imports but took only 4 per cent of its exports. South-east Asia took an even smaller percentage, because of western or Indian domination in textiles, and supplied one-tenth of Japan's imports—vegetable oils, fibres, rubber, and petroleum products.

Japan's brilliant transformation into a modern economic power completes the story of Asia's traditional trade. Yet some allusion should be made to the darker consequences of a firm belief that military strength went hand in hand with economic strength. Imperial exploitation and further industrialization enabled Japan, by 1936, to obtain more than 70 per cent of export receipts from Asia and to double the proportion of imports supplied by East Asia. Dominant military leaders then took advantage of the Second World War for temporary conquests which, besides shaking western empires, badly hurt other Asians and ended in disaster for the Japanese. After the war, stripped both of colonies and armed forces, they made a wonderful recovery which brought their country to greater heights of industrialization through peaceful trade. Only then did Japan offer other Asian countries what it was uniquely qualified to give: friendly help and guidance for attempting a better economic development than they had yet obtained from the new conditions of world trade.

List of Sources

(*denotes works which have been especially useful for this book)

A. GENERAL

(excluding purely statistical sources which are given in the relevant tables)

Baron, S. W.	*A Social and Religious History of the Jews*, vol. I. London, 1952.
Bingham, W., Conroy, H., and Ilke, F. W.	*A History of Asia*, vol. I. Boston, 1964.
Boulnois, L.	*The Silk Road*. London, 1966.
Boxer, C. R.	*Portugal and Brazil*. Ed. H. V. Livermore. Oxford, 1953.
——.	*The Dutch Seaborne Empire*. London, 1965.
Carr-Saunders, A. M.	*World Population*. Oxford, 1936.
Clark, C. G.	*The Conditions of Economic Progress*. London, 1957.
Derry, T. K., and Williams, T. I.	*A Short History of Technology*. Oxford, 1960.
Fletcher, M. E.	'The Suez Canal and World Shipping.' *Journal of Economic History*, XVIII, No. 4 (1958).
Frank, Tenney	*An Economic History of Rome*. New York, 1962.
——. (ed.)	*An Economic Survey of Ancient Rome*. vols. I–IV, Baltimore, 1933–8; vol. V, New Jersey, 1959.
Giles, H A. (trans.)	*The Travels of Fa-hsien*. London, 1923.
Gourou, P.	*The Tropical World*. London, 1966.
Graham, G. S.	'The Ascendancy of the Sailing Ship.' *Economic History Review*, IX, No. 1 (1957).

GRISWOLD, A. B., KIM, C., and POTT, P. H. — *Burma, Korea, Tibet*. London, 1964.

GROUSSET, R., — *Histoire de l'Extrême Orient*, tomes I–II. Paris, 1929.

——. *In the Footsteps of the Buddha*. London, 1932.

HEATON, H. *Economic History of Europe*. New York, 1936.

HOURANI, G. F. *Arab Seafaring*. Princeton, 1951.

HUDSON, G. F. *Europe and China*. London, 1931.

HYDE, W. W. *Ancient Greek Mariners*. New York, 1947.

KNOWLES, L. C. A. *Economic Development of the British Overseas Empire*. London, 1924.

MIRSKY, J. *The Great Chinese Travellers*. London, 1965.

MITCHELL, B. R., and DEANE, P. *Abstract of British Historical Statistics*. Cambridge, 1962.

PARKINSON, C. N. *Trade in the Eastern Seas*. London, 1937.

PARRY, J. H. *The Spanish Seaborne Empire*. London, 1966.

PIRES, TOMÉ *Suma Oriental*, vols. I–II. Ed. A. Cortesao. London, 1944.

POLO, MARCO *The Travels of Marco Polo*. Ed. R. Latham. Harmondsworth, 1958.

PURCELL, V. *South and East Asia since 1800*. Cambridge, 1965.

ROSTOVTZEFF, M. *The Social and Economic History of the Hellenistic World*, vols. I–III. Oxford, 1941.

——. *The Social and Economic History of the Roman Empire*, vols. I–II. Oxford, 1957.

SCHOFF, W. H. *The Periplus of the Erythrean Sea*. New York, 1912.

TARN, W. W., and GRIFFITH, G. T. *Hellenistic Civilization*. London, 1952.

TOUSSAINT, A. *Histoire de l'Océan Indien*. Paris, 1961.

WHEELER, M. — *Rome Beyond the Imperial Frontiers.* London, 1954.

WICKIZER, V. D., and BENNETT, M. K. — *The Rice Economy of Monsoon Asia.* Stanford, 1941.

WITTFOGEL, K. A. — *Oriental Despotism.* Yale, 1957.

YATES, P. L. — *Forty Years of Foreign Trade.* London, 1959.

YULE, H., and CORDIER, H. — *Cathay and the Way Thither,* vols. I–IV. London, 1915–16.

ZINKIN, M. — *Asia and the West.* London, 1951.

B. WEST ASIA

BURY, J. E. — *History of the Later Roman Empire,* vols. I–II. London, 1931.

CULICAN, W. — *The First Merchant Venturers.* London, 1966.

GHIRSHMAN, R. — *Iran.* Harmondsworth, 1954.

HEYD, W. — *Histoire du Commerce du Levant au Moyen-Age,* tomes I–II. Amsterdam, 1959.

HITTI, P. K. — *History of the Arabs.* London, 1951 and 1963.

——. — *The Near East in History.* New York, 1961.

HUSSEY, J. M. — *The Byzantine World.* London, 1957.

JONES, A. H. M., and MONROE, E. — *A History of Ethiopia.* Oxford, 1935.

OLIVER, R., and FAGE J. D. — *A Short History of Africa.* Harmondsworth, 1962.

OLMSTEAD, A. T. — *History of the Persian Empire.* Chicago, 1948.

OSTROGORSKY, G. — *History of the Byzantine State.* Oxford, 1956.

PORADA, E. — *Ancient Iran.* London, 1965.

RICE, D. T. — *The Byzantines.* London, 1962.

RICE, T. T. — *Everyday Life in Byzantium.* London, 1967.

RUNCIMAN, S. — *Byzantine Civilization.* London, 1933.

SYKES, P.   *A History of Persia*, vols. I–II. London, 1930.

VASILIEF, A. A.   *History of the Byzantine Empire.* Madison, 1952.

C. SOUTH ASIA

ADHYA, G. L.   *Early Indian Economics.* London, 1966.

ANSTEY, V.   * *The Economic Development of India.* London, 1942.

BAGCHI, P. C.   *India and China.* Calcutta, 1944.

BAILEY, S. D.   *Ceylon.* London, 1952.

BASHAM, A. L.   *The Wonder that was India.* London, 1954.

CHAKRAVARTI, N. P.   *India and Central Asia.* Calcutta, 1927.

CHAUDHURI, K. N.   *The English East India Company.* London, 1965.

DAS GUPTA, A.   *Malabar in Asian Trade.* Cambridge, 1967.

DAVIDS, T. W. RHYS   *Buddhist India.* London, 1903.

Dodwell, H. H. (ed.)   *The Cambridge History of India*; vol. v, *British India.* Cambridge, 1932.

DUTT, R. C.   *Later Hindu Civilization.* Calcutta, 1909.

——.   * *The Economic History of India*, vols. I and II. London, 1882.

FORREST, D. M.   *A Hundred Years of Ceylon Tea.* London, 1967.

FURBER, H.   *John Company at Work.* Cambridge, Mass., 1948.

GOITEIN, S. D.   'Mediterranean to India.' *Speculum*, XXIX (1954).

GOETZ, H.   *India.* London, 1959.

HOSKINS, H. L.   *British Routes to India.* London, 1928.

KRISHNA, B.   *Commercial Relations between India and England (1601–1757).* London, 1924.

LAMB, H. *Babur the Tiger*. London, 1961.

LUDOWYK, E. F. C. *The Story of Ceylon*. London, 1962.

——. *The Modern History of Ceylon*. London, 1966.

MAJUMDAR, R. C., RAYCHAUDHURI, H. C., and DATTA, K. *An Advanced History of India*. London, 1965.

Majumdar, R. C., and Pusalker, A. D. (eds.) *The History and Culture of the Indian People*. Bombay:

vol. II, *The Age of Imperial Unity*. 1953.

vol. III, *The Classical Age*. 1954.

vol. IV, *The Age of Imperial Kanauj*. 1955.

vol. V, *The Struggle for Empire*. 1957.

vol. VI, *The Delhi Sultanate*. 1960.

MORELAND, W. H. **India at the Death of Akbar*. London, 1920.

——. **From Akbar to Aurangzeb*. London, 1923.

MORELAND, W. H., and CHATTERJEE, A. *A Short History of India*. London, 1957.

MUKERJEE, R. *A History of Hindu Civilization*. Bombay, 1958.

PIGGOTT, S. *Prehistoric India*. Harmondsworth, 1950.

RAWLINSON, H. G. *India: A Short Cultural History*. London, 1952.

RAY, H. C. *History of Ceylon*, Part II. Colombo, 1960.

SASTRI, N. *A History of South India*. Oxford, 1966.

Singh, V. B. (ed.) *Economic History of India, 1857–1956*. Bombay, 1965.

SMITH, V. A. *The Oxford History of India*. Oxford, 1958.

SNODGRASS, D. R. *Ceylon: An Export Economy in Transition*. Illinois, 1966.

SPEAR, P.	*A History of India*, vol. 2. Harmondsworth, 1965.
———.	*The Nabobs*. Oxford, 1963.
SRIDIHARAN, K.	*A Maritime History of India*. Delhi, 1965.
THAPAR, R.	*A History of India*, vol. 1. Harmondsworth, 1966.
TRESSIDER, A. J.	*Ceylon*. Princeton, 1960.
WARMINGTON, E. H.	* *The Commerce between the Roman Empire and India*. Cambridge, 1928.
WHEELER, M.	*Civilizations of the Indus Valley*. London, 1966.
WOODRUFF, P.	*The Men Who Ruled India*. 2 vols., London, 1953 and 1954.

D. CENTRAL ASIA

CAROE, O.	*The Pathans*. London, 1958.
FAIRSERVIS, W.	*Horsemen of the Steppes*. Leicester, 1963.
FRASER-TYTLER, W. K.	*Afghanistan*. Oxford, 1953.
GRIAZNOV, M.	*L'Art Ancien de l'Altai*. Leningrad, 1958.
HAMBRIS, L.	*La Haute-Asie*. Paris, 1953.
LATTIMORE, O.	*Inner Asian Frontiers of China*. Boston, 1962.
MONGAIT, A. L.	*Archaeology in the U.S.S.R.* Harmondsworth, 1961.
MURPHY, G. G. S.	*Soviet Mongolia*. Berkeley, 1966.
PHILLIPS, E. D.	*The Royal Hordes*. London, 1965.
PRAWDIN, M.	*The Mongol Empire*. London, 1940.
RICE, T. T.	*Ancient Arts of Central Asia*. London, 1965.
RICHARDSON, H. E.	*Tibet and Its History*. Oxford, 1962.
SANKRITYAYANA, R.	*History of Central Asia*. Calcutta, 1964.
SHAKABPA, T. W. D.	*Tibet*. Yale, 1967.

SHEN, T., and LIU, S.   *Tibet and the Tibetans.* Stanford, 1953.

STEIN, M. A.   *On Ancient Caravan Tracks past the Pamirs.* Calcutta, 1932.

——.   *On Ancient Central Asian Tracks.* London, 1933.

——.   *The Indo-Iranian Borderlands.* London, 1934.

TARN, W. W.   *The Greeks in Bactria and India.* Cambridge, 1951.

WATKINS, M. B.   *Afghanistan.* Princeton, 1963.

WEEKES, R. V.   *Pakistan.* Princeton, 1964.

E. EAST ASIA

ALLEN, G. C.   *A Short Economic History of Modern Japan.* London, 1946.

ALLEN, G. C., and DONNITHORNE, A. G.   **Western Enterprise in Far Eastern Economic Development: China and Japan.* London, 1954.

BATE, H. M.   *Report from Formosa.* London, 1952.

BEASLEY, W. G.   *The Modern History of Japan.* London, 1963.

CH'AO-TING CHI   *Key Economic Areas in Chinese History.* New York, 1963.

COLLIS, M.   *Foreign Mud.* London, 1946.

Cranmer-Byng, J. L. (ed.)   *An Embassy to China.* London, 1962.

DUBS, H.   'An Ancient Chinese Gold Stock.' *Journal of Economic History,* II, No. 1 (1942).

ENDACOTT, G. B.   *A History of Hong Kong.* Oxford, 1964.

FAIRBANK, J. K., and REISCHAUER, E. O.   **East Asia: The Great Tradition.* Boston, 1958.

——., and CRAIG, A. M.   *East Asia: The Modern Transformation.* London, 1965.

FITZGERALD, C. P.   *China: A Short Cultural History.* London, 1961.

GERNET, J. *Daily Life in China on the Eve of the Mongol Invasion.* London, 1962.

GODDARD, W. G. *Formosa.* London, 1966.

GOODRICH, L. C. **A Short History of the Chinese People.* New York, 1959.

GREENBERG, M. *British Trade and the Opening of China.* Cambridge, 1951.

GROUSSET, R. *The Rise and Splendour of the Chinese Empire.* Berkeley, 1953.

LATOURETTE, K. S. *The Chinese: Their History and Culture.* New York, 1946.

LIU, J. T. C. *Reform in Sung China.* Cambridge, Mass., 1959.

LOCKWOOD, W. W. *The Economic Development of Japan.* Princeton, 1954.

——. (ed.) *The State and Economic Enterprise in Japan.* Princeton, 1965.

McCUNE, E. *The Arts of Korea.* Tokyo, 1962.

MORSE, H. B. *The Trade and Administration of the Chinese Empire.* London, 1908.

NEEDHAM, J. *Science and Civilisation in China.* Cambridge: vol. I, *Introductory Orientations,* 1954; vol. III, *Mathematics and the Sciences of the Heavens and the Earth,* 1959.

NORMAN, E. H. *Japan's Emergence as a Modern State.* New York. 1940.

PRODAN, M. *The Art of the T'ang Potter.* London, 1960.

SANSOM, G. B. *Japan: A Short Cultural History.* London, 1952.

——. *The Western World and Japan.* London, 1950.

——. **A History of Japan.* 3 vols., London, 1959, 1961, and 1963.

SPEISER, W. *China: Spirit and Society.* London, 1960.

STORRY, R. *A History of Modern Japan.* Harmondsworth, 1960.

WILLETTS, W.   *Chinese Art*, vols. I–II. Harmondsworth, 1958.

——.   'The Maritime Adventures of Grand Eunuch Ho.' *Journal of South East Asian History*, (Sept. 1964, V, No. 2).

WRIGHT, S. F.   *Hart and the Chinese Customs*. Belfast, 1950.

F. SOUTH-EAST ASIA

ALLEN, G. C., and DONNITHORNE, A. G.   *Western Enterprise in Indonesia and and Malaya. London, 1957.

ANDRUS, J. R.   *Burmese Economic Life*. Stanford, 1948.

BERVAL, R. de   *Kingdom of Laos*. Saigon, 1959.

BUSCH, N. F.   *Thailand*. New York, 1959.

CADY, J. F.   *Southeast Asia: Its Historical Development*. New York, 1964.

——.   *A History of Modern Burma*. New York, 1958.

CHAI HON-CHAN   *The Development of British Malaya, 1896–1909*. Oxford, 1964.

CHRISTIAN, J. L.   *Modern Burma*. Berkeley, 1942.

COEDÈS, G.   *Les États Hindouisés d'Indochine et d'Indonésie*. Paris, 1948.

——.   *Ankor*. London, 1963.

——.   *The Making of South East Asia*. London, 1966.

COLLIS, M.   *Siamese White*. London, 1936.

——.   *Raffles*. London, 1966.

Cowan, C. D. (ed.)   * *The Economic Development of South-East Asia*. London, 1964.

CRAWFURD, J.   *Journal of an Embassy to the Courts of Siam and Cochin China*. London, 1828.

DAUPHIN-MEUNIER, A.   *Histoire du Cambodge*. Paris, 1961.

DEYDIER, H.   *Introduction à la Connaissance du Laos*. Saigon, 1952.

ENNIS, T. E.   *French Policy and Developments in Indochina*. Chicago, 1936.

FURNIVALL, J. S.   *Colonial Policy and Practice*. Cambridge, 1948.

——.   **Netherlands India*. Cambridge, 1939.

GRAHAM, W. A.   *Siam*. 2 vols., London, 1924.

GROSLIER, B. Ph.   *Indochina*. London, 1962.

——.   *Ankor, Art and Civilization*. London, 1966.

GULLICK, J. M.   *Malaya*. London, 1963.

HALL, D. G. E.   **A History of South-East Asia*. London, 1964.

——.   *Burma*. London, 1960.

INGRAM, J. C.   **Economic Change in Thailand since 1850*. Stanford, 1955.

LE MAY, R.   *The Culture of South East Asia*. London, 1954.

LEUR, J. C. van   *Indonesian Trade and Society*. The Hague, 1955.

MacDONALD, M.   *Ankor*. London, 1958.

MAJUMDAR, R. C.   *Ancient Indian Colonies in the Far East*. Calcutta, 1944.

——.   *Hindu Colonization in South-east Asia*. Baroda, 1963.

MASSON, A.   *Histoire du Vietnam*. Paris, 1960.

MEILINK-ROELOFSZ, M. A. P. **Asian Trade and European Influence*. The Hague, 1962.

MILLS, L. A.   *British Malaya*. Singapore, 1961.

Philippines Commission.   *Report*, 1901, vol. IV.

Pym, C. (ed.)   *Henri Mouhot's Diary*. Oxford, 1966.

ROBEQUAIN, C.   **The Economic Development of French Indo-China*. Oxford, 1944.

——.   *Malaya, Indonesia, Borneo and the Philippines*. London, 1958.

SIAM SOCIETY.   *Selected Papers*. Bangkok, 1959:
     vol. III, *Early History and Ayudhya Period*.
     vol. VII, *Relationship with Portugal, Holland and the Vatican*.

	vol. VIII. *Relationship with France, England and Denmark.*
SWETTENHAM, F.	*British Malaya.* London, 1948.
THOMPSON, V.	*Thailand: The New Siam.* New York, 1941.
TREGONNING, K. G.	*A History of Modern Sabah.* Singapore, 1965.
VANDENBOSCH, A.	*The Dutch East Indies.* Berkeley, 1942.
VLEKKE, B. H. M.	*Nusantara: A History of Indonesia.* The Hague, 1959.
WAGNER, F. A.	*Indonesia.* London, 1959.
WHEATLEY, P.	**The Golden Khersonese.* Kuala Lumpur, 1961.
WILLOQUET, G.	*Histoire des Philippines.* Paris, 1961.
WINSTEDT, R.	*The Malays: A Cultural History.* London, 1961.
WONG LIN KEN	*The Trade of Singapore, 1819–69.* Singapore, 1961.
WOOD, W. A. R.	*A History of Siam.* Bangkok, 1924.

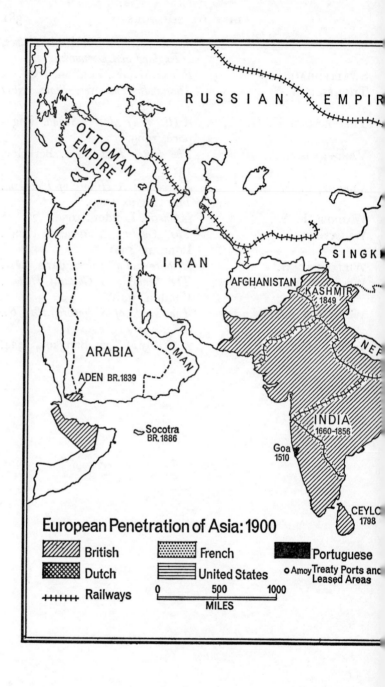

RUSSIAN EMPIR

OTTOMAN
EMPIRE

IRAN

AFGHANISTAN

SINGK

KASHMIR
1849

NE

ARABIA

OMAN

ADEN BR.1839

Socotra
BR.1886

INDIA
1660–1856

Goa
1510

CEYLO
1798

European Penetration of Asia: 1900

	British		French		Portuguese

Dutch   United States   o Amoy Treaty Ports and
Leased Areas

+++++ Railways

0   500   1000
MILES

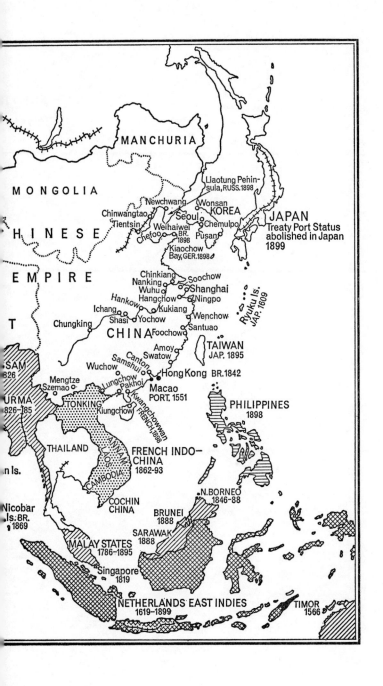

MANCHURIA

MONGOLIA

Liaotung Pehin-
sula, RUSS.1898

CHINESE

Newchwang
Chinwangtao
Tientsin
Chefoo
Weihaiwei
BR.
1898
Kiaochow
Bay, GER.1898

Wonsan
Seoul
KOREA
Chemulpo
Pusan

JAPAN
Treaty Port Status
abolished in Japan
1899

EMPIRE

Chinkiang
Nanking
Wuhu
Hankow
Hangchow
Ichang
Chungking
Shasi
Yochow
Kukiang

Soochow
Shanghai
Ningpo

Wenchow

Ryuku Is.
JAP. 1609

CHINA
Foochow
Santuao

TAIWAN
JAP. 1895

Amoy
Swatow
Canton
Samshui
Wuchow
Mengtze
Szemao
Lungchow
Pakhoi
Kiungchow
Kwangchowwan
FRENCH 1898

Hong Kong BR. 1842
Macao
PORT. 1551

SAM
826

URMA
826–85

T

TONKING

THAILAND

ANNAM

LAOS

CAMBODIA

FRENCH INDO-
CHINA
1862-93

COCHIN
CHINA

PHILIPPINES
1898

N. BORNEO
1846-88

BRUNEI
1888

n Is.

Nicobar
Is. BR.
1869

MALAY STATES
1786-1895

SARAWAK
1888

Singapore
1819

NETHERLANDS EAST INDIES
1619–1899

TIMOR
1566

Index

Abahai, King of Manchuria, 152–3
abarute, 167
Abbasid Dynasty and Empire, 78–
85; see also Arabia, Iran
Abd-al-Malik (Arab caliph), 74
Abdul Hamid (Indian historian), 173
abu-al-Abbas (Arab caliph), 75
Abyssinia (Ethiopia), 6, 10, 11, 39,
40, 55, 59, 62, 83
Acapulco (Mexican port), 188, 189
Achaemenes (Iranian king), 5
Acheh (Sumatran state), 116, 183,
192, 193, 198, 199, 225, 323
Achin (Sumatran port), 116, 143,
321
Actium, battle of, 14
Adams, William (English sailor),
204
Aden (Eudaemon Arabia), 4, 11, 12,
17, 39, 41, 80, 84, 168, 180, 182,
189
Adulis (Massawa), 11, 40
adzes, 40
Aegean Sea, 10, 57
Afghanistan, 3, 9, 18, 19, 42, 64,
168, 170, 171, 174, 179, 237, 238,
253, 255, 259, 260, 286
Africa, 6, 10, 11, 37, 38, 39, 41, 53,
55, 78, 143, 178, 182, 201, 265,
301
agalwood, see aloeswood
aghilwood, see aloeswood
Agra (Indian city), 199, 200, 296
Agung, Sultan of Bantam, 227
Ahmadabad (Indian city), 199, 200,
298
Ahmadnagar (Indian state), 177,
179, 181

Ahmad Shah Durrani, 238
Ahom (Thai state), 155
Aichi (Japanese cotton centre), 367
Ainu (Japan), 106–7
Aila (Red Sea port), 39
Ain Jalut, battle of, 132
Airlangga, King of East Java, 116
Ajanta caves, 66
Akbar (Mughal emperor), 172–4,
175, 177, 236, 242, 253, 255, 261
Alai Valley, Turkestan, 20, 21, 36
Alans (nomad people), 49, 52
Alaric, King of the Visigoths, 57
Alaungpaya, King of Burma, 223,
224, 328
Albazin (Manchurian fort), 207
Albuquerque, A. de (Portuguese
governor), 167, 176, 178, 179
Aleppo (Syrian town), 7, 170
Alexander (Greek emperor), 8–9,
14, 74, 78, 238, 253
Alexandria (Egyptian port), 11, 38,
39, 46, 54, 55, 74, 80, 139, 168,
182, 259, 263
Algeria, 74
Alichar-Pamir route, 20
Allepey (Malabar port), 239
almonds, 77, 87, 256
almug (tree), 23
Altai mountains, 2, 4, 38
aloes or aloeswood, 27, 41, 59, 80,
113, 154, 164, 165, 167, 224, 225
alum, 165, 167, 270
Amalfi (Italian port), 56
Amangkurat, Sultan of Mataram,
227
Amaravati (Indian city), 63, 70
amber, 8, 38, 57, 98, 179, 252

ambergris, 202
Amboina (Indonesian island), 181, 183, 184, 185, 190, 193, 194, 196, 197, 226, 227, 229, 307, 322
Ambon (Indonesian port), 117
Amherst, Lord (English ambassador), 272
amomum, see cardamom
Amoy (Chinese port), 188, 205, 206, 209, 273, 276, 283
Amsterdam, 191, 192, 195
Amur River, Mongolia, 152, 207, 278
Anaukpetlun, King of Burma, 215
Anawrahta, King of Burma, 154–5
Andaman Islands, 115
Anderson, A. (British historian): quoted, 215
Andhra (Indian city), 70
Ang Duong, King of Cambodia, 341
An-hsi (Chinese protectorate), 33
Anhwei (Chinese province), 278
Anjer (Indonesian port), 307
Anjuman Pass (in Kashmir), 20
Ankor, see Cambodia
Ankor Thom (Cambodian capital), 120, 123
An Lu-shan (Chinese general), 92
Annam, 27, 36, 85, 90, 93, 138, 142, 145, 153, 154, 157, 161, 224, 338, 343, 345; see also Vietnam
anthracite, 345
antimony, 42, 77
Antioch (Mediterranean port), 12, 13, 56
Antiochus III (Iranian emperor), 14
Anuradhapura (capital of Ceylon), 115
apes, 23
Apologus (al-Ubullah, Gulf port), 39, 41
apples, 77
apricots, 67, 77, 256
Arabia, 2, 4, 5, 8, 10, 11, 12, 14, 17, 22, 38, 39, 41, 42, 46, 47, 54, 55, 62, 73–9, 80, 89, 99, 179, 202, 246, 253, 255, 256, 288, 295
Arakan, 328, 329

Aral Sea, 50, 58, 127
Arameans (Semitic nomads), 4
Araxes River, 55
Arcot, 240
Ardashir (Iranian emperor), 50, 51
areca nuts, 216, 238
Arikamedu (Indian port), 44
Arkwright, Sir Richard, 266
Armalee (Central Asian town), 135
Armarapura (Burmese town), 329
Armenia, 3, 13, 51, 170, 247
armour, 18, 108, 149
aromata (aromatics), 10, 14, 47, 55, 59, 62, 89, 252, 255
Arsaces (Parthian king), 13
Arsacid dynasty and empire, see Iran
Arsinoe (Red Sea port), 6, 40
Artabanus (Iranian emperor), 50–1
Artashut (Iranian silk centre), 55
Arthasastra (Indian book), 47
Aru (Darau, Indonesian port), 143, 165
Asia Minor, 5, 7, 9, 13, 127, 128, 170
Asia, Roman Province of, 14
Asoka (Indian emperor), 15–18, 21
Assam, 22, 30, 70, 155, 236, 292, 305, 320, 329
Assassins (Moslem sect), 132
Assyria, 4, 5, 14
Astrakan (Central Asian town), 135
Asuka (Japanese capital), 103
Attila, King of the Huns, 52, 57
Augustus (Roman emperor), 14, 22, 35
Aurangzeb (Mughal emperor), 236, 237
Aurelian (Roman emperor), 54
Australasia, 292
Australia, 284, 325
Ava (Burmese capital), 215, 218, 223, 329, 330, 334
Avalites (Zeila), 40, 47
axes, 40
Axum (African state), 36, 39, 40, 55, 59
Ayuthia (Thai capital), 181, 215, 216, 217, 218, 219, 220, 221, 223, 224, 225, 329

Azania (East Africa), 40
azurite, 77

Bab al-Mandab, Straits of, 11, 55
Babur (Mughal emperor), 171–2, 261
Babylonia, 5, 6, 7, 8, 14
backgammon, 87
Bactra, *see* Balkh
Bactria (Afghanistan), 3, 6, 9, 12–14, 15, 17, 18, 19, 22, 31, 32, 33, 35, 44, 51, 62, 68, 253
Badakashan (Central Asia), 71
Baghdad, 75, 77, 81, 89, 132, 171, 251
Bagyidaw, King of Burma, 329, 330
Bahadur Shah (Mughal emperor), 236–7
Bahmani (Deccan kingdom), 168, 176, 261
Baikal, Lake, 4, 207, 208
Bakr, abu (Arab caliph), 75
Bakufu (Japanese government), 109, 351, 352, 354, 355, 356, 357, 358, 359, 360, 361, 367
Balambar, King of the Huns, 52
Balasore (Indian port), 201
Balat (Vietnam port), 340
Bali (Indonesian island), 116, 161, 228, 322
Balkh (Bactra, Afghan town), 12, 13, 14, 17, 20, 36, 48, 79, 86, 130, 131, 137, 170, 236
Baltimore, 248
Baluchistan, 8
bamboo, 22, 32, 38
Bamyan (Afghan town), 68, 131
Banda Islands, 117, 165–6, 182, 183, 184, 185, 186, 193, 194, 196, 197, 225, 226, 229, 235, 307, 322
Bandar Abbas (Persian Gulf port), 200, 201
Bangeri (Indonesian tin centre), 225
Bangkok, 222, 283, 323, 330, 341, 342, 344, 347, 349
Banka Island (Indonesian tin centre), 113, 310, 319
banking, 7, 61, 62, 97, 137, 212, 213, 249, 304, 306, 313, 316, 319, 336, 362–4
Bantam (Javanese pepper centre), 191–200, 203, 217, 220, 225–9, 234
Barakar (Indian steel centre), 297
Barbaricum (Bahardipur, Indian port), 42
Barbosa, Duarte (Portuguese traveller), 159
Bariam Khan (Mughal Minister), 172
Bari Doab Canals (India), 296
Barnes, Sir Edward (Governor of Ceylon), 302, 303
Barygaza (Broach, Indian port), 24, 39, 41, 42, 43, 46, 70, 199, 200
basil (herb), 77
Basra, al- (Persian Gulf port), 81
Bassac River (Vietnam), 338
Bassein (Burmese port), 177, 223, 224, 334
Batang River (Sumatra), 112
Batavia (Javanese port), 196–9, 203, 225–34, 263, 307, 309, 312, 322, 348
Battambang (Cambodian province), 341, 344
Battutah, ibn- (Arab traveller), 99, 137, 139–40, 168, 215
Bawdwin (Burmese mine), 335
Bayinnaung (Burmese king), 159
bdellium (gum), 42, 47, 48
beads, 39, 167
beans, 87, 123, 139, 257, 281, 282
bêche-de-mer, 322
Bedouin, 2, 5, 54
Béhaine, de, Bishop, 340
Beirut (Syrian port), 56
Belgium, 248, 249, 313, 349, 350
Benares (Indian town and district), 18, 19, 286
Bencoolen (Sumatran port), 227, 311
Bengal, 21, 30, 51, 70, 115, 161, 163–4, 166, 173, 177, 201, 218, 221, 227, 233, 235, 237, 239–49, 255, 256, 262, 265, 270, 271, 285, 286, 291, 292, 293, 297, 298, 299, 315, 332, 345, 348

26

Benson, R. (British Resident), 330

Bentinck, Lord (Governor-General of India), 285, 287, 292

benzoin (gum), 112, 157, 159, 164, 166, 215, 322, 344

Berbers (Arab people), 40

Berenice (Red Sea ports): Berenice (Ras Benas), 11, 40; Berenice the All Golden (Massawa), 11; Berenice Epideiris, 11; Berenice Trogodytica, 11

Bernier, F. (French traveller), 174

beryls, 23

betel-nuts, 270, 322

Betwar Canal (India), 296

Bhamo (Burmese town), 44, 153, 155, 157, 215, 218, 219, 332

Bhavavarman, King of Chenla, 111

Bhutan (Himalayan kingdom), 209

Bihar (Indian state and province), 115, 240

Bijapur (Indian state), 176, 177, 179, 181, 236

Billiton (Indonesian island), 310, 319, 320

Bird, George (Ceylonese planter), 303

birds' nests, 322, 327, 348

Birmingham, 266

bitumen, 77

Black River (Indochina), 154

Black Sea, 13, 35, 57, 58, 128, 254

blackwood, 41, 167

bleaching powder, 367

Bodawpaya, King of Burma, 328, 329

Bogor (town in Java), 28

Bokeo (Cambodian sapphire mines), 345

Bokhara (Central Asian town), 85, 127, 129, 130, 136, 137, 171

Bolgary (Russian state), 131

Bolor Tagh mountains (Himalayas), 64

Boloven Plateau (Laos), 344

Bolts, William (English merchant), 265

Bombay, 201, 237, 239, 241, 243, 244, 246, 247, 248, 262, 263, 287, 288, 289, 298, 334, 349

Boni (Indonesian state), 226, 229

books, 63, 89, 99, 104, 149, 355, 366

Borneo, 24, 28, 116, 142, 156, 164, 183, 191, 255, 267, 269, 311, 320, 322, 327

Borobudur (temple in Java), 114

Boromokot (Thai king), 222

Bosch, van den, J. (Governor-General of Indonesia), 313, 314, 315

Bosporus (Black Sea kingdom), 12, 58

Bowring, Sir John (E.I.C. official), 349

Brahmaputra River (India), 236, 237

bracelets, 167

brass, 40, 266, 288

Brazil, 175, 178, 182, 257, 292, 306, 326

brazilwood, 158, 167

Briggs, General, 290

bristles, 281

Britain, Great, 185, 189, 204, 236, 242, 254, 261, 266, 267, 269, 272, 273, 274, 275, 276, 277, 278, 282, 285, 288, 290, 292, 297, 302, 303, 304, 305, 306, 307, 311, 312, 315, 317, 321, 322, 323, 324, 325, 327, 328, 329, 330, 331, 333, 334, 340, 343, 344, 347, 349, 350, 358, 359, 361, 365, 366, 368; *see also* East India Company (English)

Brito, P. de (Portuguese admiral), 215

Broach, *see* Barygaza

broadcloth, 201

brocade, 18, 38, 56, 70, 77, 96, 110, 179

Broecke, P. van den (Dutch official), 199

Bronze Age, 2, 4

bronzeware, 4, 29, 30, 33, 37, 62, 89, 101, 149, 188, 255, 266, 366

Brooke, James, Rajah of Sarawak, 327

Brunei, *see* Borneo

Bruno, de, Sieur (French official), 223

Buddhism, 15–19, 21–2, 24, 25, 37, 61–73, 86, 89, 90, 100, 102, 103, 104, 105, 106–7, 109, 110, 111, 120, 151, 154, 155, 156, 157, 222, 256, 257, 331, 332, 349, 354, 361

building stones, 38

Buitzenzorg (Indonesian Botanic Garden), 312, 317, 320

Bundelkhand (Indian state), 237

Burhanpur (Indian town), 199

Burma, 15, 17, 21, 22, 24, 25, 44, 70, 149, 153, 161, 194, 200, 204, 255, 256, 269; under Pagan dynasty, 154–6; under Shan and Mon, 156; under Toungoo dynasty, 158–60, 181, 192, 206, 218, 219, 221, 223, 259; under Konbaung dynasty, 224, 267, 279, 299, 328–334, 347; under British rule, 329–339, 343, 349, 351

Burnaby, R. (E.I.C. official), 220

Burney, H. (E.I.C. official), 323, 330, 347

Bus, Viscount du, (Governor-General of Indonesia), 312, 313

Byzantium, 15, 50, 51, 52–9, 60, 87, 127–8, 134, 178, 251, 257, 258

Cabral, A. (Portuguese navigator), 175, 176

calambac, 165

Calapa (Batavia), 165

Calcutta, 237, 239, 240, 241, 242, 243, 246, 247, 248, 249, 254, 262, 263, 288, 289, 299, 311, 313, 323, 324

calico, 62, 202, 264, 265

Calicut (Indian state), 142, 143, 169, 175–7, 194, 239, 246, 259

Callinicum (Mesopotamian town), 55

Camara (Karikal, Indian port), 43

Ca-mau, Cape (Vietnam), 27

Cambay (Indian district), 42, 51, 52, 70, 163, 164, 178, 180, 199, 200, 201

Cambodia: under Funan, 24–5, 26–27; 111–12, 346; under Chenla, 112, 114; under Ankor, 117–24, 142, 155, 157, 161, 252, 259; post Ankor, 157, 160, 166, 181, 200, 204, 216, 218, 219, 222, 224, 255, 322, 347; under French, 267, 328, 339, 340, 341–2, 344–5

Cambyses (Iranian emperor), 5

camels, 2, 3, 10, 11, 12, 36, 62, 70, 89, 253, 256, 257, 296

Campbell, Lt.-Gen. C. (Governor of Ceylon), 303

camphor, 23, 80, 112, 113, 164, 165, 167, 204, 246, 255, 270, 322, 365

Cana (Hsin-al-Ghurab, Arabian port), 41

canals, 6, 11, 27, 30, 39, 78, 85, 92, 138, 346; see also irrigation, Suez Canal

Cannanor (Indian port), 176, 237

cannon, 260–2, 357

Canton (Chinese port), 31, 36, 45, 66, 80, 81, 82, 84, 93, 98, 113, 141, 144, 185, 186, 188, 191, 206, 208, 209, 214, 215, 230, 244, 246, 247, 248, 249, 254, 259, 262, 263, 264, 270–3, 275, 276, 277, 279, 284, 342, 348

Cape of Good Hope, 175, 188, 191, 233, 235

Cape Horn, 187

Capellan, G. A. van der (Governor-General of Indonesia), 312

caravans and routes, within India, 17; Arabia–Egypt–Africa, 4, 11, 12, 39, 55; Iran–Rome–Byzantium, 14, 55, 57, 58; Iran–Central Asia, 14, 35–6, 46, 53, 58, 59, 170–1; India–Central Asia, 20–1, 62, 63, 64, 68–9, 71, 174–5, 253; China–Central Asia, 32–8, 53, 62, 63, 64, 71, 72, 134, 208–9; China–Tibet–India, 44; China–Burma, 21, 22, 44, 208, 209; Burma–Thailand–Cambodia, 25; Malayan portages, 26–8

cardamom, 23, 47, 113, 165, 247, 255
cards (playing), 141
Carnatic coast (India), 241, 243
carnelians, 42, 77, 98, 167, 255
Carpathian mountains, 128
Carr-Saunders, A. M. (British demographer): quoted 267
carrots, 140, 257
carpets, 14, 36, 77, 89, 253, 255
Carthage, 53, 74
Caspian Sea (and region), 3, 6, 13, 14, 19, 34, 35, 49, 58, 87, 127
cassava (root), 317, 320, 321
cassia, 11, 43, 47, 165, 238, 302
castor oil, 293
catechu (astringent bark), 164, 167
Cathayana, 95
Catherine the Great, 358
cattle, 2, 69, 254, 284
Caucasus (mountains), 13, 49, 51, 58, 60
cayenne pepper, 213, 257
cedar, 7
celadons, 96, 146, 156
Celates (sea gipsies), 183
Celebes (Indonesia), 28, 161, 226
cement, 367
Ceram (Indonesian island), 184, 196, 197
ceramics, 29, 30, 33, 37, 96, 214, 266; see also celadons, porcelain, pottery
cereals, 2, 69, 293, 336, 369; see also corn, grain, rice, wheat
Ceylon, 8, 15, 17, 19, 22, 23, 26, 36, 40, 43, 55, 57, 59, 65, 70, 81, 82, 84, 99, 112, 115, 116, 117, 142, 143, 155, 177, 179, 255, 256; under Dutch, 200, 222, 225, 231, 232, 235; under British, 243, 254, 255, 256, 263, 268, 269, 270, 280, 292, 297, 301–9, 320, 326, 365
Chagatai, Khanate of, 132, 133, 134, 168, 170
Chaiya (Malayan port), 220
Chakravarti, N. P. (Indian archæologist): quoted 21
Chakri dynasty, see Thailand

Champa (Vietnam), 24, 25, 26, 27, 82, 85, 96, 115, 116, 119, 120, 138, 142, 143, 153, 155, 161, 166
Champassac (Laotian kingdom), 343
Chandernagore (Indian port), 239
Chandragupta I (Indian emperor), 9, 12, 255
Chandra Gupta II (Indian emperor), 51, 61
Ch'ang-an (Chinese city), 63, 72, 86, 92, 93, 100, 101, 104, 254
Chang Ch'ien (Chinese traveller), 22, 31, 32, 34
Chang Lo-hsing (Chinese bandit), 277
Chang Po-go (Korean merchant), 104
Chao Anou, King of Vientiane, 343
Chao Ju-kua (Chinese officer), 99, 114, 117, 187
Ch'ao K'uang-yin (Chinese emperor), 93
chaplets, 42
Characene (Iranian province), 14
Charax (Persian Gulf port), 39
Charles I, King of England, 201
Charles II, King of England, 201, 202
Chaul (Indian port), 176, 181
chaulmoogra oil, 140
Chaumont, Chevalier de (French ambassador), 222
Chekiang (Chinese province), 88, 150
Che-li-fo-che, see Indonesia: Srivijaya
Chenab Canal (India), 296
Chen-chou (pewter centre), 123
Cheng Ch'eng-kung (Koxunga, Chinese loyalist), 205
Cheng Ho (Chinese admiral), 99, 142–5, 151, 162, 166, 254, 259
Chen Tsung (Chinese emperor), 93
Chengtu (Chinese city), 67, 97, 209
Chenla, see Cambodia
Chera (Indian state), 23
Chernigov (Russian town), 133
Chettyars (Indian money-lenders), 334, 335, 336, 337, 338

Ch'ien-lung (Chinese emperor), 273
Chiengmai (Thai centre), 154, 156, 157, 159, 160, 218, 329
Chihli (Chinese port), 150
Chin dynasty and empire, see China
China, 1, 3, 4, 5, 12, 14, 17, 19, 20, 21, 22, 24, 25, 26, 27, 28, 29, 30, 251, 253, 254, 255, 256, 257; first empire, 31–8, 42, 43, 44, 45; first partition, 50, 53, 55, 58, 59, 62, 63, 65, 101; second empire, 67, 71, 72, 78, 80, 81, 83, 84, 85–95, 257, 360; second partition, 95–9, 127; Yuan dynasty, 131, 132, 134, 135, 136–41; Ming dynasty, 141–5, 150–1, 152–3, 161, 170, 179, 180, 183, 185, 186, 188, 190, 193, 194, 195, 199, 202, 203, 261; Chin dynasty, 153, 205, 213–15, 217, 220, 225, 226, 227, 230, 232, 234, 244, 245, 246, 247, 248, 249, 254, 260, 261, 262, 264, 266, 267, 268, 269, 270–85, 292, 295, 298, 302, 305, 322, 325, 328, 329, 331, 333, 340, 341, 342, 343, 348, 354, 358, 369, 370; Chinese abroad, 145, 187, 194, 199, 227, 228, 233, 307, 310, 312, 313, 315, 316, 319, 324, 325, 326, 327, 335, 336, 337, 338, 340, 345, 346, 349, 350, 351
chinaware, 270
chintzes, 264
Chitral (Indian town), 20
Chittagong (Indian port), 181, 216, 236, 237, 329
chives, 87, 257
Ch'oe family (Korean Ministers), 105, 145
Chola (Indian state), 23, 43, 113, 115, 116, 155, 169, 252
Cholon (Vietnam), 346
Cho-po (Indonesian kingdom), 112
Chorasmia (Central Asia), 7, 49
Choshu (Japanese clan), 357, 359, 360
Chosroes I (Iranian emperor), 51, 60
Chou (Chinese people), 30

Chou Ch'ufei (Chinese writer), 98, 114, 117
Chou Ta-kuan (Chinese envoy)', 120–4
Christianity, 54, 55, 57, 59, 73, 76, 84, 87, 95, 127, 137, 175, 192, 204, 205, 210, 217, 219, 222, 236, 301, 340, 342, 347
chrysoberyls, 43, 255
Ch'uan-chou (Zaiton, Chinese port), 98, 99, 123, 139
Chu Hsi (Chinese philosopher), 96
Chulalongkorn (Thai king), 347, 350, 351
Chu-li (Malay port), 25
Chusan Island (China), 150
Chu Yu (Chinese writer), 98
Chwostow, M. K. (Russian historian), 46
cigarettes, 282
Cimmerians (nomad people), 3
cinchona (quinine), 213, 257, 292, 305, 306, 316, 320, 321
cinnamomum, see cinnamon
cinnamon, 11, 23, 39, 40, 41, 43, 47, 48, 80, 89, 179, 200, 231, 255, 301, 302, 306, 313, 315, 316, 318
civet, 202
Clarke, Sir A. (British governor), 324
Claudius (Roman emperor), 36, 38, 43
Clive, R. (British official), 235, 240
cloth, 40, 41, 199
clothing, 8, 41, 42
cloves, 59, 113, 116, 164, 165, 166, 167, 182, 183, 184, 193, 196, 197, 198, 226, 230, 255, 306, 318
Clysma (Red Sea port), 39
coal, 264, 297, 345, 365, 367, 369, 370
Cochin (Indian port), 175, 199, 238, 239, 246
Cochinchina, see Cambodia, Vietnam
cochineal, 313, 315, 318
coconut oil, 349; see also copra, oilseeds

coconuts, 23, 179, 305, 306, 326, 327
coconut wood, 42, 83
Coedès, G. (French historian): quoted 153, 156
Coen, Jan P. (Governor-General of Indonesia), 194–7, 199, 203, 217, 225, 229, 231, 233, 253
coffee, 202, 231, 232, 234, 235, 245, 291, 292, 293, 301, 302, 303, 304, 305, 306, 307, 308, 309, 310, 312, 313, 315, 317, 318, 319, 320, 321, 322, 326, 344
Coimbatore Gap (South India), 23, 43
coins, 7, 13, 17, 41, 45, 46, 53, 61, 84, 97, 99, 111, 149, 165, 174, 272, 280, 316, 351, 352, 361, 363
coir, 83, 247, 256
Coleroon Works (Indian irrigation scheme), 287
Coloe (African town), 40
Colombo, 177, 302, 303, 304
Columbus, Christopher, 186
combs, 123
commercial revolution of Sung China, 96–7, 258
Comorin, Cape (South India), 23, 178, 238
Confucianism, 34, 96, 100, 103, 211, 340, 354, 355
Congo, 319
Constantinople, 52, 56, 57, 74, 128, 258, 261
Conti, N. (Portuguese traveller),178
Cook, Captain J. (English sailor), 233
coapl (gum), 40
Copenhagen, 249
copper, 2, 4, 8, 11, 17, 31, 40, 41, 42, 61, 67, 97, 98, 104, 111, 122, 123, 149, 164, 166, 167, 179, 195, 204, 212, 255, 316, 322, 342, 365, 367, 369
copra, 320, 321
Coptos (Nile port), 11, 39
coral, 23, 36, 41, 42, 98, 179, 201, 252
cordage, 322

coriander, 257
corn, 10, 14
Cornwallis, Lord (Governor-General of India), 242, 243
Coromandel Coast (South India), 43, 44, 142, 143, 144, 161, 164–5, 177, 190, 193, 194, 200, 221, 239, 241
Cosmas Indicopleustes (Byzantine geographer), 36, 55, 57, quoted 59
costus (root), 42, 47
cotton goods: Indian, 3, 14, 17, 40, 42, 47, 62, 83, 89, 98, 99, 159, 163, 164, 165, 166, 171, 178, 179, 182, 183, 193, 195, 201, 204, 231, 233, 240, 247, 252, 253, 254, 255, 264–5, 266, 270, 288, 298–9; British, 226, 282, 284, 288, 289, 294, 309, 317, 322, 333; other, 77, 96, 99, 140, 154, 166, 255, 281, 316, 367, 369, 370
cotton, raw, 158, 170, 212, 246, 247, 255, 263, 267, 270, 281, 288, 290, 291, 294, 307, 332, 333, 337, 345, 348, 357, 369, 370
Cotton, Sir A. T. (British engineer), 296
cowrie shells, 4, 30, 65, 70
Cranganore (Muziris, Indian port), 22, 24, 42, 43, 199, 238
Crawfurd, Dr. J. (E.I.C. official), 323, 330, 332, 340, 347, 348
crêpes, 38, 214
Crete, 7, 16
crockery, 266, 322, 333; see also pottery
Crompton, S. (British inventor), 266
Cromwell, Oliver, 201, 202, 237, 248
Crusade, Fourth, 53, 128
crystal, 36, 44, 98
Ctesiphon (Iranian city), 14, 35
cubeb (spice), 113, 165
cucumber, 77, 87, 257
Cunnale (Malabar pirate), 181
Curtius, D. (Dutch consul), 358
custard apple, 213, 257
cutch, 332

cutlery, 18, 275
Cyprus, 74
Cyrus the Great (Iranian emperor),
5, 7, 9

Dabhol (Indus port), 169, 178
Dacca (Indian port), 177, 288
Dai Viet, *see* Vietnam, 119
Daendels, H. W. (Governor-General
of Indonesia), 307, 310
daimyos (Japanese lords), 147, 150,
151, 152, 211, 212, 213, 354, 355,
356, 359, 360, 361, 363, 367
Dalhousie, Lord (Governor-
General of India), 285, 289, 290,
330, 331
Dam, P. van (V.O.C. official), 234
Daman (Indian port), 177
Damascus, 4, 170
damasks, 38, 164, 167
Damirica (South India), 43
Dangkrek Mountains (Cambodia),
117
Danube, River, 8, 49, 52
Daraut Kurghan (Central Asian
town), 20
Darius (Iranian emperor), 6–8, 9,
255
Darkot Pass (Kashmir), 20
Darjeeling (Indian town), 209
dates, 42, 77, 87, 256, 257
Deccan, 19, 61, 65, 70, 168, 178,
179, 236, 237, 238, 243, 291; *see
also* India
deerskins, 204
Defoe, Daniel (English author):
quoted 252
Dekker, D. (Dutch author), 318
Delhi, 168, 170, 171, 172, 174, 236,
237, 238, 240
Demetrios (Bactrian king), 18
Denmark, 197, 226, 227, 237, 248,
249, 349, 350
Desfarges, Marshal, 222
Deterding, Sir H. (Dutch agent),
320
Devanter, C. T. van (Dutch writer),
328

diamonds, 43, 255
Diaz de Novaes, B. (Portuguese
sailor), 175
Diocletian (Roman emperor), 47,
53, 55
Diodotus, Satrap of Bactria, 12
Diridotis (Iranian port), 8
Diu (Indian port), 177, 181; battle
of, 176, 261
Dizibul, Khan of Sogdia, 58
Djar, al- (Red Sea port), 80
Dnieper River (Russia), 52
Dniester River (Russia), 52, 131
dogs, 14
Dominican monks, 210
Don River (Russia), 52
Dorah Pass (Afghanistan), 20
Douglas, S. (British official), 302
Doumer, P. (Governor of Indo-
china), 345, 346
dragon's blood (gum), 41
Drake, Sir Francis (English sailor),
185, 192
drugs, 8, 14, 18, 39, 41, 83, 89, 98,
136, 149, 179, 255
Dundee, 290, 299
Dupuis, J. (French merchant), 342
Dupleix, J. F. (Governor of Pondi-
cherry), 223, 237, 239, 240
Dupré, Admiral (Governor of
Cochin), 342
Dutt, R. C. (Indian historian), 286
Dutthagamini, King of Ceylon, 43
Dvaravati (Mon kingdom in Thai-
land), 25
dyes, 14, 42, 179, 204, 255, 291
Dzungaria (Central Asia), 32, 49,
207, 208, 209

eaglewood, *see* aloeswood
earth oil (petroleum), 333
East India Company (Dutch,
V.O.C.), 181, 253; in India,
238–9, 240, 241, 247; in Indochina, 214–24; in Indonesia, 191–
200, 225–35, 307, 316; in Far
East, 203–4, 205, 206

East India Company (English, E.I.C.), 252; in India, 174, 200–2, 230, 235, 237, 239, 240–50, 264–265; in Indochina, 214–24, 329–330, 347; in Indonesia–Malaya, 192–3, 196, 197, 199, 200, 227, 310, 311; in Far East, 204, 206, 231, 262–3, 270–2, 279, 285–9, 291, 293, 296

East India Company (French), 219, 237

ebony, 7, 11, 42, 98, 322

Ecbatana (Hamadan, Iran), 6, 12, 14, 36

Ecole Française d'Extrême Orient, 344

Edom (Near Eastern kingdom), 4

egg-plant, 77

eggs, 281, 282

Egypt, 1, 4, 6, 7, 8, 256, 285; under Ptolemies, 9–12, 258; under Rome, 38–9, 251; under Caliphate, 73, 74, 76, 78, 80; under Fatimids, 127; under Mamluks, 132, 133; under Ottomans, 175, 176, 177, 259, 261, 285

Eisai (Japanese Buddhist), 110

Ekathotsarot, King of Thailand, 216, 217, 218

Elam (Iranian province), 14

Elburz Mountains (Iran), 132

Elephanta Island (India), 241

elephants, 10, 11, 157, 179, 255, 256

Elgin, Lord (British envoy), 277–8

Elliott, Captain Charles (British official), 272

embassies, 15, 22, 27, 32, 34, 35, 36, 37; Japan, 107; Ming, 142, 148, 149, 150; Thai, 156, 158; Majapahit, 162

embroidery, 18, 201

enamelware, 266

encomienda (estates) system, 301

England, see Britain

Ephesus (Iranian port), 6

Ephthalites (White Huns), 50, 51, 52, 58, 60

Epirus (Greece), 16

Erythrean Sea (Indian Ocean), see Periplus

Ethiopia, see Abyssinia

Euergetes II (Greek king of Egypt), 11

Euphrates River (Iraq), 1, 51, 54, 78, 133, 140

Europe: advisers, 137, 210, 350, 356; enthusiasm for China, 210; imperialism, 224, 225, 267, 370; learning, 210, 285, 349, 355, 366; role in Asian trade, 252, 253, 267, 269, 332, 337, 348; see also individual countries and commodities; fire-arms, mining plantations, shipping, etc.

Fa-hsien (Buddhist pilgrim), 63–6, 254

Faifo (port in Vietnam), 216, 224

famines, 70, 93, 173, 201, 277, 286, 290, 292, 293, 296, 297, 300, 317, 352; see also population

Fa Ngum, King of Laos, 157

Fan Shih-man, King of Funan, 25, 27

fans, 65, 104, 110, 149, 167, 366

Farama (Red Sea port), 80

Fars (Iranian province), 50

Fatimid dynasty (Egypt), 127

feathers, 164, 281

Fergana (Central Asian state), 7, 12, 33, 34, 38, 86, 127, 171, 253

Ferry, J. (French premier), 344

Fertile Crescent, 1, 4

fertilizers, 264, 309, 319, 368

figs, 77, 87, 257

fire-arms, 186, 217, 224, 252, 261, 304, 322, 333, 342, 367

firewood, 284

fish, 10, 27, 57, 205, 256, 284, 345, 346, 348, 365, 368

Fitch, R. (English traveller), 159, 190, 192

Flanders, 248

flax, 87, 170, 257

'flying cash', 97

Foochow (Chinese port), 93, 98, 273, 276
Formosa, *see* Taiwan
Fort St. George (*see also* Madras), 201, 239, 240
Fort William (Calcutta), 237, 239
Fort Yakutsk (Siberia), 207
Fort Zeelandia (Taiwan trading post), 203
fowls, 7, 30
France, 74, 80, 134, 219, 220, 221–2, 223, 227, 230, 239–40, 241, 248, 249, 262, 267, 273, 277, 281, 307, 315, 317, 325, 332, 334, 338, 339, 340–6, 349, 350, 358, 359, 365, 366
Franciscan monks, 210
Franck (Governor of Dutch Ceylon), 302
frankincense, 8, 11, 39, 40, 41, 42, 47, 48, 112
Frederick, Caesar (Venetian traveller), 159
fruit, 69, 145, 212, 253, 256, 284, 370
Fuggers (German bankers), 182
Fujiwara (Japanese clan), 102, 107–109
Fujiwara (Japanese teacher), 354
Fukien (Chinese province), 96, 150, 158, 203, 206, 209, 210
Fullerton, R. (Governor of Penang), 323
Funan, *see* Cambodia
Furnivall, J. S. (British official), 313, 317
furs, 2, 8, 32, 36, 57, 80, 89, 104, 134, 207, 208, 253, 254, 267, 282

Gaja Mada (Minister of Majapahit), 161–2
Gallienus (Roman emperor), 54
Galloola (Ceylonese district), 305
Gama, Vasco da (Portuguese explorer), 175
gamboge (resin), 322
gambier (astringent), 326

Gandhara (Graeco–Indian state), 19, 37, 64
Ganga Canal (India), 296
Ganges, River, 17, 18, 24, 43, 44, 61, 64, 70, 215, 237, 247, 285, 287, 296
garnets, 43, 255
Garnier, F. (French explorer), 342
Gautama (Buddha), 15
Gaul, 45, 52, 53
gauze, 38
Gaza (Palestinian city), 11
Gedrosia (Iranian province), 14
gems, 11, 14, 17, 23, 37, 38, 43, 44, 45, 57, 65, 77, 89, 139, 179, 181, 202, 246, 253, 255; *see also* individual gems
Gennai (Japanese scholar), 355
Genoa, 128, 133, 182, 248
Genouilly, Admiral de, 340
Genroku (Japanese era), 356
Georgia, 77, 131, 170
Germany, 38, 317, 350, 366, 368
Gerrha (Persian Gulf port), 12, 39
Gez River (Central Asia), 20
Ghassanids (Arab tribe), 54
Ghazun Mahmud, Khan of Persia, 133–4
Ghazni (Afghan state), 127, 131, 171, 238
ghee, 41
Ghund River (Central Asia), 20
Ghur (Afghan kingdom), 168
Gia Long, Emperor of Vietnam, 340
Gibbon, Edward (historian), 14
Gilgit (Kashmir), 20
ginger, 23, 39, 47, 48, 179, 255
ginseng (root), 152, 255
girdles, 40, 41
Glasgow, 250
glass, 44, 45, 170, 252, 266, 367
glassware, 8, 10, 13, 37, 38, 39, 40, 41, 42, 78, 288, 333
Goa (Indian port), 167, 176, 178, 179, 181, 190, 193, 195, 199, 246, 247, 249
goats, 2, 296

Gobi desert (Central Asia), 63, 67, 129

Godavari River (India), 238, 287

Goez, B. (Portuguese Jesuit), 174

Goitein, S. D. (Jewish historian), 46, 84

gold, 2, 3, 4, 10, 11, 13, 14, 18, 23, 27, 28, 36, 37, 38, 40, 41, 42, 45, 46, 56, 57, 62, 67, 68, 77, 89, 97, 98, 104, 111, 122, 148, 152, 159, 164, 165, 166, 167, 170, 178, 179, 183, 186, 195, 208, 212, 252, 253, 255, 322, 349, 361, 367, 369

Golden Horde (of Mongols), 133, 170

Golden Khersonese (Malaya), 44

Golkonda (Indian state), 168, 200, 236

Gompala (Ceylonese district), 303

Go Oc Eo (Cambodian port), 25, 37, 45

Gordon, Major C. (British soldier), 278

Goths, 53

Gourou, P. (French geographer), 303

grain, 8, 164, 288, 292, 293, 299

Grand Canal (China), 85, 92, 138

Grandière, Admiral de la (Governor of Indochina), 341

granite, 284

grapes, 38, 67, 77, 256

grapefruit, 140

Great Lake (Cambodia), 117, 119, 121, 123, 157

Great Wall of China, 31, 32, 49, 63, 129

Greece, 4, 5, 6, 7, 8–15, 17, 18, 19, 40, 42, 44, 54, 75, 251, 253, 258

Gresik, see Grise

Grise (Gresik, port of Java), 193, 228

Gros, Baron (French envoy), 277–8

Grose, J. H. (E.I.C. official), 246

Groslier, B. Ph. (French archæologist), 119

groundnuts, 293, 337

Grousset, R. (historian), 145

Guardafui, Cape (Africa), 40

guilds, 16, 56, 61, 96, 137, 147, 258, 356

guitars, 141

Gujarat (Indian province), 163, 164, 168, 173, 176, 177, 178, 180, 189, 190, 195, 199, 200, 201, 237, 238, 254, 255

gunpowder, 89, 94, 141, 188, 217, 260, 262, 274

gunny bags, 299, 322

Gupta dynasty and empire, see India

Gurkas (of Nepal), 243

Hadramawt (Arabian coast), 22, 41, 55

Haiphong (port of Vietnam), 36, 37, 81, 82

Hadrian (Roman emperor), 35

Haidar Ali (ruler of Mysore), 241

Hairun, Sultan of Ternate, 185

Hakkas (Chinese people), 275, 276

Hakodate (Japanese port), 358

Hakata (port of Ryukyu Islands), 149

Halmahera (Indonesian island), 229

Hamburg, 248, 249

Hami (Central Asian town), 67

Hamid, Abdul (Indian historian), 173

Hamun, Lake (Afghanistan), 51

Han dynasty and empire, see China

Hangchow (Chinese port), 95, 98, 105, 150, 276, 278

Hangkow (Yangtze port), 283, 342

Hanoi (Vietnamese city), 45, 342, 343, 345

Hargreave, J. (British inventor), 266

Hariharpur (Indian town), 201

Haripunjaya (Lampun, Mon kingdom in Thailand), 119

Harris, Townsend (American consul), 358

Harsha (Indian emperor), 69, 70, 72

Hart, Sir R. (British official), 252, 280

Harun al-Raschid (Arab caliph), 75, 76, 255

Hastings, Warren (Governor-General of India), 241, 242

Hastings, Lord (Governor-General of India), 311

Hayam Wuruk, King of Java, 161

Hayashi Razan (Japanese teacher), 355

Hecatompylos (Iranian city), 14

Heian-kyo, see Kyoto

hemp, 123, 170, 290, 301, 302, 306

Herat (Afghan town), 51, 79, 131, 170, 171

Heroonpolite Gulf (Red Sea), 11

hides, 11, 89, 99, 217, 219, 222, 255, 264, 267, 281, 288, 293, 346, 348

Hideyoshi, Shogun of Japan, 151, 152, 217

Hien-nam (port of Vietnam), 224

Himalayan Mountains, 17

Himyarite (Arab kingdom), 55

Hinduism, 15, 18, 19, 21, 24, 25, 26, 27, 28, 52, 62, 66, 72–3, 84, 111, 119, 169, 236, 237, 238, 256, 259, 260, 367

Hindu Kush Mountains, 12, 20, 52, 68, 171

Hindustan, 172; see also India

Hippalus (Greek pilot), 22

Hirado (Japanese port), 189, 203, 204

Hiram, King of Tyre, 23

Hiroshima (Japanese port), 367

Hitti, P. K. (Arab historian), 5

Hittites (people of Asia Minor), 3

Hitu (Indonesian port), 185

Hizen (Japanese clan), 357, 360, 361

Hoevell, W. R. van (Dutch missionary), 318

Hojo (Japanese clan), 109, 151

Hokkaido (island, Japan), 368

Ho-lo-tan (Indonesian kingdom), 112

Honan (Chinese province), 131

honey, 165, 256

hong merchants (China), 206, 271, 272, 279

Hong Kong, 263, 269, 272, 273, 274, 275–6, 277, 278, 279, 283–4, 285, 345, 349, 351, 370

Honshu (island, Japan), 101, 107, 151, 356

Hooghly River (India), 65, 247; port, 181, 201, 234

Hopei (Chinese province), 129, 131

horses, 2, 4, 7, 10, 11, 12, 14, 30, 32, 33, 34, 36, 38, 62, 69, 70, 89, 99, 104, 134, 149, 152, 169, 171, 178, 195, 253, 255, 256, 257

Hourani, G. (Arab historian), 83

Houtman, Cornelius de (Dutch sailor), 191

Hsien-pi (T'o-pa, Mongol nomads), 50

Hsi-Hsia (Tibetan state), 127, 130, 131; see also Tangut

Hsinbyushin, King of Burma, 329

Hsiung-nu (Mongol nomads), 19, 31, 32, 34, 36, 49, 50

Hsuan-tsang (Buddhist pilgrim), 67–72

Hsuan Tsung (Chinese emperor), 86, 90, 91, 92, 95, 255

Huai River (China), 95, 104

H'uang Ch'ao (Chinese revel), 84, 93

Huang-chih (Malayan centre), 36

Huang Ho (river, China), 4, 29, 276

Huang Tsung-hsi (Chinese envoy), 205

Hui Tsung (Chinese emperor), 95

Hudson, G. F. (British historian), 44, 45

Hué (Vietnam capital), 27, 341, 342, 343

Hu Kuang (or Hukwang, Chinese province), 272

Hulagu (Mongol Khan), 132, 133, 140

Humayun (Mughal emperor), 172, 177

Hunan (Chinese province), 277

Hungary, 52

Hung Hsiu-ch'uan (Chinese rebel), 276

Hung-wu (Chinese emperor), 141, 142

Huns, 50, 51, 52, 67, 69; see also Ephthalites, Hsiung-nu

Hwai-ngan-chau (Chinese port on Yangtze), 138
Hyderabad (Indian state), 243
Hyrcania (Caspian province), 14
Hyogo (Kobe, Japanese port), 358

Ibrahim, Sultan of Delhi, 171
I-ching (Chinese pilgrim), 22, 111–113
Iemitsu, Shogun of Japan, 355
Ieyasu, Shogun of Japan, 204, 217, 355
Ii Naosuke (Japanese Minister), 359
Ikko (Japanese clan), 261
Ili River (Central Asia), 135; region, 95, 208
Il-Khanate, see Iran
images, 104
Imhoff, Baron W. van (Governor-General of Indonesia), 234, 307
incense, 2, 38, 41, 57, 96, 98, 104, 110, 253, 255, 270; see also frankincense
India: ancient, 1, 3, 14, 15; Mauryan empire, 15–18, 32, 35, 47, 256, 257; Greek kings, 18; Kushan empire, 19–21, 51; early Tamil states, 22–3, 24, 38, 40, 42–44, 46; Gupta empire, 51–2, 58, 59, 61–3, 64–7, 69–71, 86, 89, 90, 252; Sultanate of Delhi, 139, 168, 170, 171–2, 259; Bahmani kingdom, 168, 176; Deccan sultanates, 176, 177, 179, 195, 259; empire of Vijayanagar, 116, 168, 178–9, 259; Mughal empire, 172–80, 189, 192, 200, 201, 202, 217, 221, 225, 233, 234, 235–44, 258, 259, 260, 265; late Tamil states, 194, 196, 199, 200, 201, 202, 215, 217, 225, 230, 232, 238–9, 240, 241, 259, 261; British rule, 240–51, 262, 264, 265, 266, 267, 268, 269, 270, 280, 282, 285–300, 302, 303, 305, 311, 320, 322, 323, 326, 327, 328, 329, 331, 332, 334, 335, 337, 348, 370
India Act, 242

Indian Ocean, 12, 22, 40–3, 53, 59, 79–85, 142–5, 168–9, 175–8, 192, 194–5, 248, 251, 254, 259, 263–4
indigo, 11, 42, 47, 179, 182, 199, 201, 212, 231, 245, 255, 264, 288, 291, 294, 301, 302, 308, 312, 313, 315, 317, 318, 357
Indochina, French, 267, 338–46, 351
Indonesia: 24, 28, 81, 84, 99, 101; Srivijaya, 112–17, 161, 187; Kediri, 116–17; Singosari, 161; Majapahit, 138, 142, 149, 151, 161–2, 165, 180, 252, 259, 261; Dutch influence and rule, 192, 193, 195–202, 225–35, 247, 252, 253, 262, 267–70, 301, 306–10, 311–18, 321, 322, 326, 327, 345; see also Java, Sumatra, Spice Islands
Indravarman I, King of Ankor, 118–19
inkslabs, 149
Inland Sea (Japan), 357, 359
Indus River, 1, 4, 5, 8, 42, 62, 69, 71, 86, 238, 290, 293, 296
Iran: 1, 2, 3; Achaemenian, 5–8, 30; Seleucid, 9–10, 12–13, 19; Arsacid or Parthian, 13, 34–9 passim, 42, 44, 49; Sassanian, 35, 50–2, 55, 57, 58–61, 62, 67, 70, 251; under Arabs, 73–85 passim, 86, 87, 89, 97, 127, 254; Il-Khanate, 132, 133, 134, 168; Timarid, 170; Safavid, 171, 172, 174, 175, 179, 180, 194, 200, 214, 227, 232, 236, 238, 246, 259, 260; Qajar, 267, 288, 295, 332
Ireland, 292
irisroot, 123
Irkishtam (town in Central Asia), 20
iron and ironware, 8, 10, 17, 30, 40, 58, 77, 104, 108, 123, 167, 188, 204, 255, 258, 261, 264, 266, 297, 309, 322, 345, 357, 367, 369, 370
Iron Age, 4
Iron Gates (Afghanistan), 68

Irrawaddy River (Burma), 25, 155, 328, 331, 332, 334, 338
irrigation, 1, 7, 10, 12, 13, 17, 26, 28, 30, 32, 118–19, 120, 121, 124, 130, 133, 170, 173, 178, 212, 213, 285, 286, 287, 293, 295, 296–7, 299, 300, 315, 317, 337, 345, 350
Isanavarman II, King of Chenla, 111
Ishkashm (Afghanistan), 20
Islam, 54, 73–85, 90, 100, 133, 169, 175, 256, 367; *see also* Moslems
Ismail, Shah of Iran, 171
Issyk-kul, Lake (Central Asia), 68
Italy, 40, 52, 53, 56, 128, 134, 198, 253, 257, 281, 332, 349; *see also* Roman Empire, Genoa, Venice
ivory, 4, 11, 18, 23, 27, 38, 40, 42, 43, 45, 62, 63, 89, 98, 166, 167, 179, 201, 216, 246, 255, 270, 322

Jacob, General J. (British engineer), 293
jade, 2, 3, 4, 29, 36, 38, 89, 188, 253, 255
Jahangir (Mughal emperor), 236
Jaffna (Ceylonese port), 303
Jakarta (Indonesian port), 28, 194, 196
Jambi (Malayu, Indonesian state), 112, 113, 116, 161, 165, 198, 199, 225, 228
James I, King of England, 196
James II, King of England, 221
Japan: 72, 88, 99, 100, 101, 193, 195, 202, 255, 256, 261; Soga and Taika periods, 102–3; Nara period, 105–6; Heian period, 107; Fujiwara period, 107–9; Kamakura period, 109–11, 138, 142, 145–7, 156; Ashikaga period, 147–50, 187, 190, 191; Tokugawa period, 193, 197, 202, 203, 204–5, 211–13, 216, 217, 220, 221, 222, 224, 225, 230, 232, 233, 234, 259, 351–60; Meiji period, 267, 268, 281, 282, 295, 298, 328, 360–70
Jardine, W. (British merchant), 262, 271, 272, 274

jars, 39, 154, 157, 159
jasmine, 87, 257
Java, 84, 112, 113, 161–2, 165, 183, 191, 195, 196, 197, 199, 206, 213, 225, 226–8, 229, 231–2, 234–5, 252, 254, 255, 271, 305, 308, 310–311, 313, 314, 315, 316, 317, 318, 321, 322, 328, 345; *see also* Indonesia
Jaxartes River (Central Asia), 5, 7
Jayavarman I, King of Chenla, 112
Jayavarman II (founder of Ankor), 117–18
Jayavarman IV, King of Ankor, 119
Jayavarman VII, King of Ankor, 120, 255
Jebei (Mongol general), 129
Jebel Allaki (African gold mines), 11
Jelal ed-Din, Prince of Kwarizm, 130–1
Jenghiz Khan (Mongol conqueror), 128–31, 145, 167, 170, 251
Jerusalem, 127
Jesuits, 204, 210, 219, 222, 224, 261, 274, 278
jewellery, 18, 37, 38, 63, 89, 255
Jews, 46, 61, 76, 80–1, 84, 182, 191
Jhelum Canal (India), 296
Jodhpur (Indian state), 237
Johore (Malay state), 184, 193, 311; *see also* Malaya
John of Marignolli (Franciscan missionary), 137, 139
John of Montecorvino (Franciscan missionary), 137
Josephus (Jewish historian), 80
Jourdain, J. (British sailor), 217
Juan-juan (Mongol tribe), 50
Judaism, 73
Juddah (Red Sea port), 80
Judea, 80
Julian Emperors (of Rome), 38
Jumna River (India), 65, 287, 296
jungle products, 122, 229, 246, 323, 327, 346
junks, 97–8, 139, 140, 149, 151, 164, 166, 188, 254, 270, 283, 284, 285

Jurched (Chin, Mongol tribe), 95, 105, 127, 128, 129, 131, 152, 251
Justin II (Roman emperor), 58
Justinian (Byzantine emperor), 56, 59, 87, 255
jute and jute goods, 264, 267, 288, 291, 293, 299, 370

Kabul, 6, 18, 69, 74, 79, 86, 171, 174, 238
Kaesong (Korean capital), 104, 131
Kagoshuna (Japanese town), 359
Kaidu, Khan of Chagatai, 134
Kaifeng (Chinese city), 95, 129, 131
Kajangala (Indian city), 70
Kalah Bar (Kedah? Kra?, Arab port in Malaya), 82, 84, 113, 144
Kalidasa (Indian dramatist), 66
Kalimantan, 161, 162; see also Borneo
Kalinga (Indian state), 115
Kalyan (Indian town), 289
Kanagawa (Japanese port), 358, 359
Kancipura (Indian town), 70
Kandahar (Afghan town), 175, 236
Kandy (capital of Ceylon), 155, 235, 302, 303, 304
Kanenaga (Japanese chief), 149
K'ang-hsi (Chinese emperor), 208, 210, 255, 278
Kanghwa Island (Korea), 131, 145
Kanishka, King of Kushan, 19, 20, 21, 51, 69
Kansu (Chinese province), 29, 31, 32, 44, 49, 90, 93, 127
Kan-t'o-li (Indonesian kingdom), 112
Kanto Plain (Japan), 151, 212
Kanwaha, battle of, 172
Kan Ying (Chinese envoy), 34
Kao Hsien-chih (Chinese general), 90
Kao Tsu (Chinese emperor), 31
kaolin (clay), 77, 87
Kao Tsung (Chinese emperor), 85–86
Kapisi (Begram, Afghan town), 20, 69, 71

kapok, 306, 320
Karachi, 296
Kara-Khitai (Turkish state), 127, 129
Karakorum (Mongol capital), 134
Karashar (Tarim oasis), 32, 63, 67, 90
Karenni (Burmese district), 333–4
Karghalik (Tarim oasis), 64
Karnal, battle of, 238
Karpuradvipa (camphor isle), 23
Kashgar (Tarim oasis), 19, 20, 21, 32, 34, 36, 64, 71, 74, 90, 127, 137, 254
Kashmir, 18, 19, 20, 42, 51, 52, 69, 71, 209, 243
Kasimbazar (Indian port), 201
Kassites (people of Asia Minor), 3
Katamari (Japanese leader), 102
Kattigara (Chinese port), 44, 45
Kaya (Mimana, Korean port), 101
Kayal (Cael, Indian port), 143
Ke-cho (port in Vietnam), 224
Kedah (port and state in Malaya), 25, 26, 82, 116, 167, 225, 323, 330, 344
Kediri (Javanese kingdom), 116–17, 161
Kelantan (Malayan port), 143, 344
Ken Canal (India), 296
Kerala (Indian state), 115
Kerduan (Central Asian town), 131
kerosene, 282, 337, 366
Kertanagara, King of Java, 161
Kerulen River (Mongolia), 128
kettles, 167, 254, 266
Kew (English botanical gardens), 306, 326
Khalid (Arab general), 73, 74
Khatmandu (capital of Nepal), 209
Khawak Pass (Afghanistan), 20
Khitan (Liao, Mongol tribe), 90, 93, 94, 95, 105, 127; see also Kara-Khitai
Khmer empire, see Cambodia
Khordadhbeh-ibn (Arab historian), 80
Khorog (Central Asian town), 20

Khotan (Tarim oasis), 2, 3, 16, 19, 21, 32, 34, 36, 38, 64, 71, 87, 90, 209, 253
Khurasan (Afghan state), 76, 77, 79, 130, 171
Khwarizm (Turkish state), 127, 128, 129, 131
Khyber Pass (Afghanistan), 8, 20, 64
Kiakhta (Central Asia), 207, 208, 278
Kiangsi (Chinese province), 96
Kiev, 132, 133
Kila Panja (Afghan town), 20
Kinsai (Hangchow), 138
Kinta (Malayan tin mines), 325
Kipchak, Khanate of, 132–3, 140, 170
Kirghiz (Mongol tribe), 91
Kistna River (India), 293
Kizil-Kum Desert (Central Asia), 130
knives, 254, 266, 275
Koguryo (Korean kingdom), 72, 85, 100, 101
Koh Ker (Cambodian town), 119
Kokand (Central Asian state), 33, 34
Konbaung Dynasty, see Burma
Konin (Japanese emperor), 106–7
Konyo (Japanese scholar), 355
Korat (Thai town), 222
Korea, 50, 72, 82, 86, 89, 97, 99, 100, 255, 256; Silla dynasty, 100–101, 103–4, 108; Koryo dynasty, 104–5, 131, 142, 145–6; Yi dynasty, 148–9, 152, 205, 206, 279, 364, 369, 370
Koryo dynasty, see Korea
Kotumbara (Indian town), 18
Kowloon Peninsula (China), 278
Ko-ying (Sumatran port), 28
Kra Isthmus (Malayan Peninsula), 26
krises, see swords
Krishna River (India), 287
Krom, N. J. (Dutch historian), 115
Kuala Lumpur (Malayan town), 324
Kuang-an (port of Vietnam), 340
Kublai Khan (Chinese emperor), 100, 131–2, 136–7, 145, 146, 153, 154, 155, 161, 251, 255
Kucha (Tarim oasis), 32, 63, 67–8, 90
Kuei (Chinese prince), 209
kuge (Japanese courtiers), 355
Kumarajiva (Tarim Buddhist), 63
Kung (Chinese prince), 278
Kunlun mountains (China), 1
Kustana (Indian prince), 16
Kwa-chow (Caigiu), 158
Kwangsi (Chinese province), 276, 277
Kwantung (Chinese province), 45, 206; port, 150
Kweichow (Chinese province), 213, 277
Kyoto (Japanese town), 103, 107, 359, 360
Kyushu (island of Japan), 101, 186, 204, 357

Labuan Island (Borneo), 327
lac, 30, 40, 157, 159, 166, 255, 332, 348
Laccadive Islands (Indian Ocean), 83
lacquerware, 4, 29, 33, 38, 96, 110, 123, 149, 202, 204, 255, 266, 270, 366
Lagrée, D. de (French explorer), 342
Lahore (Indian town and district), 174, 175, 238
Lajazzo (Laias, Armenian port), 137
Lambert, 247
Lancaster, J. (English sailor), 192
Lanchow (Chinese city), 34, 36, 209, 251
Lane, W.: quoted 182
Langkasuka (Malayan state), 26
Lan Xang, see Laos
Laos, 111, 112, 120, 159, 160, 206, 216, 217, 222, 224, 267, 279, 329, 340, 342, 343–4
lapis lazuli, 3, 4, 42, 77, 255

Larpent, G. G. de H. (British merchant), 287
Larut (Malayan tin mines), 325
lascars (Indian seamen), 245, 246
Lashio (Burmese town), 334, 337
laudanum, 47
Lavo (Lopburi, Mon kingdom in Thailand), 119
Lawrence, Lord (Viceroy of India), 297
Le (Vietnam dynasty), 224
lead, 14, 68, 77, 89, 98, 159, 164, 179, 201, 204, 216, 255, 267, 322, 337
leather and leatherware, 10, 57, 255
Lebanon, 7
lemon, 77, 87
Lena River (Siberia), 207
lentils, 96
lettuce, 87
Leuke Kome (Red Sea port), 39, 40
Leur, J. C. van (historian), 197, 198, 253, 263
Levant, 3, 4, 5, 11, 57, 78, 198, 259
Lhasa (Tibetan capital), 44, 90, 209
Liao (Khitan state), 93
Liaotung (Chinese province), 152, 369
lignaloes, see aloeswood
Liegnitz, battle of, 132
lignum aloe, see aloeswood
Ligor (Tambralinga, Malayan port), 26, 113, 116, 117, 156, 167, 222, 330
Li Kuang-li (Chinese general), 33
lime, 284
linens, 8, 10, 38, 42, 47, 62, 252
Linschoten, J. H. van (Dutch geographer), 190
linseed, 293
Lintin Island (China), 271, 272
Lin Tse-hsu (Chinese commissioner) 272
liquor, 96, 294, 337
Lisbon, 182
Li Tzu-ch'eng (Chinese general), 153
List, F. (German economist), 252
Liu Yen (Chinese minister), 92
Liverpool, 250

Lodi dynasty, 171; see also India
London, 192, 242, 243, 249, 250, 262, 263, 265, 270, 272, 275, 290, 305, 322, 336
long pepper, 165
Loolecondera (Ceylon estate), 305
Lopburi (Thai town), 222; see also Lavo
Lop Nor (Tarim oasis), 63
Louis XIV, King of France, 219, 222
Loulan (Chinese town), 21, 32
Lovek (Cambodian town), 216, 219
Loyang (Chinese town), 63, 92, 93
Luang Prabang (town or state in Laos), 154, 156, 159, 342, 343
lucerne, 7, 38, 257
Luchu (Ryukyu) Islands, 149, 150, 205, 206, 279, 357
Lung-men (caves, North China), 63
Lu Kuei-meng (Chinese author), 88
Lu Yu (Chinese author), 88
Luzon (Philippine island), 151
lycium (plant juice), 42

Macao, 151, 181, 185, 186, 188, 190' 194, 203, 213, 224, 227, 270, 271' 272, 284
Macartney, Lord (British envoy), 210, 271, 273
Macassar (Indonesian port), 184, 193, 196, 197, 225, 226, 227, 228, 229, 230, 307, 322
mace, 116, 164, 165, 166, 183, 184, 193, 197, 198, 226, 255
Macedonia, 15, 36
machinery, 282, 289, 294, 309, 353, 366, 369
macir (bark), 41
Mackenzie, James (Governor of Ceylon), 303
McLeod, Capt. W. (British official), 330, 332
Madagascar, 24, 39, 194, 248
Madras, 26, 51, 201, 219, 220, 223, 237, 239, 240, 241, 243, 244, 247, 248, 262, 286, 287, 293, 296, 298, 337

Madura Island (Indonesia), 161, 227, 228

Maebashi (Japanese cotton centre), 367

Maes Titanius (Greek merchant), 35–6

Magadha (Indian state), 16, 17–18, 51, 52, 65

Magellan, Straits of, 191

Magellan, F. (Spanish sailor), 184, 186

Magnesia, battle of, 14

Mahakam River (Borneo), 28

Ma Hao (caves, China), 22

Mahendraparvata, see Phnom Kulen

Mahé (Indian port), 241

Mai-mai-ch'eng (Mongolian town), 208

Maingy, A. D. (Administrator of Tennasserim), 329–30

maize, 213, 257, 346

Majapahit Empire, see Indonesia

Majumdar, R. C. (Indian historian), 21

Makran (Indian district), 1, 4, 8, 18, 42

Malabar (Indian coast), 22, 39, 41, 42, 43, 175, 176, 177, 178, 198, 199, 200, 201, 230, 237, 238, 239, 254, 255, 256, 304

malabathrum (patchouli?), 43, 47, 48

Malacca, see Malaya

Malacca, Strait of, 22, 82, 113, 114, 117, 161, 246

Malao (Berbera, African port), 40

Malaya: ancient and portage states, 24, 25, 26, 27, 28, 36, 37, 43, 82, 114, 142; Malacca, 142, 143, 144, 151, 159, 161, 162–7, 176, 181, 182–3, 185, 186, 190, 193, 198, 203, 206, 215, 216, 225, 226, 227, 228, 229, 232, 235, 307, 323, 326, 335; British influence and rule, 267, 268, 269, 270, 288, 295, 297, 301, 306, 308–9, 311, 321, 322, 323–7, 337, 344, 347, 348

Malayu, see Jambi

Maldive Islands (Indian Ocean), 4, 83, 115, 143, 177, 183

Malwa (Indian state), 52, 237, 247, 271

Mamun, al- (Arab caliph), 75

Manchester, 266, 275, 288, 298, 312, 317, 322, 332, 366, 369

Manchuria, 31, 49, 85, 86, 90, 105, 129, 255, 256, 278, 370

Mandalay, 331, 332, 334

Mangalore (Indian port), 39

manganese, 267, 298

Mang-hao (Chinese town), 342

Mangu (Mongol Khan), 131–2

Manichaeism, 87

Manila, 184, 187, 188, 190, 194, 203, 204, 206, 210, 214, 216, 226, 227, 271

Manipur (Indian district), 329

Mansur, al- (Arab caliph), 75, 81

Mansuriya (Indus port), 169

Mapillas (Moslem descendants), 169

Marathas (Hindu people), 236, 237, 238, 241, 243, 246

Marathon, battle of, 6

marble, 77

Marcus Aurelius (Roman emperor), 37, 44, 52

Marinus of Tyre (Greek merchant), 35–6

Market and Cape of Spices, see Guardafui

Martaban (Burmese port), 25, 166, 218

Martabanjars, 157, 159

Martel, Charles (French king), 74

Martin, M. (British historian), 288

Marx, Karl (German philosopher), 297, 298

Mary, Queen of England, 264

Mas'udi, al- (Arab historian), 113

Mascarenha Islands (Madagascar), 248

Masqat (Persian Gulf port), 81, 82, 144

Masulipatam (Indian port), 200, 220, 221, 239

Mataram (Indonesian kingdom), 114, 115, 197, 225, 226, 227, 228, 229, 234
matches, 282, 333, 366, 369
Matelieff, C. (Dutch admiral), 193
Ma Te-hsin (Chinese Moslem), 277
Matheson, J. (English navigator), 262, 271
Mathura (Indian kingdom), 18
mats, 281, 366
Matsukata, M. (Japanese Finance Minister), 363-4, 365, 368
Maudun, (Modun, nomad emperor), 31
Mauryan Dynasty, see India
Mecca, 73, 78, 176, 179
Media (Iranian kingdom), 5, 6, 14
medicines, 104
Medina (Arab town), 73, 80
Mediterranean Sea, 4, 5, 14, 15, 29, 35, 39, 42, 45, 53, 74, 78, 79, 84, 195, 201, 259
Megasthenes (Seleucid ambassador), 16
Meiji, Emperor, see Japan
Mekong River (Indochina), 22, 24, 27, 111, 112, 117, 119, 154, 338, 341, 342, 343, 344, 346
melon, 77, 139
Menam River (Thailand), 27, 119, 120, 219, 341, 344, 347, 349
Menander (Bactrian general), 18
Menuthias (Pemba or Zangchar), 40
merchants: position of, 257-9; see also Jews, Moslems, and individual countries
mercury, 77, 104, 110, 123, 164, 179, 201, 246, 255, 270
Mergui (Burmese port), 82, 181, 215, 220, 221, 222
Meroe (Abyssinian kingdom), 10-11
Merv (Central Asian town), 12, 35, 51, 79, 87, 131
Mesopotamia, 1, 3, 4, 5, 7, 55, 73, 76, 77, 78, 83, 132, 133, 256
metals and metalwares, 294, 322, 331, 353, 357, 366, 369; see also iron, lead, tin, etc.
Mewar (Indian state), 236
Mexico, 186-7, 188, 234, 301
Miao (Chinese tribe), 277, 278
Middleton, Sir Henry (English sailor), 254
Midnapur (Indian state), 293, 296
migration, see population
Mildura (Indonesian island), 308
millet, 67
Mimana, see Kaya
Minamoto (Japanese clan), 109
Minangkabau (Malayan states), 324
Mincing Lane, 305
Mindanao (Philippines island), 187
Mindon, King of Burma, 331, 332, 333, 334, 347
minerals, 10, 32, 134, 254, 267, 269, 337, 339, 345, 365; see also iron, lead, tin, etc.
Ming dynasty, see China
Ming-ti (Chinese emperor), 34
Minh-Mang, Emperor of Vietnam, 340
mining, 10, 67, 108, 110, 189, 297-8, 310; see also minerals
Minto, Lord (Governor-General of India), 307, 310, 311
mirrors, 4, 33, 37, 254
Mithridates I (Iranian emperor), 14
Mito (Japanese clan), 357, 359
Mitsubishi Company (Japan), 369
Mitsui (Japanese merchants), 213, 356-7
Mocha (Muza, Arab port), 202, 231
Mogadishu (East African port), 143
Mogaung (Thai state), 155
Mogok (Burmese ruby mines), 337
Moira, Lord (Governor-General of India), 243
Mo-lo-yeu, see Malayu
Molucca Islands (Indonesia), 116, 161, 162, 166, 184, 185, 186, 187, 188, 190, 191, 193, 197, 199, 206, 217, 225, 229, 230, 310, 311

Mon (people of Lower Thailand and Lower Burma), 25, 154, 155, 158, 159, 215, 223, 224, 328, 329, 331

money-lending, 61, 62, 137, 182, 199, 212, 213, 232, 249, 334, 335–336, 337, 338

Mongkut, King of Thailand, 347, 348–9, 350–1

Mongolia, 3, 4, 31, 32, 49, 85, 88, 90, 152, 207, 256, 279

Mongols, 4, 50, 105, 117, 127–37, 251, 253, 254, 257

moonstones, 43, 255

monopolies, 9, 10, 39, 43, 56, 58, 59, 60, 88, 93, 96, 182, 184, 198, 219, 227, 229, 230, 231, 235, 248, 258, 270, 276, 302, 306, 307, 311, 313, 315, 333, 342, 348, 349

Moreland, W. H. (British historian), 175, 179–80, 253

Moros (Indonesian pirates), 187, 229, 235

mosaics, 78

Moscha (Khor Reiri, Arabian port), 41

Moscow, 140, 170, 207

Moslems, 53, 75, 76, 79, 83, 84, 91, 97, 162, 168, 169, 171, 172, 173, 175, 176, 178, 181, 182, 183, 221, 225, 228, 236, 237, 252, 253, 256, 259, 260, 262, 277, 278, 302, 367; see also Islam

Mosyllum (Ras Hantara, African port), 40

Mouhot, H. (French explorer), 342

Moulmein (Burmese port), 25, 44, 330, 334, 337

Mozambique (African port), 193

Mu'awiyah (Arab caliph), 74

Mughal dynasty, see India

Muhammad (founder of Islam), 73

Muhammad, Shah of Bahmani, 261

Muhammad, King of Ghur, 168

Muhammad Ali (ruler of Egypt), 263

Muhammed Aly (Indian prince), 240

Mukden (Manchurian capital), 152–3

Mukerji, K. (Indian economist), 300

Muktafi, al- (Arab caliph), 77

Mulavarman, King of Borneo, 28

mulberry trees, 71, 91, 212

Mundus (Bender Hais, African port), 40

Münster, Treaty of, 203

Muong Nai (Thai state), 155

murrhine (glass), 40

Murshedabad (Indian town), 288

Musi River (Indonesia), 112

musk, 80, 123, 164, 167, 202

muslins, 11, 14, 17, 18, 40, 62, 83, 123; see also cotton goods

Mussel Harbour (Myos Hormos, Red Sea port), 11, 22, 40

mustard, 293

Mutawakkil, al- (Arab caliph), 77

Mutinghe, H. W. (Dutch official in Indonesia), 310

Mutsu (Japanese gold mine), 111

Muza, see Mocha

Muziris, see Cranganore

Myédé River (Burma), 331

myrrh, 8, 11, 39, 40, 41, 47, 48, 112, 270

Mysore (Indian state), 241, 243, 292

Nabataeans (Arab tribe), 4, 11, 12, 39

Nadir, Shah of Persia, 238–9, 260

Nagasaki (Japanese port), 204, 205, 214, 234, 351, 355, 358

Nagpur (Indian cotton centre), 298

Nakhon Nayok (Thai town), 222

Nakhon Srithammarat (Thai port), 181

Nalanda (Indian Buddhist centre), 69, 70, 112, 113

Namoa Island (China), 151

Nam Patane basin (Laos), 344

Nanchao (Thai kingdom), 21, 90, 93, 153–4, 155, 277

Nandabayin, King of Burma, 160, 215
Nanking (Chinese port), 66, 101, 141, 150, 209, 264, 271, 273, 274, 276, 278
Nan Shan Mountains (China), 32
Nantaungmya (Burmese king), 155
Nan-yueh (Chinese kingdom), 36
Napier, Lord (British general), 272
Naples, 56
Napoleon, Louis (French emperor), 277, 340, 341
Napoleonic Wars, 307, 310
naphtha, 77
Nara (Japanese capital), 105, 107
Narai, King of Thailand, 218, 219, 220, 221, 222, 347, 348
nard (spice), 42, 43, 47
Narikeldvipa (coconut isle, Southeast Asia), 23
Narsah (Iranian emperor), 55
Naresuen, King of Thailand, 160, 216
navigation, 22, 98, 110, 144, 175, 191, 262
Nederlandsche Handelmaatschpij (N.H.M.), 312–13, 315–16, 320
Necho (Egyptian pharaoh), 6
Needham, J. (British scientist), 44, 45, 96, 257
needles, 123, 167, 254, 266
Negapatam (Indian port), 113, 116
Negrais (Burmese island), 223
Negri Sembilan (Malayan state), 324, 326
Nepal, 69, 90, 209, 243, 279
nephrite (jade), 29
Nerchinsk, Treaty of, 207, 208, 210, 278
Nero (Roman emperor), 23
Netherlands, 184, 185, 188, 190, 191, 206, 207, 252, 253, 261, 262, 265, 267, 302, 304, 307, 310–24, 328, 349, 350, 351, 355, 358, 359; see also East India Company (Dutch)
New England, 249
New Guinea, 229

New Sarai (capital of Golden Horde), 133
New York, 337
New Zealand, 274
Nguyen (Vietnamese family), 340, 341
Nguyen-Anh, Prince, see Gia Long
Nicobar Islands (Indian Ocean), 116
Nien (Chinese bands), 277, 278
Niigata (Japanese port), 358
Nile, River, 1, 6, 10, 11, 39, 55, 263
Ningpo (Chinese port), 95, 188, 273, 276
Nippon Yusen Kaisha (Japanese company), 369
Nishapur (Central Asian town), 131
Nisibis (Iranian town), 55
Niya (Tarim oasis), 21, 71
Nizam dynasty (of South India), 238, 239, 241
Nobunaga (Japanese general), 151
nomads, as traders, 1–5
Norodom, King of Cambodia, 341, 344
North, Lord (Governor of Ceylon), 302
North America, 292
Norway, 349
Novgorod (Russian town), 140
Nubia (African kingdom or province), 10, 11, 13
Nuniz, F. (Portuguese trader), 178
Nurhachi, King of Manchuria, 152
nutmeg, 113, 116, 164, 165, 166, 167, 183, 184, 193, 196, 197, 198, 226, 229, 230, 255, 318

oak, 245
Obata, S. (Japanese historian), 86
Ocelis (Aela, Red Sea port), 22, 29
Octavian, later Augustus (Roman emperor), q.v., 14
Odaynath, Chief of Palmyra, 54
Odoric of Pordenone (Italian Franciscan), 137, 138, 139
Odovacar (Visogoth chief), 53
Ogatai (Mongol khan), 131, 132

oil (vegetable), 8, 10, 11, 267, 281, 282, 308, 309, 316, 370
oil-seeds, 212, 264, 281, 299, 305
Oirats (Mongolian tribe), 145
olives, 40, 87
Omana (Muscat?, Persian Gulf port), 39, 41, 42
Ombilin (Sumatran town), 321
Onin War (Japan), 150
onions, 87, 257
opium, 164, 199, 213, 214, 215, 245, 248, 254, 257, 262, 270, 271, 272, 275, 276, 277, 280, 281, 282, 284, 288, 294, 301, 313, 322, 340, 349
Opone (Ras Hafun, African port), 40
Oraea (Indian port), 42
orange, 77
Ordos (region, China), 93, 127
organs (reed), 141
Orissa (Indian province), 15, 17, 26, 70, 201, 237, 238, 293, 296
Orléans, 52
Ormuz (Persian Gulf port), 143, 144, 176, 181, 189, 195, 200
Osaka (Japanese port), 354, 356, 357, 358, 359
Osaka Shosen Kaisha (Japanese shipping line), 369
Ostend, 249
Ostend company, 248
ostrich feathers, 11
Ostrogorsky, G. (Russian historian), 57
Ostrogoths, 52
Ottoman Turks, 170, 182, 183, 189, 259, 260
Ouchi (Japanese clan), 150
Oudh (Indian province), 237, 240, 243, 285, 287, 296
oxen, 256
Oxus River (Amu Darya, Central Asia), 7, 60, 68

pachak (root), 164, 167
Pacific Ocean, 186, 207, 358
Padang (Sumatran town), 321

Paekche (Korean kingdom), 72, 100, 101, 102, 103
Paes, D. (Portuguese traveller), 178
Pagan (Burmese kingdom), 153, 154–6, 159
Pagan Min, King of Burma, 330, 331
Pahang (Malayan state), 143, 324
Pailin (Indo-Chinese sapphire mines), 345
paintings, 99, 104
Pakistan, see India
Palawan (Philippines island), 187
Palembang (Indonesian port), 28, 112, 116, 143, 144, 162, 165, 198, 199, 228, 307, 310, 311, 317
Palermo (Italian city), 134
Pallava (kingdom, India), 70
Pallu, Bishop (French missionary), 222
Palmerston, Lord (British Minister), 272, 277
palm sugar, 332
Palmyra (Arab city), 54
Pamir Mountains (Central Asia), 1, 12, 16, 19, 20, 34, 36, 64, 67, 78, 85, 90, 130
Panarukan (Indonesian town), 307
Pan Ch'ao (Chinese general), 34, 35
Pandya (Indian kingdom), 23, 115
Panipat, battle of, 238
Panjshir (valley, Afghanistan), 20
Pankalan Brandan (Indonesian oil field), 320
Pankor Engagement, 324
P'an-p'an (Malayan kingdom), 26
Pané (Sumatran city), 116
paper, 10, 13, 38, 78, 89, 104, 108, 123, 212, 214, 255, 266, 322, 348, 367
Paramesvara, Sultan of Malacca, 142, 162
Paris, 334, 343
pass system: Portuguese, 176–7, 181–2; Dutch, 181, 194–6, 200, 228–9, 310, 311
Parsa (Fars, Iran), 5
Parsees (Indian sect), 246, 270, 298

Parsumash (Iranian kingdom), 5
Parthians, see Iran
Pasé (Indonesian port), 166, 183
Patani (town in Malayan peninsula), 26, 162, 181, 193, 198, 215,
  216-17, 218, 225
Patna (Palimbothra, Indian town),
  44, 201
Pavie, A. (French consul), 343-4
Pax Romana, 15, 134
Pax Tartarica, 134-5
peaches, 67, 256
peacocks, 7, 23, 87
peanuts, 257
pearls, 11, 17, 23, 27, 37, 42, 43, 45,
  65, 70, 77, 89, 98, 139, 164, 165,
  167, 270, 322
pears, 67
peas, 87, 139, 257
Pedir (Sumatran port), 165, 166,
  183
Pegolotti, F. (Italian merchant),
  135-6, 254
Pegu (Burmese port), 158, 159, 166,
  179, 180, 183, 215, 223, 247, 261
Peking, 129, 134, 141, 153, 205, 208,
  209, 210, 261, 271, 274, 277, 278,
  280, 340, 343, 348
Penang (Malayan island), 192, 263,
  283, 310, 321, 323, 325, 326, 330
Peninsular & Oriental Steam Navigation Company, 263
pepper, 8, 11, 17, 23, 38, 42, 47, 57,
  139, 140, 157, 158, 179, 183, 186,
  192, 193, 195, 196, 198, 199, 200,
  201, 225, 228, 229, 230, 238, 246,
  247, 255, 270, 301, 302, 315, 318,
  322, 323, 346
Peradeniya (Ceylonese district), 302
Perak (Malayan port), 26, 225, 323,
  324, 325
perfumes, 18, 27, 41, 104, 110, 179
Pergamum (state in Asia Minor),
  12, 14
Periplus of the Erythrean Sea, The
  (c. A.D. 60), 40, 41-3, 46
Perkins, Sir W. H. (British chemist),
  291

Perlis (Malayan sultanate), 344
Peroz, Emperor of Iran, 51, 52
Perry, Commodore M. C. (Ameri-
  can sailor), 358-9
Persia, see Iran
Persian Gulf, 3, 5, 12, 17, 34, 39, 41,
  62, 79-80, 81-4, 99, 143, 144, 168,
  176, 180, 181, 182, 189, 195, 201,
  233, 246, 253, 270
Persis (Iranian province), 14
Peru, 188, 190
Pescadores Islands (China), 203
Peshawar (Taxila, Indian town), 17,
  19, 20, 64, 69, 296
pesticides, 368
Petchaburi (Thai town), 217
Petra (Arabian city), 4, 11, 12, 39, 54
petroleum, 308, 320-1, 333, 337,
  338, 339, 370
pewter, 123
Phaulkon, Constant (Greek ad-
  venturer), 220-2
Philadelphia, 249
Philadelphus I, King of Egypt, 11
Philip V, King of France, 134
Philip II, King of Spain and Portu-
  gal, 177, 182, 185, 187
Philippines, 151, 156, 185, 187-8,
  204, 206, 267, 269, 301-2, 308, 309
Phnom Bakeng (Cambodian town),
  119
Phnom Kulen (Mahendraparvata,
  Cambodian capital), 117, 118
Phnom Penh (Cambodian capital),
  157, 216, 341, 344
Phoenicia, 1, 5, 6, 12
Phu Ly (Vietnamese town), 345
pianos, 275
pigs, 284
Pi-lo-ko, King of Nanchao, 154
Pindari (Indian bands), 243
pineapple, 213, 257
P'i-pa (Bactrian lute), 38
pirates, 46, 262; Red Sea, 5, 11;
  Persian Gulf, 12; Indian Ocean,
  83, 177, 178, 181, 221; Malaya-
  Indonesia, 26, 66, 142, 162, 222,
  229-30, 323; China Sea, 27, 97,

pirates—*cont.*
  104, 142, 146–7, 148–51, 187, 213,
  274, 275, 276
Pires, Tomé (Portuguese official),
  163–7, 178, 180, 185
Pisa, 128
pistachio (nut), 7, 140, 257
pitch, 165
Pitsanulok (Thai town), 160
Pitt, W. (Prime Minister of Britain),
  242
plantations, 269, 280, 284, 291, 292,
  301–6, 313, 314, 315, 316, 318–19,
  320, 326–8, 345, 365
Plassey (India), battle of, 240
Pliny (Roman geographer), 5, 20,
  24, 36, 43, 45, 46, 47, 252, 254
plums, 67, 139
Poduca, *see* Pondicherry
P'o-hai (Mongol tribe), 90
Poitiers, battle of, 74
Poland, 132
polo, 87
Polo, Marco (Italian traveller), 95,
  137–9
pomegranate, 67, 77, 87, 257
Pondicherry (Poduca, Indian port),
  24, 43, 44, 223, 237, 239, 240, 241,
  298
P'ong Tuk (Thai town), 25
Pontus (state in Asia Minor), 3, 14
Poona (Indian state), 243
population: Asia, 267–9; Burma,
  335, 337, 339; Ceylon, 303, 304,
  308; China, 91–2, 94, 95, 96, 141,
  151, 276; French Indochina, 338,
  339, 345; Hong Kong, 284–5;
  India, 173, 200, 294, 297, 299–
  300; Indonesia, 233, 308, 327–8;
  Iran, 60; Japan, 106–7, 211, 352,
  353, 354; Malaya, 308, 325, 327;
  Philippines, 187, 308; Thailand,
  339
porcelain, 38, 87, 88, 96, 98, 99, 104,
  110, 123, 141, 149, 164, 167, 179,
  188, 195, 202, 212, 214, 224, 252,
  253, 254, 255, 257, 272, 348; *see
  also* pottery

Po-sse (Persians), 81
portages, *see* Malaya
Portugal, 151, 167, 175–80, 181–6,
  187, 188, 189, 190–1, 192, 193,
  194, 195, 197, 198, 200, 201, 202,
  203, 204, 206, 208, 215, 216, 219,
  224, 226, 229, 232, 236, 237, 238,
  247, 249, 252, 253, 257, 259, 261,
  262, 271, 335, 347, 349
potato, 186, 213, 257
pottery, 8, 13, 88, 108, 122, 146,
  156–7, 159, 164, 170, 179, 182,
  214, 245, 246, 252, 254, 255, 266
Pottinger, Sir Henry (British
  official), 275
Prabalingga (Javanese district), 307
Prapanca (Majapahit poet), 161
P'ra Pathom (Thai town), 25
Pra Phetraja, King of Thailand, 222
Prasat Thong, King of Thailand,
  217, 218
Preah Khan (Cambodian town),
  120
Preanger (Indonesian district), 310,
  312, 316
printing, 89, 141, 148, 257
Procipius (Byzantine historian):
  quoted 56, 87
Prome (Burmese town), 159
Provence (French district), 134
Prussia, 248, 343, 349
Ptolemais Theron (Epitheras of the
  Hunts, Red Sea port), 11, 40
Ptolemy (Greek geographer), 35,
  43, 44
Ptolemies (Greek kings of Egypt),
  9–12, 13, 14, 80, 258
Puket Island (Thailand–Malaya),
  220, 222, 225
Pulicat (Indian port), 194
Punjab, 8, 18, 64, 74, 78, 167, 174,
  237, 238, 243, 255, 285, 287, 290,
  298
Purnavarman (Indonesian king), 28
Pusan (Korean port), 148
P'ya Taksin (Thai king), 329
Pyrard, F. (French sailor), 182
Pyraleae Islands (Africa), 40

Pyu (Burmese kingdom), 25, 154

Quelpart Island (Korea), 150
Quilon (Indian port), 82, 115, 143, 169, 199
quinine, *see* cinchona

Raffles, Sir T. S. (British official), 310–11, 312, 313, 321
railways: Burma, 333, 334, 337; Ceylon, 304, 309; Hong Kong, 327; India, 285, 289–90, 291, 292, 293, 295, 296–7, 300; Indonesia, 309, 321; Japan, 365, 367, 368; Malaya, 324, 326; Thailand, 339, 350, 351
Rajaraja I, King of Chola, 115
Rajendra I, King of Chola, 115–16
Rajendravarman, King of Chenla, 119
Rajisthan (Indian region), 17, 243
Rajputs (Indian caste), 52, 73, 172, 237, 243, 259
Rama I (Thai king), 347
Rama II (Thai king), 347
Rama III (Thai king), 347, 348
Ramadhibodi, King of Thailand, 157–8, 216
Rama Khambeng, King of Thailand, 156, 157, 161
Rangoon (Burmese port), 44, 329, 330, 332, 333, 334, 337
Raniganj (Indian coal centre), 289, 297
rape, 293
rattan, 165, 270, 322
realgar (red sulphide of arsenic), 42
Red River (Indochina), 119, 154, 342–3, 345
Red Sea, 2, 4, 5, 6, 11, 12, 22, 39, 41, 55, 58, 62, 79, 80, 84, 168, 169, 176, 180, 181, 182, 201, 246, 253, 259, 264, 270
Reinwardt, Prof. C. (Dutch official), 312
Reyersz, C. (Dutch admiral), 203

Rezanov, N. P. (Russian envoy to Japan), 358
Rhapta (Dar-es-Salaam, African port), 40
Rhine, River, 8, 49, 52
rhinoceros horn, 40, 45, 89, 98, 322
Rhodes (Mediterranean island), 74
rhubarb, 89, 167, 255
Riau (Indonesian port), 322
rice, 7, 11, 17, 23, 30, 41, 67, 121, 147, 159, 165, 166, 179, 196, 199, 212, 213, 226, 227, 229, 247, 252, 256, 264, 267, 269, 270, 271, 284, 292, 306, 307, 309, 314–15, 316, 322, 327, 328, 350, 351, 352, 353, 365, 368, 370
Ricci, M. (Italian Jesuit), 210
Ridley, H. N. (Director of Singapore Botanic Gardens), 326
roads, 1, 6, 13, 16, 17, 20, 21, 22, 25, 31, 32, 34, 35, 39, 44, 58, 63–5, 67–9, 71–2, 108, 134, 209, 212 (Japan), 302, 307, 315, 321, 326, 331, 333, 344, 350, 351; *see also* caravans
Robequain, C. (French geographer), 301, 338
Roe, Sir Thomas (English ambassador), 175, 190, 258
Roman Empire, 13, 14, 15, 22, 23, 24, 28, 34, 35, 37, 38–48, 49, 50, 51, 52–3, 55, 57, 62, 84, 251, 252, 253, 254
roses, 48, 77
rosewater, 164
rosewood, 41
Rostovtzeff, M. (American historian), 10, 46
Royal Road (Iran), 6
rubber, 267, 306, 308, 321, 326, 327, 345, 346, 370
rubies, 3, 43, 77, 158, 159, 255, 333, 337
rugs, 18, 36, 77
Roman empire, 13, 14, 22–3, 24, 34, 35, 37, 38–48, 49, 52–3, 251, 253, 254
Runciman, S. (British historian), 57

Russia, 57, 207–8, 210, 215, 260, 278, 280, 290, 358, 369–70; see also Siberia
Ryazan (Russian town), 132
Ryukyu Islands, see Luchu Islands

Safavid dynasty and empire, see Iran
Sabah, see Borneo
Sabana (Malayan port), 44
safflower, 87, 257
saffron, 48, 87, 257
Sagala, see Sialkot
Sagaing (Burmese town), 218
sago, 166, 226
Saigon (port of Indochina), 45, 340, 342, 345, 346, 348
Sailendra dynasty, see Indonesia
Sakas (steppe tribe), 4, 14, 19, 23, 49
saké (rice wine), 357, 362
Sakhalin Island (off Japan), 369
Sakchi (Indian steel centre), 297
Salsette Island (India), 241
salt, 10, 17, 27, 88, 96, 97, 138, 247, 258, 276, 284, 289, 294, 342, 357, 370
saltpetre, 123, 141, 167, 188, 199, 201, 216, 240, 245, 262, 322
Salween River (Burma), 332
Samarkand (Central Asian town), 12, 51, 68, 78, 85, 89, 127, 130, 137, 170, 171
Samavid dynasty, see Iran
Samudra (Indonesian port), 143
Samudra Gupta (Indian emperor), 51
Samurai (Japanese soldier-class), 352, 354, 355, 356, 360, 361, 362, 363, 366, 368
sandalwood, 42, 59, 113, 123, 158, 164, 167, 179, 186, 190, 193, 195, 246, 255, 270, 322
Sanf-Fulaw Island (Indochina), 82
Sanjaya, King of Java, 114
Sansom, G. (British historian), 103, 111
Santo Domingo, 291

sappanwood (dyestuff), 98, 158, 216, 222, 231, 255, 322, 348
sapphires, 43, 159, 255, 345
Sarapis (Masirah Island, Arabia), 41
Sarawak, see Borneo
Sarhad (Afghan town), 20
Sarikol Range (Central Asia), 20
Sarmatians (Central Asian nomads), 3, 50, 52
Satha I, King of Cambodia, 216
satin, 139
Satsuma (Japanese clan), 357, 359–360, 362
Scotland, 245
screens, 104, 110
Scylax (Greek pilot), 6
Scythians (nomad tribe), 3, 4, 19, 51
seaweeds, 322, 365
Selangor (Malayan state), 324
Seleucia (capital of Iran), 12, 14, 17
Seleucid dynasty and empire, see Iran
Seleucus Nicator (Iranian emperor), 12
Seljuk Turks, 127, 128
Semarang (port of Java), 233
Sempaga (Indonesian port), 28
Seres (Chinese), 36
serichatum (?), 47
sericulture, 29, 30, 71, 87, 101, 122, 134, 154, 170, 257, 368
sesame, 7, 41, 87, 256, 257, 293
Shah Jahan (Mughal emperor), 173, 181, 236, 238
Shah Rukh (Timurid ruler), 171
shallot, 87
Shan (Thai people), see Burma
Shan States (Burma), 337
Shang dynasty, see China
Shanghai (Chinese port), 263, 274, 275, 276, 277, 278, 279, 280, 283, 333
Shansi (Chinese province), 93, 129
Shantung (Chinese province), 30, 66, 97, 104, 129, 150, 277
Shapur I (Iranian emperor), 54
Shapur II (Iranian emperor), 51

shark-skin, 204
sharks' fins, 246, 256
sheep, 2
Sheffield, 266, 275
Shensi (Chinese province), 275
Sher Shah (Afghan king of India), 172
Shibar Range (Afghanistan), 69
Shih-Huang-ti (Chinese emperor), 31
Shilka River (Manchuria), 207
Shimoda (Japanese port), 358
Shintoism, 354, 355
shipbuilding: West Asian, 42, 83; South Asian, 245, 246, 247, 262, 263, 264, 266; South-east Asian, 188, 223, 330; East Asian, 97–8, 186, 204, 357, 367, 369; European, 22, 40, 188, 223, 246, 247, 262
shipping: West Asian, 5, 6, 11, 12, 22, 55, 58, 59, 62, 79–85, 113, 144, 168–9, 175, 253; South Asian, 17, 22, 23–8, 37, 62, 123, 169, 179–180, 245–8, 253, 262, 295; South-east Asian, 24, 28, 113–14, 163–7, 309; East Asian, 37, 97–8, 103–4, 108, 110, 117, 134, 136, 137–40, 142–5, 146, 148–51, 169, 186–8, 213, 280, 282–3, 284, 365, 368, 369; European, 39–44, 55, 179, 181–9, 191, 253, 262–4, 285, 288
shoes, 366
Sialkot (Sagala, Kashmir town), 18, 52
Siam, see Thailand
Siam, Gulf of, 117, 221
Siberia, 2, 12, 13, 23, 31, 50, 89, 207, 214, 253
Siem Reap (Cambodian province), 341, 344
Sikhs (Hindu sect), 237, 238
Sikkim (Himalayan state), 44
Silesia, 132
silk goods, 4, 11, 14, 17, 18, 22, 27, 28, 29, 31, 32, 35, 37, 38, 43, 55, 56, 57, 59, 60, 62, 65, 70, 77, 80, 85, 89, 96, 99, 101, 104, 110, 123, 134, 135, 136, 139, 149, 157, 165, 188, 195, 201, 202, 204, 214, 240, 252, 253, 254, 255, 264, 265, 266, 270, 272, 281, 282, 284, 288, 294, 322, 348, 354, 368
silk, raw, etc., 29, 30, 35, 36, 37, 43, 44, 47, 56, 57, 58, 62, 71, 89, 101, 135, 136, 139, 149, 164, 179, 188, 195, 212, 224, 254, 255, 267, 270, 281, 282, 288, 294, 301, 302, 313, 352, 365, 368
Silk Road, 20, 35, 46, 86, 87, 93, 97, 128, 208, 214, 254, 278
Silla (Korean kingdom), 72, 100–1, 103
silver, 4, 7, 13, 14, 27, 38, 40, 41, 42, 45, 56, 61, 67, 68, 70, 77, 88, 89, 97, 98, 122, 152, 159, 178, 179, 186, 187, 188, 190, 195, 201, 204, 212, 214, 244, 248, 252, 255, 267, 272, 316, 337, 351, 367
Sinae (Chinese), 44
Sinai Peninsula (Red Sea), 4, 11, 54
Sind (Indian province), 8, 74, 80, 84, 168, 243, 285, 293
Singapore, 116, 162, 263, 276, 283, 311, 313, 321–2, 323, 324, 325, 326, 330, 348, 349, 351
Singosari (Javanese kingdom), 117
Sinha, Raja (ruler of Ceylon), 200
Sinju (I-ching, Chinese port), 138
Sinkiang (Chinese province), 208
Sinnapitiya (Ceylonese district), 303
Siraf (Persian Gulf port), 81, 82, 83
Siraj-ud-daula (Mughal nawab), 240
Sirhind Canal (India), 296
Sisaphon (Cambodian province), 341
Si T'ep (Thai town), 25
Sivaji (Maratha chief), 236
Skanda Gupta, Emperor of India, 52
skins, 42, 99, 207, 267, 282, 288, 294, 322; see also hides
slave trade, 11, 42, 57, 80, 83, 124, 151, 165, 171, 179, 252, 265, 301, 318, 333

smuggling, 71, 87, 151, 234, 248, 249–50, 270, 271, 272, 276, 322, 357; *see also* pirates

So (Japanese clan), 149

soap, 282, 366

Socotra Island (Dioscorida), 11, 17, 39, 41, 80

sodium sulphate, 367

Soga (Japanese family), 102, 111

Sogdia (Central Asia), 8, 58, 77, 127

Somaliland(Africa), 99

Son Canals (Bengal), 293, 296

Songtham, King of Thailand, 217, 218

Song Gianh River (Vietnam), 224

Soochow (Chinese port), 278

Sopatma (Madras), 24, 43

sorghum, 140, 213, 257

Souligna Vingsa, King of Laos, 343

soyabean, 38, 281, 370

Spain, 45, 53, 74, 77, 78, 183, 186–9, 190, 192, 193, 196, 200, 203, 204, 215, 216, 219, 226, 248, 267, 301–302, 332, 340,

Speelman, C. J. (Dutch official), 226, 229

Spice Islands (Indonesia), 117, 183, 184–6, 191, 193, 196, 198, 226, 229, 232; *see also* individual islands, Banda, etc.

spices, 14, 17, 27, 28, 47, 55, 59, 62, 80, 83, 89, 116, 136, 171, 176, 178, 179, 181, 183, 184–6, 188, 189, 191, 193–4, 195, 196–200, 225–6, 227, 228, 230, 248, 252, 253, 254, 264, 310, 311, 326

spikenard, *see* nard

spinach, 87

spinel (gem), 43, 159

Spinks, C. N. (pottery expert), 156

Spitalfield (English silk centre), 265

Srinagar (Kashmir), 20, 69

Srivijaya, *see* Indonesia

Srong-tsan-Gampo (Tibetan king), 90

Ssu-ma Ch'ien (Chinese historian), 33

Staffordshire (English pottery centre), 266

steel, 40, 98, 164, 255, 297, 309; *see also* iron

Stein, Sir Aurel (British archæologist), 4, 20, 21, 89

sticklac, 344

storax (balsam), 41, 42, 48

Strabo (Roman geographer), 22

Straits Settlements, *see* Malaya

straw, 281, 366

Suez (Kolzoum), 80, 263

Suez Canal, 264, 289, 292, 293, 299, 305, 320, 334, 365

sugar (cane), 41, 77, 87, 139, 140, 159, 171, 179, 201, 204, 224, 235, 240, 245, 246, 256, 270, 276, 282, 288, 291, 294, 301, 302, 307, 308, 309, 312, 313, 315, 316, 317, 318, 319, 321, 322, 326, 332, 333, 348, 357, 362, 366, 369, 370

Suhar (Persian Gulf port), 81

Sui dynasty, *see* China

Sukhotai (Thai capital), 155–6

Sulayman the Magnificent (Arab caliph), 259

sulphur, 77, 123, 149, 167, 204, 365

Sulu Islands (Philippines), 229, 279

Sumatra (Indonesia), 28, 84, 161, 165, 183, 186, 191, 198, 199, 225, 227, 229, 230, 232, 235, 307, 310, 311, 319, 321, 323, 324; *see also* Indonesia

Sunda Straits (Indonesia), 113, 114, 117, 165, 183, 191, 230, 311

Sung dynasty, *see* China

Sunga dynasty (India), 18

Sungei Ujang (Malayan state), 324

Surabaya (Bay of Indonesia), 116

Surat (Indian port), 199, 200, 202, 220, 225, 237, 243, 246, 254, 288, 337

Suryavarman I, King of Ankor, 119

Suryavarman II, King of Ankor, 119

Susa (Iranian city), 6, 7, 8, 17

Sutlej River (India), 296

Suvarnabhumi (South-east Asia), 23

Swat, River (India), 20, 293
Swatow (Chinese port), 144, 271, 277, 283
Sweden, 248, 349
sweet clover, 42
sweet potato, *see* potato
Swettenham, Sir F. (British official), 324, 325
Sword, Mulinghaus (smelting company), 325
swords, 40, 104, 110, 149, 164, 254
Syagras (Ras Fartak, Arabian port), 41
Sym, A. (British planter), 288
Symes, M. (British official), 329
Syria, 1, 4, 6, 7, 12, 13, 14, 16, 35, 46, 49, 54, 55, 56, 58, 60, 61, 73, 74, 76, 77, 78, 86, 132, 170, 259
Syriam (Burmese port), 215, 219, 223, 224
Szechwan (Chinese province), 22, 67, 70, 88, 92, 131, 209, 274

Tabinshwehti, King of Burma, 215
Tabriz (Iranian town), 140
Taedong River (Korea), 100
taffeta, 38, 167
Taiho Code (Japan), 103
Taikwa Edict (Japan), 102
Taipei (Chinese port), 277
Taiping movement (China), 276, 277, 278, 280, 342
Taira Kiyomori (Japanese shogun), 109
T'ai Tsung (Chinese Emperor), 67, 72, 85, 87, 90
Taiwan, 85, 151, 203, 205, 206, 209, 213, 225, 274, 276, 343, 364, 369, 370
Taj Mahal (Indian tomb), 236
Takash, Shah of Khwarizm, 127
Taklamakan desert and oasis towns, 1, 19–21, 29, 31, 32–4, 36, 37, 49, 50, 63–4, 67–8, 71–2, 78–9, 86, 90, 91, 127, 129–30, 133, 136, 208; *see also* individual towns, Silk Road
Takkola (Malayan port), 23, 44, 116

Talas River, battle of, 79, 90
Tali, Lake (China), 277, 342
Talikhan (Central Asian town), 131
Talmud, 80
tamarinds, 165
Tambralinga, *see* Ligor
Tamils, 15, 23, 43–4, 303, 304, 306; *see also* India, Ceylon
Tamralipti (Tamluk, Indian port), 17, 24, 70
Tana (Crimean port), 135, 136
Tanegashima Island (Japan), 181, 186
T'ang dynasty, *see* China, 67
Tangut (Tibetan tribe), 93, 94, 129; *see also* Hsi-hsia
Tanjore (Indian province), 115, 287
tapestries, 77, 89, 164, 201
tapioca, 320; *see also* cassava
Taprobane, *see* Ceylon
Tarain (Taraori), battle of, 168
Tarim Basin, *see* Taklamakan, Silk Road
Taruma (Javanese state), 28
Ta-shih (Persians), 81
Tashkent (Central Asian town), 51, 79, 85, 90
Tashkurghen (Central Asian town), 20, 64, 71
Tata, J. N. (Indian industrialist), 297, 298
Taun-Murun Saddle (Central Asia), 20
Tavoy (Burmese port), 160
Taxila, *see* Peshawar
Taylor, J. (Ceylon planter), 305
tea, 87, 88, 96, 97, 110, 134, 156, 202, 208, 209, 214, 215, 224, 231, 233, 244, 246, 248, 252, 262–3, 264, 267, 270, 276, 280, 281, 282, 284, 288, 292, 294, 301, 305–6, 308, 313, 315, 318, 320, 321, 322, 345, 348, 365, 368
teak, 7, 42, 83, 88, 179, 223, 246, 255, 312, 330, 334, 337, 344, 349, 350

Temmei famine (Japan), 352
Tempo famine (Japan), 352
Tempo Reform (Japan), 357
Temuchin, *see* Jenghiz Khan
Temur (Chinese emperor), 141
Tenasserim (Burmese town and district), 25, 117, 154, 181, 215, 221, 328, 329, 338, 347
Tenchi (Japanese emperor), 102
Tennant, Sir J. E. (Governor of Ceylon), 304
Ternate (Indonesian port), 117, 181, 182, 183, 184, 188, 193, 225, 226, 227, 229, 322
textiles, 38, 199, 202, 229, 230, 231, 252, 253, 255, 267, 269, 288, 289, 290, 298, 299, 316, 322, 331, 332, 333, 339, 353, 362, 366, 369, 370; *see also* cotton goods, etc.
Thailand, 24, 25, 116, 255; Sukhotai period, 154–7; Ayuthia period, 142, 157–8, 160, 161, 162, 166, 191, 200, 204, 206, 215, 216–224, 237, 261; Bangkok period, 268, 269, 279, 328, 329, 330, 333, 339, 341, 343, 344, 346–51, 365
Tharawaddy Min, King of Burma, 330
Thaton (Burmese port), 25, 154
Thibaw, King of Burma, 334
Thieu-Tri, Emperor of Vietnam, 340
Thin (China), 43
Thinae (Chinese city), 43
Three Pagoda Pass (Thailand), 25, 157, 218
T'iao-chih (Tarim kingdom), 33
Tiberius (Roman emperor), 23, 45
Tibet, 16, 44, 50, 86, 88, 90, 99, 137, 166, 175, 207, 208–9, 214, 256, 260
Tidore (Indonesian port), 183, 184, 185, 188, 193, 196, 226, 229
T'ien Shan Mountains (Central Asia), 1, 32, 67, 68, 86
Tientsin, Treaty of, 277, 278, 280, 281
Tiglath-pileser I (Assyrian king), 4

Tigris River (Iraq), 1, 14, 78, 81, 133, 140
tiles, 78, 367
timber, 7, 10, 32, 41, 83, 104, 110, 149, 227, 247, 267, 330, 331, 333, 338, 339, 365
Timor Island (Indonesia), 161, 186, 190, 193, 229, 255, 307
Timur-the-Lame (Mongol emperor), 170–1, 259
tin, 2, 3, 37, 42, 68, 89, 164, 166, 167, 179, 183, 186, 198, 201, 204, 216, 217, 220, 222, 225, 227, 246, 255, 266, 267, 270, 308, 310, 319, 320, 321, 322, 323, 324, 325, 338, 342, 344, 345, 348, 350
Tipu (ruler of Mysore), 241, 243
Tirhut (Indian province), 291
Tiridates I, King of Parthia, 14
Titianus, Maes (Greek merchant), 35
tobacco, 186, 212, 238, 247, 302, 306, 308, 309, 312, 313, 315, 316, 318, 319, 321, 322, 327, 362
Tobelo (Indonesian port), 229
Togan Temur (Chinese emperor), 141
Tokugawa (Japanese clan), *see* Japan
Tokyo (Yedo), 211, 212, 213, 354, 356, 358, 359, 360, 361
Tomoika (Japanese cotton centre), 367
Tongking, 114, 224, 342, 343, 345
tools, 254, 288
toothpaste, 366
topaz, 42, 43, 165

Van kings (of Armenia), 7
Vandals (nomad tribe), 53
Vargas, J. de B. Y. (Governor-General of Philippines), 301, 302
Varthema, Ludovico di (Italian traveller), 158
velvets, 139, 154, 179, 188
Venice, 128, 133, 175, 176, 178, 182
Vera Cruz (Mexican port), 188
vermilion, 123, 201
Versailles, 222

Verus (Roman emperor), 35
Vespasian (Roman emperor), 23, 45, 46
Victoria, Queen of England, 300
Victoria, Lake (Central Asia), 20, 71
Vientiane (Laos town), 120, 156, 343
Vietnam, 24, 26, 36, 143, 213, 216, 219, 224, 256, 267, 279, 328, 334, 338, 340–1, 343, 345–6, 351; see also Annam, Champo, Cochinchina, French Indochina, etc.
Vijaya, King of Java, 161
Vijayanagar (Indian kingdom), see India
Villalobos, R. L. de (Portuguese sailor), 187
Visigoths, 52, 53
Vladimir (Russian principality), 132
Vladivostok, 278
Volga River, 3, 131
Vypin Island (India), 199

Wadia family (Indian shipbuilders), 246
Wakhan Valley (Afghanistan), 20, 71
Wakhjir Pass (Afghanistan), 20
walnuts, 256
Wang An-shih (Chinese Minister), 94–5
Wang Chih (Chinese merchant), 151
Wang Kon (Korean king), 104
Wang Mang (Chinese emperor), 34, 36, 45
Wang Ta-Yuan (Chinese traveller), 161–2
Wareru (Mon king), 156
Warmington, E. H. (British historian), 46
water-buffalo, 30
wax, 165
weapons, 104, 108; see also fire-arms, swords, etc.
Wei Valley (China), 30
Wei dynasty, see China, 37, 50, 58, 62, 63

Weiheiwei (Chinese port), 369
Wellesley, Province (Malayan province), 326
Wellesley, Lord (Governor-General of India), 243
Welsers (German bankers), 182
Wen Chan, Princess (Tibetan consort), 90
Wen-chou (Chinese lacquer centre), 123
West Indies, 291, 301, 303
Whampoa (Chinese port), 271, 272
wheat, 17, 30, 38, 41, 64, 67, 69, 123, 139, 292, 296, 332, 333
Wheatley, P. (British geographer), 44
Wheeler, Sir M. (British archæologist), 38, 44
White, G. (English merchant), 220, 221
White, S. (English adventurer), 220, 221
Wilhelmina, Queen of the Netherlands, 328
William II, King of England, 264
William VI, King of the Netherlands, 311, 312, 313
Williams, Dr. C. (British Agent at Mandalay), 332
wines, 8, 10, 40, 41, 42, 44, 140, 159, 179, 256, 317
wolfram, 338
wood, 227
Woodruff, P. (British historian), 296
woods, precious, 89
wool, 2, 369
woollens, 13, 14, 47, 62, 70, 77, 167, 179, 244, 264, 270, 294, 322, 366, 367
Wu San-kuei (Chinese general), 153, 209
Wu-ti (Chinese emperor), 22, 31, 33–4, 36, 38, 45, 100, 257, 258

Xerxes (Iranian emperor), 7

Yamada Nagamasa (Japanese soldier), 217
Yamato (Japanese kingdom), 101

Yandabo, Treaty of, 329, 330
Yangi Hisar (Central Asian town), 20
Yang Hsiu-cheng (Taiping general), 276
Yang Kuei-fei (Chinese consort), 92
Yangtze River (China), 59, 82, 96, 97, 138, 273, 280, 281, 283
Yang Yen (Chinese Minister), 92
Yarkand (Tarim oasis), 19, 20, 21, 32, 34, 64
Yasovarman, King of Ankor, 119
Yasin (town in Kashmir), 20
Yedo, see Tokyo
Yellow Sea, 97
Yemen (Arabian state), 2, 55, 77
Yen (Chinese state in Korea), 100
Yenangyaung (Burmese oil-field), 337
Yi Song-gye (Korean emperor), 148
Yi Sun-sin (Korean admiral), 152
Yin Ching (Chinese admiral), 142
Yokohama (Japanese port), 359, 361, 364
Yokosuka (Japanese port), 358
Yoritomo (Japanese shogun), 109
Yoshimune (Japanese shogun), 352
Yoshimitsu (Japanese shogun), 147, 148, 149

Yueh-chih (nomad tribe), 31, 32, 34; see also India: Kushan empire
Yumen-Kuan (Chinese town), 32, 72
Yung-ch'ang (Chinese border post), 22
Yun-kang (cave temples, China), 63
Yung-li (Chinese emperor), 218
Yung-lo (Chinese emperor), 141, 142, 144, 145, 218
Yunnan (Chinese province), 21, 22, 32, 44, 90, 153, 155, 158, 209, 213, 218, 277, 332, 333, 342
Yunnan-fu (Chinese town), 342

Zabae (Chinese port), 44
Zaiton, see Ch'uan-chou
Zamorin of Calicut, 169, 175-7, 261
Zanzibar, 99, 175
Zenobia, Queen of Palmyra, 54
Zijlker, A. J. S. (Sumatran planter), 320
zinc, 179, 255, 270, 345
zircon, 43
zithers, 141
Zoroastrianism, 15, 76, 87
Zwaardekroon, H. (Governor-General of Indonesia), 231